INTERACTIONS

INTERACTIONS
The Aims and Patterns of Writing

JAMES D. LESTER

Austin Peay State University

Wadsworth Publishing Company
Belmont, California
A Division of Wadsworth, Inc.

Special Projects Editor: Judith McKibben
Editorial Assistant: Sharon Wallach
Production Editor: Deborah McDaniel
Managing Designer: Donna Davis
Print Buyer: Barbara Britton
Designer: Lisa Mirski
Copy Editor: Evelyn Mercer Ward
Cover Design: Donna Davis
Cover Painting: *Rooms by the Sea* by Edward Hopper, 1951 (Yale University Art
Gallery, Bequest of Stephen Carlton Clark, B.A., 1903)

Acknowledgments are listed on pages 397–400.

Printed in the United States of America   49

1 2 3 4 5 6 7 8 9 10---92 91 90 89 88

Library of Congress Cataloging-in-Publication Data

Lester, James D.
  Interactions: the aims and patterns of writing.

  Includes index.
  1. College readers.   2. English language—Rhetoric.
I. Title.
PE1417.L439   1988   808'.0427   87-21249
ISBN 0-534-08076-6

Contents

TEN

Induction and Deduction   367

Contents by Aims of Discourse

EXPRESSIVE WRITING

Writing forms that derive mainly from personal experiences and attitudes of the writer; writing as discovery, therefore exploratory, usually private, and employing autobiographical detail.

EXPLANATORY WRITING

Writing that derives from the writer's wish to reach beyond the personal to explain real-world matters; writing that informs, interprets, and theorizes.

PERSUASIVE WRITING

Writing that expresses a position, defends it, and argues convincingly; writing that becomes a form of recommendation, where the writer attempts to win over the reader.

IMAGINATIVE AND CREATIVE WRITING

Writing that responds to form and persona as much as to message; writing that searches out a new voice, experiments with a special form, or allows the language to call attention to itself.

Contents by Themes and Issues

POLITICS

TECHNOLOGY AND SCIENCE

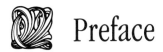 # Preface

As writing teachers, we must keep our writing programs fresh, using new texts that incorporate the most recent theories of reading and composition, while also maintaining proven, traditional pedagogy.

With this goal, I developed a book that not only uses the traditional patterns of development as writing models but also reflects contemporary thinking on the writing process. The book is called *Interactions: The Aims and Patterns of Writing* because my primary objective was to blend the patterns of rhetoric with the aims of discourse—to express, explain, persuade, and create—and to show how these parts interact.* Yet this was not all. I wanted a new pedagogy that avoided yes-no questions and busywork assignments. I wanted a book that emphasized good reading habits, featured student essays as well as professional models, and stressed the fundamentals of the writing process.

The text is organized to lead students from idea (subject), to aim, to audience, and then to pattern. As a colleague has noted, "Pattern is what helps students find form, although form also helps clarify aim and audience."

UNIQUE FEATURES

Interactions unites the ten rhetorical patterns of development with the four fundamental aims of discourse, recognizing that each pattern may serve every aim. It has these special features.

1. The chapters focus on one pattern of development but also present expressive, explanatory, persuasive, and imaginative essays to demonstrate the pattern in service of the writer's aim.

*For additional discussion of the aims of discourse, see James Kinneavy, *A Theory of Discourse*, 2d ed. (New York: Norton, 1980).

2. The essays reflect and endorse the natural flow of the writing process, from idea to aim to audience to pattern and, ultimately, to a design for the overall structure of the essay.

3. Pedagogical apparatus is included in the form of comments and analyses of the featured essay as well as directions to the student to perform specific, limited tasks related to inventing topics, taking notes, and drafting paragraphs.

4. A student essay in each chapter shows how another student has approached the assignment. Student essays are accompanied by comments of these students on their aims and strategies in planning and writing their essays.

5. Three tables of contents are included and are arranged by rhetorical patterns, the aims of discourse, and the issues dealt with in the essays; this will aid instructors in varying the sequence of courses.

6. Introductions to each essay guide effective reading habits (showing the interrelationship of good reading and effective writing), and assignments at the end of each essay reinforce careful reading.

7. Assignments at the end of each essay require students to develop their own papers rather than answer questions of analysis about the model essays.

8. The blending of patterns is emphasized, promoting the idea that essays usually employ one primary pattern of development and several minor patterns.

ARRANGEMENT OF THE BOOK

As the table of contents indicates, this book is arranged in a traditional order according to the basic patterns of development. Beyond this general structure, however, it differs from other books in several ways.

Each chapter features essays that are expressive, explanatory, persuasive, or imaginative and creative in their aim of discourse. Any individual pattern, for instance comparison/contrast, will serve all four types of aims, although sometimes aims may overlap.

In the first chapter, for example, the student will discover how description serves several aims: the expressive purpose (Annie Dillard), the explanatory purpose (John McPhee and Joan Didion), the persuasive purpose (Jonathan Schell), and the creative purpose (Robert Bly and student Christa Lednicky). The introduction to each essay introduces the subject, discusses the writer's apparent aim, and makes suggestions for reading the essay.

The "Comments and Assignments" section at the end of each essay explores the aims and patterns of the writer. Instead of asking numerous questions about an essay's meaning, rhetorical techniques, and language as in many writing texts, this book provides students with comments and explanations about specifics of the essay—things students need to know. Here's an example of one comment and its corresponding assignment:

Comment. "Salvation" is one small passage from Langston Hughes's autobiography. The deception by the twelve-year-old Langston is central to this narration. He lied and in the process lost his faith rather than strengthened it. Buried within the narration, therefore, is a life experience about childhood and rites of passage.

Assignment. Think back into your past and write down two or three episodes that are memorable and perhaps worth expressing. Make some notations about *why* the experiences stick in your mind. What lesson about life did you learn? Does it have universal appeal? Will others identify with your dilemma, problem, or activity?

These assignments motivate students to build ideas, make notes, write brief paragraphs, perform limited research, and gradually but surely build a rough draft. Armed with reasons and specific writing tasks, students can use patterns of development not as mere formulas but as methods for discovering and expanding ideas. Such busywork questions as "What is the author's tone?" or "How serious is the author in paragraph 6?" are replaced by assignments that require students to perform specific tasks connected with the creation of their own essays.

INSTRUCTIONAL AIDS

Interactions will make life easier for instructors. The assignments at the end of each essay motivate students to create ideas, notes, and rough drafts. Instructors do not have to work through a set of questions; there are no questions.

For those instructors who desire additional pedagogy, the *Instructor's Manual* features supplementary teaching tools: (1) discussion and quizzes on the content of the essays; (2) questions and answers on issues, language, and writing techniques; (3) discussion and quizzes on rhetorical patterns; (4) discussion and quizzes on aims of discourse; and (5) a brief discussion with examples on the role of research and the citation of sources.

Instructors can choose from three outlines for designing their lesson plans: (1) the primary outline that features the ten rhetorical patterns of development; (2) an alternate outline arranged by the four aims of discourse (expressive, explanatory, persuasive, and imaginative); and (3) an outline that arranges the essays by issues, such as history, the environment, ethnic issues.

CONSIDERATION OF STUDENTS

Interactions will also make life easier for students by encouraging fundamental processes: good reading habits, methods for discovering a topic and purpose, planning and note-taking, and drafting a complete paper. There is no busywork. The end-of-essay comments and assignments focus and direct writing activities. Students are not required to make a difficult analysis of the essay. Instead they are asked to generate a rough draft that emulates the aim and structure of the model essay.

In addition, students are encouraged to maintain a reading notebook (or careful marginal notes) and a writing journal. As standard tools of disciplined writers, these will help supply students with ideas and preliminary sketches.

Students can also discover how their peers have responded to these assignments, for every chapter features a student essay accompanied by comments by the student writer.

ACKNOWLEDGMENTS

I express appreciation to my family for providing an environment that encourages and stimulates the creative process. I would like to thank the following reviewers for their thoughtful and helpful comments about the development of this text: David Ackiss, Missouri Southern State College; Tracy Baker, University of Alabama at Birmingham; Richard Batteiger, Oklahoma State University; Alma Bryant, University of South Florida; Joanne Brown, Des Moines Area Community College; Ann Carlton, Oklahoma City University; Peggy Cole, Arapahoe Community College; Marya DuBose, Augusta College; Carol Holder, California State Polytechnic University; Lola Johnson, California State College—Stanislaus; Linda Peckham, Lansing Community College; Mary Ann Peters, Oklahoma State University and Technical Institute; William Pixton, Oklahoma State University; Nancy Walker, Southwest Missouri State University.

Introduction to the Student

Your college work will demand good communication skills, both verbal and written. Your best ideas deserve effective delivery in freshman themes and other assignments—essay exams, reports, and research papers. What's more, today's high-tech society demands well-written business memos, résumés, sales letters, and presentations to accompany graphs, charts, and statistical data. It's not too early to begin thinking about a professional position in management, nursing, teaching, and so forth. Accompanying that position will be demands for excellence in writing. Therefore, this book has been designed to meet two objectives: (1) to stimulate your imagination with well-written essays on a broad range of topical issues, and (2) to provide you with tools and techniques for building your own essays.

The writers represented in this text have some things in common: Each writes with a specific aim and each uses patterns of writing to achieve that aim. Good writers have an aim or a purpose for their writing, identify their audiences, and develop their essays with examples, comparisons, definitions, and other appropriate patterns of development. One writer might explain the difference between a brain and a computer, another might meditate on a natural wonder, and a third might argue the merits of nuclear disarmament.

FOUR STAGES OF PLANNING AN ESSAY

This book will help you find ideas for writing; it will explain how to establish an aim of discourse for your special audience; and it will encourage you to select the patterns of development that can best communicate your message.

Finding Ideas A good topic will assist the process of writing and strengthen the essay's content. The best topics grow out of your need to

1

address an audience on an issue of importance. This book will present you with issues and problems that will provoke response or inspire the imagination. Ideas will emerge from the model essays and from suggestions by the author. Each essay in this book, with its accompanying comments and assignments, can help you discover an idea that might launch a writing experience. You can select from essays by professionals or students. In every case you will find a brief introduction, the essay itself, and a set of comments and assignments. The comments will explain how the writer of the essay performed and the assignments will prompt you toward ideas for developing your own essay.

Establishing an Aim   Four basic aims are fundamental for any writer.

1. *Expressive* writing develops from the experiences and thoughts of the writer. It is autobiographical and expresses inner feelings about events, places, and people that have made lasting impressions. You will use the expressive aim of discourse for making entries in your journal and for notes on personal speculations. Expressive writing appears in finished form as a position paper, a reminiscence, an autobiography, or a personal narration. For example, Annie Dillard describes her walk in the woods and her discovery of a knotted snakeskin, and Langston Hughes narrates his experiences at an old-time revival. Many of the writings in this textbook have an expressive aim of discourse, and they usually are positioned as the first essay in each chapter.

2. *Explanatory* writing explains real-world matters by defining a subject, showing how it works, or analyzing its parts. You can use the explanatory aim of discourse for telling a reader how to use computer graphics, explaining the disappearance of the family farm, or writing a brief history about Alaska's efforts to become a state. Explanatory writing takes many other forms, such as biography, news stories, speeches, and essay exam answers. Explanatory essays in this book usually are positioned as the second essay in each chapter. John McPhee, for example, describes the awesome grandeur of the Alaskan grizzly, Lewis Thomas gives examples of the music of nature, and Bruce Catton compares generals Grant and Lee at their meeting in Appomattox, Virginia.

3. *Persuasive* writing addresses and attempts to convince the reader. about the truth of a proposition and even, on occasion, urges the reader to action. The persuasive writer uses personal elements and objective explanation to reinforce appeals for support, action, or belief in a cause. The writer addresses the reader directly with answers, solutions, and recommendations. For example, Jonathan

Schell advocates nuclear disarmament by describing the effects of a one-megaton bomb exploded over New York City, and Richard Rodriguez urges all ethnic and minority students to learn and embrace standard English. These writers have a cause, so the persuasive appeal controls their essays. Persuasive essays are usually the third essay in each chapter.

4. *Creative* writing approaches the same subjects and topics as the other aims of discourse but takes a different perspective: It creates a special voice or character and imaginatively experiments with form and style. Creative writing includes poetry and fiction but can extend to some forms of nonfiction prose writing, as you will find demonstrated in several essays of this book, such as Robert Bly's imaginative description of a goalie in "The Hockey Poem" or John Updike's image study of "Central Park." Creative essays sometimes appear as the fourth or fifth essay in a chapter.

The essays in this book are a mix of these four aims of discourse. The introductions to each essay will explain the writer's aim and establish a focus of your reading. The "Comments and Assignments" section that follows each essay will help you understand the writer's techniques and suggest ways for you to develop your own essay.

Addressing a Special Audience   Idea, aim, and audience all interact. Sometimes you will write about and for yourself in a journal, diary, or reading notebook. At other times, you might write about yourself in private letters, position papers, or personal narrations.

However, you will direct most of your writing, especially for college assignments, toward readers who need information. You will explain a problem, analyze it, argue the merits of one side over another, or define a complex mechanism or process. Readers of a news story want to know who, what, when, where, why, and how. In contrast, readers of an academic essay on laser beams may need classification (what are the types?), process analysis (how do lasers work?), definition (what exactly are lasers?), or causal analysis (what happens when the laser beam hits a target?).

Both explanatory and persuasive prose need an ordered structure if you hope to answer readers' questions and meet their expectations. With persuasive writing especially, readers must understand the problem, for they will want to know the issue and why it's important. Readers will also want to know your basis for assertions, will need to see some evidence, and will expect you to reach a few conclusions.

Therefore, consider always the expectations of your readers, using these guidelines.

1. Be precise so that readers understand your exact meaning and cannot make interpretations that distort your ideas.
2. Remember that readers tend to categorize ideas, so emphasize new ideas with new wording, new imagery, new examples.
3. Don't allow readers to view you as another conventional writer making safe, normal statements. Take risks and confront a problem. Let readers see you struggling to make all the pieces fit. If they see you working and sweating, they'll get down in the trenches with you. If you show deep involvement, the reader will respond.
4. Readers have short-term memories, so in longer papers provide periodic summaries or reviews of your position.

Selecting Patterns of Development   The demands of your audience and the requirements of your subject affect your choice of patterns of development. The basic patterns are methods for developing your ideas. They reflect your mental arrangement of information and ultimately your physical arrangement of paragraphs. A pattern may appear as a complete block, such as a paragraph of definition. In a full essay, however, you will need to blend and mix several of these patterns.

description

narration

example

comparison and contrast

analogy

division and classification

process analysis

definition

cause and effect

induction and deduction

Each pattern gives a distinct feature to an essay. Some add concrete detail, others compare items and ideas, and several develop a sequence of events or actions. The chapter introductions discuss each pattern.

Usually, your aim and sense of audience will interact to help focus your writing situation and thereby suggest the patterns of development most useful for your essay. A *writing situation* is your mental or written formula that spells out your subject, aim, audience, and in many cases the primary method for developing the essay. For example, one student jotted down this writing situation.

> I work at a department store in the appliance department. I want to write an essay about the differences of men and women as shoppers. My aim is to increase sales by store personnel.

This writer has a purpose: to explain methods for increasing sales. The limited audience consists of store personnel. The writer's primary pattern of development is *comparison and contrast* of men and women shoppers. In addition, the paper will benefit by use of additional patterns, such as *classification* to examine types of shoppers, *examples* of each, and a *cause-and-effect* discussion to determine why shoppers have differences. The writer will use these patterns for a purpose.

Another writer sketched this writing situation.

> I'm going to investigate the Tennessee seat belt law to determine whether the legislature gives in to the demands of automobile lobbyists or listens to the requests of citizens and voters. Maybe I'll make this a letter to the editor and argue against the power of special interest groups and political action committees.

This writer has identified an audience (concerned citizens who read editorial pages), selected a persuasive aim of discourse (to argue against the power of political action committees), and committed the essay to certain patterns of development, especially *cause and effect* (to analyze how and why lobbyists exert influence), *example* (to illustrate specific instances of lobbying techniques), and the gathering of *inductive* evidence (gathering sufficient data before making any conclusions).

Another student made this preliminary note.

> I'm going to write about the burden of being a father's favorite child. When I was about six years old and playing underneath the back porch one day, I overheard my Dad tell my neighbor, Mr. Robbins, "Jake's my favorite son." I'm Jake, and believe me, life changed after that. I had to keep this secret and also live up to Dad's expectations.

This writer's reminiscence of a personal experience will need the patterns of *narration* to relate past events and perhaps *cause and effect* for explaining the consequences of this discovery.

Like these writers, you may need one primary pattern in combination with several other patterns. For example, expressive writing about a difficult period in childhood, perhaps the trauma of divorcing parents, might need your *narration* as a primary pattern for telling a portion of your life history, but it could also feature *examples* of your trauma, *description* of each parent, and perhaps *cause and effect analysis* to explain consequences in your life as a victim of divorce.

Choices must be made, then, at every stage. The assignments that follow each essay will not only encourage your use of one primary pattern but will also advocate your use of several supporting patterns of development.

READING AN ESSAY

Good writers are good readers. Research proves that writing grows and develops as a consequence of careful and thoughtful reading. Therefore, you must read effectively in order to generate your own ideas. Reading essays by good writers will stimulate your thinking, not stifle it, because it will open the door to further exploration. Borrow an idea and amplify it, revise it to your standards, or offer a counterproposal.

Linda Flower in her book *Problem Solving Strategies for Writing* says, "Instead of remembering all the details, readers do something much more creative—they draw inferences as they read and use the writer's ideas to form their own concepts. In other words, readers remember not what *we* tell them, but what they tell *themselves*."* Research by Flower and others suggests that you are not passively absorbing information as you read. Instead, you make new information and form new meanings by rearranging ideas, by sniffing around the information presented to find extra tidbits, and by just ignoring some factual data.

Reading an essay or book is like a negotiable confrontation: The author says one thing, like "*It is possible to stop most drug addiction in the United States within a very short time* (Gore Vidal), and you respond with *maybe!* In effect, you have restructured his sentence to: "It may be possible to stop most drug addiction in the United States within a very short time." You are negotiating with the author and asking him for more input and more evidence.

If we accept the creative nature of our reading habits, the next concern becomes one of using effective techniques for better comprehension. Five processes will aid you: prereading, making marginal notes, summarizing, borrowing key terms and quotable phrases, and rereading.

Prereading   Before reading most assignments, you quickly check to see how many pages you must read. This is a legitimate strategy, for you must plan your time and effort. Other prereading strategies include

---

*Linda Flower, *Problem Solving Strategies for Writing* (New York: Harcourt Brace Jovanovich, 1981) 131.

1. Scanning introductory material for previews and summaries of the work as well as notes about an author's credentials
2. Considering the date, especially for timely topics
3. Reading the title for informative clues, especially academic titles that use precise, descriptive terms
4. Examining illustrations and photographs to enhance your initial knowledge of the subject matter
5. Formulating ideas from highlighted items (such as subheads, boxed notations, colored typefaces, and colored shading)

These techniques, which take only a few seconds, will serve you well before you begin serious reading.

Making Marginal Notes   Making your own notes in the margins of pages clarifies your initial understanding of an essay and later helps you review it. You may have noticed that many of your instructors have made extensive marginal notes in their textbooks. These notes represent extensions and responses to textual discussions. The instructors have made the texts personally dynamic. You can do the same in your own books. (Avoid writing in library publications; instead, make annotations on photocopied magazine articles or photocopied pages of books.)

As you read, don't just highlight passages in yellow felt pen. The material will merely remain there in yellow ink ready for rereading. Instead, underline only key phrases, terms, and dates. In particular, write notes in the margins that pursue a specific issue or idea. (See the marginal notes on John F. Kennedy's "Inaugural Address," which follows later.)

Use these basic techniques for marking textual matter.

Keep a pencil handy as you read and use it.

Underline key terms and key concepts but avoid underlining whole blocks of prose.

Write in the margins of your own books, especially to record *your* responses and opinions as well as to summarize the author's ideas.

Underline key terms and look up the meanings in a good dictionary. Question and challenge the meaning of a writer's statements. Question the author's evidence, the author's apparent bias, the author's voice (is this writer serious or ironic?), and especially the author's purpose. Ask questions such as: Is he serious? Where's her evidence? Can this be true?

You will find marginal notes valuable for later reference. Research suggests that we read using short-term memory, so ideas are not remembered for long after an initial reading. Writing marginal notes will help you retain key points, *even if you never return to the original material.*

Summarizing   Many textbooks provide chapter summaries, but a typical essay or book offers no convenient review. Yet you need an overview for understanding the author's general points. These techniques will help you.

1. Keep a reading notebook and fill it with notes and ideas on the subject. Let your reading stimulate your own ideas. You can also list each source, summarize it briefly, and make connections of the source to your subject.

2. Use the summaries made by an author within a work. Most good writers will pause briefly throughout their writing to review and/or summarize primary ideas. Mark these spots with highlighting or marginal notes.

3. Write an outline summary. As you read, jot down important points about each major block of material, which may represent one paragraph or several. An alternative is to list the topic sentence for each paragraph, but this is such a mechanical exercise that you may not capture the essence of the writing. Do not mix your thoughts with the summary; enclose your own words within parentheses whenever you find it necessary to blend both into one note.

4. Write a précis of the essay or book, that is, a highly condensed summary that reduces a paragraph to a sentence, tightens an article into a brief paragraph, and summarizes a book in a page or two. The précis length for an essay should be one paragraph of 50 to 100 words. A good précis captures the author's essential ideas, cuts through all preliminaries, evidence, illustrations, and excess wording in order to list the writer's topic, thesis, and conclusions.

Borrowing Key Terms and Quotable Phrases   Another way to read effectively is to itemize bits of information. Use these techniques.

1. Inventory key words. Every topic has a vernacular (a set of words so fundamental to the subject that every writer uses them). Music has its particular jargon, as does poetry, architecture, and even carpentry. An article on pollution of a mountain stream will use a vernacular, such as "toxins," "contamination," "impurities," "environment,"

and so forth. Listing fundamental terms creates a vocabulary for your writing.

2. Write down definitions to new words or to unusual, different meanings for terms that you thought you understood.

3. Look for quotable statements and jot them down as direct quotations (word for word and within quotation marks) or as paraphrases (reworded in your style). Carefully note your source because you will need this information in the paper. Quotation ought to be a purposeful act for citing

> special evidence
>
> wording that is exceptionally precise, appropriate, and distinctive in tone and style
>
> words of a leading authority on the subject
>
> evidence, statistics, and factual data that are pertinent to your study

Rereading   If you have read slowly, carefully, and followed the preceding steps, you can refer to your marginal notes, reading notebook, summaries, key terms, and quotations. A second reading, if you believe it necessary, should proceed smoothly.

Reading Notes on John F. Kennedy's "Inaugural Address"   A reading of John F. Kennedy's "Inaugural Address" follows. It reflects basic techniques by a student who has read carefully to determine Kennedy's definition of freedom. The student, after this reading and note-taking, can develop a general essay on freedom or can analyze and interpret Kennedy's use of the term.

JOHN F. KENNEDY

Inaugural Address

We observe today not a victory of party but a celebration of *His inauguration*
freedom, symbolizing an end as well as a beginning, signi- *is a "celebration*
fying renewal as well as change. For I have sworn before you *of freedom"*
and Almighty God the same solemn oath our forebears prescribed nearly a century and three-quarters ago.

The world is very different now. For man holds in his
mortal hands the power to abolish all forms of human
poverty and all forms of human life. And yet the same
revolutionary belief for which our forebears fought is still
at issue around the globe, the belief that the rights of man
come not from the generosity of the state but from the *religious*
hand of God. *freedom*

We dare not forget today that we are the heirs of that
first revolution. Let the word go forth from this time and
place, to friend and foe alike, that the torch has been
passed to a new generation of Americans, born in this
century, tempered by war, disciplined by a hard and bitter *Human rights*
peace, proud of our ancient heritage, and unwilling to *is a freedom*
witness or permit the slow undoing of those human rights
to which this nation has always been committed, and to
which we are committed today at home and around the
world.

Let every nation know, whether it wishes us well or ill, *freedom is*
that we shall pay any price, bear any burden, meet any *worth all*
hardship, support any friend, oppose any foe to assure the *these things*
survival and the success of liberty.

This much we pledge—and more.

To those old allies whose cultural and spiritual origins
we share, we pledge the loyalty of faithful friends. United,
there is little we cannot do in a host of cooperative ventures. Divided, there is little we can do, for we dare not
meet a powerful challenge at odds and split asunder.

John F. Kennedy (1917–63), the thirty-fifth president of the United
States, served less than three years of the term he began in 1961. He was
assassinated in Dallas, Texas, on November 22, 1963. During his brief
presidential career, the world was brought to the brink of nuclear war
over the presence of Soviet missiles in Cuba.

To those new states whom we welcome to the ranks of the free, we pledge our word that one form of colonial control shall not have passed away merely to be replaced by a far more iron tyranny. We shall not always expect to find them supporting our view. But we shall always hope to find them strongly supporting their own freedom, and to remember that, in the past, those who foolishly sought power by riding the back of the tiger ended up inside.

He welcomes third world nations to freedom

To those peoples in the huts and villages of half the globe struggling to break the bonds of mass misery, we pledge our best efforts to help them help themselves, for whatever period is required, not because the Communists may be doing it, not because we seek their votes, but because it is right. If a free society cannot help the many who are poor, it cannot save the few who are rich.

He would help the poor to help themselves & thus find freedom maybe use this as a quote

To our sister republics south of our border, we offer a special pledge: to convert our good words into good deeds, in a new alliance for progress, to assist free men and free governments in casting off the chains of poverty. But this peaceful revolution of hope cannot become the prey of hostile powers. Let all our neighbors know that we shall join with them to oppose aggression or subversion anywhere in the Americas. And let every other power know that this hemisphere intends to remain the master of its own house.

His "alliance for progress" will "assist free men and free governments" to escape poverty

To that world assembly of sovereign states, the United Nations, our last best hope in an age where the instruments of war have far outpaced the instruments of peace, we renew our pledge of support: to prevent it from becoming merely a forum for invective, to strengthen its shield of the new and the weak, and to enlarge the area in which its writ may run.

UN support

Finally, to those nations who would make themselves our adversary, we offer not a pledge but a request: that both sides begin anew the quest for peace, before the dark powers of destruction unleashed by science engulf all humanity in planned or accidental self-destruction.

We dare not tempt them with weakness. For only when our arms are sufficient beyond doubt can we be certain beyond doubt that they will never be employed.

But neither can two great and powerful groups of nations take comfort from our present course—both sides

freedom by strength of arms and military power but he is willing to search for peace & to negotiate

overburdened by the cost of modern weapons, both rightly alarmed by the steady spread of the deadly atom, yet both racing to alter that uncertain balance of terror that stays the hand of mankind's final war.

So let us begin anew, remembering on both sides that civility is not a sign of weakness, and sincerity is always subject to proof. Let us never negotiate out of fear, but let us never fear to negotiate.

Let both sides explore what problems unite us instead of belaboring those problems which divide us.

Let both sides, for the first time, formulate serious and precise proposals for the inspection and control of arms, and bring the absolute power to destroy other nations under the absolute control of all nations.

Let both sides seek to invoke the wonders of science instead of its terrors. Together let us explore the stars, conquer the deserts, eradicate disease, tap the ocean depths and encourage the arts and commerce.

Let both sides unite to heed in all corners of the earth the command of Isaiah to "undo the heavy burdens . . . [and] let the oppressed go free."

And if a beachhead of cooperation may push back the jungle of suspicion, let both sides join in creating a new endeavor, not a new balance of power, but a new world of law, where the strong are just and the weak secure and the peace preserved.

a "new world of law" would preserve peace & assure freedom

All this will not be finished in the first one hundred days. Nor will it be finished in the first one thousand days, nor in the life of this Administration, nor even perhaps in our lifetime on this planet. But let us begin.

In your hands, my fellow citizens, more than mine, will rest the final success or failure of our course. Since this country was founded, each generation of Americans has been summoned to give testimony to its national loyalty. The graves of young Americans who answered the call to service surround the globe.

Now the trumpet summons us again—not as a call to bear arms, though arms we need; not as a call to battle, though embattled we are; but a call to bear the burden of a long twilight struggle, year in and year out, "rejoicing in hope, patient in tribulation," a struggle against the common enemies of men: tyranny, poverty, disease and war itself.

this will be "a long twilight struggle" against forces that might destroy freedom

Can we forge against these enemies a grand and global alliance, North and South, East and West, that can assure a more fruitful life for all mankind? Will you join in that historic effort?

In the long history of the world, only a few generations have been granted the role of defending freedom in its hour of maximum danger. I do not shrink from this responsibility; I welcome it. I do not believe that any of us would exchange places with any other people or any other generation. The energy, the faith, the devotion which we bring to this endeavor will light our country and all who serve it, and the glow from that fire can truly light the world.

He will defend freedom in "its hour of maximum danger."

And so, my fellow Americans, ask not what your country can do for you; ask what you can do for your country.

My fellow citizens of the world, ask not what America will do for you, but what together we can do for the freedom of man.

Finally, whether you are citizens of America or citizens of the world, ask of us here the same high standards of strength and sacrifice which we ask of you. With a good conscience our only sure reward, with history that final judge of our deeds, let us go forth to lead the land we love, asking His blessing and His help, but knowing that here on earth God's work must truly be our own.

Citizens of all nations must work for the freedom of all people.

Summary: Kennedy says the torch of freedom has passed to a new generation that must struggle against the enemies. He welcomes the challenge and asks Americans and citizens of the world to join his quest for freedom.

WRITING AN ESSAY

In your individual essays you must find your own way at your own pace. Have you ever noticed that during your writing you will stop, reread a paragraph or two, and then start again? Your review stimulates your thinking and helps you create new ideas. Have you rushed to write a sentence before you might forget an idea? Your writing and thinking will constantly stimulate new ideas. Therefore, you should consider your first draft as a preliminary discovery draft to sketch in broad strokes your basic concerns, to set the framework for the big picture, and to focus on one subject. Subsequent drafts must supply background, add color to the foreground, and provide specific detail. The essay will grow page after page, just as an oil painting slowly but surely reaches a finished stage on canvas.

Each part of the writing process contributes to the final manuscript. The following procedure has produced many excellent essays:

1. Begin by reading the introduction to an essay that looks interesting to you or read one assigned by the instructor. The introduction will give you background information on the author, explain the author's topic and purpose, and in general establish points that you should watch for in the reading of the essay itself.

2. Read the essay in the manner outlined in the previous section. Make brief marginal notations, list key words, record your thoughts in a reading notebook or journal. In particular, write personal notes to discover your own ideas and to confront issues that you must address in an essay of your own.

3. After finishing the essay, read the first set of "Comments and Assignments" on the "Aims and Strategies of the Writer" that appears after each essay. Each comment should clarify one of the *author's* fundamental aims, while each assignment should set in motion *your* discovery of a topic and a reason for writing about it.

During this discovery stage of the writing process, the concept of *invention* applies to your work. You must *invent* the topic and the ingredients for a paper. Here are a few invention techniques.

Freewriting is a period of nonstop writing without worries about style or penmanship. The freewriting exercise gets your writing "juices" flowing and helps you develop a few specific thoughts. Start with your general subject and for five minutes or so write whatever comes to mind. Later, on examination, a few ideas might emerge from this burst of mental energy.

Brainstorming means that you gather with a few of your peers or associates for a period of discussion and examination of a topic. Discuss ideas with other people, ask questions, and listen. Later on, you must address these ideas in the paper, so find out your audience's concerns to give yourself a sense of direction.

Clustering requires that you isolate the subject's general issues or basic ideas and interrelate them into a design that groups and classifies major categories, as in the following clustering:

This design spotlights legislators as the fundamental center in the push-pull debate, which suggests a focus on legislative action. Perhaps the writer could call a local representative's office for information.

Framing a *writing situation* will uncover your role as a writer on this subject for a specific audience. You must clarify your aim and establish your methods for developing the essay. (For examples, see pages 4–5.)

4. Read the second set of "Comments and Assignments" on the "Writing Process." These comments are designed to explain a writer's organization, an essay's structure, and a writer's use of the patterns of development.

   The assignments at this stage of the process recommend preliminary writing projects and also suggest ways to structure your essay, build an intense opening, develop paragraphs of substance, establish an effective voice and point of view, and many other matters of general development.

5. Write a *rough draft*. This first version of your paper is a discovery draft in which you can record your central ideas and begin filling paragraphs with evidence. If you are prepared with notes, outlines, and rough lists, you can make this draft more complete.

6. Revision of the first draft allows you to cut and paste, delete, add new paragraphs, and in general expand and flesh out the paper. Your revision should alter and improve the paper as a whole so that (1) the introduction presents your subject and your special concerns, (2) the body builds a clear sequence of major ideas with appropriate evidence, and (3) the ending evolves logically and makes a concluding statement about the subject.

   Ideally, a period of incubation should follow your revision of the rough draft. During that time you must let the paper lie idle so that a reappraisal after a day or so provokes challenging views and new ideas.

7. Editing prepares the revised essay for typing or final writing in ink. Check paragraphs for completeness. Study sentence structure and word choices. Look for ways to change "to be" verbs (is, are, was) to strong, active verbs. Avoid passive voice. Check individual words for their appropriateness. Cut out vague words. Look for ways to break up long strings of monosyllabic words (for instance, change "in one day a life can change from one of joy to one of sad times" [sixteen words] to "one day often changes life from joy to sadness" [nine words]).

Edit to avoid discriminatory language by following a few simple steps: (a) Be accurate. (b) Use plural subjects so that nonspecific pronouns are grammatically correct (for instance, "Doctors maintain *their* surgical equipment and other lab supplies in sterile condition"). (c) Reword sentences so that a pronoun is unnecessary ("The doctor maintained all surgical equipment in sterile condition"). (d) Use a specifier (the, this, that) or the pronoun you, if appropriate ("The doctor maintained *that* surgical equipment in sterile condition" or "Each of you must maintain *your* equipment in sterile condition"). (e) At first mention, use a person's full name (Mary Jo Penzak) and thereafter use the last name only (Penzak, not Mrs. Penzak).

8. Proofread the final manuscript, whether typed or written in ink, for any last-minute errors. Remember, it's better to mar a neat page with strike-outs and corrections than to submit it in attractive but error-filled form. Your readers do not wish to edit or proofread your paper. They wish to examine your ideas and your development and expansion of them; don't burden them with extra work. Also, don't force them to judge you on penmanship, spelling, and grammar rather than on the quality of your thinking and composition skills.

Your understanding of the four aims of discourse and your ability to handle the ten basic patterns of rhetoric will prepare you for writing assignments throughout your college years and beyond. Consider a few typical assignments and effective responses.

Trace the development of slavery in South Carolina.
(Your explanation should use historical narration plus some process analysis and cause and effect.)

Compare and contrast the various sugar substitutes.
(Your explanation should depend primarily on contrast, plus classification and examples.)

Develop a position paper on euthanasia.
(Your expressive discourse will require causal analysis, plus definition, examples, and process analysis.)

Defend President Reagan's firm commitment to military spending.
(Your persuasive discourse needs a pattern of cause and effect, plus comparison and classification.)

Create a letter to promote the next meeting of the Chemistry Club.
(Your persuasive discourse will use cause and effect, plus inductive or deductive reasoning.)

Write a short story of approximately ten pages.
(Your creative discourse needs narration, plus description and a mixture of cause and effect relationships among the characters.)

Interpret Robert Frost's poem "Design."
(Your explanation should classify for analysis, use inductive evidence, and cite examples.)

Debate the issues of abortion and take a position.
(Your persuasive discourse needs deductive reasoning, plus causal analysis, classification, description, definition, and process analysis.)

Keep a log of observations during a botany field trip.
(Your expressive discourse should describe and narrate personal reactions and also use explanation to classify, compare, and give examples.)

Develop a computer program that features both loops and arrays.
(Your explanation should use process analysis, plus classification and causal analysis.)

Knowledge gained in a basic composition course will serve your cross-disciplinary needs. Once you recognize the purpose of the writing, you can use fundamental patterns of development to advance and expand the work, whether it's an essay exam answer, a report for a marketing course, or a position paper in ethics.

 Description

Three characteristics are common to most descriptive essays: The writer creates one dominant impression; reports details; and brings to life a special scene, person, or event. A brief paragraph will demonstrate these elements.

> A single knoll rises out of the plain in Oklahoma, north and west of the Wichita Range. For my people, the Kiowas, it is an old landmark, and they gave it the name Rainy Mountain. The hardest weather in the world is there. Winter brings blizzards, hot tornadic winds arise in the spring, and in summer the prairie is an anvil's edge. The grass turns brittle and brown, and it cracks beneath your feet. There are green belts along the rivers and creeks, linear groves of hickory and pecan, willow and witch hazel. At a distance in July or August the steaming foliage seems almost to writhe in fire. Great green and yellow grasshoppers are everywhere in the tall grass, popping up like corn to sting the flesh, and tortoises crawl about on the red earth, going nowhere in the plenty of time. Loneliness is an aspect of the land. All things in the plain are isolate: there is no confusion of objects in the eye, but *one* hill or *one* tree or *one* man. To look upon that landscape in the early morning, with the sun at your back, is to lose the sense of proportion. Your imagination comes to life, and this, you think, is where Creation was begun.

This paragraph by Scott Momaday from *The Way to Rainy Mountain* provides one dominant impression: the arid, isolated nature of his homeplace. Momaday reinforces the impression with focused details and fresh images—"green belts," "steaming foliage," grass "brittle and brown."

CONVEY ONE DOMINANT IMPRESSION

Momaday uses the isolated majesty of Rainy Mountain to evoke the fearful loneliness of the high plains of Oklahoma. Similarly, a dominant

19

impression should permeate your descriptive writing so that the reader knows your direction—whether you are creating a sense of isolation, innocence, horror, intimacy, love, fear, or hate. The essays that follow do this: Annie Dillard uses a dried, knotted snakeskin to convey the impression of nature's mysterious presence. Joan Didion describes absurd wedding rituals to paint a picture of Las Vegas as a bizarre town that never sleeps. The persuasive words of Jonathan Schell reinforce the somber message of his essay—the shocking effects of nuclear explosion. Such subjective description drawn from personal responses differs from objective description, which is discussed on the next page.

SUPPLY PLENTY OF FOCUSED DETAILS

Momaday reinforces his dominant impression—loneliness—with carefully chosen details: the hot dry prairie land, sparse hickory and pecan trees, grasshoppers, tortoises. This imagery invites readers to view the scene through Momaday's eyes as he stands alone on the Oklahoma prairie. He doesn't merely say the weather is hot and the land is dry; he wraps the words around you so you almost feel and see the heat and dryness.

The necessity of focused details means that your writing should maintain a consistent point of view. Locate a place and let your description move the reader. This focus is evident in this student writer's re-creation of the nostalgia of an old country store.

> After stepping across a sleeping shepherd dog and pushing against a door held together by tin signs saying "RC Cola," "Colonial Bread," and "Lucky Strikes," I entered the musky store. I ducked around whole country hams hanging from low rafters, pinched off a small chunk of cheese from a huge block near the aisle, and almost stumbled over a tub of overripe Jonathans.

This description moves the reader through the doorway, around the hams, past the cheese, and below to the apples. Description is rarely stationary. Even if the objects being described do not move, the observer's eyes do. Description should create a sense of movement.

OFFER FRESH METAPHORICAL IMAGES

Figurative language uses imagery to give freshness and originality to the writing. A *simile* expresses a comparison of two items that are not of the same general class but that have something in common. It joins these items by connecting them with words such as "like" or "as if":

"The professor's chalk scratched against the board like a bluejay screeching from the woods." A *metaphor* makes an implied comparison by speaking as though the two items actually belonged together: "The professor's owl eyes, on the alert for any unwarranted movement, peered across the room."

In the short paragraph that opened this chapter, Momaday uses similes and metaphors: the prairie is an anvil's edge, the grass cracks beneath your feet, the rivers have green belts, the grasshoppers pop up like corn to sting the flesh. Descriptive writing often uses comparisons that link items not usually associated: popcorn with grasshoppers, the harsh edges of the prairie with a blacksmith's anvil. In one of the following essays, Robert Bly describes a hockey goalie as wearing an African Mask, skating on rhinoceros legs, and, as Bly puts it: "Sadly sweeping the ice in front of his house, he is the old witch in the woods, waiting for the children to come home." In every case, of course, the writer's imagery must reinforce the meaning and thesis of the essay. Bly's imagery builds the impression of the goalie as a lonely, strange outcast who is not involved in the game except for sporadic, violent moments.

USE OBJECTIVE DESCRIPTION FOR SCIENTIFIC WRITING

Objective description is exact, factual, and detailed, being shorn of personal, subjective overtones. The purpose is to report precisely what you see: under a microscope, within a dissected frog, in the water of a local lake. The specificity of objective writing forces you to focus on concrete detail, not how you feel about a dead frog or the lake. Although Jonathan Schell's underlying purpose is to ban nuclear weapons, he gives the impression of objective description in his vivid re-creation of a bomb dropped on New York City. Schell achieves an effect of flat, unemotional language that gives the *appearance* of objectivity.

To review: You can write an effective descriptive essay by limiting yourself to a dominant impression and letting selected details grow out of your narrowed focus. Adding fresh similes or metaphors will enhance the essay. Your descriptive essay will need

1. Plenty of details that focus on one dominant impression
2. A consistent point of view that helps maintain the reader's visual perspective
3. A few figures of speech that will enrich your style with fresh comparisons

Sometimes writers use description as a tool for expressing personal feelings about a special place. Such writing thereby reveals private responses to the subject while drawing a picture for the reader. With a writing focus turned inward to her own thoughts as well as outward to her surroundings, the writer shares and reveals something special— a moment in time that is precious and worth capturing in words. Put another way, the writer's subjective reactions decorate and color the topic to the point that we learn as much about the writer as we do about the object or scene described.

In the following passage Annie Dillard describes a February stroll through the woods near her farm in Virginia. She moves us visually to her discovery of a knotted snakeskin found on the forest floor. The scene causes her to describe her personal feeling about the mysterious cycle of nature. The snakeskin is her primary image. Her speculations on springtime develop from a personal response to the visual experiences. Consequently, her pattern of development is description.

As you read the essay, make marginal notes that explain the descriptive focus of each paragraph. For example, paragraph 1: "Walking in the woods, Dillard discovers a knotted snakeskin lying beside an abandoned fish aquarium."

Annie Dillard, a native of Pittsburgh, lived for several years in Virginia on her farm, Tinker Creek. Her interest in the environment is reflected in many of her essays. "Untying the Knot" is from her book Pilgrim at Tinker Creek *(1974), for which she won the Pulitzer Prize. She has also published* Tickets for a Prayer Wheel *(1974),* Holy the Firm *(1977),* Living by Fiction *(1982), and* Teaching a Stone to Talk *(1982).*

ANNIE DILLARD

Untying the Knot

Yesterday I set out to catch the new season, and instead I found an old   1
snakeskin. I was in the sunny February woods by the quarry; the snakeskin was lying in a heap of leaves right next to an aquarium someone had thrown away. I don't know why that someone hauled the aquarium deep into the woods to get rid of it; it had only one broken glass side. The snake found it handy, I imagine; snakes like to rub against something rigid to help them out of their skins, and the broken aquarium looked like the nearest likely object. Together the snakeskin and the aquarium made an interesting scene on the forest floor. It looked like

an exhibit at a trial—circumstantial evidence—of a wild scene, as though a snake had burst through the broken side of the aquarium, burst through his ugly old skin, and disappeared, perhaps straight up in the air, in a rush of freedom and beauty.

The snakeskin had unkeeled scales, so it belonged to a nonpoison- 2 ous snake. It was roughly five feet long by the yardstick, but I'm not sure because it was very wrinkled and dry, and every time I tried to stretch it flat it broke. I ended up with seven or eight pieces of it all over the kitchen table in a fine film of forest dust.

The point I want to make about the snakeskin is that, when I found 3 it, it was whole and tied in a knot. Now there have been stories told, even by reputable scientists, of snakes that have deliberately tied themselves in a knot to prevent larger snakes from trying to swallow them— but I couldn't imagine any way that throwing itself into a half hitch would help a snake trying to escape its skin. Still, ever cautious, I figured that one of the neighborhood boys could possibly have tied it in a knot in the fall, for some whimsical boyish reason, and left it there, where it dried and gathered dust. So I carried the skin along thoughtlessly as I walked, snagging it sure enough on a low branch and ripping it in two for the first of many times. I saw that thick ice still lay on the quarry pond and that the skunk cabbage was already out in the clearings, and then I came home and looked at the skin and its knot.

The knot had no beginning. Idly I turned it around in my hand, 4 searching for a place to untie; I came to with a start when I realized I must have turned the thing around fully ten times. Intently, then, I traced the knot's lump around with a finger: it was continuous. I couldn't untie it any more than I could untie a doughnut; it was a loop without beginning or end. These snakes *are* magic, I thought for a second, and then of course I reasoned what must have happened. The skin had been pulled inside-out like a peeled sock for several inches; then an inch or so of the inside-out part—a piece whose length was coincidentally equal to the diameter of the skin—had somehow been turned right-side out again, making a thick lump whose edges were lost in wrinkles, looking exactly like a knot.

So. I have been thinking about the change of seasons. I don't want 5 to miss spring this year. I want to distinguish the last winter frost from the out-of-season one, the frost of spring. I want to be there on the spot the moment the grass turns green. I always miss this radical revolution; I see it the next day from a window, the yard so suddenly green and lush I could envy Nebuchadnezzar down on all fours eating grass. This year I want to stick a net into time and say "now," as men plant flags on the ice and snow and say, "here." But it occurred to me that I could no more catch spring by the tip of the tail than I could untie the apparent knot in the snakeskin; there are no edges to grasp. Both are continuous loops.

I wonder how long it would take you to notice the regular recurrence of the seasons if you were the first man on earth. What would it be like to live in open-ended time broken only by days and nights? You could say, "it's cold again; it was cold before," but you couldn't make the key connection and say, "it was cold this time last year," because the notion of "year" is precisely the one you lack. Assuming that you hadn't yet noticed any orderly progression of heavenly bodies, how long would you have to live on earth before you could feel with any assurance that any one particular long period of cold would, in fact, end? "While the earth remaineth, seedtime and harvest, and cold and heat, and summer and winter, and day and night shall not cease": God makes this guarantee very early in Genesis to a people whose fears on this point had perhaps not been completely allayed.

It must have been fantastically important, at the real beginnings of human culture, to conserve and relay this vital seasonal information, so that the people could anticipate dry or cold seasons, and not huddle on some November rock hoping pathetically that spring was just around the corner. We still very much stress the simple fact of four seasons to schoolchildren; even the most modern of modern new teachers, who don't seem to care if their charges can read or write or name two products of Peru, will still muster some seasonal chitchat and set the kids to making paper pumpkins, or tulips, for the walls. "The people," wrote Van Gogh in a letter, "are very sensitive to the changing seasons." That we are "very sensitive to the changing seasons" is, incidentally, one of the few good reasons to shun travel. If I stay at home I preserve the illusion that what is happening on Tinker Creek is the very newest thing, that I'm at the very vanguard and cutting edge of each new season. I don't want the same season twice in a row; I don't want to know I'm getting last week's weather, used weather, weather broadcast up and down the coast, old-hat weather.

But there's always unseasonable weather. What we think of the weather and behavior of life on the planet at any given season is really all a matter of statistical probabilities; at any given point, anything might happen. There is a bit of every season in each season. Green plants—deciduous green leaves—grow everywhere, all winter long, and small shoots come up pale and new in every season. Leaves die on the tree in May, turn brown, and fall into the creek. The calendar, the weather, and the behavior of wild creatures have the slimmest of connections. Everything overlaps smoothly for only a few weeks each season, and then it all tangles up again. The temperature, of course, lags far behind the calendar seasons, since the earth absorbs and releases heat slowly, like a leviathan breathing. Migrating birds head south in what appears to be dire panic, leaving mild weather and fields full of insects and seeds; they reappear as if in all eagerness in January, and poke about morosely in the snow. Several years ago our October woods would have made a dismal colored photograph for a sadist's calendar: a killing frost came before the leaves had even begun to brown; they dropped from every tree like crepe, blackened and limp. It's all a chancy, jumbled affair at best, as things seem to be below the stars.

Time is the continuous loop, the snakeskin with scales endlessly 9
overlapping without beginning or end, or time is an ascending spiral if you will, like a child's toy Slinky. Of course we have no idea which arc on the loop is our time, let alone where the loop itself is, so to speak, or down whose lofty flight of stairs the Slinky so uncannily walks.

The power we seek, too, seems to be a continuous loop. I have 10
always been sympathetic with the early notion of a divine power that exists in a particular place, or that travels about over the face of the earth as a man might wander—and when he is "there" he is surely not here. You can shake the hand of a man you meet in the woods; but the spirit seems to roll along like the mythical hoop snake with its tail in its mouth. There are no hands to shake or edges to untie. It rolls along the mountain ridges like a fireball, shooting off a spray of sparks at random, and will not be trapped, slowed, grasped, fetched, peeled, or aimed. "As for the wheels, it was cried unto them in my hearing, O wheel." This is the hoop of flame that shoots the rapids in the creek or spins across the dizzy meadows; this is the arsonist of the sunny woods: catch it if you can.

AIMS AND STRATEGIES OF THE WRITER

Comment. According to the title of her book, she is a "pilgrim" who has journeyed to her Tinker Creek farm where she seeks enlightenment. On this day a personal quest draws her into the woods for a February walk. However, she does not find exactly the spring season she went looking for; she finds instead a knotted snakeskin.

Assignment 1. Consider for a moment your walk today to a class session. Did you pause to observe and look closely at the things around you? If not, make a commitment to take a walk at some time today for the purpose of close observation—of natural signs, of people, and of the unusual. Be like a pilgrim in a sacred place where all things have meaning. Your observations will aid in your discovery of a subject.

Comment. The snakeskin is central to Dillard's descriptive essay because she uses it to suggest additional ideas. In effect, she allows universal values to develop from her examination of the snakeskin, pointing out that "the power we seek, too, seems to be a continuous loop."

Assignment 2. Recall and describe in a brief paragraph or a journal entry an unusual object or scene that you recently observed. Explain why it stays in your memory and the reasons for your subjective response to the scene.

Comment. A writer's point of view ("I," "he," "she," "it," "you") often reflects descriptive purposes. References to "he" and "it" suggest objectivity. References to "you" imply direction and instruction. Dillard purposely uses "I" in order to reveal personal involvement.

Assignment 3. Change "I" in Dillard's opening sentence to "you" and then change "I" to "she." Explain how each change affects the direction the essay can take.

Comment. Dillard's descriptive essay about a snakeskin expresses personal attitudes that would be inappropriate for a scientific laboratory report about a species of snake. The difference between personal and scientific description suggests something about the writer's concern for the needs of the readers.

Assignment 4. Find an objective, scientific description of a snake in a science book or encyclopedia. You can easily see the differences between a science writer's purposes and those of Dillard. Write two descriptions, one subjective and one objective. Relate first how you feel about a roach crawling on your bathroom floor; then write an objective description of the roach, explaining its role in the cycle of nature.

THE WRITING PROCESS

Comment. Dillard's opening paragraph explains that she went into the woods in search of the new spring season. Her fifth paragraph returns to that idea as she confesses, "I could no more catch spring by the tip of the tail than I could untie the apparent knot in the snakeskin; there are no edges to grasp." Later, in paragraph 9, she returns to the "continuous loop" of the snakeskin.

Assignment 5. Outline or diagram Dillard's essay either showing her opening, body, and conclusion or explaining the contents of each paragraph. Your outline should reveal how Dillard's central snakeskin image—the dominant impression—frames her philosophical musings.

Comment. Dillard uses the snakeskin as a symbol; that is, it really is an old dried snakeskin twisted into a knot, but it also represents the mysteries of nature.

Assignment 6. Select a natural phenomenon—maybe a squirrel with a jaw full of acorns—and write a brief paragraph exploring what this image suggests to you about life.

Comment. The setting of a descriptive essay affects the writer's message. Dillard uses the quiet, rural setting of a southern forest. The setting is appropriate for her reflections about natural wonders.

Assignment 7. Change the setting of this essay and explain how the change affects the tone and message of the essay. For example, suppose you were to find a snakeskin in your kitchen sink after you had been on vacation for two weeks.

Comment. Dillard offers extensive commentary about one incongruity of the forest scene—the presence of an abandoned fish aquarium near the snakeskin. She uses this juxtaposition of a household item with a natural wonder to create a fresh metaphoric image in which she imagines a wild scene of the snake bursting from the aquarium into free, unrestrained beauty.

Assignment 8. Consider the many ways in which modern gadgetry conflicts with natural habitation—for instance, a beer can's pop top attracting a trout or a wild deer grazing near a scummy, contaminated pond. Write a paragraph that speculates on how modern technology conflicts with nature.

Comment. In paragraph 5 Dillard uses a technique known as *allusion*, in which a writer makes reference to a historic person or event. In this case she alludes to Nebuchadnezzar, a Babylonian king who had spells of madness during which he imagined himself an ox and would actually eat the grass in the fields.

Assignment 9. Draw on your knowledge of history and literature to make connections between a contemporary and an ancient scene or object. For example, you might refer to professional football players as Octavian gladiators, the new city hall as the town labyrinth, or a talkative friend as another Shakespeare. Write a brief paragraph that extends the comparison of your two items. (However, you must depend on your background for references and anticipate the knowledge of your audience. For instance, if your readers have not read Hawthorne's *The Scarlet Letter*, an allusion to Hester's "A" will make little sense.)

Comment. Some topics require unusual or specialized words relating to the subject. Dillard goes walking in the woods near the *quarry* (a deep pit from which stone has been extracted). She reports that the snakeskin has *unkeeled scales* (scales that do not have a ridge, making the snake's body very smooth and shiny).

Assignment 10. Select a subject for descriptive writing and determine specialized wording that may be required. For example, floating along a river will differ in a barge, raft, flatboat, or keelboat. Use a dictionary, thesaurus, or encyclopedia to discover special words. Writers are a diligent breed; they love finding just the right word even if it means searching several biology or psychology books. Caution: You must select new words carefully and use them correctly.

Comment. In her final three paragraphs, Dillard creates a number of fresh, metaphoric images.

> "the earth absorbs and releases heat slowly, like a leviathan breathing"

> "they [leaves] dropped from every tree like crepe, blackened and limp"

> "time is an ascending spiral if you will, like a child's toy Slinky"

> "It [divine power] rolls along the mountain ridges like a fireball"

Assignment 11. Try completing these similes after the word "like" with your own images. In addition, choose one of these similes (yours or Dillard's) and write a brief paragraph that explains the effect of the comparison.

In the mid 1970s John McPhee spent a considerable time living in and researching the state of Alaska. "Grizzly" describes one part of that experience. On a hiking trip he and two companions suddenly encounter a grizzly bear, which stands only a hundred yards away, foraging for food. McPhee maintains, in general, an objective description of the bear's appearance, eating habits, and behavior when confronted by humans. Yet just beneath the surface of objective description is McPhee's primary thesis—the awesome grandeur of Alaska. The bear is just one manifestation of the state's alluring—and wild— magnificence.

As you read, make marginal notes on two aspects of McPhee's descriptive writing. First, highlight his descriptive passages on the bear and its habits. Second, note his description of human beings and their reactions to bears. Look too for those passages in which McPhee paints the grandeur of Alaska.

McPhee is a professional writer whose works include various topics: Oranges (1967) studies the history of the fruit; Levels of the Game (1969) examines tennis; The Curve of Binding Energy (1974) probes nuclear waste problems; and The Place de la Concord Suisse (1984) is a portrait of the Swiss Army. "Grizzly" is from McPhee's book on Alaska, Coming into the Country (1976).

JOHN McPHEE

 Grizzly

We passed first through stands of fireweed, and then over ground that 1
was wine-red with the leaves of bearberries. There were curlewberries, too, which put a deep-purple stain on the hand. We kicked at some wolf scat, old as winter. It was woolly and white and filled with the hair of a snowshoe hare. Nearby was a rich inventory of caribou pellets and, in increasing quantity as we moved downhill, blueberries—an outspreading acreage of blueberries. Fedeler stopped walking. He touched my arm. He had in an instant become even more alert than he usually was, and obviously apprehensive. His gaze followed straight on down our intended course. What he saw there I saw now. It appeared to me to be a hill of fur. "Big boar grizzly," Fedeler said in a near-whisper. The bear was about a hundred steps away, in the blueberries, grazing. The head was down, the hump high. The immensity of muscle seemed to vibrate slowly—to expand and contract, with the grazing. Not berries alone

but whole bushes were going into the bear. He was big for a barren-ground grizzly. The brown bears of Arctic Alaska (or grizzlies; they are no longer thought to be different) do not grow to the size they will reach on more ample diets elsewhere. The barren-ground grizzly will rarely grow larger than six hundred pounds.

"What if he got too close?" I said.   2

Fedeler said, "We'd be in real trouble."   3

"You can't outrun them," Hession said.   4

A grizzly, no slower than a racing horse, is about half again as fast as   5
the fastest human being. Watching the great mound of weight in the blueberries, with a fifty-five-inch waist and a neck more than thirty inches around, I had difficulty imagining that he could move with such speed, but I believed it, and was without impulse to test the proposition. Fortunately, a light southerly wind was coming up the Salmon valley. On its way to us, it passed the bear. The wind was relieving, coming into our faces, for had it been moving the other way the bear would not have been placidly grazing. There is an old adage that when a pine needle drops in the forest the eagle will see it fall; the deer will hear it when it hits the ground; the bear will smell it. If the boar grizzly were to catch our scent, he might stand on his hind legs, the better to try to see. Although he could hear well and had an extraordinary sense of smell, his eyesight was not much better than what was required to see a blueberry inches away. For this reason, a grizzly stands and squints, attempting to bring the middle distance into focus, and the gesture is often misunderstood as a sign of anger and forthcoming attack. If the bear were getting ready to attack, he would be on four feet, head low, ears cocked, the hair above his hump muscle standing on end. As if that message were not clear enough, he would also chop his jaws. His teeth would make a sound that would carry like the ringing of an axe.

One could predict, but not with certainty, what a grizzly would do.   6
Odds were very great that one touch of man scent would cause him to stop his activity, pause in a moment of absorbed and alert curiosity, and then move, at a not undignified pace, in a direction other than the one from which the scent was coming. This is what would happen almost every time, but there was, to be sure, no guarantee. The forest Eskimos fear and revere the grizzly. They know that certain individual bears not only will fail to avoid a person who comes into their country but will approach and even stalk the trespasser. It is potentially inaccurate to extrapolate the behavior of any one bear from the behavior of most, since they are both intelligent and independent and will do what they choose to do according to mood, experience, whim. A grizzly that has ever been wounded by a bullet will not forget it, and will probably

know that it was a human being who sent the bullet. At sight of a human, such a bear will be likely to charge. Grizzlies hide food sometimes—a caribou calf, say, under a pile of scraped-up moss—and a person the bear might otherwise ignore might suddenly not be ignored if the person were inadvertently to step into the line between the food cache and the bear. A sow grizzly with cubs, of course, will charge anything that suggests danger to the cubs, even if the cubs are nearly as big as she is. They stay with their mother two and a half years.

None of us had a gun. (None of the six of us had brought a gun on the trip.) Among nonhunters who go into the terrain of the grizzly, there are several schools of thought about guns. The preferred one is: Never go without a sufficient weapon—a high-powered rifle or a shotgun and plenty of slug-loaded shells. The option is not without its own inherent peril. A professional hunter, some years ago, spotted a grizzly from the air and—with a client, who happened to be an Anchorage barber—landed on a lake about a mile from the bear. The stalking that followed was evidently conducted not only by the hunters but by the animal as well. The professional hunter was found dead from a broken neck, and had apparently died instantly, unaware of danger, for the cause of death was a single bite, delivered from behind. The barber, noted as clumsy with a rifle, had emptied his magazine, missing the bear with every shot but one, which struck the grizzly in the foot. The damage the bear did to the barber was enough to kill him several times. After the corpses were found, the bear was tracked and killed. To shoot and merely wound is worse than not to shoot at all. A bear that might have turned and gone away will possibly attack if wounded.

Fatal encounters with bears are as rare as they are memorable. Some people reject the rifle as cumbersome extra baggage, not worth toting, given the minimal risk. And, finally, there are a few people who feel that it is wrong to carry a gun, in part because the risk is low and well worth taking, but most emphatically because they see the gun as an affront to the wild country of which the bear is sign and symbol. This, while strongly felt, is a somewhat novel attitude. When Robert Marshall explored the Brooks Range half a century ago, he and his companions fired at almost every bear they saw, without pausing for philosophical reflection. The reaction was automatic. They were expressing mankind's immemorial fear of this beast—man and rattlesnake, man and bear. Among modern environmentalists, to whom a figure like Marshall is otherwise a hero, fear of the bear has been exceeded by reverence. A notable example, in his own past and present, is Andy Russell, author of a book called *Grizzly Country*. Russell was once a professional hunter, but he gave that up to become a photographer, specializing in grizzlies. He says that he has given up not only shooting bears but even carrying a gun. On rare instances when grizzlies charge toward him, he shouts at them and stands his ground. The worst thing to do, he says, is to run, because anything that runs on open tundra suggests game to a bear. Game does not tend to stand its ground in the presence of grizzlies. Therefore, when the bear comes at you, just stand there. Charging something that does not move, the bear will theoretically stop and reconsider. (Says Russell.) More important, Russell believes that the bear will *know* if you have a gun, even if the gun is concealed:

> Reviewing our experiences, we had become more and more convinced that carrying arms was not only unnecessary in most grizzly country but was certainly no good for the desired atmosphere and proper protocol in obtaining good film records. If we were to obtain such film and fraternize successfully with the big bears, it would be better to go unarmed in most places. The mere fact of having a gun within reach, cached somewhere in a pack or a hidden holster, causes a man to act with unconscious arrogance and thus maybe to smell different or to transmit some kind of signal objectionable to bears. The armed man does not assume his proper role in association with the wild ones, a fact of which they seem instantly aware at some distance. He, being wilder than they, whether he likes to admit it or not, is instantly under even more suspicion than he would encounter if unarmed. 9
>
> One must follow the role of an uninvited visitor—an intruder—rather than that of an aggressive hunter, and one should go unarmed to ensure this attitude. 10

Like pictures from pages riffled with a thumb, all of these things went through my mind there on the mountainside above the grazing bear. I will confess that in one instant I asked myself, "What the hell am I doing *here?*" There was nothing more to the question, though, than a hint of panic. I knew why I had come, and therefore what I was doing there. That I was frightened was incidental. I just hoped the fright would not rise beyond a relatively decorous level. I sensed that Fedeler and Hession were somewhat frightened, too. I would have been troubled if they had not been. Meanwhile, the sight of the bear stirred me like nothing else the country could contain. What mattered was not so much the bear himself as what the bear implied. He was the predominant thing in that country, and for him to be in it at all meant that there had to be more country like it in every direction and more of the same kind of country all around that. He implied a world. He was an affirmation to the rest of the earth that his kind of place was extant. There had been a time when his race was everywhere in North America, but it had been hunted down and pushed away in favor of something else. For example, the grizzly bear is the state animal of California, whose country was once his kind of place; and in California now the grizzly is extinct. 11

The animals I have encountered in my wilderness wanderings have   12
been reluctant to reveal all the things about them I would like to know. The
animal that impresses me most, the one I find myself liking more and more,
is the grizzly. No sight encountered in the wilds is quite so stirring as those
massive, clawed tracks pressed into mud or snow. No sight is quite so
impressive as that of the great bear stalking across some mountain slope
with the fur of his silvery robe rippling over his mighty muscles. His is a
dignity and power matched by no other in the North American wilderness.
To share a mountain with him for a while is a privilege and an adventure
like no other.

I have followed his tracks into an alder hell to see what he had been   13
doing and come to the abrupt end of them, when the maker stood up thirty
feet away with a sudden snort to face me.

To see a mother grizzly ambling and loafing with her cubs across the   14
broad, hospitable bosom of a flower-spangled mountain meadow is to see
life in true wilderness at its best.

If a wolf kills a caribou, and a grizzly comes along while the wolf is   15
feeding on the kill, the wolf puts its tail between its legs and hurries
away. A black bear will run from a grizzly, too. Grizzlies sometimes kill
and eat black bears. The grizzly takes what he happens upon. He is an
opportunistic eater. The predominance of the grizzly in his terrain is
challenged by nothing but men and ravens. To frustrate ravens from
stealing his food, he will lie down and sleep on top of a carcass, occasionally swatting the birds as if they were big black flies. He prefers a
vegetable diet. He can pulp a moosehead with a single blow, but he is
not lusting always to kill, and when he moves through his country he
can be something munificent, going into copses of willow among un-
fleeing moose and their calves, touching nothing, letting it all breathe
as before. He may, though, get the head of a cow moose between his
legs and rake her flanks with the five-inch knives that protrude from
the ends of his paws. Opportunistic. He removes and eats her entrails.
He likes porcupines, too, and when one turns and presents to him a
pygal bouquet of quills, he will leap into the air, land on the other side,
chuck the fretful porcupine beneath the chin, flip it over, and, with a
swift ventral incision, neatly remove its body from its skin, leaving
something like a sea urchin behind him on the ground. He is nothing
if not athletic. Before he dens, or just after he emerges, if his mountains
are covered with snow he will climb to the brink of some impossible
schuss, sit down on his butt, and shove off. Thirty-two, sixty-four, ninety-
six feet per second, he plummets down the mountainside, spray snow
flying to either side, as he approaches collision with boulders and trees.
Just short of catastrophe, still going at bonecrushing speed, he flips to
his feet and walks sedately onward as if his ride had not occurred.

His population density is thin on the Arctic barren ground. He needs   16
for his forage at least fifty and perhaps a hundred square miles that are
all his own—sixty-four thousand acres, his home range. Within it, he
will move, typically, eight miles a summer day, doing his traveling
through the twilight hours of the dead of night. To scratch his belly he
walks over a tree—where forest exists. The tree bends beneath him as
he passes. He forages in the morning, generally; and he rests a great
deal, particularly after he eats. He rests fourteen hours a day. If he
becomes hot in the sun, he lies down in a pool in the river. He sleeps
on the tundra—restlessly tossing and turning, forever changing position. What he could be worrying about I cannot imagine.

His fur blends so well into the tundra colors that sometimes it is   17
hard to see him. Fortunately, we could see well enough the one in front
of us, or we would have walked right to him. He caused a considerable
revision of our travel plans. Not wholly prepared to follow the advice of
Andy Russell, I asked Fedeler what one should do if a bear were to
charge. He said, "Take off your pack and throw it into the bear's path,
then crawl away, and hope the pack will distract the bear. But there is
no good thing to do, really. It's just not a situation to be in."

We made a hundred-and-forty-degree turn from the course we had   18
been following and went up the shoulder of the hill through ever-
thickening brush, putting distance behind us in good position with the
wind. For a time, we waded through hip-deep willow, always making
our way uphill, and the going may have been difficult, but I didn't
notice. There was adrenalin to spare in my bloodstream. I felt that I was
floating, climbing with ease, like Hession. I also had expectations now
that another bear, in the thick brush, might come rising up from any
quarter. We broke out soon into a swale of blueberries. Hession and
Fedeler, their nonchalance refreshed, sat down to eat, paused to graze.
The berries were sweet and large.

"I can see why he's here," Hession said.   19
"These berries are so big."   20
"Southern exposure."   21
"He may not be the only one."   22
"They can be anywhere."   23
"It's amazing to me," Fedeler said. "So large an animal, living up   24
here in this country. It's amazing what keeps that big body alive." Fede-
ler went on eating the blueberries with no apparent fear of growing fat.
The barren-ground bear digs a lot of roots, he said—the roots of milk
vetch, for example, and Eskimo potatoes. The bear, coming out of his
den into the snows of May, goes down into the river bottoms, where
overwintered berries are first revealed. Wolf kills are down there, too.

By the middle of June, his diet is almost wholly vegetable. He eats willow buds, sedges, cotton-grass tussocks. In the cycle of his year, roots and plants are eighty percent of what he eats, and even when the salmon are running he does not sate himself on them alone but forages much of the time for berries. In the fall, he unearths not only roots but ground squirrels and lemmings. It is indeed remarkable how large he grows on the provender of his yearly cycle, for on this Arctic barren ground he has to work much harder than the brown bears of southern Alaska, which line up along foaming rivers—hip to hip, like fishermen in New Jersey—taking forty-pound king salmon in their jaws as if they were nibbling feed from a barnyard trough. When the caribou are in fall migration, moving down the Salmon valley toward the Kobuk, the bear finishes up his year with one of them. Then, around the first of November, he may find a cave or, more likely, digs out a cavern in a mountain-side. If he finds a natural cave, it may be full of porcupines. He kicks them out, and—extending his curious relationship with this animal—will cushion his winter bed with many thousands of their turds. If, on the other hand, he digs his den, he sends earth flying out behind him and makes a shaft that goes upward into the side of the mountain. At the top of the shaft, he excavates a shelf-like cavern. When the outside entrance is plugged with debris, the shaft becomes a column of still air, insulating the upper chamber, trapping the bear's body heat. On a bed of dry vegetation, he lays himself out like a dead pharaoh in a pyramid. But he does not truly hibernate. He just lies there. His mate of the summer, in her den somewhere, will give birth during winter to a cub or two—virtually hairless, blind, weighing about a pound. But the male has nothing to do. His heart rate goes down as low as eight beats a minute. He sleeps and wakes, and sleeps again. He may decide to get up and go out. But that is rare. He may even stay out, which is rarer—to give up denning for that winter and roam his frozen range. If he does this, sooner or later he will find a patch of open water in an otherwise frozen river, and in refreshing himself he will no doubt wet his fur. Then he rolls in the snow, and the fur acquires a thick plate of ice, which is less disturbing to the animal than to the forest Eskimo, who has for ages feared—feared most of all—the "winter bear." Arrows broke against the armoring ice, and it can be heavy enough to stop a bullet.

We moved on now, in continuing retreat, and approached the steep incline of the tributary valley we'd been skirting when the bear rewrote our plans. We meant to put the valley between us and him and reschedule ourselves on the other side. It was in fact less a valley than an extremely large ravine, which plunged maybe eight hundred feet, and

25

then rose up an even steeper incline some fifteen hundred feet on the other side, toward the top of which the bushy vegetation ceased growing. The walking looked promising on the ridge beyond.

I had hoped we might see a den site, and this might have been the place. It had all the requisites but one. It was a steep hillside with southern exposure, and was upgrown with a hell of alders and willows. Moreover, we were on the south side of the Brooks Range divide, which is where most of the dens are. But we were not high enough. We were at something under two thousand feet, and bears in this part of Alaska like to den much higher than that. They want the very best drainage. One way to become a "winter bear" is to wake up in a flooded den. 26

The willow-alder growth was so dense and high that as we went down the hillside we could see no farther than a few yards ahead. It was wet in there from the recent rain. We broke our way forward with the help of gravity, crashing noisily, all but trapped in the thicket. It was a patch of jungle, many acres of jungle, with stems a foot apart and as thick as our arms, and canopies more than twelve feet high. This was bear habitat, the sort of place bears like better than people do. Our original choice had been wise—to skirt this ravine-valley—but now we were in it and without choice. 27

"This is the sort of place to come upon one of them unexpectedly," Hession said. 28

"And there is no going back," Fedeler said. "You can't walk uphill in this stuff." 29

"Good point," Hession said. 30

I might have been a little happier if I had been in an uninstrumented airplane in heavy mountain cloud. We thunked and crashed for fifteen minutes and finally came out at the tributary stream. Our approach flushed a ptarmigan, willow ptarmigan; and grayling—at sight of us— shot around in small, cold pools. The stream was narrow, and alders pressed over it from either side. We drank, and rested, and looked up the slope in front of us, which must have had an incline of fifty degrees. The ridge at the top looked extremely far away. Resting, I became aware of a considerable ache in my legs and a blister on one of my heels. On the way uphill we became separated, Hession angling off to the right, Fedeler and I to the left. We groped for handholds among bushes that protruded from the flaky schist, and pulled ourselves up from ledge to ledge. The adrenalin was gone, and my legs were turning to stone. I was ready to dig a den and get in it. My eyes kept addressing the ridgeline, far above. If eyes were hands they could have pulled me there. Then, suddenly, from far below, I saw Jack Hession lightly ambling along the ridge—in his tennis shoes, in his floppy cotton hat. He was looking around, killing time, waiting up for us. 31

Things seemed better from the ridge. The going would be level for 32
a time. We sat down and looked back, to the north, across the deep
tributary valley, and with my monocular tried to glass the grazing bear.
No sight or sign of him. Above us now was a broadly conical summit,
and spread around its western flank was a mile, at least, of open alpine
tundra. On a contour, we headed south across it—high above, and two
miles east of, the river. We saw what appeared to be a cairn on the next
summit south, and decided to go to it and stand on it and see if we
could guess—in relation to our campsite—where we were. Now the
walking felt good again. We passed a large black pile of grizzly scat.
"When it's steaming, that's when you start looking around for a tree,"
Hession said. This particular scat had sent up its last vapors many days
before. Imagining myself there at such a time, though, I looked around
idly for a tree. The nearest one behind us that was of more than dwarf
or thicket stature was somewhere in Lapland. Ahead of us, however,
across the broad dome of tundra, was a dark stand of white spruce, an
extremity of the North American forest, extending toward us. The trees
were eight hundred yards away. Black bears, frightened, sometimes
climb trees. Grizzlies almost never climb trees.

AIMS AND STRATEGIES OF THE WRITER

Comment. McPhee begins the essay by establishing the setting, place,
and atmosphere. Descriptive writers must convey a firm sense of the
environment and the interrelationship of all parts. McPhee also makes
it clear that he and his guides are intruders into this natural wilderness.

Assignment 1. Write two paragraphs, one that establishes a descriptive
setting where you belong and feel comfortable and one that is foreign
and dangerous to your well-being.

Comment. Rarely are writers able to witness a spectacular scene and
immediately render it into words with meaning and depth; research
and additional study are usually necessary. Such is the case here, since
McPhee tells more about the grizzly than he could have gleaned from
one encounter.

Assignment 2. Note those passages in McPhee's essay that suggest
additional study on his part. Now write a paragraph describing your
own encounter with an animal in the wild. Consider this important
point: Would additional research on the subject give your paragraph
more authenticity?

Comment. Dillard (pages 22–25) writes in a quiet, retrospective manner about an old snakeskin. McPhee, however, writes to explain something for his readers, not to meditate about it. He has a point beyond the speculation about his chance encounter with a bear. He wants to explain Alaska, and the bear is one symbol of the state's wildness.

Assignment 3. Write a brief paragraph that compares and contrasts the aims and general strategies of the two writers, Dillard and McPhee.

Comment. A writer must meet the needs of the readers. Dillard anticipates an intellectual reader who enjoys philosophical speculation. McPhee, however, appears to have in mind a different reader, one who is adventurous and curious about the wilds of Alaska. Few writers merely describe in a vacuum; they color their work with subjective feelings.

Assignment 4. Write a brief paragraph on a subject, first using objective description; then rewrite it, this time including your subjective impressions. Your topic might be a thing (your sewing machine), animal (a wild deer on your front lawn), or place (an abandoned rock quarry).

THE WRITING PROCESS

Comment. McPhee does not describe a bear hunt nor does he narrate an episode in which he is chased by a bear. Yet he discusses the encounter as though it were an adventure story.

Assignment 5. Examine the beginning paragraph by McPhee, then write a similar paragraph on a different subject. Use McPhee's style and tone as much as possible.

Comment. McPhee focuses on one specific bear, maintaining a dominant impression so that the grizzly comes to represent the untamed grandeur of Alaska.

Assignment 6. Select one animal and explain briefly how it represents the basic character of a place. It could be a toy poodle in a reclining chair, a friend's pet raccoon that ventures cautiously from the woods each morning for snacks, or a wild goose that wings silently across a lake in the early morning mist.

Comment. McPhee uses a circular pattern in his essay. In the opening, a guide warns McPhee to stop; in the closing, a guide offers several ideas. In effect, McPhee's personal description of the bear is wrapped within the adventurous journey into the wilds.

Assignment 7. Recall a personal experience that caused you to live intensely for a brief period—an encounter with a burglar or a wild animal, an automobile crash, getting tackled in a football game. Write a brief introduction to establish the setting, especially how you happened to be in that place; then devote a full paragraph to describing this object. Then return to the setting and subsequent events.

Comment. McPhee orders his description by establishing certain characteristics of the grizzly, who is unpredictable, unchallenged, munificent [or generous], opportunistic, athletic, and a nomadic traveler.

Assignment 8. Select one of the bear's characteristics and explain briefly how McPhee uses concrete details that illustrate the bear's talents. Note especially any metaphorical images.

Comment. McPhee involves himself in the descriptive essay and brings to life one particular bear that he encounters in the Alaskan woods. The discussion of the grizzly could appear in other forms.

Assignment 9. Find an encyclopedia entry on the grizzly bear and write a brief paragraph that explores the differences between that objective entry and McPhee's more subjective description.

Comment. McPhee quotes twice from another expert, Andy Russell, who has far more experience with grizzly bears than most men. The quotations reinforce McPhee's story.

Assignment 10. Begin writing your descriptive explanation of a subject. Research it as necessary and, where appropriate, reproduce a relevant quotation or two.

Writers sometimes prefer to remove themselves from the immediate scene, stand back at a distance, and report their findings. Joan Didion does this in her description of marriage Las Vegas style. Even when she brings personal observation of an episode into the description, she remains aloof and distant, preferring to seem somewhat objective while nonetheless making a subjective judgment about the city.

Didion wishes to criticize the contemporary scene, unlike Dillard who philosophizes and McPhee who explains. Didion's essay reaches beyond environmental concerns to make social judgments about life-styles in one city. Her technique, a description of the Las Vegas wedding business, allows readers to discover the nature of this desert town, which devotes itself to immediate gratification. Her description thereby moves beyond observation to value judgment.

As you read the essay, make marginal notes to highlight the exaggerations Didion uses for ironic effect. The accumulation of these satiric thrusts shows how she portrays the absurdity of marriage in Las Vegas.

Didion, a novelist, essayist, and screenwriter, lives and works in California, which provides the setting for most of her subtle, ironic comments about the American scene. She collaborated on the movies A Star Is Born *(1976) and* True Confession *(1981). Her novels include* Play It as It Lays *(1971) and* A Book of Common Prayer *(1976). Her nonfiction work includes* The White Album *(1979),* Salvador *(1983), and the book from which "Marrying Absurd" is reprinted,* Slouching towards Bethlehem *(1967).*

JOAN DIDION

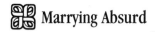 Marrying Absurd

To be married in Las Vegas, Clark County, Nevada, a bride must swear   1
that she is eighteen or has parental permission and a bridegroom that
he is twenty-one or has parental permission. Someone must put up five
dollars for the license. (On Sundays and holidays, fifteen dollars. The
Clark County Courthouse issues marriage licenses at any time of the
day or night except between noon and one in the afternoon, between
eight and nine in the evening, and between four and five in the morning.) Nothing else is required. The State of Nevada, alone among these
United States, demands neither a premarital blood test nor a waiting
period before or after the issuance of a marriage license. Driving in
across the Mojave from Los Angeles, one sees the signs way out on the
desert, looming up from that moonscape of rattlesnakes and mesquite,

even before the Las Vegas lights appear like a mirage on the horizon: "Getting Married? Free License Information First Strip Exit." Perhaps the Las Vegas wedding industry achieved its peak operational efficiency between 9:00 P.M. and midnight of August 26, 1965, an otherwise unremarkable Thursday which happened to be, by Presidential order, the last day on which anyone could improve his draft status merely by getting married. One hundred and seventy-one couples were pronounced man and wife in the name of Clark County and the State of Nevada that night, sixty-seven of them by a single justice of the peace, Mr. James A. Brennan. Mr. Brennan did one wedding at the Dunes and the other sixty-six in his office, and charged each couple eight dollars. One bride lent her veil to six others. "I got it down from five to three minutes," Mr. Brennan said later of his feat. "I could've married them *en masse*, but they're people, not cattle. People expect more when they get married."

What people who get married in Las Vegas actually do expect— 2 what, in the largest sense, their "expectations" are—strikes one as a curious and self-contradictory business. Las Vegas is the most extreme and allegorical of American settlements, bizarre and beautiful in its venality and in its devotion to immediate gratification, a place the tone of which is set by mobsters and call girls and ladies' room attendants with amyl nitrite poppers in their uniform pockets. Almost everyone notes that there is no "time" in Las Vegas, no night and no day and no past and no future (no Las Vegas casino, however, has taken the obliteration of the ordinary time sense quite so far as Harold's Club in Reno, which for a while issued, at odd intervals in the day and night, mimeographed "bulletins" carrying news from the world outside); neither is there any logical sense of where one is. One is standing on a highway in the middle of a vast hostile desert looking at an eighty-foot sign which blinks "Stardust" or "Caesar's Palace." Yes, but what does that explain? This geographical implausibility reinforces the sense that what happens there has no connection with "real" life; Nevada cities like Reno and Carson are ranch towns, western towns, places behind which there is some historical imperative. But Las Vegas seems to exist only in the eye of the beholder. All of which makes it an extraordinarily stimulating and interesting place, but an odd one in which to want to wear a candlelight satin Priscilla of Boston wedding dress with Chantilly lace insets, tapered sleeves and a detachable modified train.

And yet the Las Vegas wedding business seems to appeal to precisely 3 that impulse. "Sincere and Dignified Since 1954," one wedding chapel advertises. There are nineteen such wedding chapels in Las Vegas, intensely competitive, each offering better, faster, and, by implication, more sincere services than the next: Our Photos Best Anywhere, Your

Wedding on a Phonograph Record, Candlelight with Your Ceremony, Honeymoon Accommodations, Free Transportation from Your Motel to Courthouse to Chapel and Return to Motel, Religious or Civil Ceremonies, Dressing Rooms, Flowers, Rings, Announcements, Witnesses Available, and Ample Parking. All of these services, like most others in Las Vegas (sauna baths, payroll-check cashing, chinchilla coats for sale or rent) are offered twenty-four hours a day, seven days a week, presumably on the premise that marriage, like craps, is a game to be played when the table seems hot.

But what strikes one most about the Strip chapels, with their wishing wells and stained-glass paper windows and their artificial bouvardia, is that so much of their business is by no means a matter of simple convenience, of late-night liaisons between show girls and baby Crosbys. Of course there is some of that. (One night about eleven o'clock in Las Vegas I watched a bride in an orange minidress and masses of flame-colored hair stumble from a Strip chapel on the arm of her bridegroom, who looked the part of the expendable nephew in movies like "Miami Syndicate." "I gotta get the kids," the bride whimpered. "I gotta pick up the sitter, I gotta get to the midnight show." "What you gotta get," the bridegroom said, opening the door of a Cadillac coupe de ville and watching her crumple on the seat, "is sober.") But Las Vegas seems to offer something other than "convenience"; it is merchandising "niceness," the facsimile of proper ritual, to children who do not know how else to find it, how to make the arrangements, how to do it "right." All day and evening long on the Strip, one sees actual wedding parties, waiting under the harsh lights at a crosswalk, standing uneasily in the parking lot of the Frontier while the photographer hired by The Little Church of the West ("Wedding Place of the Stars") certifies the occasion, takes the picture: the bride in a veil and white satin pumps, the bridegroom usually in a white dinner jacket, and even an attendant or two, a sister or a best friend in hot-pink *peau de soie*, a flirtation veil, a carnation nosegay. "When I Fall in Love It Will Be Forever," the organist plays, and then a few bars of Lohengrin. The mother cries; the stepfather, awkward in his role, invites the chapel hostess to join them for a drink at the Sands. The hostess declines with a professional smile; she has already transferred her interest to the group waiting outside. One bride out, another in, and again the sign goes up on the chapel door: "One moment please—Wedding."

I sat next to one such wedding party in a Strip restaurant the last time I was in Las Vegas. The marriage had just taken place; the bride still wore her dress, the mother her corsage. A bored waiter poured out a few swallows of pink champagne ("on the house") for everyone but the bride, who was too young to be served. "You'll need something with more kick than that," the bride's father said with heavy jocularity to his new son-in-law; the ritual jokes about the wedding night had a certain Panglossian character, since the bride was clearly several months pregnant. Another round of pink champagne, this time not on the house, and the bride began to cry. "It was just as nice," she sobbed, "as I hoped and dreamed it would be."

AIMS AND STRATEGIES OF THE WRITER

Comment. Irony of situation exposes some incongruity, some twist of fate, or a result that differs with expectations. It applies to those instances when the absurd and abnormal become the norm, as with Didion's ironic view of Las Vegas. She presents scene after scene of absurd behavior to illustrate the special character of Las Vegas, which she describes as a town that endorses strange behavior because "what happens there has no connection with 'real' life."

Assignment 1. Write a paragraph establishing a scene for ironic commentary. You might, for example, describe a mass of drunken fans at a football game, a line of shoppers at a bargain sale, a gaggle of professors gathered for morning coffee.

Comment. Didion uses Las Vegas marriage ceremonies to maintain one dominant impression, but her aim extends beyond explaining the irony of the marriages to a statement about Las Vegas as a city, which she calls "the most extreme and allegorical of American settlements." By "allegorical" she means that the city stands as a symbol for the excesses and extremes of human behavior, an oasis that "seems to exist only in the eye of the beholder."

Assignment 2. Use the opening paragraph that you wrote for assignment 1 above and write a second paragraph that extends your observations into the realm of social judgment. That is, what do drunken fans represent? What is the significance of the crush of shoppers? Why are the professors clustered?

Comment. Didion's writing reflects a critical attitude. She breaks down the issues into manageable parts, searches for weaknesses as well as strengths, and gives the audience an honest judgment about the subject. Her description exposes one shallow aspect of American culture as represented by the garish city. However, her criticism is muted by the humorous, ironic illustrations that decorate the piece.

Assignment 3. Writing humor is difficult, but if you feel confident, write a complete descriptive essay that has a satiric tone. Be careful to make your subject representative and symbolic of a type. Condemn the excesses and extremes of human behavior in general, not the actions of a particular group. Humor laughs with the crowd; it does not isolate and attack one particular set of people.

Comment. "Marrying Absurd" is one essay in Didion's *Slouching towards Bethlehem*. The book's title is taken from a poem by W. B. Yeats, "The Second Coming," in which a frightening, amoral beast slouches toward Bethlehem to be born.

The Second Coming

Turning and turning in the widening gyre
The falcon cannot hear the falconer;
Things fall apart; the center cannot hold;
Mere anarchy is loosed upon the world,
The blood-dimmed tide is loosed, and everywhere
The ceremony of innocence is drowned;
The best lack all conviction, while the worst
Are full of passionate intensity.

Surely some revelation is at hand;
Surely the Second Coming is at hand.
The Second Coming! Hardly are those words out
When a vast image out of *Spiritus Mundi*
Troubles my sight: somewhere in sands of the desert
A shape with lion body and the head of a man,
A gaze blank and pitiless as the sun,
Is moving its slow thighs, while all about it
Reel shadows of the indignant desert birds.
The darkness drops again; but now I know
That twenty centuries of stony sleep
Were vexed to nightmare by a rocking cradle,
And what rough beast, its hour come round at last,
Slouches towards Bethlehem to be born?

Assignment 4. Write a paragraph that explains "Marrying Absurd" in light of Didion's allusion to this poem.

THE WRITING PROCESS

Comment. Didion differs from descriptive writers who might concentrate on one image, for she illustrates several types of absurd marriages, overwhelming the reader with descriptive examples.

Assignment 5. List Didion's examples of Las Vegas weddings and explain how each contributes another critical view.

Comment. Didion opens her essay much like an objective report, almost as though she intends to explain the steps necessary for getting married in Las Vegas. Slowly she builds the absurdity, which peaks when Mr. Brennan marries sixty-seven couples on one night. The reader gradually warms to the unfolding ironic discovery. This opening device is called *verisimilitude*, that is, something that has the appearance of, but is not actually, straightforward truth.

Assignment 6. Try writing the opening to your satiric description (see assignments 1 and 2) as a straightforward report of facts. Then find a way to twist and turn the illustrations gradually for ironic intent.

Comment. The wedding descriptions provided by Didion may or may not be true episodes. Writers often take some liberties with fact, especially when using ironic *hyperbole* (intentional exaggeration not intended to be taken literally). Writers of irony depend on hyperbole as a staple device.

Assignment 7. Review your descriptive essay for elements you might exaggerate for effect. Remember, excess breeds contempt, so keep your illustrations and episodes slightly absurd but not totally ridiculous. For example, describing a gaggle of professors gathered for morning coffee might include reference to chattering geese, but the image of a drooling vulture may overstep both relevancy and propriety. Exaggeration has its limits. It can be useful to have someone read and react to your early draft.

Comment. Like other descriptive writers, Didion enjoys an occasional metaphor or allusion.

> Marriage, she says, is *like craps*, a game to be played when the table seems hot.
>
> She refers to one bridegroom as one "who looked the part of the expendable nephew in movies like 'Miami Syndicate.'"
>
> She alludes to marriage jokes that have "a Panglossian character, since the bride was clearly several months pregnant." (Pangloss, the optimist tutor in Voltaire's *Candide*, constantly preached that this world was the best of all possible places despite the constant misfortunes that afflicted him.)

Assignment 8. Write a humorous description using figurative language to show the foolish but human pursuit of immediate gratification. Start by noting an instance of foolishness. Add to it other examples. Remember to maintain a dominant impression by focusing on one issue—buying, eating, playing, dancing, loving, and so forth.

Some writers use description as a persuasive tool. Perhaps a writer describes an object or event in all its horrifying detail, thereby hoping to convince the reader that such a circumstance is unacceptable. The argument in such cases need not be stated directly; the description or illustration makes the point.

Writers also use description to ameliorate or endorse. For instance, a description of the quiet grandeur of a natural scene might endorse environmental concerns.

In this excerpt, Jonathan Schell describes in unremitting, illustrated sequences the effects of a one-megaton bomb detonated on New York City. His unstated message comes through clearly: The fate of the earth depends on nuclear control. By his objective, informative tone and startlingly detailed descriptions, Schell attempts to awaken readers to the profound consequences of a nuclear war. (On this same topic, see also Carl Sagan's "The Nuclear Winter," in Chapter 9.)

Since the paragraphs of this essay are fairly long, make a brief summary of each paragraph in your reading notebook or in the margins. Note those instances where Schell's description, while appearing objective, conveys frightening scenes for shock value to enforce his persuasive appeal. There is something to be learned here about dispassionate description used in the service of argument.

Jonathan Schell is a contemporary writer of social, political, and environmental commentary. This essay is from his book The Fate of the Earth *(1982).*

JONATHAN SCHELL

 A Description of the Effects of a One-Megaton Bomb

What happened at Hiroshima was less than a millionth part of a holocaust at present levels of world nuclear armament. The more than millionfold difference amounts to more than a difference in magnitude; it is also a difference in kind. The authors of "Hiroshima and Nagasaki" observe that "an atomic bomb's massive destruction and indiscriminate slaughter involves the sweeping breakdown of all order and existence—in a word, the collapse of society itself," and that therefore "the essence of atomic destruction lies in the totality of its impact on man and society." This is true also of a holocaust, of course, except that the totalities in question are now not single cities but nations, ecosystems, and the earth's ecosphere. Yet with the exception of fallout, which was relatively light at Hiroshima and Nagasaki (because both the bombs were air-burst), the immediate devastation caused by today's bombs would be of a sort similar to the devastation in those cities. The immediate effects of a twenty-megaton bomb are not different in kind from those of a twelve-and-a-half-kiloton bomb; they are only more extensive. (The proportions of the effects do change greatly with yield, however. In small bombs, the effects of the initial nuclear radiation are important, because it strikes areas in which people might otherwise have remained alive, but in larger bombs—ones in the megaton range—the consequences of the initial nuclear radiation, whose range does not increase very much with yield, are negligible, because it strikes areas in which everyone will have already been burned or blasted to death.) In bursts of both weapons, for instance, there is a radius within which the thermal pulse can ignite newspapers: for the twelve-and-a-half-kiloton weapon, it is a little over two miles; for the twenty-megaton weapon, it is twenty-five miles. (Since there is no inherent limit on the size of a nuclear weapon, these figures can be increased indefinitely, subject only to the limitations imposed by the technical capacities of the bomb builder—and of the earth's capacity to absorb the blast. The Soviet Union, which has shown a liking for sheer size in so many of its undertakings, once detonated a sixty-megaton bomb.) Therefore, while the total effect of a holocaust is qualitatively different from the total effect of a single bomb, the experience of individual people in a holocaust would be, in the short term (and again excepting the presence of lethal fallout wherever the bombs were ground-burst), very much like the experience of individual people in Hiroshima. The Hiroshima people's experience, accordingly, is of much more than historical interest. It is a picture of what our whole world is always poised to become—a backdrop of scarcely imaginable horror lying just behind the surface of our normal life, and capable of breaking through into that normal life at any second. Whether we choose to think about it or not, it is an omnipresent, inescapable truth about our lives today that at every single moment each one of us may suddenly become the deranged mother looking for her burned child; the professor with the ball of rice in his hand whose wife has just told him "Run away, dear!" and died in the fires; Mr. Fukai running back into the firestorm; the naked man standing on the blasted plain that was his city, holding his eyeball in his hand; or, more likely, one of millions of corpses. For whatever our "modest hopes" as human beings may be, every one of them can be nullified by a nuclear holocaust.

One way to begin to grasp the destructive power of present-day   2 nuclear weapons is to describe the consequences of the detonation of a one-megaton bomb, which possesses eighty times the explosive power of the Hiroshima bomb, on a large city, such as New York. Burst some eighty-five hundred feet above the Empire State Building, a one-megaton bomb would gut or flatten almost every building between Battery Park and 125th Street, or within a radius of four and four-tenths miles, or in an area of sixty-one square miles, and would heavily damage buildings between the northern tip of Staten Island and the George Washington Bridge, or within a radius of about eight miles, or in an area of about two hundred square miles. A conventional explosive delivers a swift shock, like a slap, to whatever it hits, but the blast wave of a sizable nuclear weapon endures for several seconds and "can surround and destroy whole buildings" (Glasstone). People, of course, would be picked up and hurled away from the blast along with the rest of the debris. Within the sixty-one square miles, the walls, roofs, and floors of any buildings that had not been flattened would be collapsed, and the people and furniture inside would be swept down onto the street. (Technically, this zone would be hit by various overpressures of at least five pounds per square inch. Overpressure is defined as the pressure in excess of normal atmospheric pressure.) As far away as ten miles from ground zero, pieces of glass and other sharp objects would be hurled about by the blast wave at lethal velocities. In Hiroshima, where buildings were low and, outside the center of the city, were often constructed of light materials, injuries from falling buildings were often minor. But in New York, where the buildings are tall and are constructed of heavy materials, the physical collapse of the city would certainly kill millions of people. The streets of New York are narrow ravines running between the high walls of the city's buildings. In a nuclear attack, the walls would fall and the ravines would fill up. The people in the buildings would fall to the street with the debris of the buildings, and the people in the street would be crushed by this avalanche of people and buildings. At a distance of two miles or so from ground zero, winds would reach four hundred miles an hour, and another two miles away they would reach a hundred and eighty miles an hour. Meanwhile, the fireball would be growing, until it was more than a mile wide, and rocketing upward, to a height of over six miles. For ten seconds, it would broil the city below. Anyone caught in the open within nine miles of ground zero would receive third-degree burns and would probably be killed; closer to the explosion, people would be charred and killed instantly. From Greenwich Village up to Central Park, the heat would be great enough to melt metal and glass. Readily inflammable materials, such as newspapers and dry leaves, would ignite in all five boroughs (though in only a small part of Staten Island) and west to the Passaic River, in New Jersey, within a radius of about nine and a half miles from ground zero, thereby creating an area of more than two hundred and eighty square miles in which mass fires were likely to break out.

If it were possible (as it would not be) for someone to stand at Fifth   3
Avenue and Seventy-second Street (about two miles from ground zero) without being instantly killed, he would see the following sequence of events: A dazzling white light from the fireball would illumine the scene, continuing for perhaps thirty seconds. Simultaneously, searing heat would ignite everything flammable and start to melt windows, cars, buses, lampposts, and everything else made of metal or glass. People in the street would immediately catch fire, and would shortly be reduced to heavily charred corpses. About five seconds after the light appeared, the blast wave would strike, laden with the debris of a now nonexistent midtown. Some buildings might be crushed, as though a giant fist had squeezed them on all sides, and others might be picked up off their foundations and whirled uptown with the other debris. On the far side of Central Park, the West Side skyline would fall from south to north. The four-hundred-mile-an-hour wind would blow from south to north, die down after a few seconds, and then blow in the reverse direction with diminished intensity. While these things were happening, the fireball would be burning in the sky for the ten seconds of the thermal pulse. Soon huge, thick clouds of dust and smoke would envelop the scene, and as the mushroom cloud rushed overhead (it would have a diameter of about twelve miles) the light from the sun would be blotted out, and day would turn to night. Within minutes, fires, ignited both by the thermal pulse and by broken gas mains, tanks of gas and oil, and the like, would begin to spread in the darkness, and a strong, steady wind would begin to blow in the direction of the blast. As at Hiroshima, a whirlwind might be produced which would sweep through the ruins, and radioactive rain, generated under the meteorological conditions created by the blast, might fall. Before long, the individual fires would coalesce into a mass fire, which, depending largely on the winds, would become either a conflagration or a firestorm. In a conflagration, prevailing winds spread a wall of fire as far as there is any combustible material to sustain it; in a firestorm, a vertical updraft caused by the fire itself sucks the surrounding air in toward a central point, and the fires therefore converge in a single fire of extreme heat. A mass fire of either kind renders shelters useless by burning up all the oxygen in the air and creating toxic gases, so that anyone inside the shelters is asphyxiated, and also by heating the ground to such high temperatures that the shelters turn, in effect, into ovens, cremating the people inside them. In Dresden, several days after the firestorm raised there by Allied conventional bombing, the interiors of some bomb

shelters were still so hot that when they were opened the inrushing air caused the contents to burst into flame. Only those who had fled their shelters when the bombing started had any chance of surviving. (It is difficult to predict in a particular situation which form the fires will take. In actual experience, Hiroshima suffered a firestorm and Nagasaki suffered a conflagration.)

In this vast theater of physical effects, all the scenes of agony and   4
death that took place at Hiroshima would again take place, but now involving millions of people rather than hundreds of thousands. Like the people of Hiroshima, the people of New York would be burned, battered, crushed, and irradiated in every conceivable way. The city and its people would be mingled in a smoldering heap. And then, as the fires started, the survivors (most of whom would be on the periphery of the explosion) would be driven to abandon to the flames those family members and other people who were unable to flee, or else to die with them. Before long, while the ruins burned, the processions of injured, mute people would begin their slow progress out of the outskirts of the devastated zone. However, this time a much smaller proportion of the population than at Hiroshima would have a chance of escaping. In general, as the size of the area of devastation increases, the possibilities for escape decrease. When the devastated area is relatively small, as it was at Hiroshima, people who are not incapacitated will have a good chance of escaping to safety before the fires coalesce into a mass fire. But when the devastated area is great, as it would be after the detonation of a megaton bomb, and fires are springing up at a distance of nine and a half miles from ground zero, and when what used to be the streets are piled high with burning rubble, and the day (if the attack occurs in the daytime) has grown impenetrably dark, there is little chance that anyone who is not on the very edge of the devastated area will be able to make his way to safety. In New York, most people would die wherever the blast found them, or not very far from there.

If instead of being burst in the air the bomb were burst on or near   5
the ground in the vicinity of the Empire State Building, the overpressure would be very much greater near the center of the blast area but the range hit by a minimum of five pounds per square inch of overpressure would be less. The range of the thermal pulse would be about the same as that of the air burst. The fireball would be almost two miles across, and would engulf midtown Manhattan from Greenwich Village nearly to Central Park. Very little is known about what would happen to a city that was inside a fireball, but one would expect a good deal of what was there to be first pulverized and then melted or vaporized. Any human beings in the area would be reduced to smoke and ashes; they would simply disappear. A crater roughly three blocks in diameter and

two hundred feet deep would open up. In addition, heavy radioactive fallout would be created as dust and debris from the city rose with the mushroom cloud and then fell back to the ground. Fallout would begin to drop almost immediately, contaminating the ground beneath the cloud with levels of radiation many times lethal doses, and quickly killing anyone who might have survived the blast wave and the thermal pulse and might now be attempting an escape; it is difficult to believe that there would be appreciable survival of the people of the city after a megaton ground burst. And for the next twenty-four hours or so more fallout would descend downwind from the blast, in a plume whose direction and length would depend on the speed and the direction of the wind that happened to be blowing at the time of the attack. If the wind was blowing at fifteen miles an hour, fallout of lethal intensity would descend in a plume about a hundred and fifty miles long and as much as fifteen miles wide. Fallout that was sublethal but could still cause serious illness would extend another hundred and fifty miles downwind. Exposure to radioactivity in human beings is measured in units called rems—an acronym for "roentgen equivalent in man." The roentgen is a standard measurement of gamma- and X-ray radiation, and the expression "equivalent in man" indicates that an adjustment has been made to take into account the differences in the degree of biological damage that is caused by radiation of different types. Many of the kinds of harm done to human beings by radiation—for example, the incidence of cancer and of genetic damage—depend on the dose accumulated over many years; but radiation sickness, capable of causing death, results from an "acute" dose, received in a period of anything from a few seconds to several days. Because almost ninety percent of the so-called infinite-time dose of radiation from fallout—that is, the dose from a given quantity of fallout that one would receive if one lived for many thousands of years—is emitted in the first week, the one-week accumulated dose is often used as a convenient measure for calculating the immediate harm from fallout. Doses in the thousands of rems, which could be expected throughout the city, would attack the central nervous system and would bring about death within a few hours. Doses of around a thousand rems, which would be delivered some tens of miles downwind from the blast, would kill within two weeks everyone who was exposed to them. Doses of around five hundred rems, which would be delivered as far as a hundred and fifty miles downwind (given a wind speed of fifteen miles per hour), would kill half of all exposed able-bodied young adults. At this level of exposure, radiation sickness proceeds in the three stages observed at Hiroshima. The plume of lethal fallout could descend, depending on the direction of the wind, on other parts of New York State and parts of

New Jersey, Pennsylvania, Delaware, Maryland, Connecticut, Massachusetts, Rhode Island, Vermont, and New Hampshire, killing additional
millions of people. The circumstances in heavily contaminated areas,
in which millions of people were all declining together, over a period
of weeks, toward painful deaths, are ones that, like so many of the
consequences of nuclear explosions, have never been experienced.

A description of the effects of a one-megaton bomb on New York   6
City gives some notion of the meaning in human terms of a megaton of
nuclear explosive power, but a weapon that is more likely to be used
against New York is the twenty-megaton bomb, which has one thousand
six hundred times the yield of the Hiroshima bomb. The Soviet Union
is estimated to have at least a hundred and thirteen twenty-megaton
bombs in its nuclear arsenal, carried by Bear intercontinental bombers.
In addition, some of the Soviet SS-18 missiles are capable of carrying
bombs of this size, although the actual yields are not known. Since the
explosive power of the twenty-megaton bombs greatly exceeds the
amount necessary to destroy most military targets, it is reasonable to
suppose that they are meant for use against large cities. If a twenty-
megaton bomb were air-burst over the Empire State Building at an
altitude of thirty thousand feet, the zone gutted or flattened by the blast
would have a radius of twelve miles and an area of more than four
hundred and fifty square miles, reaching from the middle of Staten
Island to the northern edge of the Bronx, the eastern edge of Queens,
and well into New Jersey, and the zone of heavy damage from the blast
wave (the zone hit by a minimum of two pounds of overpressure per
square inch) would have a radius of twenty-one and a half miles, or, an
area of one thousand four hundred and fifty square miles, reaching to
the southernmost tip of Staten Island, north as far as southern Rockland
County, cast into Nassau County, and west to Morris County, New Jersey.
The fireball would be about four and a half miles in diameter and
would radiate the thermal pulse for some twenty seconds. People
caught in the open twenty-three miles away from ground zero, in Long
Island, New Jersey, and southern New York State, would be burned to
death. People hundreds of miles away who looked at the burst would
be temporarily blinded and would risk permanent eye injury. (After the
test of a fifteen-megaton bomb on Bikini Atoll, in the South Pacific, in
March of 1954, small animals were found to have suffered retinal burns
at a distance of three hundred and forty-five miles.) The mushroom
cloud would be seventy miles in diameter. New York City and its sub-
urbs would be transformed into a lifeless, flat, scorched desert in a few
seconds.

If a twenty-megaton bomb were ground-burst on the Empire State   7

Building, the range of severe blast damage would, as with the one-megaton ground blast, be reduced, but the fireball, which would be almost six miles in diameter, would cover Manhattan from Wall Street to northern Central Park and also parts of New Jersey, Brooklyn, and Queens, and everyone within it would be instantly killed, with most of them physically disappearing. Fallout would again be generated, this time covering thousands of square miles with lethal intensities of radiation. A fair portion of New York City and its incinerated population, now radioactive dust, would have risen into the mushroom cloud and would now be descending on the surrounding territory. On one of the few occasions when local fallout was generated by a test explosion in the multi-megaton range, the fifteen-megaton bomb tested on Bikini Atoll, which was exploded seven feet above the surface of a coral reef, "caused substantial contamination over an area of more than seven thousand square miles," according to Glasstone. If, as seems likely, a twenty-megaton bomb ground-burst on New York would produce at least a comparable amount of fallout, and if the wind carried the fallout onto populated areas, then this one bomb would probably doom upward of twenty million people, or almost ten percent of the population of the United States.

AIMS AND STRATEGIES OF THE WRITER

Comment. Schell's primary purpose is to convince the reader of the dangers of nuclear warfare. He uses description to carry his message, re-creating with detailed exactness the effects of an atomic explosion.

Assignment 1. Generate a list of topics for which you could provide convincing and detailed description to awaken the reader to real dangers. Write an exploratory paragraph on one of your topics or one of the following: (1) the disposal of toxins into a village stream, (2) the early release of dangerous criminals, (3) the use of some weight reduction methods, or (4) the kidnapping of young children.

Comment. Schell attempts to meet the needs of his audience, which he apparently sees as a body of concerned citizens rather than a select group of scientists. (He published the essay in a popular magazine, *The New Yorker*, not in a scientific journal.) For this reason, he vividly portrays complex events, leaving little to the reader's imagination.

Assignment 2. Develop a brief writing situation for an essay on the topic chosen for assignment 1. Explain your persona as writer. (Schell assumes the persona of knowledgeable scientist.) Describe your audience, general or specialized. Finally, present your intent and tell what you hope to accomplish by your persuasive essay.

Comment. Writers like Schell who feel strongly about a subject often use impassioned language and imperative appeals.

Assignment 3. Examine paragraph 1 of Schell's essay and note instances when Schell's tone rises slightly in passionate appeal and use of stark descriptions.

THE WRITING PROCESS

Comment. Schell creates one dominant impression, provides plenty of specific details, and focuses on a scarcely imaginable scene.

Assignment 4. Write a brief paragraph that explains the focus of Schell's essay, commenting on why that perspective would be physically impossible (see the opening of paragraph 3).

Comment. Schell begins his essay with a discussion of the Hiroshima and Nagasaki atomic bombings, a comparison that gives credibility to his later speculative descriptions. Without this concrete, historical evidence of the Japanese bombings, the reader could dismiss Schell's description as mere fancy.

Assignment 5. Write a brief opening paragraph for one of your topics for assignment 1. Establish a sense of reality about a recent event so that your descriptive speculations of future consequences will have an authoritative base.

Comment. The structure of a persuasive piece usually includes a *proposition* (for instance, that nuclear war is horrible), an *assumption* (that reasonable people want to end the arms race), *credibility* (Schell knows what he's talking about), and *evidence* (which he provides in vivid, almost frightening imagery).

Assignment 6. Write an essay that uses description for a persuasive appeal to the reader. Test your descriptive persuasion against the four criteria above. Research your topic if you feel you need to establish your credibility. Read the beginnings of Chapters 9 and 10, which offer additional guidelines for cause-effect analysis and inductive/deductive reasoning.

Writers use description for informative and creative purposes. Imaginative writers look at things from various perspectives, finding a different focus or odd angle and surprising us with a fresh image or metaphor. In some cases the creative aim is so dominant that an essay becomes a prose poem or has the appearance of a short story. Good prose, not poetry, is the medium, but the writer delights in descriptive imagery and flights of fancy more than hard-hitting persuasion or philosophical musings. Such is the case in the following short descriptive piece by Robert Bly.

"The Hockey Poem" is rich in metaphorical language; Bly compares hockey players to pike swimming, hawks hurrying for the mouse, amoebas on the pale slide, and so forth. Yet his dominant image is the goalie, whom he slowly transforms allegorically into a woman weeping over the children of men.

Reading or writing this kind of prose requires the writer's attentive allegiance to the language, for words motivate the entire work. Bly uses his words and images to surprise and delight us, reflecting his sense of writing as a "leaping around the unconscious." Despite the entertainment value, works such as Bly's are also meant to present arguments and to inform.

As you read, make marginal comments, noting Bly's frequent similes and metaphors—the rich figurative language that prompts him to call this piece a prose poem.

Bly has published several books of poetry: Silence in the Snowy Fields (1962), The Light Around the Body (1968), and Sleepers Joining Hands (1974). "The Hockey Poem" is from his collection of prose poems, The Morning Glory (1975).

ROBERT BLY

🎴 The Hockey Poem

The Boston College team has gold helmets, under which the long black   1
hair of the Roman centurion curls out ... and they begin. How weird the goalies look with their African masks! The goalie is so lonely anyway, guarding a basket with nothing in it, his wide lower legs wide as ducks'.... No matter what gift he is given, he always rejects it.... He has a number like 1, a name like Mrazek, sometimes wobbling his legs waiting for the puck, or curling up like a baby in the womb to hold it, staying a second too long on the ice.

The goalie has gone out to mid-ice, and now he sails sadly back to   2
his own box, slowly, he looks prehistoric with his rhinoceros legs, he
looks as if he's going to become extinct, and he's just taking his time. . . .

When the players are at the other end, he begins sadly sweeping the   3
ice in front of his house, he is the old witch in the woods, waiting for
the children to come home. . . .

Suddenly they all come hurrying back, toward us, knees dipping,   4
like oil wells, they rush toward us wildly, fins waving, they are pike
swimming toward us, their gill fins expanding like the breasts of opera
singers, no, they are twelve hands practicing penmanship on the same
piece of paper. . . . They flee down the court toward us like birds, swirling two and two, hawks hurrying for the mouse, hurrying down wind-
valleys, swirling back and forth like amoeba on the pale slide, as they
sail in the absolute freedom of water and the body, untroubled by the
troubled mind, only the body, with wings as if there were no grave, no
gravity, only the birds sailing over the cottage far in the deep woods. . . .

Now they attack the goalie, and he's desperate . . . looking wildly   5
over his left shoulder, rushing toward the other side of his cave, like a
mother hawk whose chicks are being taken by two snakes . . . suddenly
he flops on the ice like a man trying to cover a whole double bed. . . .
He has the puck. He stands up, turns to his right, and drops it on the
ice at the right moment, he saves it for one of his children, a mother
hen picking up a seed and then dropping it. . . .

But the men are all too clumsy, they can't keep track of the puck . . .   6
no, it is the *puck*, the puck is too fast, it is too fast for human beings, it
humiliates them constantly. They are all a little like country boys at the
fair watching the con man—the puck always turns up under the wrong
walnut shell. . . .

They come down court again, one man guiding the puck this time   7
. . . and Ledingham comes down beautifully, like the canoe through
white water, or the lover going upstream, every stroke right, like the
stallion galloping up the valley surrounded by his mares, how beautiful,
like the body and soul crossing in a poem. . . .

The player in position pauses, aims, pauses, cracks his stick on the   8
ice, and a cry as the puck goes in! The goalie stands up disgusted, and
throws the puck out. . . .

The player with a broken stick hovers near the cage. When the play   9
shifts, he skates over to his locked-in teammates, who look like a nest
of bristling owls, owl babies, and they hold out a stick to him. . . .

Sometimes the players crash together, their hockey sticks raised like   10
lobster claws. They fight with slow motions, as if undersea . . . they're
fighting over some woman back in the motel no one can see . . . but

like lobsters they forget what they're battling for, the clack of the armor plate distracts them, and they feel a pure rage. . . .

Or a fighter sails over to the penalty box, where ten-year-old boys   11
wait, to sit with the criminal, who is their hero. . . . They know society is wrong, the wardens are wrong, the judges hate individuality. . . .

And this man with his peaked mask, with slits, how fantastic he is,   12
like a white insect, who has given up on evolution in this life, his family hopes to evolve *after* death . . . in the grave. He's as ominous as a Middle Ages knight, the Black Prince . . . his enemies defeated him in daylight, but every one of them died in their beds that night. . . . At his father's funeral, he carried his own head under his arm. . . .

He is the old woman in the shoe, whose house is never clean, no   13
matter what she does. Perhaps this goalie is not a man at all, but a woman, all women, in her cage everything disappears in the end, we all long for it, all these movements on the ice will end, all the arena seats will come down, the chamber walls bare. . . . This goalie with his mask is a woman weeping over the children of men, that are cut down like grass, gulls standing with cold feet on the ice. . . . And at the end, she is still waiting, brushing away the leaves, waiting for the new children developed by speed, by war. . . .

AIMS AND STRATEGIES OF THE WRITER

Comment. A contest of any sort reminds us about the general struggle of life. In this description Bly associates the hockey goalie with a figure who tends life—the eternal woman. "This goalie with his mask is a woman weeping over the children of men." The implications are chilling.

Assignment 1. Write a brief paragraph comparing Dillard's snakeskin, McPhee's grizzly, and Bly's hockey goalie. How do the images differ? How are they similar? What lessons of life do each suggest?

Comment. Although he wants to inform the reader, Bly wishes also to entertain the reader with words that sparkle and phrases that delight. He does not persuade, nor does he consciously offer personal philosophy.

Assignment 2. Explain how "The Hockey Poem" would change if Bly adopted a persuasive attitude such as that of Schell. Also explain how it would change if Bly wished instead to explain the rules of hockey.

Comment. Some writers use visual imagery to express subjective feelings. Bly belongs to this group, at least in this piece.

Assignment 3. The aim of many writers is to use visual orientation so that scenes come alive. For instance, instead of saying "I feel lousy and depressed" you could say "My mind is a wet blanket tonight." Practice visual orientation; this will help you sharpen the details of your descriptive essays. For example, provide imagery for the following situations: disgust with a person who lied to you, affection for a friend, your reactions to a cold room.

THE WRITING PROCESS

Comment. Inventions of language and image are often accidental and unexpected; they can seldom be forced. Imagine, for example, Bly as he sat watching a hockey match, squinting his eyes perhaps to make everything a bit fuzzy and allowing images to come and go.

Assignment 4. Describe something familiar to you, maybe the layout of your neighborhood or house. Work your way through the setting image by image. A single incident or focus should slowly emerge, which will form the dominant impression. Around this impression build a tight, honed description.

Comment. Bly views the game of hockey through different eyes than the average spectator. A general description of the game, such as the scoring methods or the rules, is not his purpose. He sees the game and the players in metaphoric, not literal, terms.

Assignment 5. List the metaphors Bly uses to describe the goalie. Also list the metaphors used to describe the other players. Note places where Bly might have used general description but does not.

Comment. Emotion can be shown by one image. Bly allows a single detail to develop and carry the point. The goalie is an old witch waiting for the children to come; later, the goalie portrays all women who weep for the children of men.

Assignment 6. Write a short descriptive essay in Bly's style. Let your scene develop slowly; don't force it. Allow your mind to drift among the spectrums of words, along the edges of your imagination. Even one fresh image or metaphor can make the difference in a piece of writing.

Christa Lednicky writes a brief psychological piece about her secret heart, her double image that sometimes threatens to engulf her. Like Robert Bly in the previous work, she writes in an imaginative manner and uses two techniques: (1) She creates a persona who tells the story, and (2) she uses an abstract narrative form rather than a straightforward explanation of human problems.

The danger of such writing is that some readers might not understand the interpretations. Yet this problem exists for any imaginative writer who is preoccupied with form, characterization, and imagery rather than straightforward communication. Lednicky takes certain risks, challenges the reader, and accepts misinterpretations and false applications of her writing.

Her aim of discourse requires plenty of rich descriptive passages as she narrates this one evening of human fears and frustrations. Implied throughout this piece is her thesis: the contrasting emotions of a conscious heart in conflict with a secret one.

As you read, make notes marking Lednicky's shift from "I" to "she" and back again. In addition, summarize her images to find how they reflect the duality of the narrator's mood.

CHRISTA LEDNICKY, STUDENT

 ## Secret Heart

Lying in the cold narrow bed that I'd pulled close to the window, I   1
watched the clouds scar the sky with a pattern of dusk. Soon the moon, full and bloated, cast its light through the cold glass panes and onto my blanket.

I'd told her she's not to come tonight. Not tonight. In my conscious   2
mind I hoped she would not come again, yet my secret heart wanted to hear the sound of her feet on the stairs. Sometimes I deceive myself into thinking that I hear her gentle knock on my door, as shy and quiet as the first night I met her. Not tonight.

Tonight is the night of the moon, and I feel . . . changed. Soon I will   3
sleep, and my secret heart will take care of me and guard me from the demons that come with the moon. It will not let me wonder where the scents come from . . . or the blood. It will not let me look in the mirror to see the frighteningly haggard stranger that stands there. My secret heart will not hurt me.

On such nights as these, the city seems spread before me, waiting   4
for me. I think of the dreaming people in their darkened rooms behind

locked doors. Do those locked doors protect them from their dreams? I think not.

Glancing up to the sky, I watch the last of the evening rays glimmer   5 on the edge and drop into nothingness. The moon drives darkness across the window, and I rejoice.

I look down the length of my body and see the pale blue shadows   6 cast mystery upon thighs that shiver in the cold dampness of the room. What would she look like, I wonder, in this light? Mysterious and beautiful, I think. Changed.

In that moment, as I close my eyes and begin my visions of her, I   7 hear the quiet rap of her knuckles on the door. The sound is so very faint, but it is enough. My secret heart begins to cry out, "No, not tonight!" but it is shadowed by the grin twisting this face that seems no longer mine.

I move into the circle of darkness surrounding the bed and creep   8 toward the door separating us. My secret heart whispers that locked doors never protect people from their dreams . . . or their nightmares.

CHRISTA LEDNICKY TALKS ABOUT
HER AIMS AND STRATEGIES

I wanted to explore the images that float along the edges of the brain, but I simply refused in this instance to write a traditional essay. I created a story to show the problem in action rather than just tell about it. But I had to argue my case with the instructor, who returned it marked "fiction." My position was that yes, it sounds or reads like fiction, but it does make a serious point about the human psyche. After I said that I was explaining psychic duality by looking through the mind of a special character, the instructor let me submit it.

Comment. Lednicky establishes her thesis first, the duality and disharmony of the individual mind. She then frames a descriptive narration to depict her point. She did not write a short story, as such, but an essay in story form.

Assignment 1. Frame a thesis that you might use for any essay, then, following Lednicky's style, write from the point of view of an involved persona. For example, if you condemn kidnapping of children, write a piece from the viewpoint of an eight-year-old child who is snatched from a car while the mother has run briefly into a store. Do *not* write a short story and hope it has a thesis.

Comment. A brief narration like Lednicky's sometimes appears as the introduction to a long essay or article on a serious subject. For example,

Lednicky or another writer could follow her descriptive narrative with a serious and scholarly discussion of schizophrenia.

Assignment 2. Write a descriptive paragraph that could serve as an introductory setting or anecdote for a serious discussion. The opening will interact with the body of the essay. For example, your thesis may center on the dangers of certain weight reduction programs, so your opening paragraph could describe one person in the process of making a decision about using weight-loss pills, controlled meals, health club, and so forth.

CHAPTER TWO

 Narration

In narration, the story-telling pattern of discourse, a voice (persona) presents a series of events in chronological order, keeping the focus on essentials of character, setting, and action. Usually a conflict of some type motivates the action. A brief passage from "Salvation" by Langston Hughes demonstrates these elements.

> The preacher preached a wonderful rhythmical sermon, all moans and shouts and lonely cries and dire pictures of hell, and then he sang a song about the ninety and nine safe in the fold, but one little lamb was left out in the cold. Then he said: "Won't you come? Won't you come to Jesus? Young lambs, won't you come?" And he held out his arms to all us young sinners there on the mourners' bench. And the little girls cried. And some of them jumped up and went to Jesus right away. But most of us just sat there.
>
> A great many old people came and knelt around us and prayed, old women with jet-black faces and braided hair, old men with work-gnarled hands. And the church sang a song about the lower lights are burning, some poor sinners to be saved. And the whole building rocked with prayer and song.
>
> Still I kept waiting to *see* Jesus.

This brief passage establishes that a child is speaking to us in a first-person voice about the happenings at a church service. The focus moves from actions of the preacher, to the response of the child's peers, to the ministrations of the congregation. We anticipate some kind of action by the speaker. (The entire selection follows later in this chapter.)

REPORT A SERIES OF EVENTS

Whether called a story, plot, or episode, one essential ingredient of your narration will be a set of actions that intensifies in its progression. The

63

tricky part is to select key events, memorable experiences, and unique perspectives that your readers will find entertaining and informative. Depending on the writer's purpose, the series of events might be drawn from personal experience (autobiography) or comic events about real or imaginary characters (humor). In other cases the writer can report on significant events from the past that have shaped our society (history) or tell the story of one person's life (biography).

In almost every case, the events should develop with intensifying progression toward a significant moment, one that enlightens the reader about an experience of life, a philosophical awakening, a moment of truth, or an everlasting theme.

USE PACING TO MAINTAIN
PROGRESSION OF THE STORY LINE

Not every moment is important. Just as the descriptive writer selects focused details, so must a narrator select significant events while passing over the dull ones. Pacing requires that you skip even exciting periods of time *if they do not advance the main idea of your narration.* For example, a runner's efforts to reach the finish line of a marathon race must dominate the narrative, so key segments of the twenty-six miles, not every mile, should be highlighted. And a fight among the fans gathered to watch the race should not be included unless the fight affected the runner's performance.

Pacing helps you keep elements of the story in proportion. In the passage above, Hughes does not dwell for long on the preacher's sermon because he wants to bring the focus back to his own character. Historians do the same thing by developing important moments and ignoring the less important. For example, in an essay in this chapter, Carin Quinn introduces Levi Strauss in 1848 in New York, follows him to California in 1850, jumps to 1870, to 1902, to the 1930s, and then skips forward to the present. Quinn tightens and narrows the portrait of Strauss so that brief periods in this man's career represent the whole.

The word *foreshortening* is often applied to this practice of passing over periods of time by using transitional words or phrases such as "at last," "later," "soon," or "after a short time."

ESTABLISH A VOICE FOR TELLING THE STORY

As the writer you are the narrator of events. You can remain outside, as an uninvolved observer who reports, or you can place yourself into the narration, becoming a *persona* in the action; you can even serve as the speaker, as Hughes did in the passage that began this chapter. Personal narration usually requires the first-person "I" point of view. Reserve the first-person "we" for any editorial writing you do. Both Scott Momaday (pages 72–77) and Richard Rodriguez (pages 86–96) employ the first-person voice. Historic narration and biography normally use the third-person point of view ("he" or "she"), such as the third-person point of view used by Quinn in the historical essay on pages 80–83. Creative writers have greater leeway with voice; they might speak in the first-person voice of a main character, build the story with third-person observations, or omnisciently enter the minds of several different characters. (See, for example, Mark Twain's handling of voice in "Coyote," pages 99–101.)

USE A TIME SEQUENCE

Chronological order moves your writing from earlier to later, from older to newer, and from past to present. You can change the normal time sequence by several methods. *In medias res* ("into the middle of things") begins narration in the midst of action. (For example, skip over the preparations for a trip to the coast as well as minor events along the way; begin your story instead with your first steps into the pounding surf.) *Flashback* stops the narrative flow, regresses backward to a time in the past, and then returns to the main stream of the story. Use it when starting a story in the present and then regressing into past events. *Flashforward* does the opposite of flashback; use it when forecasting events that will occur later in the story. For example, Hughes begins "Salvation" by saying: "I was saved from sin when I was going on thirteen. But not really saved. It happened like this."

The opening statement is a *flashforward*; it signals something to occur soon. Hughes then flashes back in time to the night of a church revival. His technique is representative of another device—*foreshadowing*—which signals to the reader that certain events will occur later in the narration. Use foreshadowing to warn readers, for example, that a climate of tragedy hangs over the story, for instance: "A gray mist hovered in the air as I drove toward the outskirts of town." Finally, *historical causal chains* enable a historian to explore why things happened as they did, why one event led to the next, which in turn motivated other events. For instance, Quinn shows the causal chain of events in the building of the Levi's jeans empire. Causal chains can be used in essays that narrate the history of a business or the biography of a noted person.

COMBINE DESCRIPTION WITH NARRATION TO CREATE SETTING

Effective narration presents an environment for its readers. A writer's careful selection of descriptive detail, as explained in Chapter 1, will bring alive the scenes and atmosphere of the narration. The writing selections in this chapter create effective settings. For example, Hughes provides the religious fervor of a church revival; Momaday paints a stark picture of the land near Rainy Mountain, Oklahoma; Rodriguez invites the reader into his Hispanic home; Twain furnishes rich descriptive touches to his story of the dog and coyote; and Randall Williams describes the atmosphere of the Alabama woods where he secluded himself for one summer.

USE DIALOGUE

Allow the characters of the narration to speak with one another. Dialogue gives a natural, relaxed tone to the story. However, conform to this rule: Dialogue should advance the progression of the narration. Idle, purposeless dialogue will irritate the reader. In addition, use standard writing conventions for dialogue: Place every statement within quotation marks and begin a new paragraph each time a different person speaks. (Study Hughes's essay for an example of effective dialogue.)

To review: Your narrative essay will need

1. A voice, which might be your own first-person "I," third-person "he" or "she," or a blend of the two points of view (to be used when writing about yourself and another person)
2. A chronological order of events, which can be interrupted by flashbacks or speeded up by foreshortening
3. A focus on how one central event affects a person or how several persons participate in a sequence of events

Writers use narration as a tool for expressing personal feelings about the special times of their lives. When drawing from personal experience, a writer usually expresses a fact of life, a lesson, perhaps even an awakening to life's complexities.

In the following passage, Langston Hughes establishes a personal voice to narrate a series of events that affected him deeply as a young boy. The aim of his narration is to interpret one aspect of his own character. He admits his deceptive behavior in church during a revival. The experience haunts him thereafter. His confusion and human weakness give the narration universal appeal. Readers recognize and share his recollection of a rite of passage from youth to adulthood because Hughes shows it in action and does not merely generalize about it. As a result, the piece reads like a story, in this case a true one.

In reading the essay, note the author's handling of dialogue. Marginally note his shifts from first-person voice to third-person; he bounces the focus back and forth from private thoughts to the words and actions of others.

Langston Hughes (1902–67), an accomplished poet and short story writer, was a native of Joplin, Missouri. He served for many years as a columnist for The New York Post. *"Salvation" is from his autobiography,* The Big Sea *(1940), which recounts experiences of his youth and his short stint as a sailor.*

LANGSTON HUGHES

Salvation

I was saved from sin when I was going on thirteen. But not really saved.   1
It happened like this. There was a big revival at my Auntie Reed's church. Every night for weeks there had been much preaching, singing, praying, and shouting, and some very hardened sinners had been brought to Christ, and the membership of the church had grown by leaps and bounds. Then just before the revival ended, they held a special meeting for children, "to bring the young lambs to the fold." My aunt spoke of it for days ahead. That night I was escorted to the front row and placed on the mourners' bench with all the other young sinners, who had not yet been brought to Jesus.

My aunt told me that when you were saved you saw a light, and   2
something happened to you inside! And Jesus came into your life! And God was with you from then on! She said you could see and hear and feel Jesus in your soul. I believed her. I had heard a great many old

67

people say the same thing and it seemed to me they ought to know. So I sat there calmly in the hot, crowded church, waiting for Jesus to come to me.

The preacher preached a wonderful rhythmical sermon, all moans 3 and shouts and lonely cries and dire pictures of hell, and then he sang a song about the ninety and nine safe in the fold, but one little lamb was left out in the cold. Then he said: "Won't you come? Won't you come to Jesus? Young lambs, won't you come?" And he held out his arms to all us young sinners there on the mourners' bench. And the little girls cried. And some of them jumped up and went to Jesus right away. But most of us just sat there.

A great many old people came and knelt around us and prayed, old 4 women with jet-black faces and braided hair, old men with work-gnarled hands. And the church sang a song about the lower lights are burning, some poor sinners to be saved. And the whole building rocked with prayer and song.

Still I keep waiting to *see* Jesus. 5

Finally all the young people had gone to the altar and were saved, 6 but one boy and me. He was a rounder's son named Westley. Westley and I were surrounded by sisters and deacons praying. It was very hot in the church, and getting late now. Finally Westley said to me in a whisper: "God damn! I'm tired o' sitting here. Let's get up and be saved." So he got up and was saved.

Then I was left all alone on the mourners' bench. My aunt came and 7 knelt at my knees and cried, while prayers and songs swirled all around me in the little church. The whole congregation prayed for me alone, in a mighty wail of moans and voices. And I kept waiting serenely for Jesus, waiting, waiting—but he didn't come. I wanted to see him, but nothing happened to me. Nothing! I wanted something to happen to me, but nothing happened.

I heard the songs and the minister saying: "Why don't you come? My 8 dear child, why don't you come to Jesus? Jesus is waiting for you. He wants you. Why don't you come? Sister Reed, what is this child's name?"

"Langston," my aunt sobbed. 9

"Langston, why don't you come? Why don't you come and be saved? 10 Oh, Lamb of God! Why don't you come?"

Now it was really getting late. I began to be ashamed of myself, 11 holding everything up so long. I began to wonder what God thought about Westley, who certainly hadn't seen Jesus either, but who was now sitting proudly on the platform, swinging his knickerbockered legs and grinning down at me, surrounded by deacons and old women on their knees praying. God had not struck Westley dead for taking his name in vain or for lying in the temple. So I decided that maybe to save further trouble, I'd better lie, too, and say that Jesus had come, and get up and be saved.

So I got up. 12

Suddenly the whole room broke into a sea of shouting, as they saw 13
me rise. Waves of rejoicing swept the place. Women leaped in the air.
My aunt threw her arms around me. The minister took me by the hand
and led me to the platform.

When things quieted down, in a hushed silence, punctuated by a 14
few ecstatic "Amens," all the new young lambs were blessed in the name
of God. Then joyous singing filled the room.

That night, for the last time in my life but one—for I was a big boy 15
twelve years old—I cried. I cried, in bed alone, and couldn't stop. I
buried my head under the quilts, but my aunt heard me. She woke up
and told my uncle I was crying because the Holy Ghost had come into
my life, and because I had seen Jesus. But I was really crying because I
couldn't bear to tell her that I had lied, that I had deceived everybody
in the church, and I hadn't seen Jesus, and that now I didn't believe
there was a Jesus any more, since he didn't come to help me.

AIMS AND STRATEGIES OF THE WRITERS

Comment. "Salvation" is one small passage from Hughes's autobiography. The deception by the twelve-year-old Langston is central to this narration. He lied and in the process lost his faith rather than strengthened it. Buried within the narration, therefore, is a life experience about childhood and rites of passage.

Assignment 1. Think back into your past and write down two or three episodes that are memorable and perhaps worth expressing. Make some notations about *why* the experiences stick in your mind. What lesson about life did you learn? Does it have universal appeal? Will others identify with your dilemma, problem, or activity?

Comment. Truth is sometimes stranger than fiction. Personal narration explains those unusual true-life events that stay in our memories. These events usually have universal appeal because they reflect moments of human triumph or failure.

Assignment 2. Consider a period of your own life as a good story. Try to tell it that way as you create a rough draft. Describe a setting and develop yourself as a central character in the story. Establish a problem or confrontation, progress toward a moment of dramatic intensity, and then resolve the conflict.

Comment. Narration used in nonfiction has a serious purpose. The author explores a thesis and uses the story to make a point. However, nonfiction narration requires a light hand when presenting philosophical insights. Hughes, for example, wants us to recognize moral despair and religious frustration, feelings that afflict most people at one time or another, but he chooses to show us with a story rather than tell us in a serious essay.

Assignment 3. The effective lessons in life are discovered, not forced on us. Your personal narrative essay should reflect this. Therefore, write down the point you wish to make and then *don't* use it in your paper. A narrative essay does not always need an *expressed* thesis if the message is clear. Let your reader discover the lesson; don't become didactic. Determine early that your dialogue and action will make the point, without an expressed moral.

THE WRITING PROCESS

Comment. Hughes narrates the story in first-person voice, which enables him to achieve his purpose: the expression of personal emotions.

Assignment 4. Starting at the beginning of "Salvation," change the point of view to the third-person "he." (For example, "Langston was saved from sin when he was going on thirteen.") As you work through the story changing "I" to "he," note how your third-person narration affects the distance between the boy and the reader. The narrator now intervenes to tell about Langston and his problems.

Comment. The descriptive setting of "Salvation" presents the boy sitting on the front row at church at night. The preacher "moans and shouts" with "lonely cries" and sings about "one little lamb . . . left out in the cold" while little girls cry. The young boy hears moans and voices, and when he finally stands, "waves of rejoicing swept the place" and "women leaped in the air." The skillful descriptive detail makes the atmosphere come alive for the reader.

Assignment 5. Select one episode from your past (use the list from assignment 1) and develop descriptive details about the setting. Where did it happen? What time of day was it? What was the weather like that day? What season was it? Who else was present? In particular, jot down any descriptive details of the setting that will bring the scene to life.

Comment. Hughes employs dialogue at several points in the narration. He encloses each statement with quotation marks and begins a new paragraph when somebody new speaks (note especially paragraphs 8 through 10).

Assignment 6. Write a brief scene that requires dialogue. That is, have your "I" narrator speak to another person in a series of brief paragraphs. Keep in mind that dialogue should contribute to the progression of the story and in some way advance your general thesis.

Comment. Hughes develops his narration around one short episode that has human drama and makes a point about a child's initiation into the adult world.

Assignment 7. Make your personal narration of about the same length as the one by Hughes, keeping it centered around one brief moment of time that awakened you to some fact of life or taught you an important lesson.

Rather than write about himself, Momaday writes the story of his grandmother. In so doing, he indirectly describes himself and his Indian heritage. Reminiscence, one kind of autobiography, often imbues the episode with nostalgic longing for a time that is gone forever. This type of narration re-creates special times, notable persons, and remembered places, blending description with biography and personal experience. Reminiscence attempts to capture in words a moment or two of one's life, thereby preserving forever a distinctive place or cherished person.

The following passage, "My Kiowa Grandmother," serves as the preface to Momaday's anthology of Indian folklore, The Way to Rainy Mountain *(1969). He uses the dignity of the old woman to symbolize pride in himself and all others of Indian ancestry, meanwhile touching the hearts of his readers, reminding them of lost tribes, lost religions, and lost hope.*

As you read, make marginal notes on Momaday's use of description, biographical and narrative details, and autobiographical remembrances. These notes will help you see the shifting focus from land, to grandmother, to writer.

N. Scott Momaday, a Kiowa Indian who was raised on a reservation, now teaches college English. In 1969 he received the Pulitzer Prize for his novel House Made of Dawn.

N. SCOTT MOMADAY

My Kiowa Grandmother

A single knoll rises out of the plain in Oklahoma, north and west of the   1
Wichita range. For my people, the Kiowas, it is an old landmark, and
they gave it the name Rainy Mountain. The hardest weather in the world
is there. Winter brings blizzards, hot tornadic winds arise in the spring,
and in the summer the prairie is an anvil's edge. The grass turns brittle
and brown, and it cracks beneath your feet. There are green belts along
the rivers and creeks, linear groves of hickory and pecan, willow and
witch hazel. At a distance in July or August the steaming foliage seems
almost to writhe in fire. Great green and yellow grasshoppers are everywhere in the tall grass, popping up like corn to sting the flesh, and
tortoises crawl about on the red earth, going nowhere in the plenty of
time. Loneliness is an aspect of the land. All things in the plain are
isolate; there is no confusion of objects in the eye, but *one* hill or *one*

tree or *one* man. To look upon that landscape in the early morning, with the sun at your back, is to lose the sense of proportion. Your imagination comes to life, and this, you think, is where Creation was begun.

I returned to Rainy Mountain in July. My grandmother had died in the spring, and I wanted to be at her grave. She had lived to be very old and at last infirm. Her only living daughter was with her when she died, and I was told that in death her face was that of a child.

I like to think of her as a child. When she was born, the Kiowas were living the last great moment of their history. For more than a hundred years they had controlled the open range from the Smoky Hill River to the Red, from the headwaters of the Canadian to the fork of the Arkansas and Cimarron. In alliance with the Comanches, they had ruled the whole of the Southern Plains. War was their sacred business, and they were the finest horsemen the world has ever known. But warfare for the Kiowas was preeminently a matter of dispositon rather than of survival, and they never understood the grim, unrelenting advance of the U.S. Cavalry. When at last, divided and ill provisioned, they were driven onto the Staked Plains in the cold of autumn, they fell into panic. In Palo Duro Canyon they abandoned their crucial stores to pillage and had nothing then but their lives. In order to save themselves, they surrendered to the soldiers at Fort Sill and were imprisoned in the old stone corral that now stands as a military museum. My grandmother was spared the humiliation of those high gray walls by eight or ten years, but she must have known from birth the affliction of defeat, the dark brooding of old warriors.

Her name was Aho, and she belonged to the last culture to evolve in North America. Her forebears came down from the high country in western Montana nearly three centuries ago. They were a mountain people, a mysterious tribe of hunters whose language has never been classified in any major group. In the late seventeenth century they began a long migration to the south and east. It was a journey toward the dawn, and it led to a golden age. Along the way the Kiowas were befriended by the Crows, who gave them the culture and religion of the Plains. They acquired horses, and their ancient nomadic spirit was suddenly free of the ground. They acquired Tai-me, the sacred sun-dance doll, from that moment the object and symbol of their worship, and so shared in the divinity of the sun. Not least, they acquired the sense of destiny, therefore courage and pride. When they entered upon the southern plains they had been transformed. No longer were they slaves to the simple necessity of survival; they were a lordly and danger-ous society of fighters and thieves, hunters and priests of the sun.

According to their origin myth, they entered the world through a hollow log. From one point of view, their migration was the fruit of an old prophecy, for indeed they emerged from a sunless world.

Though my grandmother lived out her long life in the shadow of   5
Rainy Mountain, the immense landscape of the continental interior lay like memory in her blood. She could tell of the Crows, whom she had never seen, and of the Black Hills, where she had never been. I wanted to see in reality what she had seen more perfectly in the mind's eye, and drove fifteen hundred miles to begin my pilgrimage.

Yellowstone, it seemed to me, was the top of the world, a region of   6
deep lakes and dark timber, canyons and waterfalls. But, beautiful as it is, one might have the sense of confinement there. The skyline in all directions is close at hand, the high wall of the woods and deep cleavages of shade. There is a perfect freedom in the mountains, but it belongs to the eagle and the elk, the badger and the bear. The Kiowas reckoned their stature by distances they see, and they were bent and blind in the winderness.

Descending eastward, the highland meadows are a stairway to the   7
plain. In July the inland slope of the Rockies is luxuriant with flax and buckwheat, stonecrop and larkspur. The earth unfolds and the limit of the land recedes. Clusters of trees, and animals grazing far in the distance, cause the vision to reach away and wonder to build upon the mind. The sun follows a longer course in the day, and the sky is immense beyond all comparison. The great billowing clouds that sail upon it are shadows that move upon the grain like water, dividing light. Farther down, in the land of the Crows and Blackfeet, the plain is yellow. Sweet clover takes hold of the hills and bends upon itself to cover and seal the soil. There the Kiowas paused on their way; they had come to the place where they must change their lives. The sun is at home on the plains. Precisely there does it have the certain character of a god. When the Kiowas came to the land of the Crows, they could see the dark lees of the hills at dawn across the Bighorn River, the profusion of light on the grain shelves, the oldest deity ranging after the solstices. Not yet would they veer southward to the caldron of the land that lay below; they must wean their blood from the northern winter and hold the mountains a while longer in their view. They bore Tai-me in procession to the east.

A dark mist lay over the Black Hills, and the land was like iron. At   8
the top of a ridge I caught sight of Devil's Tower upthrust against the gray sky as if in the birth of time the core of the earth had broken through its crust and the motion of the world was begun. There are things in nature that engender an awful quiet in the heart of man; Devil's Tower is one of them. Two centuries ago, because they could

not do otherwise, the Kiowas made a legend at the base of the rock. My grandmother said:

"Eight children were there at play, seven sisters and their brother.   9
Suddenly the boy was struck dumb; he trembled and began to run upon his hands and feet. His fingers became claws, and his body was covered with fur. There was a bear where the boy had been. The sisters were terrified; they ran, and the bear after them. They came to the stump of a great tree, and the tree spoke to them. It bade them climb upon it, and as they did so, it began to rise into the air. The bear came to kill them, but they were just beyond its reach. It reared against the tree and scored the bark all around with its claws. The seven sisters were borne into the sky, and they became the stars of the Big Dipper." From that moment, and so long as the legend lives, the Kiowas have kinsmen in the night sky. Whatever they were in the mountains, they could be no more. However tenuous their well-being, however much they had suffered and would suffer again, they had found a way out of the wilderness.

My grandmother had a reverence for the sun, a holy regard that now   10
is all but gone out of mankind. There was a wariness in her, and an ancient awe. She was a Christian in her later years, but she had come a long way about, and she never forgot her birthright. As a child she had been to the sun dances; she had taken part in that annual rite, and by it she had learned the restoration of her people in the presence of Tai-me. She was about seven when the last Kiowa sun dance was held in 1887 on the Washita River above Rainy Mountain Creek. The buffalo were gone. In order to consummate the ancient sacrifice—to impale the head of a buffalo bull upon the Tai-me tree—a delegation of old men journeyed into Texas, there to beg and barter for an animal from the Goodnight herd. She was ten when the Kiowas came together for the last time as a living sun-dance culture. They could find no buffalo; they had to hand an old hide from the sacred tree. Before the dance could begin, a company of soldiers rode out from Fort Sill under orders to disperse the tribe. Forbidden without cause the essential act of their faith, having seen the wild herds slaughtered and left to rot upon the ground, the Kiowas backed away forever from the tree. That was July 20, 1890, at the great bend of the Washita. My grandmother was there. Without bitterness, and for as long as she lived, she bore a vision of deicide.

Now that I can have her only in memory, I see my grandmother in   11
the several postures that were peculiar to her: standing at the wood stove on a winter morning and turning meat in a great iron skillet; sitting at the south window, bent above her beadwork, and afterwards, when her vision failed, looking down for a long time into the fold of

her hands; going out upon a cane, very slowly as she did when the weight of age came upon her; praying. I remember her most often at prayer. She made long, rambling prayers out of suffering and hope, having seen many things. I was never sure that I had the right to hear, so exclusive were they of all mere custom and company. The last time I saw her she prayed standing by the side of her bed at night, naked to the waist, the light of a kerosene lamp moving upon her dark skin. Her long black hair, always drawn and braided in the day, lay upon her shoulders and against her breasts like a shawl. I do not speak Kiowa, and I never understood her prayers, but there was something inherently sad in the sound, some merest hesitation upon the syllables of sorrow. She began in a high and descending pitch, exhausting her breath to silence; then again and again—and always the same intensity of effort, of something that is, and is not, like urgency in the human voice. Transported so in the dancing light among the shadows of her room, she seemed beyond the reach of time. But that was illusion; I think I knew then that I should not see her again.

Houses are like sentinels in the plain, old keepers of the weather watch. There, in a very little while, wood takes on the appearance of great age. All colors wear soon away in the wind and rain, and then the wood is burned gray and the grain appears and the nails turn red with rust. The window panes are black and opaque; you imagine there is nothing within, and indeed there are many ghosts, bones given up to the land. They stand here and there against the sky, and you approach them for a longer time than you expect. They belong in the distance; it is their domain. 12

Once there was a lot of sound in my grandmother's house, a lot of coming and going, feasting and talk. The summers there were full of excitement and reunion. The Kiowas are a summer people; they abide the cold and keep to themselves, but when the season turns and the land becomes warm and vital they cannot hold still; an old love of going returns upon them. The aged visitors who came to my grandmother's house when I was a child were made of lean and leather, and they bore themselves upright. They wore great black hats and bright ample shirts that shook in the wind. They rubbed fat upon their hair and wound their braids with strips of colored cloth. Some of them painted their faces and carried the scars of old and cherished enmities. They were an old council of warlords, come to remind and be reminded of who they were. Their wives and daughters served them well. The women might indulge themselves; gossip was at once the mark and compensation of their servitude. They made loud and elaborate talk among themselves, full of jest and gesture, fright and false alarm. They went abroad in fringed and flowered shawls, bright beadwork and German silver. 13

They were at home in the kitchen, and they prepared meals that were banquets.

There were frequent prayer meetings, and nocturnal feasts. When I 14 was a child I played with my cousins outside, where the lamplight fell upon the ground and the singing of the old people rose up around us and carried away into the darkness. There were a lot of good things to eat, a lot of laughter and surprise. And afterwards, when the quiet returned, I lay down with my grandmother and could hear the frogs away by the river and feel the motion of the air.

Now there is a funeral silence in the rooms, the endless wake of 15 some final word. The walls have closed in upon my grandmother's house. When I returned to it in mourning, I saw for the first time in my life how small it was. It was late at night, and there was a white moon, nearly full. I sat for a long time on the stone steps by the kitchen door. From there I could see out across the land; I could see the long row of trees by the creek, the low light upon the rolling plains, and the stars of the Big Dipper. Once I looked at the moon and caught sight of a strange thing. A cricket had perched upon the handrail, only a few inches away. My line of vision was such that the creature filled the moon like a fossil. It had gone there, I thought, to live and die, for there, of all places, was its small definition made whole and eternal. A warm wind rose up and purled like the longing within me.

The next morning, I awoke at dawn and went out on the dirt road to 16 Rainy Mountain. It was already hot, and the grasshoppers began to fill the air. Still it was early in the morning, and birds sang out of the shadows. The long yellow grass on the mountain shone in the bright light, and a scissortail hied above the land. There, where it ought to be, at the end of a long and legendary way, was my grandmother's grave. She had at last succeeded to that holy ground. Here and there on the dark stones were ancestral names. Looking back once, I saw the mountain and came away.

AIMS AND STRATEGIES OF THE WRITER

Comment. Scott Momaday chose to write about somebody other than himself, his Kiowa grandmother, in order to narrate certain events of her life and thereby to make his point about his race and America's heritage.

Assignment 1. Choose somebody from your life, either a relative or friend, who appears worthy of biographical treatment in the pattern of Momaday's writing. Begin making notes on your recollections for some purpose—to reaffirm your heritage, to express your affection, to relate a person's life-style or their sense of humor. Your notes should be descriptive, relating how the person looked, and also narrative, telling episodes and events. These notes will provide concrete detail for your biographical writing.

Comment. Momaday carefully selects the places and events that help him portray his grandmother so that this portrait of her represents the Kiowa nation and his own ancestry.

Assignment 2. Write a paragraph that describes the significance of your biographical subject. Why do you remember the person? What did you learn from the person? Why is that person's life worth sharing with others? Go beyond the mere fact that the person is your grandfather or neighbor and explain the universal values you gained by the relationship.

Comment. Momaday's reminiscence of events and other people differs from autobiography because he expresses memories of another time and place rather than just commenting about himself. Biography nevertheless expresses personal feelings and attitudes, for Momaday reveals as much about himself as he does about his grandmother.

Assignment 3. Begin writing sketches for your biography in a style of reminiscence. Put yourself into the story and tell how another person affected you. (For example: "I remember the first time I met my neighbor, Mr. Robb.")

THE WRITING PROCESS

Comment. The *pacing* and selection of detail by Momaday are noteworthy. His technique focuses on a few crucial episodes that reveal the meaning of his grandmother's life. Obviously, he could not discuss everything about her. Instead, he develops in about six pages her relationship to the land, to Kiowa legend, and to her religion.

Assignment 4. Use *pacing* to control your biographical essay. Write down a list of key ingredients, especially two pieces of description for setting and for subject and at least two or three narrative episodes, that show how the subject touched your life. Don't try to tell everything you remember; allow a few episodes to carry the point.

Comment. Momaday does not use dialogue extensively in his essay, but he does present the voice of his grandmother in paragraph 8 and suggests her voice indirectly in paragraph 10.

Assignment 5. Develop dialogue that allows the subject of your personal biography to speak. Remember two conventions: The dialogue should advance the progression of your essay, and each speech should be enclosed within quotation marks.

Comment. Using a blend of description and narration, Momaday opens with description of the land (see the discussion in Chapter 1, pages 19–20), then shifts to his reminiscence of his grandmother and her relationship to the land. He ends the essay with a final descriptive look at Rainy Mountain, his ancestral home.

Assignment 6. Consider the role of description in your narrative plot. Can you stop action to describe place and person? Will the description contribute to the special character of your subject? In the fashion of Momaday, write a descriptive paragraph for your opening and another for your closing.

Comment. Momaday uses time sequences effectively. He returns to Rainy Mountain because his grandmother has died, then uses flashback techniques to recreate her presence in the story.

Assignment 7. Determine the time sequences of your personal biography. Can you begin in medias res, perhaps at age eight while you are bouncing on your grandfather's knee? Should you foreshadow his death (if that void in your life will be the point of the narration)? Can you, like Momaday, return to the scene of remembered joy and then flashback to happier times? Would a flashforward, as in the opening by Hughes (pages 67–69) be effective for your beginning? Take the time to organize a plan or outline for your essay.

Comment. Momaday's essay serves as a model for personal biography. He uses the first-person "I" for his reminiscence, employs the third-person "she" to describe his grandmother, uses description effectively, and relates several narrative episodes.

Assignment 8. Using Momaday's essay as a model, write your personal reminiscence of a memorable person. Allow your persona, your personal voice in the first-person "I," to enter the story but keep your primary focus on the character, actions, and words of your subject.

S*ome writers choose to write history, a sequential narration of past events concerning a particular person, country, event, or organization. These writers narrate objectively, without personal involvement. The next essay, a historical narration by Carin Quinn, traces the life of Levi Strauss and the development of the Levi's blue jeans empire. Quinn combines a biography of one person with the history of a manufacturing phenomenon.*

Writers such as Quinn look to the past for information (reading old documents, diaries, and journals and collecting other bits of evidence), then piece together what happened years ago to explain the events and to comment on their significance.

Quinn makes the case that Levi's blue jeans are a true American symbol, ranking with Coca-Cola and McDonald's hamburgers. The essay narrates Levi's life, gives the history of blue jean manufacturing, and serves as a lesson in marketing and entrepreneurship.

In reading this essay, make marginal notes about major figures, dates, and key events. In addition, summarize or paraphrase the essay's thesis—what makes this historical narration important and worthy of mention? (For an example of one reader's brief summary, see page 13.)

Carin Quinn is both historian and freelance writer. Her work in American studies demonstrates that her purpose is one of explanation, not of expression of personal feelings or narration of her own life. "The Jeaning of America—and the World" appeared in American Heritage *(April–May 1978).*

CARIN QUINN

🀫 The Jeaning of America—and the World

This is the story of a sturdy American symbol which has now spread throughout most of the world. The symbol is not the dollar. It is not even Coca-Cola. It is a simple pair of pants called blue jeans, and what the pants symbolize is what Alexis de Tocqueville called "a manly and legitimate passion for equality." Blue jeans are favored equally by bureaucrats and cowboys; bankers and deadbeats; fashion designers and beer drinkers. They draw no distinctions and recognize no classes; they are merely American. Yet they are sought after almost everywhere in the world—including Russia, where authorities recently broke up a teen-aged gang that was selling them on the black market for two hundred dollars a pair. They have been around for a long time, and it seems likely that they will outlive even the necktie. 1

This ubiquitous American symbol was the invention of a Bavarian- 2
born Jew. . . . His name was Levi Strauss.

He was born in Bad Ocheim, Germany, in 1829, and during the 3
European political turmoil of 1848 decided to take his chances in New
York, to which his two brothers already had emigrated. Upon arrival,
Levi soon found that his two brothers had exaggerated their tales of an
easy life in the land of the main chance. They were landowners, they
had told him; instead, he found them pushing needles, thread, pots,
pans, ribbons, yarn, scissors, and buttons to housewives. For two years
he was a lowly peddler, hauling some 180 pounds of sundries door-to-
door to eke out a marginal living. When a married sister in San Francisco offered to pay his way West in 1850, he jumped at the opportunity,
taking with him bolts of canvas he hoped to sell for tenting.

It was the wrong kind of canvas for that purpose, but while talking 4
with a miner down from the mother lode, he learned that pants—
sturdy pants that would stand up to the rigors of the diggings—were
almost impossible to find. Opportunity beckoned. On the spot, Strauss
measured the man's girth and inseam with a piece of string and, for six
dollars in gold dust, had them tailored into a pair of stiff but rugged
pants. The miner was delighted with the result, word got around about
"those pants of Levi's," and Strauss was in business. The company has
been in business ever since.

When Strauss ran out of canvas, he wrote his two brothers to send 5
more. He received instead a tough, brown cotton cloth made in Nîmes,
France—called *serge de Nîmes* and swiftly shortened to "denim" (the
word "jeans" derives from *Gênes*, the French word for Genoa, where a
similar cloth was produced). Almost from the first, Strauss had his cloth
dyed the distinctive indigo that gave blue jeans their name, but it was
not until the 1870s that he added the copper rivets which have long
since become a company trademark. The rivets were the idea of a
Virginia City, Nevada, tailor, Jacob W. Davis, who added them to pacify
a mean-tempered miner called Alkali Ike. Alkali, the story goes, com-
plained that the pockets of his jeans always tore when he stuffed them
with ore samples and demanded that Davis do something about it. As a
kind of joke, Davis took the pants to a blacksmith and had the pockets
riveted; once again, the idea worked so well that word got around; in
1873 Strauss appropriated and patented the gimmick—and hired Davis
as a regional manager.

By this time, Strauss had taken both his brothers and two brothers- 6
in-law into the company and was ready for his third San Francisco store.
Over the ensuing years the company prospered locally, and by the time
of his death in 1902, Strauss had become a man of prominence in
California. For three decades thereafter the business remained profitable

though small, with sales largely confined to the working people of the West—cowboys, lumberjacks, railroad workers, and the like. Levi's jeans were first introduced to the East, apparently, during the dude-ranch craze of the 1930s, when vacationing Easterners returned and spread the word about the wonderful pants with rivets. Another boost came in World War II, when blue jeans were declared an essential commodity and were sold only to people engaged in defense work. From a company with fifteen salespeople, two plants, and almost no business east of the Mississippi in 1946, the organization grew in thirty years to include a sales force of more than twenty-two thousand, with fifty plants and offices in thirty-five countries. Each year, more than 250,000,000 items of Levi's clothing are sold—including more than 83,000,000 pairs of riveted blue jeans. They have become, through marketing, word of mouth, and demonstrable reliability, the common pants of America. They can be purchased prewashed, prefaded, and preshrunk for the suitably proletarian look. They adapt themselves to any sort of idiosyncratic use; women slit them at the inseams and convert them into long skirts, men chop them off above the knees and turn them into something to be worn while challenging the surf. Decorations and ornamentations abound.

The pants have become a tradition, and along the way have acquired   7
a history of their own—so much so that the company has opened a museum in San Francisco. There was, for example, the turn-of-the-century trainman who replaced a faulty coupling with a pair of jeans; the Wyoming man who used his jeans as a towrope to haul his car out of a ditch; the Californian who found several pairs in an abandoned mine, wore them, then discovered they were sixty-three years old and still as good as new and turned them over to the Smithsonian as a tribute to their toughness. And then there is the particularly terrifying story of the careless construction worker who dangled fifty-two stories above the street until rescued, his sole support the Levi's belt loop through which his rope was hooked.

Today "those pants of Levi's" have gone across the seas—although   8
the company has learned that marketing abroad is an arcane art. The conservative dress jeans favored in northern France do not move on the Côte d'Azur; Sta-Prest sells well in Switzerland but dies in Scandinavia; button fronts are popular in France, zippers in Britain.

Though Levi Strauss & Co. has since become Levi Strauss Interna-   9
tional, with all that the corporate name implies, it still retains a suitably fond regard for its beginnings. Through what it calls its "Western Image Program," employing western magazine advertisements, local radio and television, and the promotion of rodeos, the company still pursues

the working people of the West who first inspired Levi Strauss to make pants to fit the world.

AIMS AND STRATEGIES OF THE WRITER

Comment. Generally, historians write narrative episodes about political figures and great national events, but Quinn chooses to write industrial history. She selects a product of the clothing industry and, by dipping into the past, traces the history of the product.

Assignment 1. Select a historic subject that interests you and begin reading about it. You may prefer to write of a person, such as Ulysses Grant; a product, such as McDonald's hamburgers; or an event, such as Halloween. This assignment requires some research. You cannot depend entirely on your personal feelings or opinions because readers will want accurate, authentic information.

Comment. Quinn advances more than dry historic facts by referring to blue jeans as a "sturdy American symbol." The subject has social significance, and the writer fully establishes the national, worldwide appeal of Levi's blue jeans. The historian acts as the interpreter of this significance.

Assignment 2. Jot down notes about the significance of your historic subject. For example, how has the McDonald's hamburger affected American society and its eating habits? One purpose of your work as historian is to interpret, evaluate, and judge events of the past and put them into perspective for the reader.

Comment. The writer of informative narration must resolve conflicts in evidence, solve factual problems, and in general act as an investigator. Quinn ventured far back into the past to trace facts and data, explore records, and settle disputes in evidence. This task requires an inquisitive, exploratory mind.

Assignment 3. Spend about thirty minutes in the library researching your topic. Search the card catalog for books. For magazine articles, examine *Readers' Guide to Periodical Literature*. For newspaper reports, search *New York Times Index*. For scholarly journal articles examine either *Humanities Index* or *Social Sciences Index*. Write down facts and general knowledge, not scholarly quotations. You might want to add a brief bibliography of sources at the end of your essay.

THE WRITING PROCESS

Comment. Historical narration, as opposed to autobiography, requires a different voice for the writer. Quinn steps away from the story and speaks objectively in the third person. She talks not about herself but about Levi Strauss and his blue jeans.

Assignment 4. Study the narrative point of view in paragraph 3 of Quinn's essay, then write a similar passage for your essay, using the third person "he," "she," "it," or "they." Keep the focus on the subject, not on your feelings about the subject.

Comment. Quinn uses pacing to control the essay. After an introduction, the writer moves by dates: the birth of Strauss in 1829, his move to America in 1848, the move west in 1850, the patent in 1873, and his death in 1902. Note especially that Quinn keeps a focus on Strauss's business activities; the essay is not merely a biography of one man's life but the history of a product.

Assignment 5. Work out the pacing and overall plan for your essay. For example, if you are writing the history of the McDonald's hamburger chain, begin with the original McDonald's, introduce Ray Kroc, the founder, and follow the highlights of his progress in franchising the chain across America. Whatever your topic, you must remember that you cannot include everything, so pick the crucial scenes and develop those with vivid details.

Comment. Study the basic form of Quinn's essay and note first the introduction of the subject—blue jeans—then the biography of a key figure—Levi Strauss—and finally, the role of blue jeans in today's world.

Assignment 6. Consider Quinn's essay sequence: contemporary subject, history of the subject, and the role the subject plays today. Will that pattern (present, past, present) work in your essay? If it doesn't work, look for other sequences, perhaps the more traditional past-to-present pattern.

Comment. Another way to consider Quinn's development of the essay is to examine her use of historic causal chains: the emigration to America, the move west with material for tents, the use of denim for jeans, the addition of rivets, and so forth.

Assignment 7. Apply historic causal chains to your essay. For example, study the history of a fashion phenomenon—such as the Izod alligator, western boots, or panty hose—and note the significant dates in the history of the product. If you want to keep your topic centered on a local subject, select a manufacturing firm in your area and, after interviews and research, write a brief history of the company, focusing on key events and especially on one key person.

Some writers use their interpretation of history and personal experience to argue an issue with the reader. The technique is narration, but the aim is persuasion. In the next essay Richard Rodriguez narrates events from his childhood to establish evidence of his expertise in matters of private and public languages. He has lived with the problems, so he now wishes to persuade his readers about a point or two, especially as concerns the teaching of English as a second language.

A persuasive aim requires the writer to speak out and advance and defend his fundamental proposition with an imperative and impassioned voice. In this essay, Rodriguez places great value on public English, as opposed to bilingualism, for Hispanics and other minorities. If you live in the United States, he says, your primary language must be English. Children cannot maintain a balance between two languages. He defends his position with sound reasons and realistic evidence, in this case the events of his childhood. (See also the essay by Rachel Jones, pages 297–299.)

As you read the essay, make marginal notes that (1) record the affirmation and reaffirmation of Rodriguez's thesis, (2) record his frequent comparisons of one public language with bilingualism, and (3) record his use of narrative episodes to display and defend his position.

Richard Rodriguez was raised in Sacramento, California, the son of Spanish-speaking parents. He has gained a literary reputation for his essays and his autobiographical work, Hunger of Memory (1981).

RICHARD RODRIGUEZ

Aria: A Memoir of a Bilingual Childhood

I remember, to start with, that day in Sacramento, in a California now 1
nearly thirty years past, when I first entered a classroom—able to understand about fifty stray English words. The third of four children, I had been preceded by my older brother and sister to a neighborhood Roman Catholic school. But neither of them had revealed very much about their classroom experiences. They left each morning and returned each afternoon, always together, speaking Spanish as they climbed the five steps to the porch. And their mysterious books, wrapped in brown shopping-bag paper, remained on the table next to the door, closed firmly behind them.

An accident of geography sent me to a school where all my class- 2
mates were white and many were the children of doctors and lawyers and business executives. On that first day of school, my classmates must

certainly have been uneasy to find themselves apart from their families, in the first institution of their lives. But I was astonished. I was fated to be the "problem student" in class.

The nun said, in a friendly but oddly impersonal voice: "Boys and   3 girls, this is Richard Rodriguez." (I heard her sound it out: *Rich-heard Road-ree-guess.*) It was the first time I had heard anyone say my name in English. "Richard," the nun repeated more slowly, writing my name down in her book. Quickly I turned to see my mother's face dissolve in a watery blur behind the pebbled-glass door.

Now, many years later, I hear of something called "bilingual educa-   4 tion"—a scheme proposed in the late 1960s by Hispanic-American social activists, later endorsed by a congressional vote. It is a program that seeks to permit non-English-speaking children (many from lower class homes) to use their "family language" as the language of school. Such, at least, is the aim its supporters announce. I hear them, and am forced to say no: It is not possible for a child, any child, ever to use his family's language in school. Not to understand this is to misunderstand the public uses of schooling and to trivialize the nature of intimate life.

Memory teaches me what I know of these matters. The boy reminds   5 the adult. I was a bilingual child, but of a certain kind: "socially disad-vantaged," the son of working-class parents, both Mexican immigrants.

In the early years of my boyhood, my parents coped very well in   6 America. My father had steady work. My mother managed at home. They were nobody's victims. When we moved to a house many blocks from the Mexican-American section of town, they were not intimidated by those two or three neighbors who initially tried to make us unwelcome. ("Keep your brats away from my sidewalk!") But despite all they achieved, or perhaps because they had so much to achieve, they lacked any deep feeling of ease, of belonging in public. They regarded the people at work or in crowds as being very distant from us. Those were the others, *los gringos.* That term was interchangeable in their speech with another, even more telling: *los americanos.*

I grew up in a house where the only regular guests were my rela-   7 tions. On a certain day, enormous families of relatives would visit us, and there would be so many people that the noise and the bodies would spill out to the backyard and onto the front porch. Then for weeks no one would come. (If the doorbell rang, it was usually a salesman.) Our house stood apart—gaudy yellow in a row of white bungalows. We were the people with the noisy dog, the people who raised chickens. We were the foreigners on the block. A few neighbors would smile and wave at us. We waved back. But until I was seven years old, I did not know the name of the old couple living next door or the names of the kids living across the street.

In public, my father and mother spoke a hesitant, accented, and not   8
always grammatical English. And then they would have to strain, their
bodies tense, to catch the sense of what was rapidly said by *los gringos*.
At home, they returned to Spanish. The language of their Mexican past
sounded in counterpoint to the English spoken in public. The words
would come quickly, with ease. Conveyed through those sounds was
the pleasing, soothing, consoling reminder that one was at home.

During those years when I was first learning to speak, my mother   9
and father addressed me only in Spanish; in Spanish I learned to reply.
By contrast, English (*inglés*) was the language I came to associate with
gringos, rarely heard in the house. I learned my first words of English
overhearing my parents speaking to strangers. At six years of age, I
knew just enough words for my mother to trust me on errands to stores
one block away—but no more.

I was then a listening child, careful to hear the very different sounds   10
of Spanish and English. Wide-eyed with hearing, I'd listen to sounds
more than to words. First, there were English (gringo) sounds. So many
words still were unknown to me that when the butcher or the lady at
the drugstore said something, exotic polysyllabic sounds would bloom
in the midst of their sentences. Often the speech of people in public
seemed to me very loud, booming with confidence. The man behind
the counter would literally ask, "What can I do for you?" But by being
so firm and clear, the sound of his voice said that he was a gringo; he
belonged in public society. There were also the high, nasal notes of
middle-class American speech—which I rarely am conscious of hearing today because I hear them so often, but could not stop hearing
when I was a boy. Crowds at Safeway or at bus stops were noisy with
the birdlike sounds of *los gringos*. I'd move away from them all—all
the chirping chatter above me.

My own sounds I was unable to hear, but I knew that I spoke English   11
poorly. My words could not extend to form complete thoughts. And the
words I did speak I didn't know well enough to make distinct sounds.
(Listeners would usually lower their heads to hear better what I was
trying to say.) But it was one thing for *me* to speak English with difficulty; it was more troubling to hear my parents speaking in public: their
high-whining vowels and guttural consonants; their sentences that got
stuck with "eh" and "ah" sounds; the confused syntax; the hesitant
rhythm of sounds so different from the way gringos spoke. I'd notice,
moreover, that my parents' voices were softer than those of gringos we
would meet.

I am tempted to say now that none of this mattered. (In adulthood I   12
am embarrassed by childhood fears.) And, in a way, it didn't matter
very much that my parents could not speak English with ease. Their

linguistic difficulties had no serious consequences. My mother and father made themselves understood at the county hospital clinic and at government offices. And yet, in another way, it mattered very much. It was unsettling to hear my parents struggle with English. Hearing them, I'd grow nervous, and my clutching trust in their protection and power would be weakened.

There were many times like the night at a brightly lit gasoline station   13 (a blaring white memory) when I stood uneasily hearing my father talk to a teenage attendant. I do not recall what they were saying, but I cannot forget the sounds my father made as he spoke. At one point his words slid together to form one long word—sounds as confused as the threads of blue and green oil in the puddle next to my shoes. His voice rushed through what he had left to say. Toward the end, he reached falsetto notes, appealing to his listener's understanding. I looked away at the lights of passing automobiles. I tried not to hear any more. But I heard only too well the attendant's reply, his calm, easy tones. Shortly afterward, headed for home, I shivered when my father put his hand on my shoulder. The very first chance that I got, I evaded his grasp and ran on ahead into the dark, skipping with feigned boyish exuberance.

But then there was Spanish: *español*, the language rarely heard away   14 from the house; *español*, the language which seemed to me therefore a private language, my family's language. To hear its sounds was to feel myself specially recognized as one of the family, apart from *los otros*. A simple remark, an inconsequential comment could convey that assurance. My parents would say something to me and I would feel embraced by the sounds of their words. Those sounds said: *I am speaking with ease in Spanish. I am addressing you in words I never use with* los gringos. *I recognize you as someone special, close, like no one outside. You belong with us. In the family. Ricardo.*

At the age of six, well past the time when most middle-class children   15 no longer notice the difference between sounds uttered at home and words spoken in public, I had a different experience. I lived in a world compounded of sounds. I was a child longer than most. I lived in a magical world, surrounded by sounds both pleasing and fearful. I shared with my family a language enchantingly private—different from that used in the city around us.

Just opening or closing the screen door behind me was an impor-   16 tant experience. I'd rarely leave home all alone or without feeling reluctance. Walking down the sidewalk, under the canopy of tall trees, I'd warily notice the (suddenly) silent neighborhood kids who stood warily watching me. Nervously, I'd arrive at the grocery store to hear there the sounds of the gringo, reminding me that in this so-big world I was a foreigner. But if leaving home was never routine, neither was coming back. Walking toward our house, climbing the steps from the sidewalk, in summer when the front door was open, I'd hear voices beyond the screen door talking in Spanish. For a second or two I'd stay, linger there listening. Smiling, I'd hear my mother call out, saying in Spanish, "Is that you, Richard?" Those were her words, but all the while her sounds would assure me: *You are home now. Come closer inside With us.* "*Sí*," I'd reply.

Once more inside the house, I would resume my place in the family.   17
The sounds would grow harder to hear. Once more at home, I would grow less conscious of them. It required, however, no more than the blurt of the doorbell to alert me all over again to listen to sounds. The house would turn instantly quiet while my mother went to the door. I'd hear her hard English sounds. I'd wait to hear her voice turn to soft-sounding Spanish, which assured me, as surely as did the clicking tongue of the lock on the door, that the stranger was gone.

Plainly it is not healthy to hear such sounds so often. It is not healthy   18
to distinguish public from private sounds so easily. I remained cloistered by sounds, timid and shy in public, too dependent on the voices at home. And yet I was a very happy child when I was at home. I remember many nights when my father would come back from work, and I'd hear him call out to my mother in Spanish, sounding relieved. In Spanish, his voice would sound the light and free notes that he never could manage in English. Some nights I'd jump up just hearing his voice. My brother and I would come running into the room where he was with our mother. Our laughing (so deep was the pleasure!) became screaming. Like others who feel the pain of public alienation, we transformed the knowledge of our public separateness into a consoling reminder of our intimacy. Excited, our voices joined in a celebration of sounds. *We are speaking now the way we never speak out in public— we are together*, the sounds told me. Some nights no one seemed willing to loosen the hold that sounds had on us. At dinner we invented new words that sounded Spanish, but made sense only to us. We pieced together new words by taking, say, an English verb and giving it Spanish endings. My mother's instructions at bedtime would be lacquered with mock-urgent tones. Or a word like *sí*, sounded in several notes, would convey added measures of feeling. Tongues lingered around the edges of words, especially fat vowels. And we happily sounded that military drum roll, the twirling roar of the Spanish *r*. Family language, my family's sounds: the voices of my parents and sisters and brother. Their voices insisting: *You belong here. We are family members. Related. Special to one another. Listen!* Voices singing and sighing, rising and straining, then surging, teeming with pleasure which burst syllables into fragments of laughter. At times it seemed there was steady quiet

only when, from another room, the rustling whispers of my parents faded and I edged closer to sleep.

Supporters of bilingual education imply today that students like me 19 miss a great deal by not being taught in their family's language. What they seem not to recognize is that, as a socially disadvantaged child, I regarded Spanish as a private language. It was a ghetto language that deepened and strengthened my feeling of public separateness. What I needed to learn in school was that I had the right, and the obligation, to speak the public language. The odd truth is that my first-grade classmates could have become bilingual, in the conventional sense of the word, more easily than I. Had they been taught early (as upper middle-class children often are taught) a "second language" like Spanish or French, they could have regarded it simply as another public language. In my case, such bilingualism could not have been so quickly achieved. What I did not believe was that I could speak a single public language.

Without question, it would have pleased me to have heard my teach- 20 ers address me in Spanish when I entered the classroom. I would have felt much less afraid. I would have imagined that my instructors were somehow "related" to me; I would indeed have heard their Spanish as my family's language. I would have trusted them and responded with ease. But I would have delayed—postponed for how long?—having to learn the language of public society. I would have evaded—and for how long?—learning the great lesson of school: that I had a public identity.

Fortunately, my teachers were unsentimental about their responsi- 21 bility. What they understood was that I needed to speak public English. So their voices would search me out, asking me questions. Each time I heard them I'd look up in surprise to see a nun's face frowning at me. I'd mumble, not really meaning to answer. The nun would persist. "Richard, stand up. Don't look at the floor. Speak up. Speak to the entire class, not just to me!" But I couldn't believe English could be my language to use. (In part, I did not want to believe it.) I continued to mumble. I resisted the teacher's demands. (Did I somehow suspect that once I learned this public language my family life would be changed?) Silent, waiting for the bell to sound, I remained dazed, diffident, afraid.

Because I wrongly imagined that English was intrinsically a public 22 language and Spanish was intrinsically private, I easily noted the difference between classroom language and the language of home. At school, words were directed to a general audience of listeners. ("Boys and girls . . .") Words were meaningfully ordered. And the point was not self-expression alone, but to make oneself understood by many others. The teacher quizzed: "Boys and girls, why do we use that word in this sentence? Could we think of a better word to use there? Would the sentence change its meaning if the words were differently arranged?

Isn't there a better way of saying much the same thing?" (I couldn't say. I wouldn't try to say.)

Three months passed. Five. A half year. Unsmiling, ever watchful, my   23 teachers noted my silence. They began to connect my behavior with the slow progress my brother and sisters were making. Until, one Saturday morning, three nuns arrived at the house to talk to our parents. Stiffly they sat on the blue living-room sofa. From the doorway of another room, spying on the visitors, I noted the incongruity, the clash of two worlds, the faces and voices of school intruding upon the familiar setting of home. I overheard one voice gently wondering, "Do your children speak only Spanish at home, Mrs. Rodriguez?" While another voice added, "That Richard especially seems so timid and shy."

That Rich-heard!   24

With great tact, the visitors continued, "Is it possible for you and   25 your husband to encourage your children to practice their English when they are home?" Of course my parents complied. What would they not do for their children's well-being? And how could they question the Church's authority which those women represented? In an instant they agreed to give up the language (the sounds) which had revealed and accentuated our family's closeness. The moment after the visitors left, the change was observed. "*Ahora*, speak to us only *en inglés*," my father and mother told us.

At first, it seemed a kind of game. After dinner each night, the family   26 gathered together to practice "our" English. It was still then *inglés*, a language foreign to us, so we felt drawn to it as strangers. Laughing, we would try to define words we could not pronounce. We played with strange English sounds, often over-anglicizing our pronunciations. And we filled the smiling gaps of our sentences with familiar Spanish sounds. But that was cheating, somebody shouted, and everyone laughed.

In school, meanwhile, like my brother and sisters, I was required to   27 attend a daily tutoring session. I needed a full year of this special work. I also needed my teachers to keep my attention from straying in class by called out, "*Rich-heard!*"—their English voices slowly loosening the ties to my other name, with its three notes, *Ri-car-do*. Most of all, I needed to hear my mother and father speak to me in a moment of seriousness in "broken"—suddenly heartbreaking—English. This scene was inevitable. One Saturday morning I entered the kitchen where my parents were talking, but I did not realize that they were talking in Spanish until, the moment they saw me, their voices changed and they began speaking English. The gringo sounds they uttered startled me. Pushed me away. In that moment of trivial misunderstanding and profound insight, I felt my throat twisted by unsounded grief. I simply turned and left the room. But I had no place to escape to where I could grieve in Spanish. My brother and sisters were speaking English in another part of the house.

Again and again in the days following, as I grew increasingly angry, 28 I was obliged to hear my mother and father encouraging me: "Speak to us *en inglés*." Only then did I determine to learn classroom English. Thus, sometime afterward it happened: one day in school, I raised my hand to volunteer an answer to a question. I spoke out in a loud voice and I did not think it remarkable when the entire class understood. That day I moved very far from being the disadvantaged child I had been only days earlier. Taken hold at last was the belief, the calming assurance, that I *belonged* in public.

Shortly after, I stopped hearing the high, troubling sounds of *los* 29 *gringos*. A more and more confident speaker of English, I didn't listen to how strangers sounded when they talked to me. With so many English-speaking people around me, I no longer heard American accents. Conversations quickened. Listening to persons whose voices sounded eccentrically pitched, I might note their sounds for a few seconds, but then I'd concentrate on what they were saying. Now when I heard someone's tone of voice—angry or questioning or sarcastic or happy or sad—I didn't distinguish it from the words it expressed. Sound and word were thus tightly wedded. At the end of each day I was often bemused, and always relieved, to realize how "soundless," though crowded with words, my day in public had been. An eight-year-old boy, I finally came to accept what had been technically true since my birth: I was an American citizen.

But diminished by then was the special feeling of closeness at home. 30 Gone was the desperate, urgent, intense feeling of being at home among those with whom I felt intimate. Our family remained a loving family, but one greatly changed. We were no longer so close, no longer bound tightly together by the knowledge of our separateness from *los gringos*. Neither my older brother nor my sisters rushed home after school any more. Nor did I. When I arrived home, often there would be neighborhood kids in the house. Or the house would be empty of sounds.

Following the dramatic Americanization of their children, even my 31 parents grew more publicly confident—especially my mother. First she learned the names of all the people on the block. Then she decided we needed to have a telephone in our house. My father, for his part, continued to use the word gringo, but it was no longer charged with bitterness or distrust. Stripped of any emotional content, the word simply became a name for those Americans not of Hispanic descent. Hearing him, sometimes, I wasn't sure if he was pronouncing the Spanish word *gringo*, or saying gringo in English.

There was a new silence at home. As we children learned more and more English, we shared fewer and fewer words with our parents. Sentences needed to be spoken slowly when one of us addressed our mother or father. Often the parent wouldn't understand. The child would need to repeat himself. Still the parent misunderstood. The young voice, frustrated, would end up saying, "Never mind"—the subject was closed. Dinners would be noisy with the clinking of knives and forks against dishes. My mother would smile softly between her remarks; my father, at the other end of the table, would chew and chew his food while he stared over the heads of his children. 32

My mother! My father! After English became my primary language, I no longer knew what words to use in addressing my parents. The old Spanish words (those tender accents of sound) I had earlier used— *mamá* and *papá*—I couldn't use any more. They would have been all-too-painful reminders of how much had changed in my life. On the other hand, the words I heard neighborhood kids call their parents seemed equally unsatisfactory. "Mother" and "father," "ma," "papa," "pa," "dad," "pop" (how I hated the all-American sound of that last word)—all these I felt were unsuitable terms of address for *my* parents. As a result, I never used them at home. Whenever I'd speak to my parents, I would try to get their attention by looking at them. In public conversations, I'd refer to them as my "parents" or my "mother" and "father." 33

My mother and father, for their part, responded differently, as their children spoke to them less. My mother grew restless, seemed troubled and anxious at the scarceness of words exchanged in the house. She would question me about my day when I came home from school. She smiled at my small talk. She pried at the edges of my sentences to get me to say something more. ("What . . . ?") She'd join conversations she overheard, but her intrusions often stopped her children's talking. By contrast, my father seemed to grow reconciled to the new quiet. Though his English somewhat improved, he tended more and more to retire into silence. At dinner he spoke very little. One night his children and even his wife helplessly giggled at his garbled English pronunciation of the Catholic "Grace before Meals." Thereafter he made his wife recite the prayer at the start of each meal, even on formal occasions when there were guests in the house. 34

Hers became the public voice of the family. On official business it was she, not my father, who would usually talk to strangers on the 35 phone or in stores. We children grew so accustomed to his silence that years later we would routinely refer to his "shyness." (My mother often tried to explain: both of his parents died when he was eight. He was raised by an uncle who treated him as little more than a menial servant. He was never encouraged to speak. He grew up alone—a man of few words.) But I realized my father was not shy whenever I'd watch him speaking Spanish with relatives. Using Spanish, he was quickly effusive. Especially when talking with other men, his voice would spark, flicker, flare alive with varied sounds. In Spanish he expressed ideas and feelings he rarely revealed when speaking English. With firm Spanish sounds he conveyed a confidence and authority that English would never allow him.

The silence at home, however, was not simply the result of fewer   36 words passing between parents and children. More profound for me was the silence created by my inattention to sounds. At about the time I no longer bothered to listen with care to the sounds of English in public, I grew careless about listening to the sounds made by the family when they spoke. Most of the time I would hear someone speaking at home and didn't distinguish his sounds from the words people uttered in public. I didn't even pay much attention to my parents' accented and ungrammatical speech—at least not at home. Only when I was with them in public would I become alert to their accents. But even then their sounds caused me less and less concern. For I was growing increasingly confident of my own public identity.

I would have been happier about my public success had I not re-   37 called, sometimes, what it had been like earlier, when my family conveyed its intimacy through a set of conveniently private sounds. Sometimes in public, hearing a stranger, I'd hark back to my lost past. A Mexican farm worker approached me one day downtown. He wanted directions to some place. "*Hijito*, . . ." he said. And his voice stirred old longings. Another time I was standing beside my mother in the visiting room of a Carmelite convent, before the dense screen which rendered the nuns shadowy figures. I heard several of them speaking Spanish in their busy, singsong, overlapping voices, assuring my mother that, yes, yes, we were remembered, all our family was remembered, in their prayers. Those voices echoed faraway family sounds. Another day a dark-faced old woman touched my shoulder lightly to steady herself as she boarded a bus. She murmured something to me I couldn't quite comprehend. Her Spanish voice came near, like the face of a never-before-seen relative in the instant before I was kissed. That voice, like so many of the Spanish voices I'd hear in public, recalled the golden age of my childhood.

Bilingual educators say today that children lose a degree of "individ- 38
uality" by becoming assimilated into public society. (Bilingual schooling is a program popularized in the seventies, that decade when
middle-class "ethnics" began to resist the process of assimilation—the
"American melting pot.") But the bilingualists oversimplify when they
scorn the value and necessity of assimilation. They do not seem to
realize that a person is individualized in two ways. So they do not
realize that, while one suffers a diminished sense of *private* individuality by being assimilated into public society, such assimilation makes
possible the achievement of *public* individuality.

Simplistically again, the bilingualists insist that a student should be 39
reminded of his difference from others in mass society, of his "heritage." But they equate mere separateness with individuality. The fact is
that only in private—with intimates—is separateness from the crowd a
prerequisite for individuality; an intimate "tells" me that I am unique,
unlike all others, apart from the crowd. In public, by contrast, full
individuality is achieved, paradoxically, by those who are able to consider themselves members of the crowd. Thus it happened for me. Only
when I was able to think of myself as an American, no longer an alien
in gringo society, could I seek the rights and opportunities necessary
for full public individuality. The social and political advantages I enjoy
as a man began on the day I came to believe that my name is indeed
Rich-heard Road-ree-guess. It is true that my public society today is
often impersonal; in fact, my public society is usually mass society. But
despite the anonymity of the crowd, and despite the fact that the individuality I achieve in public is often tenuous—because it depends on
my being one in a crowd—I celebrate the day I acquired my new name.
Those middle-class ethnics who scorn assimilation seem to me filled
with decadent self-pity, obsessed by the burden of public life. Dangerously, they romanticize public separateness and trivialize the dilemma
of those who are truly socially disadvantaged.

If I rehearse here the changes in my private life after my American- 40
ization, it is finally to emphasize a public gain. The loss implies the
gain. The house I returned to each afternoon was quiet. Intimate
sounds no longer greeted me at the door. Inside there were other
noises. The telephone rang. Neighborhood kids ran past the door of
the bedroom where I was reading my schoolbooks—covered with
brown shopping-bag paper. Once I learned the public language, it
would never again be easy for me to hear intimate family voices. More
and more of my day was spent hearing words, not sounds. But that may
only be a way of saying that on the day I raised my hand in class
and spoke loudly to an entire roomful of faces, my childhood started
to end.

AIMS AND STRATEGIES OF THE WRITER

Comment. Rodriguez narrates a period of his life to make a point about language and about his identity crisis with his Spanish heritage. He uses the narration as a framework for his primary purpose—a persuasive plea against bilingualism. When writing becomes a form of recommendation, the distance narrows between writer and reader because the writer is speaking almost directly to the reader in an attempt to defend a position and, in some cases, to issue a call to action.

Assignment 1. Examine your past for personal experiences that might trigger a persuasive stance. List a few issues that concern you, especially problems that have affected you personally: prejudice, abuse, theft, deceit or love, friendship, faith. Think of a personal experience that would illustrate the issue in action. Argue the pros and cons of summer jobs, family ties, peer relationships, summer camps, and other rites of passage.

Comment. One primary aim of any persuasive writer is to establish credibility with the audience. Rodriguez, for example, gains credibility by his firsthand knowledge of the subject, his appearance of good character, and his consideration of all the issues.

Assignment 2. Choose a topic for development and begin to establish your credibility by explaining your background and experience with the subject. The narrative pattern now comes into play, for you must tell a brief story of your experiences. Next, express respect for the views of others by demonstrating your understanding of all sides (even though you may disagree with some views) so that you remove the reader's resistance. In particular, avoid a rigid, one-sided position that builds a barrier rather than removes one.

Comment. A persuasive writer like Rodriguez must balance his appeals to reason, ethics, and emotion. He explains that it was not *reasonable* to expect him to learn English in his environment. It was not *ethical* to deny him the opportunities available if he learned English (and his parents recognized this fact). It was, throughout, an *emotional* transition for the boy to change from "Ri-car-do" to "Rich-heard."

Assignment 3. Study your preliminary plans for a persuasive essay. Will your narrative develop an appeal to reason? To ethics? To emotion? Consult with others on your projected topic as a means of testing your ideas.

Comment. The evidence and proof for a persuasive essay drawn from personal experience are contained in the narrative elements. If the personal episodes related by Rodriguez are compelling and convincing, the reader will accept the writer's proposition.

Assignment 4. List at least three episodes from the Rodriguez story that convince you about his sincerity. Examine your own essay plans for similar evidence.

THE WRITING PROCESS

Comment. A narrative writer's pacing is crucial. An examination of the pacing in Rodriguez's essay reveals four major movements: (1) his Spanish identity, (2) the commitment by his parents to speak English in the home, (3) his rapid adoption of the new language, and (4) his diminished identity with his Spanish heritage.

Assignment 5. Outline your essay to determine the major portions of your narrative development. Don't try to tell everything; instead, select key episodes of your experience and allow them to represent the whole.

Comment. Your voice, whether you write in first person or third person, will affect the persuasive purpose. Rodriguez uses first person because personal experience serves as his primary evidence.

Assignment 6. Consider your options. You can (1) narrate your essay in first person so that your experience gives you a voice of authority or (2) narrate in third person to argue the effects of a situation on another person. For example, you can make a point in the first-person voice about your participation as coach in the Special Olympics or in third person about a handicapped child's participation.

Comment. A narrative essay expresses and defends a proposition or thesis. Rodriguez makes his position clear: "Only when I was able to think of myself as an American, no longer an alien in *gringo* society, could I seek the rights and opportunities necessary for full public individuality."

Assignment 7. Develop your own persuasive proposition as a closing for your essay. Use the final three paragraphs of the Rodriguez essay as a model. After that, write your complete draft to build evidence toward the conclusion. Then revise it and prepare a finished manuscript.

Description and narration in the hands of the humorist often change from patterns of factual explanation to ones of exaggeration, metaphor, and drama. Mark Twain's report on the coyote of the old West typifies this style, for he brings readers a fresh new look at this predator of the prairie.

Twain (his real name was Samuel Clemens) is best known for his novels Tom Sawyer *and* Huckleberry Finn, *but he wrote several travel books, including one on the Holy Land and Europe,* Innocents Abroad *(1869); one on his walking tour of Europe,* A Tramp Abroad *(1880); and one about his service as riverboat pilot on the Mississippi River,* Life on the Mississippi *(1883).*

After a trip to the West in 1861–66, Mark Twain wrote Roughing It *(1872), from which "Coyote" is reprinted. He used these travel chronicles to develop stories, humorous anecdotes, legends, character sketches, and descriptions about life in those times and places.*

Underlying Twain's humor are serious themes. He especially enjoys an exploration into persons's aspirations versus their actual achievements. In "Coyote," the dog fruitlessly chases the coyote, representing the distance between ideals and actual accomplishments.

In reading Twain's essay, record a few features of his style: (1) the exaggeration of details for effect, (2) his use of figurative language, (3) his personification of the animals.

MARK TWAIN

 Coyote

Another night of alternate tranquillity and turmoil. But morning came, 1
by and by. It was another glad awakening to fresh breezes, vast expanses
of level greensward, bright sunlight, an impressive solitude utterly without visible human beings or human habitations, and an atmosphere of
such amazing magnifying properties that trees that seemed close at
hand were more than three miles away. We resumed undress uniform,
climbed atop of the flying coach, dangled our legs over the side,
shouted occasionally at our frantic mules, merely to see them lay their
ears back and scamper faster, tied our hats on to keep our hair from
blowing away, and leveled an outlook over the world-wide carpet about
us for things new and strange to gaze at. Even at this day it thrills me
through and through to think of the life, the gladness and the wild
sense of freedom that used to make the blood dance in my veins on
those fine overland mornings!

Along about an hour after breakfast we saw the first prairie-dog   2
villages, the first antelope, and the first wolf. If I remember rightly, this
latter was the regular *coyote* (pronounced ky-o-te) of the farther deserts. And if it *was*, he was not a pretty creature, or respectable either,
for I got well acquainted with his race afterward, and can speak with
confidence. The coyote is a long, slim, sick and sorry-looking skeleton,
with a gray wolf-skin stretched over it, a tolerably bushy tail that forever
sags down with a despairing expression of forsakenness and misery, a
furtive and evil eye, and a long, sharp face, with slightly lifted lip and
exposed teeth. He has a general slinking expression all over. The coyote
is a living, breathing allegory of Want. He is *always* hungry. He is always
poor, out of luck and friendless. The meanest creatures despise him,
and even the fleas would desert him for a velocipede. He is so spiritless
and cowardly that even while his exposed teeth are pretending a threat,
the rest of his face is apologizing for it. And he is *so* homely!—so
scrawny, and ribby, and coarse-haired, and pitiful. When he sees you he
lifts his lip and lets a flash of his teeth out, and then turns a little out of
the course he was pursuing, depresses his head a bit, and strikes a long,
soft-footed trot through the sage-brush, glancing over his shoulder at
you, from time to time, till he is about out of easy pistol range, and then
he stops and takes a deliberate survey of you; he will trot fifty yards and
stop again—another fifty and stop again; and finally the gray of his
gliding body blends with the gray of the sage-brush, and he disappears.
All this is when you make no demonstration against him; but if you do,
he develops a livelier interest in his journey, and instantly electrifies his
heels and puts such a deal of real estate between himself and your
weapon, that by the time you have raised the hammer you see that you
need a minie rifle, and by the time you have got him in line you need a
rifled cannon, and by the time you have "drawn a bead" on him you see
well enough that nothing but an unusually long-winded streak of lightning could reach him where he is now. But if you start a swift-footed
dog after him, you will enjoy it ever so much—especially if it is a dog
that has a good opinion of himself, and has been brought up to think
he knows something about speed. The coyote will go swinging gently
off on that deceitful trot of his, and every little while he will smile a
fraudful smile over his shoulder that will fill that dog entirely full of
encouragement and worldly ambition, and make him lay his head still
lower to the ground, and stretch his neck further to the front, and pant
more fiercely, and stick his tail out straighter behind, and move his
furious legs with a yet wilder frenzy, and leave a broader and broader,
and higher and denser cloud of desert sand smoking behind, and marking his long wake across the level plain! And all this time the dog is only
a short twenty feet behind the coyote, and to save the soul of him he

cannot understand why it is that he cannot get perceptibly closer; and he begins to get aggravated, and it makes him madder and madder to see how gently the coyote glides along and never pants or sweats or ceases to smile; and he grows still more and more incensed to see how shamefully he has been taken in by an entire stranger, and what an ignoble swindle that long, calm, soft-footed trot is; and next he notices that he is getting fagged, and that the coyote actually has to slacken speed a little to keep from running away from him—and *then* that town-dog is mad in earnest, and he begins to strain and weep and swear, and paw the sand higher than ever, and reach for the coyote with concentrated and desperate energy. This "spurt" finds him six feet behind his gliding enemy, and two miles from his friends. And then, in the instant that a wild new hope is lighting up his face, the coyote turns and smiles blandly upon him once more, and with a something about it which seems to say: "Well, I shall have to tear myself away from you, bub—business is business, and it will not do for me to be fooling along this way all day"—and forthwith there is a rushing sound, and the sudden splitting of a long crack through the atmosphere, and behold that dog is solitary and alone in the midst of a vast solitude!

It makes his head swim. He stops, and looks all around; climbs the nearest sand-mound, and gazes into the distance; shakes his head reflectively, and then, without a word, he turns and jogs along back to his train, and takes up a humble position under the hindmost wagon, and feels unspeakably mean, and looks ashamed, and hangs his tail at half-mast for a week. And for as much as a year after that, whenever there is a great hue and cry after a coyote, that dog will merely glance in that direction without emotion, and apparently observe to himself, "I believe I do not wish any of the pie."

AIMS AND STRATEGIES OF THE WRITER

Comment. One fundamental aim of Twain in *Roughing It* is to depict the West in a travelogue that moves from place to place and develops scene by scene. The episode with the coyote represents one scene.

Assignment 1. Consider the situations, events, people, and animals that you would include in a travelogue of a trip you've taken. Especially note scenes and events that provide local color and give your story a special flavor.

Comment. Twain's overt purpose is almost always entertainment. He wants to amuse his readers. In this case, he makes the dog and coyote into characters, giving them a cartoon flavor.

Assignment 2. Employ a tone in your essay that meets your objectives. Do you want to amuse the reader with hyperbole? Or do you want a serious travelogue? If you write in the style of Twain, your piece will present a trivial, lighthearted, and often purposely distorted view.

Comment. Underneath the banter and good-natured fun of Mark Twain's story of the coyote, there is a serious point. The dog has high ideals, but he soon learns that catching a coyote is no easy task. The distance between his expectations and his accomplishments represents the fundamental Twain thesis: Humans, like animals, often exaggerate their own importance.

Assignment 3. Like a cake, good humor has two layers. On the surface the icing of exaggeration and irony makes us smile and laugh with delight. Underneath the icing is the cake—the realism that makes us realize that life is not simple and one dimensional. As you develop your travelogue, perhaps a narrative description of your hometown, dramatize a past event or historical episode that relates to the place and conveys a sense of its distinctive heritage.

THE WRITING PROCESS

Comment. Twain begins the piece with a focus on the coyote—its looks, disposition, and general character. Then he adds the narrative episode that brings the drama of a fruitless chase.

Assignment 4. In developing your travelogue, you will probably easily develop descriptive elements. More difficult will be the use of narration. Somewhere in the essay, tell a story that, like Twain's, reveals the true nature of the place. Write a brief narrative anecdote that you can insert into your longer essay.

Comment. Twain is master of hyperbole; he uses exaggeration for effect, such as saying that the coyote is "a long, slim, sick and sorry-looking skeleton . . . *so* homely!—so scrawny, and ribby, and coarse-haired, and pitiful" that even fleas desert him for a velocipede (tricycle).

Assignment 5. You may wish to consider using hyperbole, that is, exaggerating for effect. Create an exaggerated story, a piece of humor, that characterizes the place.

Comment. In this piece Twain uses elements of the fable (that is, he features animals as characters and conveys a moral). Twain personifies both coyote and dog. The dog learns (the moral) that his expectations exceed his ability.

Assignment 6. Try writing a fable to blend into your travelogue. Give human qualities to an animal or animals and have them speak and act. For example, you might have an old dog portray a sleepy town or use a busy anthill to represent a thriving, bustling community.

The following essay by Randall Williams represents expressive discourse that uncovers one writer's thoughts and feelings. In form it is autobiographical. Its attitude is quiet and restrospective, but humor and irony are also prominent. Its primary pattern of development is personal narration, but it features many detailed examples and descriptive observations.

Williams does not classify himself as an average college student. He dropped out of school for a time, worked in industry, retreated to a rural life-style in Alabama (which is the subject of this essay), and then made his way back to college. He does not consider himself a serious writer, yet he does experiment with poetry and fiction as well as other expository forms.

Faced with a writing assignment that called for a minimum of five pages, Williams turned to his journal, one that he packed full with entries during his summer retreat into the Alabama woods. The result is an interesting and absorbing look into one man's isolation and loneliness. Rather than allow his desire for privacy to defeat him, he confronted it and used solitude for "reflection, purification, and redemption."

In your reading of this student's essay, note narrative passages as well as breaks in the narrative when he describes a scene or his thoughts. In addition, try to spot those parts where he has obviously drawn material from his journal.

RANDALL WILLIAMS, STUDENT

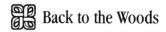 Back to the Woods

When life's hectic pace begins to outdistance my own, when obligations   1
force me into long, tense evenings of work, and when society suppresses my spirit, stuffing me into some insignificant niche, my thoughts turn to that brief but highly rewarding time I spent alone in the woods of northern Alabama. For six months I lived there, virtually isolated from the human world, concerning myself merely with the small matters of my subsistence and reading in the books I brought along. Not a noble soul seeking secret knowledge or visionary splendor, I began upon my hermitage to find relief from a way of life that threatened to overwhelm me. I hoped for a place to repair the splitting seams of my being.

A year before my reclusion I had returned to school, one more time, with high expectations. After six months of digging ditches in the fetid muck of a chemical plant, I was ready again for college life. Amidst rapping jackhammers, rumbling bulldozers, and swarming clouds of red dust, my body begged for rest. School might provide me the opportunity.

But disillusionment came quickly. I was not the young genius of my dreams. Talent, however large, can only be tapped by exercise of discipline, but I lacked discipline. I procrastinated; I cross-examined and chastised myself; in fact, I became both prosecutor and victim in one person, a merciless inquisitor interrogating the hapless victim.

As doubts and self-criticism increased, so did my isolation from the world. Attending class became a great feat of will. Classrooms of people unnerved me. After a few hours on campus among the flow of students and instructors, my senses became frighteningly acute: A crowded hallway sometimes emitted a deafening, cacaphonous roar; the morning sunlight pouring through a dusty pane at the other side of a room was painfully dazzling. I found myself rushing frantically back to my small, unkempt room to bed and sleep, my only escape from the helter-skelter world.

Fortunately, I maintained control of my life. I was unhinged, but not completely apart. I sensed life, a self, a possibility. I thought of the woods where I could piece together a new perspective and renew my energy. In the woods, unhurried and obligated to no outside interest, I could mine my own interior. Having to answer to no one, I could answer to myself.

Besides, a retreat to the woods would be practical. My savings were depleted, and the university stipend provided room and board only for excellence in studies. I would soon be forced to seek work. A friend owned eighty acres of woodland in rural northeastern Alabama, and I imagined that I could erect a shelter, live frugally, and incur minimum expenses. After days of tortured deliberations, I arranged with my friend to oversee his property for the summer.

I withdrew from college, sold a few unnecessary belongings, and sought out my brother, who lived near the woods. An experienced woodsman, he helped me purchase essentials—staples (beans, rice, canned goods), tools (axe, saw, and hammer), and shelter (sheets of plastic and rope). In his battered pickup truck we drove into the rugged hill country onto a narrow dirt lane. We passed squalid, gaunt trailer-houses patched with pitch. Barefoot children stood staring like startled deer in grassless yards. We forded a small stream and found an old logging road clotted with briars and scrub pine. We crashed pell-mell through the undergrowth until the truck could go no farther. We continued by foot to reach a clearing near a small stream that my friend had assured me would be the best spot for a campsite.

My generous brother spent several days with me, helping to erect a shelter of plastic sheets pulled across a frame of young saplings. We picked berries and explored the countryside. Then, with firm handshake and assurance of return, he was gone. I walked the ridge and listened to the low groan of his engine until it disappeared, to be replaced by the call of a whippoorwill. I was alone.   8

How did self-imposed exile affect me? I never imagined how disquieting a long stretch of solitude could be. With no one near, I felt exposed. Each time I assumed a reflective pose, taking a moment to sit upon a fallen log or to recline in the warm sun on a grassy knoll, I was overwhelmed by a sense of foreboding. Some stalking predator lurked not in the lingering shade of the forest, but in my conscience. Only by strenuous activity, by setting a brisk pace, by going about my chores, especially hauling water, and by preparing my frugal meals was I able to rid myself of this feeling of foreboding.   9

Then one morning, washing in a clear pool in the spring and catching the bleary reflection of myself—thin, disheveled, and haunted—I recognized this foreboding. It was the demanding, skeptical conscience I had hoped to leave behind when I came to the woods. But here it was, ready to assume control again, ready to condemn with uncompromising ideals, unsympathetic evaluations, and biting sarcasm. In full view of this shadowy phantom, I tried to lose myself in exhausting excursions, frivolous projects around the campsite, and in the evenings, the works of Shakespeare that I read in the dim light of my kerosene lamp. Yet even in the words of Shakespeare, I encountered this counterpart of my soul, the words of the cynical Jacques in *As You Like It*:   10

> A fool, a fool! I met a fool i' the forest,   11
> A motely fool; a miserable world.   12

and I recognized the doubts of Hamlet:

> Yea, and perhaps   13
> Out of weakness and my melancholy   14
> As he is very potent with such spirits,   15
> Abuses me to damn me!   16

A psychological dualism plagued me—not that I disliked myself, but myself disliked me. Then suicidal moths swept in from the dark, fluttered thickly onto my kerosene lamp, and snuffed it to darkness.

By morning, I knew activity was not enough to allay my moods. I desired companionship. I began to count each day, hoping for my   17 brother's return. I speculated on his appearance. The slightest shiver of the leaves, the muttering of the stream in its bed of stone, even the sound of my pulse would become the sound of his truck approaching. When he failed to show, I would be crushed.

This brother-expectant condition plagued me, yet began to disappear. The transition took place slowly as I settled into a rigid routine. I rose at first light and washed in the stream, took a short walk, and then returned to the campsite to prepare breakfast. One day I ate hot cereal; the next, I ate buttered bread with honey; the menu never varied. I drank two cups of coffee, no more, no less, and then sat in the shade of a gnarled blackjack oak to write in my notebooks. Near noon, I would amble to the cool shade of a hollow and read until the sun began its slow journey down the western sky and the temperature had cooled. Then I would take a long walk. I always prepared dinner as the first twilight began to slip furtively up the ridges, then I would read awhile, and go to bed. Such a rigid routine for me was truly remarkable. Most amazing was the fact that the routine had become firmly established without my awareness.   18

Slowly my acute self-consciousness disappeared. I became a diligent observer of the world around me. I would sit and watch scuttling crayfish feeding in a limpid pool, or enjoy an agile nuthatch probe the underside of a wild cherry branch, and then break my intense observation to discover that an afternoon was gone, and I had not noticed its passing.   19

Once painfully aware of the passage of time, I now became part of it. I lost track of time, of days, of weeks. Time no longer mattered. Having the process of nature to regulate my activities, time became cyclical, not linear. The sun rose and set; the same shadows crawled across the forest floor; rain and sun, day and night, appeared alternately. Yet each day possessed its distinct individuality, for there were subtle but magnificent phenomena to observe: the pink-throated finch lounged and sunned on my makeshift table, a wren built her nest and hatched her young in the cane of my shelter's roof, a family of gray squirrels chatted with me daily.   20

The oppressive, foreboding sense of self that I once suffered became lost in the world around me. However, rather than feeling that I had lost a part of myself, I felt that I had acquired a world.   21

The long days slowly marked the heat of summer. A drought parched the land so that my bare feet stirred up clouds of dust on walks to the stream, which soon dried up. The smooth stones in its bed bleached to thousands of upturned Buddha-bellies. I walked farther for water now, filling containers at a wrist-sized stream that broke from a rocky seam. The trip, at least half a mile, was arduous.   22

As summer deepened, the biting insects increased in number and   23
ferocity; persistent ticks and mosquitoes leeched my blood; small del-
vers dug into my skin. Like the withered foliage around me, I longed
for a shower, an hour of moisture to wash the dust from cracked skin
and give relief to irritated sores. Every evening about an hour before
dark, thunderheads gathered on the horizon. Then moist gusts of wind
shook the brittle green leaves, and thunder grumbled at flashes of
lightning. Several times I frantically prepared for a storm, lashing belongings beneath sheets of plastic, only to have the storm dissipate
quickly. Eliot's lines from "The Waste Land" became poignant. One
evening after smoothing my dry, bitten skin with ointment, I scanned
one of my books for Eliot's lines.

> Here one can neither stand nor lie nor sit   24
> There is not even silence in the mountains   25
> But dry sterile thunder without rain.   26

Then a deluge lasted for days, wind tore away my roof, and the ground
became so saturated that I stood in ankle-deep water. It soaked bed-
ding, books and paper, and even the wicks of my lanterns. For several
evenings I sat in the dark under my poncho, eating beans from a can.

Yet, despite the drought and deluge, despite the incursions of biting   27
insects, and despite the torrid days and damp nights, I was not disheart-
ened. Instead, I became intrigued with the powerful and often whimsical phenomena of nature, which made me feel small and bewildered.
Yet its power coursed through my blood. In my insignificance in the
face of that indifferent power, I discovered a majestic vision of the
world.

During August, I watched colors fade under blinding light and press-   28
ing heat. Then I felt the chilly nights of early September. Autumn would
soon arrive, and I did not have the shelter and supplies to support
myself during cool weather. Yet I felt good here; I felt a sense of happiness, one I had scoffed about as a surly student.

I realized, however, that if I stayed much longer in the woods, I   29
might never leave. I would grow old and eccentric in the shelter of the
forest. Although I did not find that idea repulsive, I felt restricted. I
longed for a greater range of possibilities for my life, which only society
and culture could provide.

Yet I feared leaving my home in the woods; I feared a renewed   30
affliction of the malady that had driven me to the woods in the first
place. I had escaped the labyrinth of self and had discovered the world
of nature, which helped me discover a new and very real self. I did not
wish to lose it.

Finally, I left the woods before hard winter set in. I have not re-   31 turned. The world is now variously new and exciting, but old and tiring at times. It is new territory, but not without the old pitfalls. The modern world too often takes from us that part which is the most important, the human part. Instead of providing tasks that fulfill us, it gives monotonous labor; instead of opportunity for dialogue, it gives us silence or one-sided monologue; instead of human relations, it gives us isolation, which differs from solitude. Solitude, I discovered, is time for reflection, purification, and redemption. Unlike isolation, it mirrors the discovery of one's reflective self.

RANDALL WILLIAMS TALKS ABOUT HIS AIMS AND STRATEGIES

I faced a few problems in writing this personal essay. I had plenty of source material in my private notebooks, but I had to make a commitment to open my journal and my life to others. If you have read the essay, you know that I'm a private person. Nevertheless, I wanted to write the piece; perhaps I even needed to write it. On a practical level, I knew I could get five pages of material out of my journal.

Next I had to formulate and articulate in words a thesis about the experience. Subconsciously, I felt good about myself and my stay in the woods, but what universal interest would that hold for others? Few people today escape into the woods for an entire summer. Yet most people get frustrated with the hurly-burly world spinning around them. At some point during my review of the notebooks, the thesis came to me—something about the value of solitude and an inner peace of mind, as opposed to feelings of loneliness. With that idea, everything began to fall into place. I could open with my frustrations at work and then at college. The stay in the woods would be the central substance of the piece. Then my decision to leave the woods would establish the theme on solitude.

My decision to use the pattern of narration was dictated by the subject, as was the retrospective mood. My writing problems were twofold. The first: What to use from the notebook? It was loaded with tidbits on my daily habits and observations as well as notes on my readings. For example, I dismissed entries like these:

> *June 11*. Feel cramps in my stomach. Hope it's not the dreaded Alabama quick-step; had the shits first week here and don't want them again.
> *June 12*. Lay reading most of yesterday. Dipped into Shakespeare again. What a master of the language he was! He constantly turns a phrase or twists a word. Wonder if anybody has studied the verbal irony of Hamlet? The guy speaks with double entendres all the time.

June 13. Rain today, but not heavy, not bad. I even walked along the ridge and watched the stream fill the hollow and rush madly north—toward Tennessee? the Tennessee River?

These entries were no help to me, and there were many like them. Others I liked and wanted to use but found no place for, such as this one:

July 2. Walked down the log road and along the dirt road for about four miles today. I even reached a few leaning clapboard houses slapped haphazardly into eroding hillsides where they stand precariously propped on rock pilings, their spindly TV antennae and crooked stovepipes extending above their tin roofs. Often, rusting automobiles sit disassembled in front yards, their dented bodies resting on concrete blocks, and, occasionally, muddy logging trucks stand parked in the shade of huge elms or maples. The few farms I saw were small. Usually a few gaunt cows, their dull hides stretched over protruding ribs, stood in weedy lots near sagging, gray barns.

I rather liked that descriptive passage, but it would not fit into the narration.

Eventually, I roughed out the essay. Then I faced my second problem—it was too long! It seemed to drag on and on, yet each paragraph made its point. Then it dawned on me—I was too verbose, too wordy. Perhaps my experience differs from other writers, who must add descriptive detail, but my notebooks had served me well. They contain, in truth, more than one essay; yet their wordiness is distracting and requires heavy editing. Sometimes I feel more like an editor than a writer, so maybe I'm learning what it means to write not just for myself but for others as well. While writing for myself, I could let emotions and ideas flow forth in almost any form. While writing an essay, I discovered how tough it is to edit my words and sentences. I like the finished paper, but I love the spontaneity of my notebook entries.

Comment. Williams wrote his journal first and then, when faced with a writing assignment, searched his entries for an idea, a central aim, and a thesis sentence. He found his basic idea in the phrase: "the value of solitude and an inner peace of mind." He then pulled from his journal the items that would develop his primary perception.

Assignment 1. To write in the manner of Williams, you will need journal entries that highlight a special time in your life. If you have such a journal, you can set to work. If not, collect journal entries for several weeks or make notes about a special time in your life. Whatever method you use, survey your entries for a common thread, a central concern, and a thesis sentence.

Comment. William's autobiographical writing features progressive narrative actions, yet he pauses periodically to describe a scene or his mood at the moment.

Assignment 2. As you prepare a rough draft about a special time in your life, stop the narrative action periodically to meditate on your feelings or to describe the setting. The action is insignificant unless the reader understands fully the situation in terms of place, time, and mood of the writer.

Comment. The personal voice of Williams appears natural and comfortable. He condemns himself at times but also recognizes his own best qualities. He has a speculative mind, loves literature, and describes with precision.

Assignment 3. Express yourself honestly in your draft about a personal experience. Speak in first-person "I," relate both good and unpleasant experiences, and show the reader each scene with carefully drawn description.

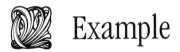 # Example

Essays built by examples have several common characteristics: First, examples illustrate the thesis so that it comes to life with specific images, events, and narrative episodes. Second, a good example has concreteness; it *shows* the reader. This helps the writer avoid abstractness and create vivid, concrete images. Third, good examples narrow the thesis to specifics and essentials. Consider Thomas Jefferson's charges against the King of Great Britain in his "Declaration of Independence."

> He has combined with others [the British Parliament] to subject us to a jurisdiction foreign to our constitution, and unacknowledged by our laws; giving his Assent to their Acts of pretended Legislation:
> For Quartering large bodies of armed troops among us:
> For protecting them, by a mock Trial, from punishment for any Murders which they should commit on the Inhabitants of these States:
> For cutting off our Trade with all parts of the world:
> For imposing Taxes on us without our Consent:
> For depriving us in many cases, of the benefits of Trial by Jury.

Jefferson continues with examples that build a strong case to support his stand. (The Declaration in its entirety occurs later in this chapter.) Removing Jefferson's examples leaves only generalizations and vague charges against the king.

FIT THE EXAMPLES TO YOUR PURPOSE

As shown in the preceding excerpt, examples supply strong evidence for Jefferson's argument. Like description (see Chapter 1), examples must be focused and appropriate to the whole. Writers need to consider the abstraction ladder as they scan the spectrum of possibilities. For instance,

The specific example "Papa Brewster" might meet the demands of readers far better than the abstract word "relative."

USE A VARIETY OF EXAMPLE FORMS

In some cases a *miscellany* of image fragments can create one dominant impression (see especially Updike's essay later in this chapter). *Descriptive examples* help you set the scene and create images for the reader. *Narrative examples* provide brief episodes that highlight your general thesis. *Character portraits* enliven the essay with human drama.

KEEP EXAMPLES ORDERED AND UNDER CONTROL

Splashing examples haphazardly throughout your essay may add concreteness but will not necessarily contribute to your point. Use a *random set* of examples, as in the Jefferson essay, to build an overall impression. Use an *incremental pattern* of examples to build from least to most, nonessential to essential, or minor to major. Use a *negative/positive* sequence of examples to show what your subject is not and what it really is. Use a *chronological order* to provide examples from the past through the present. Use one long *illustration*, which is an expanded example, rather than a cluster of small items.

MAKE CLEAR TO THE READER THAT YOU ARE GIVING EXAMPLES

Use appropriate signaling devices when you introduce examples, such as "for example," "for instance," "to illustrate," "thus," "hence," and "a case in point." Do not overuse these phrases, at risk of irritating the reader and breaking up the flow of your ideas.

INDICATE THE PURPOSE FOR A LONG LIST OF EXAMPLES

Too many examples in a row can turn your essay into an absurd laundry list of miscellaneous tidbits unless your examples interrelate and sup-

Example **115**

port a central thesis. The piece by John Updike (pages 139–141) demonstrates this point; it features images that *are* the whole. The document by Jefferson (pages 133–136) uses examples as fundamental evidence to prove a point.

To review: Use examples as a pattern of development to

1. Illustrate the central idea of the essay
2. Provide concrete detail
3. Narrow the focus of your study
4. Build incremental patterns of importance, show a negative/positive sequence, or establish a chronological order of specific events

Lorraine Hansberry was a gifted writer who died of cancer at age thirty-four. Her husband, Robert Nemiroff, gathered selections of her writings from her journals and compiled them into a book. Six journal entries from that book are reproduced here.

Writers of autobiography find examples invaluable. Hansberry, for example, dips into her past and plucks out meaningful events and experiences. The fragments of her life become a record and backdrop for the present. Hansberry's journal is typical of expressive writing, covering the spectrum of the writer's imagination. She uncovers her personality as she gives examples of the places she lived, the games she played, and the way she responded to family and friends. These personal memories of places, events, and people are the tidbits of self-discovery that motivate the writer and bring satisfaction to the reader.

As you finish reading the first journal entry, write a one-sentence précis to summarize its central idea. For the five subsequent entries, explain how one example expands on Hansberry's central idea as expressed in your précis.

Hansberry (1930–65) achieved her greatest literary success with the drama "A Raisin in the Sun" (1959). Her passages about childhood days in Chicago are from To Be Young, Gifted, and Black: Lorraine Hansberry in Her Own Words *(1969).*

LORRAINE HANSBERRY

 To Be Young, Gifted, and Black

1

For some time now—I think since I was a child—I have been pos- 1
sessed of the desire to put down the stuff of my life. That is a common-
place impulse, apparently, among persons of massive self-interest;
sooner or later we all do it. And, I am quite certain, there is only one
internal quarrel: how much of the truth to tell? How much, how much,
how much! It *is* brutal, in sober uncompromising moments, to reflect
on the comedy of concern we all enact when it comes to our precious
images!

Even so, when such vanity as propels the writing of such memoirs 2
is examined, certainly one would wish at least to have some boast of
social serviceability on one's side. I shall set down in these pages what
shall seem to me to be the truth of my life and essences . . . which are

to be found, first of all, on the Southside of Chicago, where I was born. . . .

2

All travelers to my city should ride the elevated trains that race along   3
the back ways of Chicago. The lives you can look into!

I think you could find the tempo of my people on their back   4
porches. The honesty of their living is there in the shabbiness.
Scrubbed porches that sag and look their danger. Dirty gray wood
steps. And always a line of white and pink clothes scrubbed so well,
waving in the dirty wind of the city.

My people are poor. And they are tired. And they are determined   5
to live.

Our Southside is a place apart: each piece of our living is a protest.   6

3

I was born May 19, 1930, the last of four children.   7

Of love and my parents there is little to be written: their relationship   8
to their children was utilitarian. We were fed and housed and dressed
and outfitted with more cash than our associates and that was all. We
were also vaguely taught certain vague absolutes: that we were better
than no one but infinitely superior to everyone; that we were the products of the proudest and most mistreated of the races of man; that there
was nothing enormously difficult about life; that one *succeeded* as a
matter of course.

Life was not a struggle—it was something that one *did*. One won an   9
argument because, if facts gave out, one invented them—with color!
The only sinful people in the world were dull people. And, above all,
there were two things which were never to be betrayed: the family and
the race. But of love, there was nothing ever said.

If we were sick, we were sternly, impersonally and carefully nursed   10
and doctored back to health. Fevers, toothaches were attended to with
urgency and importance; one always felt *important* in my family.
Mother came with a tray to your room with the soup and Vick's salve or
gave the enemas in a steaming bathroom. But we were not fondled, any
of us—head held to breast, fingers about that head—until we were
grown, all of us, and my father died.

At his funeral I at last, in my memory, saw my mother hold her sons   11
that way, and for the first time in her life my sister held me in her arms

I think. We were not a loving people: we were passionate in our hostilities and affinities, but the caress embarrassed us.

We have changed little. . . .   12

4

Seven years separated the nearest of my brothers and sisters and myself;   13
I wear, I am sure, the earmarks of that familial station to this day. Little has been written or thought to my knowledge about children who occupy that place: the last born separated by an uncommon length of time from the next youngest. I suspect we are probably a race apart.

The last born is an object toy which comes in years when brothers   14
and sisters who are seven, ten, twelve years older are old enough to appreciate it rather than poke out its eyes. They do not mind diapering you the first two years, but by the time you are five you are a pest that has to be attended to in the washroom, taken to the movies and "sat with" at night. You are not a person—you are a nuisance who is not particular fun any more. Consequently, you swiftly learn to play alone. . . .

5

My childhood Southside summers were the ordinary city kind, full of   15
the street games which other rememberers have turned into fine ballets these days, and rhymes that anticipated what some people insist on calling modern poetry:

> Oh, Mary Mack, Mack, Mack   16
> With the silver buttons, buttons, buttons   17
> All down her back, back, back.   18
> She asked her mother, mother, mother   19
> For fifteen cents, cents, cents   20
> To see the elephant, elephant, elephant   21
> Jump the fence, fence, fence.   22
> Well, he jumped so high, high, high   23
> 'Til he touched the sky, sky, sky   24
> And he didn't come back, back, back   25
> 'Til the Fourth of Ju—ly, ly, ly!   26

I remember skinny little Southside bodies by the fives and tens of   27
us panting the delicious hours away:

"May I?"   28

And the voice of authority: "Yes, you may—you may take one giant step."   29

One drew in all one's breath and tightened one's fist and pulled the 30 small body against the heavens, stretching, straining all the muscles in the legs to make—one giant step.

It is a long time. One forgets the reason for the game. (For children's 31 games are always explicit in their reasons for being. To play is to win something. Or not to be "it." Or to be high pointer, or outdoer, or sometimes—just *the winner*. But after a time one forgets.)

Why was it important to take a small step, a teeny step, or the most 32 desired of all—one GIANT step?

A giant step *to where?* 33

6

Evenings were spent mainly on the back porches where screen doors 34 slammed in the darkness with those really very special summertime sounds. And, sometimes, when Chicago nights got too steamy, the whole family got into the car and went to the park and slept out in the open on blankets. Those were, of course, the best times of all because the grownups were invariably reminded of having been children in the South and told the best stories then. And it was also cool and sweet to be on the grass and there was usually the scent of freshly cut lemons or melons in the air. Daddy would lie on his back, as fathers must, and explain about how men thought the stars above us came to be and how far away they were.

I never did learn to believe that anything could be as far away as 35 *that*. Especially the stars. . . .

AIMS AND STRATEGIES OF THE WRITER

Comment. Lorraine Hansberry kept journals and notebooks to record her impressions and ideas about her own life and times. Her writing explores her private world and builds a body of autobiographical details. In such writing the writer strips away pretense and says, "Here I am as I really am, without sham, false face, or act."

Assignment 1. For the next several days, keep a journal that chronicles some of your favorite memories. Select and record descriptive scenes, narrate brief episodes, draw a character sketch, and in general provide examples of your childhood. These examples will inevitably uncover something about you and your personality.

Comment. By defining fleeting thoughts and brief experiences of the past, Hansberry brings focus and clarity to her thinking. Interpreting one complicated period in her life probably helped her interpret other periods. Thus she comes to certain conclusions: "Life was not a struggle—it was something that one *did*" and "there were two things which were never to be betrayed: the family and the race."

Assignment 2. After several days of journal writing, read through your entries for universal truths of human conduct. Your ability to remember and record certain events of the past means that they hold special meaning for you. What is that meaning? Examine your journal entries for a central thought, something that ties them together in the manner of Hansberry's opening paragraph. Your reading notes, as suggested in the introduction to this essay, can help give you a sense of direction for this assignment: thesis opening followed by a series of examples.

Comment. A reminiscence enhances with special meaning one episode, place, or person in your life. In her Part 5, for example, Hansberry looks back nostalgically to capture a childhood memory and thereby to preserve it forever.

Assignment 3. Include in your journal entries at least one reminiscence. Recall one episode with a special person (see Momaday, pages 72–77). Recall a special place (see Dillard, pages 22–25). Recall a time when your life turned into chaos and disorder, yet you learned something from it (see Hughes, pages 67–69).

THE WRITING PROCESS

Comment. A cluster of examples should illustrate the character of the main subject; in this excerpt, the examples reveal the nature of the writer. Your notes in the margins should explain how each of Hansberry's entries supports her central idea.

Assignment 4. Record the main idea developed by each of Hansberry's six sections. For example, in Part 1 she suggests her desire that some "social serviceability" grow from "the truth of my life and essences." Next, consider the types of examples she uses; look especially for descriptive examples, narrative episodes, and character portraits. How do all entries as a whole convey one general theme? Write a one-sentence précis to summarize the work's central idea.

Comment. A writer's examples should *show* the reader with specific images, not abstractions and generalizations. For example, in Part 4 Hansberry uses the concrete image of herself as a new baby. During her babyhood she served as an object toy for her siblings, but then she became a pest to them.

Assignment 5. Examine your autobiographical journal entries for how well you've provided clear images. If episodes seem vague and general, review Chapter 1 for techniques on writing description or read the introduction of Chapter 2 for use of narration.

Comment. Examples should always have a purpose. Hansberry uses her descriptive reminiscences to claim both her Chicago heritage and her roots as a black.

Assignment 6. After you have developed at least seven entries in your autobiographical journal, write a thesis sentence summarizing the whole.

Comment. A finished manuscript drawn from autobiographical notes can be presented as a random set of numbered pieces, as Hansberry has done, or as a unified whole, as shown by Dillard (pages 22–25), Momaday (pages 72–77), and Williams (pages 104–109).

Assignment 7. Transform your random journal notes into a finished autobiographical essay. Select journal entries that will serve your purpose. Establish a thesis for the materials and present them as a unified whole.

Harold Krents combines two aims of discourse in his essay on blindness—the expressive and the persuasive. Drawing upon his experiences, he provides several examples that enforce his argument for tolerance and understanding of the blind. In particular, he explores with a sense of humor the recurring reactions to his blindness: many assume that since he cannot see, he also cannot hear or talk.

Krents fits the examples to his purpose in an attempt to destroy misconceptions about the handicapped: "The toughest misconception of all is the view that because I can't see, I can't work."

He experienced that problem firsthand. After earning both undergraduate and law degrees at Harvard, he did not easily find a position in a law firm. His struggle for acceptance inspired a broadway play, Butterflies Are Free. *Krents adds, "I am prototype for the main character of Leonard Gershe's play* Butterflies Are Free. *I gave the story its inspiration—the play's plot is not my story; its spirit is" (*Contemporary Artists, *Vol. 37–40R).*

As you read the essay, make marginal notes to Krents's use of example. Does each example advance his thesis? Does each example provide vivid detail? Does Krents use a variety of examples?

Krents wrote this essay in 1976 for the New York Times. *He has also written a book,* To Race the Wind, *which was published in 1972 by Putnam.*

HAROLD KRENTS

🔳 Darkness at Noon

Blind from birth, I have never had the opportunity to see myself and 1
have been completely dependent on the image I create in the eye of the observer. To date it has not been narcissistic.

There are those who assume that since I can't see, I obviously also 2
cannot hear. Very often people will converse with me at the top of their lungs, enunciating each word very carefully. Conversely, people will also often whisper, assuming that since my eyes don't work, my ears don't either.

For example, when I go to the airport and ask the ticket agent for 3
assistance to the plane, he or she will invariably pick up the phone, call a ground hostess and whisper: "Hi, Jane, we've got a 76 here." I have concluded that the word "blind" is not used for one of two reasons: Either they fear that if the dread word is spoken, the ticket agent's retina

will immediately detach, or they are reluctant to inform me of my condition of which I may not have been previously aware.

On the other hand, others know that of course I can hear, but believe   4
that I can't talk. Often, therefore, when my wife and I go out to dinner, a waiter or waitress will ask Kit if "*he* would like a drink" to which I respond that "indeed *he* would."

This point was graphically driven home to me while we were in   5
England. I had been given a year's leave of absence from my Washington law firm to study for a diploma in law degree at Oxford University. During the year I became ill and was hospitalized. Immediately after admission, I was wheeled down to the X-ray room. Just at the door sat an elderly woman—elderly I would judge from the sound of her voice. "What is his name?" the woman asked the orderly who had been wheeling me.

"What's your name?" the orderly repeated to me.   6

"Harold Krents," I replied.   7

"Harold Krents," he repeated.   8

"When was he born?"   9

"When were you born?"   10

"Nov. 5, 1944," I responded.   11

"Nov. 5, 1944," the orderly intoned.   12

This procedure continued for approximately five minutes at which   13
point even my saint-like disposition deserted me. "Look," I finally blurted out, "this is absolutely ridiculous. Okay, granted I can't see, but it's got to have become pretty clear to both of you that I don't need an interpreter."

"He says he doesn't need an interpreter," the orderly reported to   14
the woman.

The toughest misconception of all is the view that because I can't   15
see, I can't work. I was turned down by over forty law firms because of my blindness, even though my qualifications included a cum laude degree from Harvard College and a good ranking in my Harvard Law School class.

The attempt to find employment, the continuous frustration of being   16
told that it was impossible for a blind person to practice law, the rejection letters, not based on my lack of ability but rather on my disability, will always remain one of the most disillusioning experiences of my life.

Fortunately, this view of limitation and exclusion is beginning to   17
change. On April 16, the Department of Labor issued regulations that mandate equal-employment opportunities for the handicapped. By and large, the business community's response to offering employment to the disabled has been enthusiastic.

I therefore look forward to the day, with the expectation that it is   18
certain to come, when employers will view their handicapped workers
as a little child did me years ago when my family still lived in Scarsdale.

I was playing basketball with my father in our backyard according   19
to procedures we had developed. My father would stand beneath the
hoop, shout, and I would shoot over his head at the basket attached to
our garage. Our next-door neighbor, aged five, wandered over into our
yard with a playmate. "He's blind," our neighbor whispered to her
friend in a voice that could be heard distinctly by Dad and me. Dad
shot and missed. I did the same. Dad hit the rim. I missed entirely. Dad
shot and missed the garage entirely. "Which one is blind?" whispered
back the little friend.

I would hope that in the near future when a plant manager is touring   20
the factory with the foreman and comes upon a handicapped and non-
handicapped person working together, his comment after watching
them work will be, "Which one is disabled?"

AIMS AND STRATEGIES OF THE WRITER

Comment. In an interview with *Life* magazine Krents described his
feelings when at age nine he learned that he would be totally blind: "I
bawled my head off. But I remember lying in bed that night and growing up. I knew I had to grow up or fold up—to be dependent or
independent" (*Life* 6 Feb. [1970]: 57).

Assignment 1. Write a brief note explaining how Krents expands this
idea in "Darkness at Noon."

Comment. Essays that grow out of personal experience often express
reflective and meditative themes. However, Krents goes one step further
to argue an issue. His memories trigger the push for a change in the
attitudes of others.

Assignment 2. Begin the rough draft of an essay in the pattern of
"Darkness at Noon." Narrate examples of personal experience and use
them to argue a point. For example, explain the plight of America's
young work force that, like you, faced numerous rejections to job applications because "you have no experience!"

Comment. In paragraphs 2, 18, and 20, Krents expresses his fundamental aim—that prejudice against the handicapped will cease.

Assignment 3. You may or may not express the thesis of your essay so
directly, yet you should write it out clearly in your notes. During the

drafting stage make the decision to include it or not. Your examples and general discourse may imply your persuasive appeal.

THE WRITING PROCESS

Comment. Examples drawn from experience can be serious or humorous. Although he explores a serious subject, Krents employs examples that make the reader chuckle and even laugh aloud, reminding us that his spirit is upbeat and positive, not negative.

Assignment 4. In developing your essay that uses examples to persuade, build a unified set of examples that are either humorous, like Krents's, or serious.

Comment. Krents concretely shows his readers the problem through examples, rather than talking abstractly. Each episode displays images of the public's reaction to him and, in turn, to all handicapped people.

Assignment 5. Examine your rough draft to determine how well you have balanced examples with abstract discourse. In "Darkness at Noon," count the number of paragraphs that discuss the issues and the number that illustrate.

Comment. Krents orders his examples to reinforce his general idea. People assume that handicapped persons are totally incompetent: a blind person cannot hear, cannot talk, cannot work.

Assignment 6. Order for a purpose the examples of your rough draft. If possible, use an incremental pattern that builds from the least important to the most important example.

Comment. Krents has cataloged the episodes of his life, either in his notebooks or in his head. He draws from that rich repertory as necessary.

Assignment 7. To develop an essay in the tradition of Krents, record over a period of several days the images and anecdotes that fit your thesis. After you have a clear mission and a sufficient body of examples, draft the essay.

Lewis Thomas uses examples to explain a difficult concept. He advances the idea that there is somewhere a continual cosmic music, a sort of universal symphony that motivates the many sounds and signals heard on earth. He suggests that one characteristic of biology is "the urge to make a kind of music."

To defend his speculations, he uses examples from the animal kingdom, citing the musical sounds of termites, birds, toads, whales, beetles, and many more. He even includes the lowly earthworm, which makes faint staccato sounds. The numerous examples from nature supply evidence for his theories about the cosmic role of music. As you read, make marginal notes that pinpoint the different examples, for each one furthers his analysis of a world rhythm that suggests harmonic order in the universe as a whole.

Lewis Thomas is a physician, professor, and award-winning essayist. He taught medicine at the University of Minnesota, served as dean of the Yale Medical School, and now serves as chancellor of the Memorial Sloan-Kettering Cancer Center. In 1970 he began contributing to the New England Journal of Medicine *essays that examined scientific topics but couched in the language of the humanities. "The Music of* This Sphere*" is from* The Lives of a Cell *(1974), a collection of essays which won a National Book Award. Thomas also published* Medusa and the Snail *(1979) and* The Youngest Science: Notes of a Medicine Watcher *(1983).*

LEWIS THOMAS

The Music of *This* Sphere

It is one of our problems that as we become crowded together, the sounds we make to each other, in our increasingly complex communication systems, become more random-sounding, accidental or incidental, and we have trouble selecting meaningful signals out of the noise. One reason is, of course, that we do not seem able to restrict our communication to information-bearing, relevant signals. Given any new technology for transmitting information, we seem bound to use it for great quantities of small talk. We are only saved by music from being overwhelmed by nonsense.

It is a marginal comfort to know that the relatively new science of bioacoustics must deal with similar problems in the sounds made by other animals to each other. No matter what sound-making device is placed at their disposal, creatures in general do a great deal of gabbling,

126

and it requires long patience and observation to edit out the parts lacking syntax and sense. Light social conversation, designed to keep the party going, prevails. Nature abhors a long silence.

Somewhere, underlying all the other signals, is a continual music. 3 Termites make percussive sounds to each other by beating their heads against the floor in the dark, resonating corridors of their nests. The sound has been described as resembling, to the human ear, sand falling on paper, but spectrographic analysis of sound records has recently revealed a high degree of organization in the drumming; the beats occur in regular, rhythmic phrases, differing in duration, like notes for a tympani section.

From time to time, certain termites make a convulsive movement of 4 their mandibles to produce a loud, high-pitched clicking sound, audible ten meters off. So much effort goes into this one note that it must have urgent meaning, at least to the sender. He cannot make it without such a wrench that he is flung one or two centimeters into the air by the recoil.

There is obvious hazard in trying to assign a particular meaning to 5 this special kind of sound, and problems like this exist throughout the field of bioacoustics. One can imagine a woolly-minded Visitor from Outer Space, interested in human beings, discerning on his spectrograph the click of that golf ball on the surface of the moon, and trying to account for it as a call of warning (unlikely), a signal of mating (out of the question), or an announcement of territory (could be).

Bats are obliged to make sounds almost ceaselessly, to sense, by 6 sonar, all the objects in their surroundings. They can spot with accuracy, on the wing, small insects, and they will home onto things they like with infallibility and speed. With such a system for the equivalent of glancing around, they must live in a world of ultrasonic bat-sound, most of it with an industrial, machinery sound. Still, they communicate with each other as well, by clicks and high-pitched greetings. Moreover, they have been heard to produce, while hanging at rest upside down in the depths of woods, strange, solitary, and lovely bell-like notes.

Almost anything that an animal can employ to make a sound is put 7 to use. Drumming, created by beating the feet, is used by prairie hens, rabbits, and mice; the head is banged by woodpeckers and certain other birds; the males of deathwatch beetles make a rapid ticking sound by percussion of a protuberance on the abdomen against the ground; a faint but audible ticking is made by the tiny beetle *Lepinotus inquilinus*, which is less than two millimeters in length. Fish make sounds by clicking their teeth, blowing air, and drumming with special muscles against tuned inflated air bladders. Solid structures are set to vibrating by toothed bows in crustaceans and insects. The proboscis of the death's-head hawk moth is used as a kind of reed instrument, blown through to make high-pitched, reedy notes.

Gorillas beat their chests for certain kinds of discourse. Animals 8
with loose skeletons rattle them, or, like rattlesnakes, get sounds from externally placed structures. Turtles, alligators, crocodiles, and even snakes make various more or less vocal sounds. Leeches have been heard to tap rhythmically on leaves, engaging the attention of other leeches, which tap back, in synchrony. Even earthworms make sounds, faint staccato notes in regular clusters. Toads sing to each other, and their friends sing back in antiphony.

Birdsong has been so much analyzed for its content of business 9
communication that there seems little time left for music, but it is there. Behind the glossaries of warning calls, alarms, mating messages, pronouncements of territory, calls for recruitment, and demands for dispersal, there is redundant, elegant sound that is unaccountable as part of the working day. The thrush in my backyard sings down his nose in meditative, liquid runs of melody, over and over again, and I have the strongest impression that he does this for his own pleasure. Some of the time he seems to be practicing, like a virtuoso in his apartment. He starts a run, reaches a midpoint in the second bar where there should be a set of complex harmonics, stops, and goes back to begin over, dissatisfied. Sometimes he changes his notation so conspicuously that he seems to be improvising sets of variations. It is a meditative, questioning kind of music, and I cannot believe that he is simply saying, "thrush here."

The robin sings flexible songs, containing a variety of motifs that he 10
rearranges to his liking; the notes in each motif constitute the syntax, and the possibilities of variation produce a considerable repertoire. The meadow lark, with three hundred notes to work with, arranges these in phrases of three to six notes and elaborates fifty types of song. The nightingale has twenty-four basic songs, but gains wild variety by varying the internal arrangement of phrases and the length of pauses. The chaffinch listens to other chaffinches, and incorporates into his memory snatches of their songs.

The need to make music, and to listen to it, is universally expressed 11
by human beings. I cannot imagine, even in our most primitive times, the emergence of talented painters to make cave paintings without there having been, near at hand, equally creative people making song. It is, like speech, a dominant aspect of human biology.

The individual parts played by other instrumentalists—crickets or 12
earthworms, for instance—may not have the sound of music by themselves, but we hear them out of context. If we could listen to them all at

once, fully orchestrated, in their immense ensemble, we might become aware of the counterpoint, the balance of tones and timbres and harmonics, the sonorities. The recorded songs of the humpback whale, filled with tensions and resolutions, ambiguities and allusions, incomplete, can be listened to as a *part* of music, like an isolated section of an orchestra. If we had better hearing, and could discern the descants of sea birds, the rhythmic tympani of schools of mollusks, or even the distant harmonics of midges hanging over meadows in the sun, the combined sound might lift us off our feet.

There are, of course, other ways to account for the songs of whales. They might be simple, down-to-earth statements about navigation, or sources of krill, or limits of territory. But the proof is not in, and until it is shown that these long, convoluted, insistent melodies, repeated by different singers with ornamentations of their own, are the means of sending through several hundred miles of undersea such ordinary information as "whale here," I shall believe otherwise. Now and again, in the intervals between songs, the whales have been seen to breach, leaping clear out of the sea and landing on their backs, awash in the turbulence of their beating flippers. Perhaps they are pleased by the way the piece went, or perhaps it is celebration at hearing one's own song returning after circumnavigation; whatever, it has the look of jubilation.

I suppose that my extraterrestrial Visitor might puzzle over my records in much the same way, on first listening. The 14th Quartet might, for him, be a communication announcing, "Beethoven here," answered, after passage through an undersea of time and submerged currents of human thought, by another long signal a century later, "Bartok here."[1]

If, as I believe, the urge to make a kind of music is as much a characteristic of biology as our other fundamental functions, there ought to be an explanation for it. Having none at hand, I am free to make one up. The rhythmic sounds might be the recapitulation of something else—an earliest memory, a score for the transformation of inanimate, random matter in chaos into the improbable, ordered dance of living forms. Morowitz[2] has presented the case, in thermodynamic terms, for the hypothesis that a steady flow of energy from the inexhaustible source of the sun to the unfillable sink of outer space, by way of the earth, is mathematically destined to cause the organization of matter into an increasingly ordered state. The resulting balancing act

13

14

15

---

[1]Béla Bartók (1881–1945), Hungarian composer.

[2]Harold J. Morowitz (1927–   ), American biochemist, Yale University.

involves a ceaseless clustering of bonded atoms into molecules of higher and higher complexity, and the emergence of cycles for the storage and release of energy. In a nonequilibrium steady state, which is postulated, the solar energy would not just flow to the earth and radiate away; it is thermodynamically inevitable that it must rearrange matter into symmetry, away from probability, against entropy, lifting it, so to speak, into a constantly changing condition of rearrangement and molecular ornamentation. In such a system, the outcome is a chancy kind of order, always on the verge of descending into chaos, held taut against probability by the unremitting, constant surge of energy from the sun.

If there were to be sounds to represent this process, they would 16 have the arrangement of the Brandenburg Concertos[3] for my ear, but I am open to wonder whether the same events are recalled by the rhythms of insects, the long, pulsing runs of birdsong, the descants of whales, the modulated vibrations of a million locusts in migration, the tympani of gorilla breasts, termite heads, drumfish bladders. A "grand canonical ensemble" is, oddly enough, the proper term for a quantitative model system in thermodynamics, borrowed from music by way of mathematics. Borrowed back again, provided with notation, it would do for what I have in mind.

AIMS AND STRATEGIES OF THE WRITER

Comment. Thomas has a serious overall purpose in the development of all his essays: He wants to bridge the gap between the mysteries of science and the limited knowledge of the general reader. To accomplish this task, he depends on an informal language and everyday images and examples. "The Music of *This* Sphere" is exemplary, for its reading level is within the grasp of most readers. Thomas was a forerunner of the type of writer who writes for *Omni, Psychology Today, Scientific American*, and other publications. Such writers bring difficult theories into focus for all readers, not just for specialists.

Assignment 1. Go to your library and browse through a few of the contemporary magazines that present scientific ideas in manageable language. Find one article of interest and make notes about the writer's use of numerous examples to explain the difficult and obscure subject.

---

[3]Celebrated composition by Johann Sebastian Bach (1685–1750), great German composer.

Comment. Thomas wishes to explain the role of music in the cosmic order of things. (He does not refer to it as noise but as *music.*) His purpose requires the rhetorical pattern of example.

Assignment 2. Begin laying the groundwork for a complex topic that you will develop, in part, by the use of examples. Prewriting techniques, such as free writing, brainstorming, and listing ideas may help you develop such possible topics as DNA, existentialism, urban legends, junk mail, euthanasia, or steroids.

Comment. The roots of traditional essay writing lie more in an exploration of ideas than in the ratification of a thesis. Thomas belongs to the traditional school. His aim is exploration of a scientific phenomenon. In paragraph 14, for example, he admits to finding no explanation for the biological urge to make music, so he makes up his own reason.

Assignment 3. Some of your essays should reflect intellectual speculation and exploration of ideas. A tidy essay that advances a dull thesis will be less successful than one that grapples hesitantly with difficult ideas. Therefore, search out a topic that will stretch your imagination, such as the ethics of charity, environmental checks and balances, the impossibility of innocence, territorial imperatives on campus, and others that challenge you.

THE WRITING PROCESS

Comment. Thomas uses a basic order for his essay. First, he introduces a topic worthy of exploration; second, he provides numerous examples that illustrate his theory; and third, he speculates on his theory.

Assignment 4. Plan an essay that uses Thomas's approach. Introduce your subject, provide plenty of examples, and then conclude with speculations and considerations.

Comment. Thomas writes carefully and makes connections of examples and ideas at every stage of the essay.

Assignment 5. Fit your examples to your purpose by using each example to defend and exemplify your ideas. Expand your thinking in every instance to show the reader how your examples correspond to the subject and the central issue.

Comment. Because Thomas writes about music, his description of sounds requires a knowledge of musical terminology. In paragraph 3, for example, he uses "percussive sounds," "resonating corridors," "drumming," "beats," "rhythmic phrases," and "a tympani section."

Assignment 6. Like Thomas, you may need to consider the descriptive words of your subject. For example, suppose your topic is "environmental checks and balances." You might want to use effectively such words and phrases as "harmony," "counterpoise," "equilibrium," or "symmetry." Every paper you write should expand your vocabulary and your ability to use words effectively. In addition, readers expect your vocabulary to reflect the subject.

Examples serve the persuasive writer or speaker. In this essay Jefferson and his fellow contributors employ a list of examples to chronicle the injustices by the British against the colonies. Although presented in a random order, the examples slowly build into an overwhelming body of evidence that justifies Jefferson's appeal to reasonable people everywhere. He needs hard evidence to call into action a small body of revolutionaries.

For the persuasive writer, the response of the reader becomes a crucial ingredient. Therefore, Jefferson must do more than explain; he must urge the audience into intellectual activity and even physical action. Appeals to reason, ethics, and emotion in this essay invite audience participation. Yet no matter how impassioned Jefferson becomes, logic and reason must prevail if he hopes for the success of his point. He must advance and defend his fundamental proposition with sound reasons. In this case, his examples build undeniable inductive evidence about specific problems. Taking away the catalog of "facts" would weaken Jefferson's essay immeasurably.

In reading the essay, note especially its three-part structure: introduction of a fundamental proposition, list of examples, and concluding declaration.

Thomas Jefferson (1743–1826) served as third president of the United States. The "Declaration of Independence" remains Jefferson's best-known work. Congress began debating his draft on 28 June 1776 and adopted it with only minor changes on 4 July 1776.

THOMAS JEFFERSON

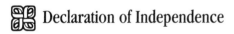 Declaration of Independence

In Congress, July 4, 1776

The Unanimous Declaration of the Thirteen
United States of America

When in the Course of human events, it becomes necessary for one 1
people to dissolve the political bands which have connected them with
another, and to assume among the powers of the earth, the separate
and equal station to which the Laws of Nature and of Nature's God
entitle them, a decent respect to the opinions of mankind requires that
they should declare the causes which impel them to the separation.

We hold these truths to be self-evident, that all men are created 2
equal, that they are endowed by their Creator with certain unalienable
Rights, that among these are Life, Liberty and the pursuit of Happiness.

That to secure these rights, Governments are instituted among Men, 3
deriving their just powers from the consent of the governed.

That whenever any Form of Government becomes destructive of 4
these ends, it is the Right of the People to alter or to abolish it, and to
institute new Government, laying its foundation on such principles and
organizing its powers in such form, as to them shall seem most likely
to effect their Safety and Happiness. Prudence, indeed, will dictate that
Governments long established should not be changed for light and
transient causes; and accordingly all experience hath shewn, that mankind are more disposed to suffer, while evils are sufferable, than to
right themselves by abolishing the forms to which they are accustomed.
But when a long train of abuses and usurpations, pursuing invariably
the same Object evinces a design to reduce them under absolute Des-
potism, it is their right, it is their duty, to throw off such Government,
and to provide new Guards for their future security.

Such has been the patient sufferance of these Colonies; and such is 5
now the necessity which constrains them to alter their former Systems
of Government. The history of the present King of Great Britain is a
history of repeated injuries and usurpations, all having in direct object
the establishment of an absolute Tyranny over these States. To prove
this, let Facts be submitted to a candid world.

He has refused his Assent to Laws, the most wholesome and neces- 6
sary for the public good.

He has forbidden his Governors to pass Laws of immediate and 7
pressing importance, unless suspended in their operation till his Assent
should be obtained; and when so suspended, he has utterly neglected
to attend to them.

He has refused to pass other Laws for the accommodation of large 8
districts of people, unless those people would relinquish the right of
Representation in the Legislature, a right inestimable to them and formidable to tyrants only.

He has called together legislative bodies at places unusual, uncom- 9
fortable, and distant from the depository of their public Records, for
the sole purpose of fatiguing them into compliance with his measures.

He has dissolved Representative Houses repeatedly, for opposing 10
with manly firmness his invasions on the rights of the people.

He has refused for a long time, after such dissolutions, to cause 11
others to be elected; whereby the Legislative powers, incapable of An-
nihilation, have returned to the People at large for their exercise; the

State remaining in the mean time exposed to all the dangers of invasion from without, and convulsions within.

He has endeavoured to prevent the population of these States; for 12 that purpose obstructing the Laws for Naturalization of Foreigners; refusing to pass others to encourage their migrations hither, and raising the conditions of new Appropriations of Lands.

He has obstructed the Administration of Justice, by refusing his 13 Assent to Laws for establishing Judiciary powers.

He has made Judges dependent on his Will alone, for the tenure of 14 their offices, and the amount and payment of their salaries.

He has erected a multitude of New Offices, and sent hither swarms 15 of Officers to harass our people, and eat out their substance.

He has kept among us, in times of peace, Standing Armies without 16 the Consent of our legislatures.

He has affected to render the Military independent of and superior 17 to the Civil power.

He has combined with others[1] to subject us to a jurisdiction foreign 18 to our constitution, and unacknowledged by our laws; giving his Assent to the Acts of pretended Legislation:

For Quartering large bodies of armed troops among us: 19

For protecting them, by a mock Trial, from punishment for any 20 Murders which they should commit on the Inhabitants of these States:

For cutting off our Trade with all parts of the world: 21

For imposing Taxes on us without our Consent: 22

For depriving us in many cases, of the benefits of Trial by Jury: 23

For transporting us beyond Seas to be tried for pretended offenses: 24

For abolishing the free System of English Laws in a neighboring 25 Province[2] establishing therein an Arbitrary government, and enlarging its Boundaries so as to render it at once an example and fit instrument for introducing the same absolute rule into these Colonies:

For taking away our Charters, abolishing our most valuable Laws, 26 and altering fundamentally the Forms of our Governments:

For suspending our own Legislatures, and declaring themselves invested with power to legislate for us in all cases whatsoever. 27

He has abdicated Government here, by declaring us out of his Protection and waging War against us: 28

He has plundered our seas, ravaged our Coasts, burnt our towns, 29 and destroyed the lives of our people.

[1] The British Parliament.

[2] The Quebec Act (1774) promised concessions to the French Catholics and reestablished the French civil law, thus alienating the Province of Quebec from the seaboard colonies in the growing controversy.

He is at this time transporting large Armies of foreign Mercenaries[3]   30
to compleat the works of death, desolation and tyranny, already begun
with circumstances of Cruelty and perfidy scarcely paralleled in the
most barbarous ages, and totally unworthy the Head of a civilized
nation.

He has constrained our fellow Citizens taken Captive on the high   31
Seas to bear Arms against their Country, to become the executioners of
their friends and Brethren, or to fall themselves by their Hands.

He has excited domestic insurrections amongst us, and has endeav-   32
oured to bring on the inhabitants of our frontiers, the merciless Indian
Savages, whose known rule of warfare, is an undistinguished destruction of all ages, sexes and conditions. In every stage of these Oppres-
sions We have Petitioned for Redress in the most humble terms: Our
repeated Petitions have been answered only by repeated injury. A
Prince, whose character is thus marked by every act which may define
a Tyrant, is unfit to be the ruler of a free people. Nor have We been
wanting in attentions to our British brethren. We have warned them
from time to time of attempts by their legislature to extend an unwar-
rantable jurisdiction over us. We have reminded them of the circumstances of our emigration and settlement here. We have appealed to
their native justice and magnanimity, and we have conjured them by the
ties of our common kindred to disavow these usurpations, which,
would inevitably interrupt our connections and correspondence. They
too have been deaf to the voice of justice and of consanguinity. We must,
therefore, acquiesce in the necessity, which denounces our Separation,
and hold them, as we hold the rest of mankind, Enemies in War, in
Peace Friends.

We, therefore, the Representatives of the United States of America,   33
in General Congress Assembled, appealing to the Supreme Judge of
the world for the rectitude of our intentions, do, in the Name and by
Authority of the good People of these Colonies, solemnly publish and
declare, That these United Colonies are, and of Right ought to be Free
and Independent States; that they are Absolved from all Allegiance to
the British Crown, and that all political connection between them and
the State of Great Britain, is and ought to be totally dissolved; and that
as Free and Independent States, they have full Power to levy War, conclude Peace, contract Alliances, establish Commerce, and to do all other
Acts and Things which Independent States may of right do.

And for the support of this Declaration, with a firm reliance on the   34
protection of divine Providence, we mutually pledge to each other our
Lives, our Fortunes and our sacred Honor.

[3]German soldiers, Hessians, hired by the British for colonial service.

AIMS AND STRATEGIES OF THE WRITER

Comment. Jefferson said his purpose was "to place before mankind the common sense of the subject, in terms so plain and firm as to command their assent."

Assignment 1. Create a list of subjects that you feel strongly about. Topics might include teenage drinking laws, use of steroids by athletes, genetic engineering, or divorced parents and their children. Select one topic that you might develop with a full set of examples.

Comment. Jefferson and other patriots needed the support of all colonists. Therefore, the Declaration's examples build evidence for the colonists as well as for the British.

Assignment 2. Identify the audience for your persuasive topic, as selected in assignment 1. Can you furnish evidence and rally supporters to action? Can you defend your position to win recognition and understanding from your opponents and others who are currently neutral? The interaction of subject and audience will affect the examples you use.

Comment. The key ingredients for persuasion serve Jefferson's purposes: a *proposition* (to declare independence from Great Britain), an *assumption* (that all humans desire freedom from the tyranny of government), *credibility* (knowledge of the subject and a consideration of the issues), *evidence* (a large body of examples), and *appeals to reason, ethics, and emotion* (the opening and closing statements).

Assignment 3. Develop a brief paragraph that explains your writing situation. Include basic ingredients, especially your proposition and source of evidence. Note this example:

> We assume that parents love their children, yet evidence mounts that in far too many cases the opposite it true. Research uncovers one example after another in which children receive neither respect nor love. We need reasonable methods for identifying, supporting, and educating neglected and abused children.

Pattern your preliminary paragraph on this example; it will clarify your purpose and set the direction for the entire essay.

THE WRITING PROCESS

Comment. Jefferson overpowers us with evidence, but the beginning and closing are the crucial ingredients that set forth the primary issue and announce the conclusion.

Assignment 4. Outline the overall plan for your paper. Where will examples appear? If you have subtopics, will you need examples for each subtopic?

Comment. Jefferson uses a random order for his set of negative examples, for the accumulation of transgressions by the British caused the revolt, not any particular action.

Assignment 5. Consider other possibilities for arranging your essay. Can you employ chronological order for the examples to show a progressive sequence over time? Will a positive/negative sequence establish a contrast of a few good features against a number of negative examples? Will an incremental pattern show increasingly severe conditions?

Comment. In its form as well as content Jefferson's essay justifies a revolution. He establishes a proposition, gives examples, makes his declaration, and issues a call to action.

Assignment 6. Write your persuasive essay so that it makes a declaration, one that would free society, for instance, from rude smokers, pornography, child abusers, terrorism, or some similar threat. Use plenty of examples for evidence in the style of Jefferson.

In the work that follows, John Updike makes no apparent effort to merge his descriptive examples into a unified prose passage, yet his implied thesis, centered around an early spring morning, gives the prose piece its unity. He catalogs a series of impressions that create a sense of the whole.

In general, one should avoid cataloging a long list of examples, especially when no purpose for the list is expressed. Yet Updike does just this and succeeds for two reasons: First, his images are tightly focused to create a portrait of one time and place—Central Park on the first day of spring. Second, the work features rich use of imagery and metaphorical language.

Updike uses examples as pictures, as symbols of life, and sensual images that readers can almost seem to touch, see, hear, smell, and taste. Painters capture memorable scenes in pigment; Updike accomplishes his portrait with words.

As you read the essay, note the type of appeal made by each image; most illustrations are visual but some relate to the other senses. In the margin list the images in which irony of situation exposes human error and foolish behavior.

"Central Park" first appeared as part of the column "Talk of the Town" in The New Yorker (for which Updike served for several years as writer and editor) and is reprinted from Updike's book Assorted Prose (1965).

JOHN UPDIKE

 Central Park

On the afternoon of the first day of spring, when the gutters were still 1
heaped high with Monday's snow but the sky itself was swept clean, we
put on our galoshes and walked up the sunny side of Fifth Avenue to
Central Park. There we saw:

Great black rocks emerging from the melting drifts, their craggy 2
skins glistening like the backs of resurrected brontosaurs.

A pigeon on the half-frozen pond strutting to the edge of the ice and 3
looking a duck in the face.

A policeman getting his shoe wet testing the ice. 4

Three elderly relatives trying to coax a little boy to accompany his 5
father on a sled ride down a short but steep slope. After much balking,
the boy did, and, sure enough, the sled tipped over and the father got
his collar full of snow. Everybody laughed except the boy, who sniffled.

Four boys in black leather jackets throwing snowballs at each other. 6
(The snow was ideally soggy, and packed hard with one squeeze.)

Seven men without hats. 7

Twelve snowmen, none of them intact. 8

Two men listening to the radio in a car parked outside the Zoo; Mel 9
Allen was broadcasting the Yanks-Cardinals game from St. Petersburg.

A tahr (*Hemitragus jemlaicus*) pleasantly squinting in the sunlight. 10

An aoudad absently pawing the mud and chewing. 11

A yak with its back turned. 12

Empty cages labelled "Coati," "Orang-outang," "Ocelot." 13

A father saying to his little boy, who was annoyed almost to tears by 14
the inactivity of the seals, "Father (Father Seal, we assumed) is very
tired; he worked hard all day."

Most of the cafeteria's out-of-doors tables occupied. 15

A pretty girl in black pants falling on them at the Wollman Memo- 16
rial Rink.

"Bill & Doris" carved on a tree. "Rex & Rita" written in the snow. 17

Two old men playing, and six supervising, a checkers game. 18

The Michael Friedsam Foundation Merry-Go-Round, nearly empty 19
of children but overflowing with calliope music.

A man on a bench near the carrousel reading, through sunglasses, a 20
book on economics.

Crews of shinglers repairing the roof of the Tavern-on-the-Green. 21

A woman dropping a camera she was trying to load, the film unroll- 22
ing in the slush and exposing itself.

A little colored boy in aviator goggles rubbing his ears and saying, 23
"He really hurt me." "No, he didn't," his nursemaid told him.

The green head of Giuseppe Mazzini staring across the white soft- 24
ball field, unblinking, though the sun was in its eyes.

Water murmuring down walks and rocks and steps. A grown man 25
trying to block one rivulet with snow.

Things like brown sticks nosing through a plot of cleared soil. 26

A tire track in a piece of mud far removed from where any auto- 27
mobiles could be.

Footprints around a Keep Off sign. 28

Two pigeons feeding each other. 29

Two showgirls, whose faces had not yet thawed the frost of their 30
makeup, treading indignantly through the slush.

A plump old man saying "Chick, chick" and feeding peanuts to 31
squirrels.

Many solitary men throwing snowballs at tree trunks. 32

Many birds calling to each other about how little the Ramble has 33
changed.

One red mitten lying lost under a poplar tree.   34

An airplane, very bright and distant, slowly moving through the   35
branches of a sycamore.

AIMS AND STRATEGIES OF THE WRITER

Comment. The first paragraph of Updike's piece explains his purpose: He wants to share with his readers a few impressions of his walk in Central Park on the first day of spring. It's a modest proposal and disclaims any aims of high moral or intellectual purpose. Like a friend, he wants to share something delightful.

Assignment 1. List a few subjects that might lend themselves to your own image study, for example, the town on a snowy morning, a restaurant at noon, a department store during the Christmas rush, and so on.

Comment. A cluster of examples should illustrate the character of the whole. Updike accomplishes this task by painting with words a series of images about Central Park. His detached amusement about human behavior is implied in many of the scenes, such as "Footprints around a 'Keep Off' sign" or "Many solitary men throwing snowballs at tree trunks."

Assignment 2. Choose one subject from your list of possibilities and begin sketching scenes and images. Silently question each for its value to your implied thesis. Do you want to show the frenzy of Christmas shoppers? The freshness of the new-fallen snow?

Comment. One purpose of image studies is entertainment. The writer wishes to delight the reader with penetrating visual scenes and surprising figurative language.

Assignment 3. Consider the freshness of your images. Have you focused on the scene from an unusual angle? Can you offer metaphoric comparisons that will surprise the reader? Can you be specific and concrete in even the smallest details? Make notes and write brief paragraphs that bring into focus some of your key scenes.

THE WRITING PROCESS

Comment. Updike is a patient writer. He allows a detail to develop and carry itself. He knows that emotion can be shown by one image. For example, when the policeman gets his shoe wet while testing the ice, we understand his frustration and embarrassment, yet Updike never uses these words.

Assignment 4. As you work to develop your various scenes, consider first an emotion—anger, frustration, pride—and then express that emotion with a visual scene, not the word. Rather than tell us a girl became angry, say instead, "She suddenly threw the ashtray against the wall."

Comment. A special aim for Updike is to look at things from different perspectives, to see Central Park in unusual and highly detailed ways. He does not merely see a man on a park bench; he sees "A man on a bench near the carrousel reading through sunglasses a book on economics."

Assignment 5. Select one subject from your list for assignment 1 and begin building your images and special views. Use concrete, specific words that appeal to sight, sound, touch, smell, and taste. Be specific in details of place, character, color, action.

Comment. Updike sees various scenes in metaphorical terms. He does not merely see a pigeon; he sees one "strutting," and the sky is "swept clean," and black rocks "emerge" from the melting snow drifts.

Assignment 6. Try to see things in metaphorical terms. That is, compare one item with another from a different plane of experience: brown sticks that "nose" through the snow or perhaps water that "murmurs." Write your descriptive examples with a variety of images and metaphorical comparisons.

Comment. A good example has concreteness; it *shows* the reader, not merely tells in words. Updike does not talk of "beauty" nor tell "how nice it is to be alive." He allows the examples to carry the message.

Assignment 7. Begin writing your essay of images. Do so as a visually oriented, not exclusively feeling-oriented, writer. The images you provide of external scenes will reveal your inner thoughts; therefore, you need not express them in a didactic or preaching manner.

Bob Wakeman decided to have some fun with his instructor's discussion of spelling devices for special effects, which include such orthographical devices as anagrams *(transposing letters),* portmanteau words *(jamming two words tightly together),* acronyms *(words formed from initial letters), and other* neologisms *(newly coined words).*

Wakeman uses an imaginatively conceived aim of discourse to make his point: that spoken English is a growing, vibrant, and highly creative form of language communication. However, his indirect message must be discovered by the reader, for Wakeman does not explain it with traditional essay development.

As a persona or actor in the story, he responds to the dialogue of friends and family. He concentrates on numerous examples of orthographical words or phrases to flesh out his short narration. Consequently, his writing style features a traditional element of humorous writing, hyperbole *(which means to exaggerate for effect). His handling of dialogue and his examples of unusual words distinguish his style.*

As you read the essay make marginal notes on several features: (1) his uncommon spelling of certain words, (2) his use of dialogue, and (3) his first-person voice with its ironic tone.

BOB WAKEMAN, STUDENT

 ## Orthographical Devices

I'm not really sure what caused it; perhaps it was the gentle prodding   1
of Dr. Lester, my writing instructor, or maybe it was the current tall, cool glass of scotch I was sipping, but regardless of cause, I was, for a period, assailed by the forces of a thing I can only call transmongrology. Let me explain. It began as I was dozing on the deck and overheard my neighbor, Mrs. Ledbettor, talking to her cat: "Does ou ant to go out wiz mama?" she asked. Just that, nothing more, but the words hung in my mind as though trying to tell me something. Then suddenly a news item flashed across my mind. It dealt with an Air Force plane that had crashed in Washington state, but flashing through my mind was the acronymiously mutated report as it would have been written by the military: "A FAC jet from SAC 5 made a ECL at SEATOC after being TUF by PU, but the fire was extinguished by a SAC ACFFT."

I took a gulp of scotch as I tried to digest what was happening to   2
me, but my reverie was interrupted when my daughter's boyfriend shouted from the back door: "Hey Bobbie, jeet jet?"

And my daughter shouted back, "Not jet, jew?"   3
"Negatron, let's grababurger."   4
"Neato, neato, I kindigit!"   5
At that moment my glass slipped from my hand, crashed on the   6
cement, and the sound brought me abruptly awake. I realized that I had
been dreaming and that people just didn't mongrelize a language that
way. I let out a sigh of relief as my wife called out, "Hey Bob, juanta
drink?"
And I said, "Abso-gawddamn-lutely!"   7

BOB WAKEMAN TALKS ABOUT HIS AIMS AND STRATEGIES

All my life I spent my writing time with dictionaries, trying to spell
words properly. My assignment as a report writer in the military taught
me that good writing demanded precise words, exact phrasing, and no
misspellings. So imagine my surprise to hear a professor talk at length
about stylistic variations of word formation and spelling. After my
shock, I came to love it, especially portmanteau words like 'universy-
lum." What a clever disguise for criticism!

I began to listen to people mispronounce words, and I spotted
instance after instance of special spellings in various magazine articles
and sports writing in the newspaper. Then, when the time arrived for
another writing assignment, I launched this one.

I had no intentions of writing a straight essay. I wanted to show this
guy trapped by a weird, acute consciousness of word distortions. I
guess it turned out okay. My instructor read it to the class, it got a terrific
laugh, and the instructor wanted a copy.

Comment. Wakeman, like other writers, has discovered that an imaginative writer in the creative stance can bend and distort the usual rules
of grammar. Beginning writers are too often conventional in form and
style, so their essays are dull. Language and grammer should serve you
stylistically. But consider this point about Wakeman's essay: He does
not abandon convention completely, for then he might entirely fail to
communicate.

Assignment 1. Write a page of experimental prose that features examples of language variations. Experiment, like Wakeman, with spelling. Put words on the page in unconventional positions. Try writing a
poem. Be a master of the language, not its slave, and use it creatively in
some manner.

Comment. Many of Wakeman's examples appear as spoken words in dialogue form.

Assignment 2. Write a brief dialogue in an attempt to capture the rhythm, pace, and sound of spoken words. To verify its accuracy, you may need to read it aloud and perhaps ask a friend to read it back to you.

Comment. When writers like Wakeman show us images or word play, the pace quickens, requiring less space and verbiage. Compare the length of Wakeman's writing, for example, with that of Williams (page 104–109), in which telling as well as showing is required.

Assignment 3. Write a creative, experimental piece that features examples of both language variations and dialogue. Keep it short, for language gymnastics cannot be sustained very long by either you or the reader.

CHAPTER FOUR

Comparison and Contrast

Comparison helps us make choices in everyday life. In written discourse, comparison examines relationships of complex items, such as the architectural design of two buildings or the economic effects of two different tax plans. Your essays will require this technique for showing similarities and differences. For example, you might explore the idea that each generation views its heroes in different ways, or you might stipulate that society needs a balance of liberals and conservatives more than it needs Democrats and Republicans. Your comparison will sometimes require you to rank one item over another for the sake of your argument. In the following excerpt Suzanne Britt compares thin people to fat people:

> In the first place, thin people aren't fun. They don't know how to goof off, at least in the best, fat sense of the word. They've always got to be adoing. Give them a coffee break, and they'll jog around the block. Supply them with a quiet evening at home, and they'll fix the screen door and lick S&H green stamps. They say things like "there aren't enough hours in the day." Fat people never say that. Fat people think the day is too damn long already.
>
> Thin people make me tired. They've got speedy little metabolisms that cause them to bustle briskly. They're forever rubbing their bony hands together and eying new problems to "tackle." I like to surround myself with sluggish, inert, easygoing fat people, the kind who believe that if you clean it up today, it'll just get dirty again tomorrow.

As demonstrated in this brief passage (the whole essay follows later in this chapter), certain characteristics distinguish comparison, contrast, and analogy. *Comparison* draws parallels between two items to show similar features of, for example, two governments, two waterway systems, or two circulatory systems. While comparison pulls subjects together, contrast splits them apart. *Contrast* develops the differences, contrasting, for instance, barge traffic on the Ohio River with that of the

Missouri River or exploring the differences in the leg muscle design of three types of frogs. Bruce Catton (pages 156–159) uses contrast as his primary rhetorical tool to show the differences between two famous generals, Lee and Grant. *Analogy* is metaphorical comparison of two items that are wholly unlike one another. A full discussion of analogy is found in Chapter 5, where you will find writers comparing the human brain with a computer or comparing people in a crowded city with rats in a maze.

USE COMPARISON AND CONTRAST FOR A REASON

Comparative techniques serve three primary purposes.

1. They inform by clarifying subjects and issues. For example, you might make distinctions between knowledge and wisdom as a way of defining them.
2. Comparative writing often judges the superiority of one side over another. Ernest Hemingway (see pages 167–168) rates Christmas in America over one spent in Paris.
3. The comparative paper can provide practical advice to help a reader make a choice. For example, a work might compare Persian, Siamese, and tabby cats in order to explain personality differences and thereby help the reader choose an appropriate pet.

In addition, the comparison/contrast pattern serves three minor purposes: (1) to present conditions in terms of the past or present or future (a view of Main Street in 1950 and today), (2) to explain which properties one subject shares with another (an evaluation of three computer software programs), and (3) to make abstract or complex issues clear by presenting a balanced contrast of items (an analysis of Civil War issues).

ORDER COMPARISON TO ENHANCE YOUR PURPOSE

There are several methods of ordering or focusing. A *central subject focus* uses comparison or contrast to enhance one key topic. For example, you might wish to explain rock music by comparing it with a variety of other forms such as country, contemporary, or classical music. Hemingway's essay uses this pattern, comparing Christmas in Paris with the holiday traditions—cranberries, turkey, and desserts—of Christmas in America.

A *two-subject focus* is a first one, then another pattern, usually requiring a four-part structure, as follows:

introduction

focus on first item

focus on second item

comparative discussion

Catton uses this method for contrasting Generals Grant and Lee. This technique is appropriate whenever two dominating subjects control the issues.

Point-by-point order sequences the items being compared into classifications and divisions. For example, your business paper that compares a corporation with a sole proprietorship might move from ownership to liability to taxes, and so forth, as follows:

Business ownership: sole proprietorship or incorporation

　Ownership

　　sole proprietor

　　corporation

　Tax advantages

　　sole proprietor

　　corporation

　Liability for lawsuits and business failures

　　sole proprietor

　　corporation

As you can see, the main items are compared under each point. This approach works well for topics that require discussion of several significant issues, especially when the issues warrant headline treatment and will help order the essay.

Process analysis can be structured by a series of comparative stages. Use this method for essays that compare activities (such as water skiing and snow skiing, tennis backhand and forehand). In outline form, this analysis looks similar to a point-by-point order, except that each point follows in progressive order.

　Hitting the backhand and forehand

　　Stance, setup, and grip

　　　backhand

　　　forehand

> The swing
>> backhand
>> forehand
> Follow through
>> backhand
>> forehand

See the essay by Devoe (pages 257–260) for his brief comparative analysis of a box turtle with a snapping turtle.

A *past-to-present* pattern compares the way things used to be with the contemporary scene. Use it to compare modern and old items (the calculator and the slide rule), to compare attitudes (the work ethic today and yesterday), or to compare social issues (large farm families of the past and the modern family). Mark Twain uses a past-to-present form to compare the river of his youth with one he sees in his maturity as a riverboat pilot (pages 152–153).

Other possible patterns exist, but generally one of the above plans, or a variation thereof, will serve your purposes.

CONFORM TO THREE RULES FOR COMPARISON PAPERS

Basic elements for comparison/contrast studies are: balanced parts, effective connectors, and clear reasons for the comparison.

Balanced parts means that the compared parts are equal in importance. Catton compares two Civil War generals, Lee and Grant. Comparing two horses—a thoroughbred with a quarter horse—would have balance, but comparing a quarter horse with an English sheepdog might cause imbalance unless you compared their inbred instincts for herding cattle and sheep.

Effective connectors allow one idea to flow directly into the next so that comparative elements precisely balance with each other. Use such words and phrases as "in contrast," "on the other hand," "similarly," "likewise," "on the contrary," "both," "although," and "one of the differences." (Again, overuse of these connectors can make your writing stilted and jerky.)

Reasons for the comparison need clear expression at some point in the essay. Mark Twain opens his essay with his thesis.

> Now when I had mastered the language of this water, and had come to know every trifling feature that bordered the great river as familiarly as I knew the letters of the alphabet, I had made a valuable acquisition. But I had lost something, too. I had lost something which could never be restored to me

while I lived. All the grace, the beauty, the poetry, had gone out of the majestic river!

In contrast, Catton waits until the end of his essay to emphasize our debt to Generals Lee and Grant. Hemingway, writing on Christmas in Paris, expresses his thesis early and also at the closing. Britt (pages 162–164) mentions her point repeatedly. In all cases, these writers clearly enunciate their purposes for the comparative studies.

To review: You should use comparison as a pattern of development to inform, judge, or offer practical advice. Order the whole to fit the needs of your subject and audience, using

a central subject focus

a two-subject focus

point-by-point order

stages of a process

a past-to-present order

You should balance your treatment of compared items, use effective connectors, and express clearly the significance of the comparison.

Samuel Clemens worked as a riverboat pilot, but he also wrote fiction and nonfiction works under the pen name of Mark Twain. His novels The Adventures of Tom Sawyer and The Adventures of Huckleberry Finn rank as American classics. He grew up in Hannibal, Missouri, where the mighty Mississippi River influenced his life. The brief comparative essay that follows offers Twain's personal reflection on his river.

Writing autobiographically, he explains how his youthful visions of majestic wonders and delights of the river changed into a mature pilot's views of practical sights and mundane sounds. His utilitarian concerns about navigating his vessel through shallows and around sandbars replaced the poetry of the river of his youth.

Twain, like any expressive writer who reflects on personal experience, touches on the idealism of his youth and the romantic appeal of the river, yet he must adjust as a grown man to practical concerns. Twain meditates on a rite of passage that all humans experience in one form or another.

As you read the essay, mark the two-subject focus on Twain's past-to-present comparison with marginal notes about his two views of river "sunsets," "slanting marks," "tumbling boils," and other descriptive images. Note too how he shifts from his riverboat trade at the end to talk about doctors, a tactic that adds universality to his thesis.

Twain wrote "Two Ways of Viewing the River" as part of his journal, Old Times on the Mississippi. He later incorporated the essay into Life on the Mississippi (1883).

MARK TWAIN

Two Ways of Viewing the River

Now when I had mastered the language of this water and had come to know every trifling feature that bordered the great river as familiarly as I knew the letters of the alphabet, I had made a valuable acquisition. But I had lost something, too. I had lost something which could never be restored to me while I lived. All the grace, the beauty, the poetry, had gone out of the majestic river! I still kept in mind a certain wonderful sunset which I witnessed when steamboating was new to me. A broad expanse of the river was turned to blood; in the middle distance the red hue brightened into gold, through which a solitary log came floating, black and conspicuous; in one place a long, slanting mark lay sparkling upon the water; in another the surface was broken by boiling,

1

tumbling rings, that were as many-tinted as an opal; where the ruddy flush was faintest, was a smooth spot that was covered with graceful circles and radiating lines, ever so delicately traced; the shore on our left was densely wooded and the somber shadow that fell from this forest was broken in one place by a long, ruffled trail that shone like silver; and high above the forest wall a clean-stemmed dead tree waved a single leafy bough that glowed like a flame in the unobstructed splendor that was flowing from the sun. There were graceful curves, reflected images, woody heights, soft distances, and over the whole scene, far and near, the dissolving lights drifted steadily, enriching it every passing moment with new marvels of coloring.

I stood like one bewitched. I drank it in, in a speechless rapture. 2 The world was new to me and I had never seen anything like this at home. But as I have said, a day came when I began to cease from noting the glories and the charms which the moon and the sun and the twilight wrought upon the river's face; another day came when I ceased altogether to note them. Then, if that sunset scene had been repeated, I should have looked upon it without rapture, and should have commented upon it inwardly after this fashion: "This sun means that we are going to have wind tomorrow; that floating log means that the river is rising, small thanks to it; that slanting mark on the water refers to a bluff reef which is going to kill somebody's steamboat one of these nights, if it keeps on stretching out like that; those tumbling 'boils' show a dissolving bar and a changing channel there; the lines and circles in the slick water over yonder are a warning that that troublesome place is shoaling up dangerously; that silver streak in the shadow of the forest is the 'break' from a new snag and he has located himself in the very best place he could have found to fish for steamboats; that tall dead tree, with a single living branch, is not going to last long, and then how is a body ever going to get through this blind place at night without the friendly old landmark?"

No, the romance and beauty were all gone from the river. All the 3 value any feature of it had for me now was the amount of usefulness it could furnish toward compassing the safe piloting of a steamboat. Since those days, I have pitied doctors from my heart. What does the lovely flush in a beauty's cheek mean to a doctor but a "break" that ripples above some deadly disease? Are not all her visible charms sown thick with what are to him the signs and symbols of hidden decay? Does he ever see her beauty at all, or doesn't he simply view her professionally and comment upon her unwholesome condition all to himself? And doesn't he sometimes wonder whether he has gained most or lost most by learning his trade?

AIMS AND STRATEGIES OF THE WRITER

Comment. Exploring one's private world is a primary aim of expressive writing. Personal notes and journal entries build a body of autobiographical details. In this selection, Twain presents the Mississippi River through the eyes of a riverboat pilot.

Assignment 1. Briefly describe a place that was special to you as a child. The purpose of this reminiscence is to compare your attitudes as a child with your understanding today as an adult. For example, you might think of the yard of the home where you were raised, going from place to place, remembering special details or significant events. Write down important memories. If you have revisited that childhood spot in recent years, contrast that special place as it exists today.

Comment. Like most writers, Twain wants to define his own life. Writing in the first-person voice, he explains how knowledge has destroyed his illusions. Twain wanted to act as a philosopher and social critic, so one reward of writing about himself was a renewed confidence in what he stood for.

Assignment 2. By defining fleeting thoughts and brief experiences of the past, you bring focus and clarity to your thinking. If you can interpret one complicated period of your life, it will probably help you interpret other episodes. Select one episode from your past and make notes about it. In particular, write a paragraph to explain the event's significance to you as a child and today as an adult.

Comment. A retrospective attitude with touches of reminiscence seems almost common to most autobiographical writing, but an ironic, self-deprecating attitude can also be adopted. Twain displays this by revealing the irony of his education. "I had mastered the language of the river," he tells us, but "the grace, the beauty, the poetry had gone out of the majestic river."

Assignment 3. Write a paragraph on your past and present feelings about an autobiographical event. Were you naive as a child? Are you now more serious and meditative? Should you admit weakness, error, or insensitivity? If so, remember that a sense of humor takes the edge off embarrassing admissions. As a writer, you might confess, "I came up short, but I understand, and I can smile about it now."

THE WRITING PROCESS

Comment. Twain's knowledge of the river from two perspectives— idealism and pragmatism—leads him into the comparative process.

Assignment 4. Write a brief paragraph explaining your reasons for comparing a youthful view of your subject with your mature approach to it. Does age bring wisdom, cynicism, bitterness over lost dreams? Do you recall with delight the escapes of childhood? Suggest such a thesis in your opening and then discuss it more fully in the conclusion.

Comment. Recalling special times and places requires a writer to blend into the essay other patterns of development, especially *description* and *example*, as demonstrated by Twain's essay.

Assignment 5. If necessary, review Chapter 1 on description and Chapter 3 on example. Then write an analysis of Twain's use of the two patterns in his first paragraph. Can you employ description and example in your autobiographical essay? How? Write a rough outline that details specific examples that you want to develop and special scenes that require full description.

Comment. Personal narration shows a sequence of one's life. However, a comparative narration must compare your life with that of somebody else or compare one period of your life with another period. Twain uses the latter technique.

Assignment 6. If necessary, review Chapter 2 on narration to determine how this technique might improve your essay. Can you narrate events of the past in comparison with current events? For example, a tennis player might compare the ability to handle pressure during a high school match and during a college match.

Comment. Twain limits his essay to a topic that has a common comparative base—two views of the river. Too often writers believe they need momentous events, yet Twain demonstrates that simple events are ample.

Assignment 7. Develop a very brief writing situation that establishes an overall plan for your essay. For example:

> I want to speak in the first person about my mother who, when I was fourteen, treated me like a child even though I knew full well that I was a grown, mature, and responsible adult. Now that I'm older, though insecure and uncertain about my future, she seeks my advice and counsel.

After developing your writing situation, write a draft, and then polish it.

The following essay by Bruce Catton has become a classic example of comparison/contrast techniques. It uses a basic two-subject focus of introduction—subject one (General Lee), subject two (General Grant)—and a comparative discussion. Catton compares the men as generals and leaders, men who have made difficult decisions costing the lives of countless soldiers. He contrasts their backgrounds to show Lee as the aristocratic Virginian stepping out of an age of chivalry into a brutal new world and to portray Grant as the raw-boned frontier hero who owes no allegiance to tradition.

Catton uses comparison and contrast for a reason. He wants to explain that the tenacity and fidelity of both men were ingredients that made America great. They fought with passion for their causes, and after the battles were over they expressed their dedication to peace for the whole nation. Consequently, Catton makes clear his reasons for using comparison as a pattern of development: Those persons who divide a country can also unite it.

As you read, note the fundamental differences of the two generals as explained in Catton's first twelve paragraphs and also the generals' similarities as developed in paragraphs 13 through 16. In addition, explain why each man fought so tenaciously for his cause.

Bruce Catton (1899–1978) was originally a newspaper reporter who became interested in history. Slowly and surely he developed an expertise in Civil War matters. "Grant and Lee: A Study in Contrasts" is from the book The American Story *(1956).*

BRUCE CATTON

Grant and Lee: A Study in Contrasts

When Ulysses S. Grant and Robert E. Lee met in the parlor of a modest house at Appomattox Court House, Virginia, on April 9, 1865, to work out the terms for the surrender of Lee's Army of Northern Virginia, a great chapter in American life came to a close, and a great new chapter began. 1

These men were bringing the Civil War to its virtual finish. To be sure, other armies had yet to surrender, and for a few days the fugitive Confederate government would struggle desperately and vainly, trying to find some way to go on living now that its chief support was gone. But in effect it was all over when Grant and Lee signed the papers. And the little room where they wrote out the terms was the scene of one of the poignant, dramatic contrasts in American History. 2

156

They were two strong men, these oddly different generals, and they   3
represented the strengths of two conflicting currents that, through
them, had come into final collision.

Back of Robert E. Lee was the notion that the old aristocratic concept   4
might somehow survive and be dominant in American life.

Lee was tidewater Virginia, and in his background were family, cul-   5
ture, and tradition ... the age of chivalry transplanted to a New World
which was making its own legends and its own myths. He embodied a
way of life that had come down through the age of knighthood and the
English country squire. America was a land that was beginning all over
again, dedicated to nothing much more complicated than the rather
hazy belief that all men had equal rights and should have an equal
chance in the world. In such a land Lee stood for the feeling that it was
somehow of advantage to human society to have a pronounced inequality in the social structure. There should be a leisure class, backed
by ownership of land; in turn, society itself should be keyed to the land
as the chief source of wealth and influence. It would bring forth (according to this ideal) a class of men with a strong sense of obligation to
the community; men who lived not to gain advantage for themselves,
but to meet the solemn obligations which had been laid on them by the
very fact that they were privileged. From them the country would get
its leadership; to them it could look for the higher values—of thought,
of conduct, of personal deportment—to give it strength and virtue.

Lee embodied the noblest elements of this aristocratic ideal.   6
Through him, the landed nobility justified itself. For four years, the
Southern states had fought a desperate war to uphold the ideals for
which Lee stood. In the end, it almost seemed as if the Confederacy
fought for Lee; as if he himself was the Confederacy ... the best thing
that the way of life for which the Confederacy stood could ever have to
offer. He had passed into legend before Appomattox. Thousands of
tired, underfed, poorly clothed Confederate soldiers, long since past
the simple enthusiasm of the early days of the struggle, somehow considered Lee the symbol of everything for which they had been willing
to die. But they could not quite put this feeling into words. If the Lost
Cause, sanctified by so much heroism and so many deaths, had a living
justification, its justification was General Lee.

Grant, the son of a tanner on the Western frontier, was everything   7
Lee was not. He had come up the hard way and embodied nothing in
particular except the eternal toughness and sinewy fiber of the men
who grew up beyond the mountains. He was one of a body of men who
owed reverence and obeisance to no one, who were self-reliant to a
fault, who cared hardly anything for the past but who had a sharp eye
for the future.

These frontier men were the precise opposites of the tidewater 8
aristocrats. Back of them, in the great surge that had taken people over
the Alleghenies and into the opening Western country, there was a deep,
implicit dissatisfaction with a past that had settled into grooves. They
stood for democracy, not from any reasoned conclusion about the
proper ordering of human society, but simply because they had grown
up in the middle of democracy and knew how it worked. Their society
might have privileges, but they would be privileges each man had won
for himself. Forms and patterns meant nothing. No man was born to
anything, except perhaps to a chance to show how far he could rise.
Life was competition.

Yet along with this feeling had come a deep sense of belonging to a 9
national community. The Westerner who developed a farm, opened a
shop, or set up in business as a trader, could hope to prosper only as
his own community prospered—and his community ran from the At-
lantic to the Pacific and from Canada down to Mexico. If the land was
settled, with towns and highways and accessible markets, he could
better himself. He saw his fate in terms of the nation's own destiny. As
its horizons expanded, so did his. He had, in other words, an acute
dollars-and-cents stake in the continued growth and development of his
country.

And that, perhaps, is where the contrast between Grant and Lee 10
becomes most striking. The Virginia aristocrat, inevitably, saw himself
in relation to his own region. He lived in a static society which could
endure almost anything except change. Instinctively, his first loyalty
would go to the locality in which that society existed. He would fight to
the limit of endurance to defend it, because in defending it he was
defending everything that gave his own life its deepest meaning.

The Westerner, on the other hand, would fight with an equal tenac- 11
ity for the broader concept of society. He fought so because everything
he lived by was tied to growth, expansion, and a constantly widening
horizon. What he lived by would survive or fall with the nation itself.
He could not possibly stand by unmoved in the face of an attempt to
destroy the Union. He would combat it with everything he had, because
he could only see it as an effort to cut the ground out from under
his feet.

So Grant and Lee were in complete contrast, representing two dia- 12
metrically opposed elements in American life. Grant was the modern
man emerging; beyond him, ready to come on the stage, was the great
age of steel and machinery, of crowded cities and a restless burgeoning
vitality. Lee might have ridden down from the old age of chivalry, lance
in hand, silken banner fluttering over his head. Each man was the

perfect champion of his cause, drawing both his strengths and his weaknesses from the people he led.

Yet it was not all contrast, after all. Different as they were—in back- 13 ground, in personality, in underlying aspiration—these two great soldiers had much in common. Under everything else, they were marvelous fighters. Furthermore, their fighting qualities were really very much alike.

Each man had, to begin with, the great virtue of utter tenacity and 14 fidelity. Grant fought his way down the Mississippi Valley in spite of acute personal discouragement and profound military handicaps. Lee hung on in the trenches at Petersburg after hope itself had died. In each man there was an indomitable quality . . . the born fighter's refusal to give up as long as he can still remain on his feet and lift his two fists.

Daring and resourcefulness they had, too; the ability to think faster 15 and move faster than the enemy. These were the qualities which gave Lee the dazzling campaigns of Second Manassas and Chancellorsville and won Vicksburg for Grant.

Lastly, and perhaps greatest of all, there was the ability, at the end, to 16 turn quickly from war to peace once the fighting was over. Out of the way these two men behaved at Appomattox came the possibility of a peace of reconciliation. It was a possibility not wholly realized, in the years to come, but which did, in the end, help the two sections to become one nation again . . . after a war whose bitterness might have seemed to make such a reunion wholly impossible. No part of either man's life became him more than the part he played in their brief meeting in the McLean house at Appomattox. Their behavior there put all succeeding generations of Americans in their debt. Two great Americans, Grant and Lee—very different, yet under everything very much alike. Their encounter at Appomattox was one of the great moments of American history.

AIMS AND STRATEGIES OF THE WRITER

Comment. Catton's purposes fit three categories: to inform, to judge and evaluate, and to lecture about the significance of the generals.

Assignment 1. Begin your search for a comparative topic. Select one that will require explanation, evaluation, and a discussion of basic issues. For example: (1) Select two persons who engaged in historical conflict and write a paper that examines their differences, or (2) develop an essay about two persons whose life-styles are in conflict. Use local subjects that are known to you, if possible.

Comment. Catton aims to compare two men who defended their beliefs with mental and physical talents. Yet Catton does more than report history; he interprets the role of these two generals in the shaping of a nation, especially the manner in which they represent two social currents and political philosophies.

Assignment 2. Determine how your comparative study of two persons will report the historic facts and also interpret the social role played by your subjects. If necessary, study Catton's essay for his careful interpretation of each man's background.

Comment. As an objective reporter, Catton avoids any emotional affiliation with one side or the other. He maintains a balance that offers praise for both men and credits them both for bringing peace through reconciliation.

Assignment 3. Study the draft of your comparative paper for evidence of balanced treatment or of bias. If you wish to favor one side, you will need to make value judgments using a point-by-point order.

Comment. Catton demonstrates the skills of an investigative reporter, a vital talent for any historian or biographer. His research work is evident in the many minute descriptions of the two men.

Assignment 4. If your subject lends itself to research, spend an hour or so in the library gathering details of dates, places, events, people, dress, time of day, and so forth. An encyclopedia might be sufficient, but you may also investigate a history book and dip into journal articles (as indexed in *Humanities Index* and *America: History and Life*).

THE WRITING PROCESS

Comment. The order for Catton's essay is as follows:

Introduction of the subject and principles (paragraphs 1 through 3)
Description of General Lee (paragraphs 4 through 6)
Description of General Grant (paragraphs 7 through 9)
Contrast of the two generals (paragraphs 10 through 12)
Comparison of the two generals (paragraphs 13 through 16)

Assignment 5. Apply a similar formula to your comparative essay. Do you have the necessary information? Will the formula work? If not, consider other plans, such as point-by-point, process analysis, or past-to-present.

Comment. Catton writes history, which is one type of narration.

Assignment 6. Examine Catton's use of the following narrative techniques (see Chapter 2): (1) flashbacks, (2) flashforwards, (3) time signals, (4) in medias res, (5) foreshortening, and (6) historic causal chains. Examine your planned essay for places to employ these techniques in your comparative paper.

Comment. Catton has carefully researched his subject, used both comparison and contrast to develop the topic, and makes clear his reasons for the comparison.

Assignment 7. Write your comparative paper with balanced subjects, in-depth analysis, comparison and contrast, and a clearly stated reason for making the comparison.

Some writers use comparison to make evaluations and argue a point. Suzanne Britt does this in the following essay in which she compares fat and lean people. She compares the two types point by point on such issues as energy, sense of humor, logic, and personality. She supplies numerous examples in every instance, and she insists that thin people are uptight, oppressive, and dangerous. At the same time, she would convince us that fat people are convivial, fun loving, relaxed, and generous.

Her first-person voice betrays her own weighty bias, but she uses that position to launch her attack. In effect, she takes on the world of the lean and hungry to defend herself and her world. The persuasive appeal is enhanced by her irony and sense of humor.

As you read Britt's essay, make marginal notes that reflect the point-by-point ordering of the essay and its consistent negative/positive positioning of the "thin/fat" debate. In your reading notebook write a one-sentence summary of Britt's primary idea. Then, to see clearly her special bias as reflected in the language, list key words that she associates with "thin" and with "fat."

Suzanne Britt is a freelance writer and a teacher of writing. "That Lean and Hungry Look" first appeared in Newsweek (9 October 1978).

SUZANNE BRITT

That Lean and Hungry Look

Caesar was right. Thin people need watching. I've been watching them 1 for most of my adult life, and I don't like what I see. When these narrow fellows spring at me, I quiver to my toes. Thin people come in all personalities, most of them menacing. You've got your "together" thin person, your mechanical thin person, your condescending thin person, your tsk-tsk thin person, your efficiency-expert thin person. All of them are dangerous.

In the first place, thin people aren't fun. They don't know how to 2 goof off, at least in the best, fat sense of the word. They've always got to be adoing. Give them a coffee break, and they'll jog around the block. Supply them with a quiet evening at home, and they'll fix the screen door and lick S&H green stamps. They say things like "there aren't enough hours in the day." Fat people never say that. Fat people think the day is too damn long already.

Thin people make me tired. They've got speedy little metabolisms 3 that cause them to bustle briskly. They're forever rubbing their bony hands together and eying new problems to "tackle." I like to surround myself with sluggish, inert, easygoing fat people, the kind who believe that if you clean it up today, it'll just get dirty again tomorrow.

Some people say the business about the jolly fat person is a myth, that all of us chubbies are neurotic, sick, sad people. I disagree. Fat people may not be chortling all day long, but they're a hell of a lot *nicer* than the wizened and shriveled. Thin people turn surly, mean and hard at a young age because they never learn the value of a hot-fudge sundae for easing tension. Thin people don't like gooey soft things because they themselves are neither gooey nor soft. They are crunchy and dull, like carrots. They go straight to the heart of the matter while fat people let things stay all blurry and hazy and vague, the way things actually are. Thin people want to face the truth. Fat people know there is no truth. One of my thin friends is always staring at complex, unsolvable problems and saying, "The key thing is . . ." Fat people never say that. They know there isn't any such thing as the key thing about anything.   4

Thin people believe in logic. Fat people see all sides. The sides fat people see are rounded blobs, usually gray, always nebulous and truly not worth worrying about. But the thin person persists. "If you consume more calories than you burn," says one of my thin friends, "you will gain weight. It's that simple." Fat people always grin when they hear statements like that. They know better.   5

Fat people realize that life is illogical and unfair. They know very well that God is not in his heaven and all is not right with the world. If God was up there, fat people could have two doughnuts and a big orange drink anytime they wanted it.   6

Thin people have a long list of logical things they are always spouting off to me. They hold up one finger at a time as they reel off these things, so I won't lose track. They speak slowly as if to a young child. The list is long and full of holes. It contains tidbits like "get a grip on yourself," "cigarettes kill," "cholesterol clogs," "fit as a fiddle," "ducks in a row," "organize" and "sound fiscal management." Phrases like that.   7

They think these 2,000-point plans lead to happiness. Fat people know happiness is elusive at best and even if they could get the kind thin people talk about, they wouldn't want it. Wisely, fat people see that such programs are too dull, too hard, too off the mark. They are never better than a whole cheesecake.   8

Fat people know all about the mystery of life. They are the ones acquainted with the night, with luck, with fate, with playing it by ear. One thin person I know once suggested that we arrange all the parts of a jigsaw puzzle into groups according to size, shape and color. He figured this would cut the time needed to complete the puzzle by at least 50 percent. I said I wouldn't do it. One, I like to muddle through.   9

Two, what good would it do to finish early? Three, the jigsaw puzzle isn't the important thing. The important thing is the fun of four people (one thin person included) sitting around a card table, working a jigsaw puzzle. My thin friend had no use for my list. Instead of joining us, he went outside and mulched the boxwoods. The three remaining fat people finished the puzzle and made chocolate, double-fudged brownies to celebrate.

The main problem with thin people is they oppress. Their good 10 intentions, bony torsos, tight ships, neat corners, cerebral machinations and pat solutions loom like dark clouds over the loose, comfortable, spread-out, soft world of the fat. Long after fat people have removed their coats and shoes and put their feet up on the coffee table, thin people are still sitting on the edge of the sofa, looking neat as a pin, discussing rutabagas. Fat people are heavily into fits of laughter, slapping their thighs and whooping it up, while thin people are still politely waiting for the punch line.

Thin people are downers. They like math and morality and reasoned 11 evaluation of the limitations of human beings. They have their skinny little acts together. They expound, prognose, probe and prick.

Fat people are convivial. They will like you even if you're irregular 12 and have acne. They will come up with a good reason why you never wrote the great American novel. They will cry in your beer with you. They will put your name in the pot. They will let you off the hook. Fat people will gab, giggle, guffaw, gallumph, gyrate and gossip. They are generous, giving and gallant. They are gluttonous and goodly and great. What you want when you're down is soft and jiggly, not muscled and stable. Fat people know this. Fat people have plenty of room. Fat people will take you in.

AIMS AND STRATEGIES OF THE WRITER

Comment. Britt makes clear her purpose: She wants to defend fat people against bias and prejudice. She goes on the offensive to attack lean people.

Assignment 1. Consider several topics you might develop in the comparative pattern of Britt. Choose one that involves your life-style, perhaps big football linemen versus fast little runningbacks, tennis players who charge the net and those who hover along the baseline, tuba players versus trumpet players, people who drive BMW automobiles and those who drive pickup trucks.

Comment. Britt writes with wit and a good sense of humor, yet she makes a serious point. She uses irony that has a sting to it; that is, we know she's exaggerating, yet her strong presentation makes a persuasive appeal.

Assignment 2. Write a thesis for a humorous but judgmental comparison. Make two lists, one for each side, that exaggerate the excesses; hyperbole can be one feature of your essay.

Comment. The persuasive writer appeals directly to the audience, provokes the reader, and demands participation in the debate. "Fat people are better," Britt argues, and invites your response.

Assignment 3. Draft your comparative, persuasive paper. Build on your supply of examples and evidence for both sides (see assignment 2). Then take a clear stand on one side, even though you know some readers will disagree.

Comment. Voice and attitude in persuasive discourse can become harsh, insistent, unrelenting. Yet writers like Britt, because they are confident, bold, and assured, speak with intensity and personal involvement that impels the essay forward.

Assignment 4. Determine the best voice for your subject. Should you be serious or humorous, quiet or strident, rational or emotional? Ironic exaggeration requires that you say things with tongue in cheek. The reader needs to recognize your humorous nature, yet to write satire, you must expose human vice and folly and bring fresh awareness to your reader.

THE WRITING PROCESS

Comment. While comparison pulls subjects together, contrast develops the differences between two subjects and splits them apart. Britt has carefully crafted her essay to divide, attack, and conquer.

Assignment 5. Write a brief paragraph in the style of Jordan's fifth paragraph, one that bounces back and forth from one side to the other, from negative ideas to positive ones.

Comment. An essay of contrast can be ordered in several ways, as noted in the introduction to this chapter. Britt uses a point-by-point order to sequence her major areas—sense of humor, logic, happiness, personality.

Assignment 6. Develop a writing plan that establishes the order for your comparative, persuasive essay. Will a sequence of point-by-point work for you? Or do you need process analysis, past-to-present, central subject focus, or some other order?

Comment. Britt keeps her essay in balance by avoiding subtopics or gray areas; her subjects are either skinny people or heavy people. She doesn't cloud the issue by introducing those persons whose weight is normal. She pushes her readers into one camp or the other.

Assignment 7. Doublecheck the focus of your essay. Do you cloud the issue by bringing in exceptions? Should you? Exceptions will mute the effect of your push-pull debate by introducing a third, perhaps moderate, alternative.

Comment. A negative-positive sequence is a valuable technique for this type of essay. Britt says something negative about thin people and follows with a positive about fat people. Note that she always ends with the positive.

Assignment 8. Write your complete draft of a comparative, persuasive paper. Look for sequences and techniques that will strengthen the contrast of your subjects. Provide plenty of descriptive examples and perhaps include a narrative episode or two. As always, edit the draft extensively and proofread the finished manuscript carefully.

Shortly after World War I, Ernest Hemingway served in Europe as a foreign correspondent for the Toronto Star Weekly. Drawing on his personal experiences, and perhaps his own loneliness for home, in this piece he describes a young couple that spends a rather dreary Christmas away from family, friends, and the familiar trappings of Christmas in America.

This short narrative makes an implicit comparison. Hemingway knows very well that readers will form their own images of Christmas in America, so he focuses most of the descriptive details on Paris during the Christmas season. He does not use point-by-point contrast. Rather, he describes the beauty of Paris with its falling snow, the Seine, and Notre Dame, but he also suggests that Paris is "very lonely at Christmas time."

As a creative artist Hemingway chooses to speak mainly through the voices of his characters. Accordingly, the dialogue between the young man and woman carries the story. Their conversation slowly but surely advances toward Hemingway's thesis in the final sentence: "You do not know what Christmas is until you lose it in some foreign land."

As you read this piece, mark some of the rich phrases that distinguish Hemingway's style, such as "buses rumble like green juggernauts" or "softly curtaining snow." Make marginal notes to mark the three divisions of the essay, from the descriptive setting of the opening, to the dialogue of the body, and the street scene in the closing.

"Christmas in Paris" is reprinted from By-Line: Ernest Hemingway (1967), edited by William White.

ERNEST HEMINGWAY

Christmas in Paris

Paris with the snow falling. Paris with the big charcoal braziers outside the cafés, glowing red. At the café tables, men huddled, their coat collars turned up, while they finger glasses of *grog Americain* and the newsboys shout the evening papers. 1

The buses rumble like green juggernauts through the snow that sifts down in the dusk. White house walls rise through the dusky snow. Snow is never more beautiful than in the city. It is wonderful in Paris to stand on a bridge across the Seine looking up through the softly curtaining snow past the grey bulk of Louvre, up the river spanned by many bridges and bordered by the grey houses of old Paris to where Notre Dame squats in the dusk. 2

It is very beautiful in Paris and very lonely at Christmas time.   3

The young man and his girl walk up the Rue Bonaparte from the   4
Quai in the shadow of the tall houses to the brightly lighted little Rue
Jacob. In a little second floor restaurant, The Veritable Restaurant of the
Third Republic, which has two rooms, four tiny tables and a cat, there
is a special Christmas dinner being served.

"It isn't much like Christmas," said the girl.   5

"I miss the cranberries," said the young man.   6

They attack the special Christmas dinner. The turkey is cut into a   7
peculiar sort of geometrical formation that seems to include a small
taste of meat, a great deal of gristle, and a large piece of bone.

"Do you remember turkey at home?" asks the young girl.   8

"Don't talk about it," says the boy.   9

They attack the potatoes which are fried with too much grease.   10

"What do you suppose they're doing at home?" says the girl.   11

"I don't know," said the boy. "Do you suppose we'll ever get home?"   12

"I don't know," the girl answered. "Do you suppose we'll ever be   13
successful artists?"

The proprietor entered with the dessert and a small bottle of   14
red wine.

"I had forgotten the wine," he said in French.   15

The girl began to cry.   16

"I didn't know Paris was like this," she said. "I thought it was gay and   17
full of light and beautiful."

The boy put his arm around her. At least that was one thing you   18
could do in a Parisian restaurant.

"Never mind, honey," he said. "We've been here only three days.   19
Paris will be different. Just you wait."

They ate the dessert, and neither one mentioned the fact that it was   20
slightly burned. Then they paid the bill and walked downstairs and out
into the street. The snow was still falling. And they walked out into the
streets of old Paris that had known the prowling of wolves and the
hunting of men and the tall old houses that had looked down on it all
and were stark and unmoved by Christmas.

The boy and the girl were homesick. It was their first Christmas   21
away from their own land. You do not know what Christmas is until you
lose it in some foreign land.

AIMS AND STRATEGIES OF THE WRITER

Comment. An imaginative writer like Hemingway wants to create
scenes with specific imagery, characterization, and dialogue. In this

case he expresses a thesis—that Christmas abroad is lonely and dreary—and he enhances the piece with a brief episode in the lives of two Americans.

Assignment 1. Consider topics for a paper in the Hemingway pattern: roommates who remain at school during the Thanksgiving holiday period, two boys playing hooky from school but talking constantly about their classmates. The primary setting must establish a comparison/contrast with a secondary setting.

Comment. Hemingway intends to tell a story that will reinforce his statements that Paris is lonely at Christmas time. In between the expressions of his thesis, which appears both early and late in the piece, he sandwiches a single incident of life, a young couple having Christmas dinner at a little second-floor restaurant.

Assignment 2. Develop an essay that will be enlivened by a single episode of life. Keep in mind that a single incident is powerful enough to carry your message. Don't force it into a complex plot; let one episode represent the whole.

Comment. The use of comparison, whether implied or expressed, requires a reason. Hemingway expresses his reason in both paragraph 3 and the final paragraph.

Assignment 3. Would Hemingway's message remain clear without those expressed statements? Should you express your reasons for developing a comparison, or can you remain silent and let the reader discover it? The words and actions of your characters can reveal basic ideas.

THE WRITING PROCESS

Comment. Hemingway builds his setting to assure readers of a realistic time and place.

Assignment 4. Examine Hemingway's piece for descriptive paragraphs that establish where and who, the time and weather, the sounds and scenes. Note the descriptive elements of Hemingway's opening. Look again to your own draft and, if appropriate, write a descriptive opening for your paper to establish a setting.

Comment. Dialogue stands out as one technique that good writers nurture and develop. Hemingway masters terse, quick phrasing in the alternating dialogue of two people. One critic called it "inspired baby talk" that few other writers can duplicate.

Assignment 5. Study Hemingway's handling of dialogue. Note how he shifts quickly from man to woman and back again, and each comment provokes a response to develop a natural rhythm. Try writing a block of dialogue for your essay. (Each person's statement should be enclosed within quotation marks, and a new paragraph should begin for each speaker.) Try the dialogue on a classmate. Read parts as a drama. Is it effective? Does it make its point? Is it realistic without being boring?

Comment. Narration usually requires a chronological sequence of events. The characters act, react, and build the story by their actions. In Hemingway's story, however, there is little action. The characters eat dinner, the girl cries, and they walk from the restaurant into the streets of old Paris.

Assignment 6. Consider using a narrative sequence in your essay. Create one significant event that will motivate a response by one or more characters. For example, a woman out of town on Valentine's Day might phone her boyfriend only to discover that he is not at home. That phone call might be the nucleus around which to build your essay.

Comment. Many writers enjoy using special images or symbols. For example, Hemingway uses the snow in a special way. Like the loneliness of the young couple, the snow remains unrelenting and continuous, covering everything with white.

Assignment 7. Can you isolate a special image for your story, perhaps a ringing telephone or a wilted rose on a doorstep? If so, try to use it in more than one place of the story, especially in the opening or closing.

LuEllyn Boyer has written a short expressive paper comparing the past, when she grew up in the shadow of her sister, with the present, in which she can explore her own psychological adjustment over the years and write about it. A secondary comparison of LuEllyn with her sister dominates the background of the piece. In two short pages LuEllyn covers fifteen years of her life. She recalls her childhood when she needed a role model, and she describes her maturity as an independent young woman.

To develop this essay about herself, Boyer opens in the present with a narrative anecdote, uses flashback to recreate her feelings of childish devotion to an older sister, and then returns to the present. Along the way, she embellishes the pattern of comparison with a blending of description, narration, and example.

During your reading of Boyer's essay, make marginal notes to record her various patterns of development. Also mark the three sections of the essay and note briefly the role of each section in the development of the thesis.

LU ELLYN BOYER, STUDENT

Her Shadow

One of my favorite pastimes is to talk to small children, with their honesty and sweet, innocent actions. Today, as I was taking a moment to speak to one of these delightful creatures, I caught myself asking a question I used to dread: "What are you going to be when you grow up?" My mind was jarred all the way back to my childhood, and I can clearly remember my reply to this question. It wasn't the typical and general answer that is most commonly given by children, such as a nurse or a teacher, but my constant reply was, "Just like Carolyn!" . . . Carolyn is my one and only big sister, eight years older than I. She was the apple of my eye, and I wanted to be just like her some day. When people would hear my future occupational choice, they would all join in a harmonious chorus of, "Isn't that cute?" But I got the clear impression that nobody believed my quest, so I set out to fulfill it in spite of these confounded "grown-ups."

My questful journey began at the early age of five. I used to walk behind my sister and do everything that she did, sometimes being mistaken for her shadow. I would sit unusually contented and listen to her play endless scales and compositions on our old black upright piano. I remember how people would say, "She can sure make that

1

2

171

piano talk!" Now this was beyond all my comprehensions, just being five years old, and I decided I was going to make this piano talk also. I would wait until she was finished, and then I would sit on the old black varnished bench, with my toes dangling far above the peddles, plunking out whatever I heard her play. By the age of six, I became quite good at playing by ear, but Carolyn was so wrapped up in her first boyfriend that she didn't even notice me anymore. I never understood why I couldn't go to the movies with them or even sit in between them on the front porch swing. . . . I kept following her around constantly, everywhere . . . and then Carolyn called me "Tag" and "Copycat." What did I do wrong? Mama dried my tears and explained to me how Carolyn was growing up and how I would have to leave her alone sometimes. This separation was especially hard for me, and the piano became my best friend. A year or two later, a sweet, old neighbor of ours came by for an afternoon chat, and as I completed my very own rendition of a Beethoven composition, she clapped her hands and said, "Why, you really *are* going to be like Carolyn some day." I ran crying from the room. I wanted to be *me*, not Carolyn! I had to recreate my future, this time making a name for myself. I refused to take piano lessons and voice lessons and instead taught myself how to make the piano talk and sing. By the age of thirteen I had started writing songs and was no longer referred to as "Carolyn's little sister."

Now I'm "grown up," and at the age of twenty and many songs later, 3 I still find myself fighting the "little sister" title, but I find that I don't mind as much now; it's almost refreshing to hear these words. I'm proud to be Carolyn's little sister, and I realize that it truly was her life, her example, her influence that helped me become what I am today. I smile and thank God for my big sister.

I used to walk behind my sister—now I walk beside her instead.   4

LU ELLYN BOYER TALKS ABOUT HER AIMS AND STRATEGIES

The writing assignment, to write reflectively about an important influence on my life, forced me to reach back and reevaluate my love/envy relationship with my older sister, Carolyn. Note that I label it as "love/ envy," not "love/hate." Carolyn is dear to me. I love her beyond words, but her awesome talent engulfed me in my childhood. I wanted to be so much like Carolyn that I couldn't be myself.

After my first draft, my instructor gave me good news and bad news. He said that I had a good personal narration, but I did not have an essay as such. I needed to reach out to the audience with universal values, explore the problem for my readers, and not merely write a private memoir. Consequently, I focused on my learning experience by comparing my childish fantasies with present-day realities. Rather than merely telling about Carolyn, I expanded the opening and added a two-paragraph conclusion to make my point that everybody needs to grow up.

Comment. Boyer uses comparison for a reason—to inform the reader about a personal learning experience, one that has universal value. In effect, the expressive aim of discourse balances with a past-to-present order.

Assignment 1. Write a few notes about childhood fantasies that have been altered by your present-day knowledge. The Santa Claus myth may come readily to mind, but search out other concerns, perhaps differences in your childhood views and your contemporary views of honesty, the work ethic, marriage vows, or heroes.

Comment. Boyer uses an effective opening, an anecdote about her visit with children.

Assignment 2. If you choose to develop an essay in the manner of Boyer's paper, you might develop a short opening episode that can capture the reader's attention and also set your thesis in motion.

Comment. Boyer explains in her comments above that her first draft failed in its universal appeal. She merely wrote about her jealous competition with Carolyn without considering her reader's desire for meaning and significance of the adventure.

Assignment 3. Study your own episode for universal values. Have other people in all likelihood shared an experience similar to yours? If so, build on that concept in order to draw the reader into the essay. Your past experiences are also your readers' past experiences, so your handling of these events can be informative and even inspirational to others.

 # Analogy

Analogy uses comparison to clarify a concept, function, or theory. A teacher, for example, might explain the lens of a camera by comparing it with the human eye. Analogy abandons the balanced components used in comparison, focuses on an unfamiliar or complex subject, and explains it by its similarity to something well known or easily understood. Consider this example:

> A tree is an underground creature with its tail in the air. All its intelligence is in its roots. All the senses it has are in its roots. Think what sagacity it shows in its search after food and drink! Somehow or other, the rootlets, which are its tentacles, find out that there is a brook at a moderate distance from the trunk of the tree, and they make for it with all their might. They find every crack in the rocks where there are a few grains of the nourishing substance they care for, and insinuate themselves into its deepest recesses. When spring and summer come, they let their tails grow, and delight in whisking them about in the wind, or letting them be whisked about by it; for these tails are poor passive things, with very little will of their own, and bend in whatever direction the wind chooses to make them. The leaves make a deal of noise whispering. I have sometimes thought I could understand them, as they talk with each other, and that they seemed to think they made the wind as they wagged forward and back. Remember what I say. The next time you see a tree waving in the wind, recollect that it is the tail of a great underground, many-armed polypus-like creature, which is as proud of its caudal appendage, especially in the summertime, as a peacock of his gorgeous expanse of plumage.
>
> —*Oliver Wendell Holmes,* Over the Teacups

This analogy between a tree and an animal is direct and clear. Holmes's purpose is to emphasize the underground root system as the most important part of a tree.

175

DISTINGUISH ANALOGY FROM METAPHOR

A metaphor is a very concise figurative comparison that appeals briefly to the reader's imagination. An analogy is a long figurative comparison, usually a paragraph or more in length, that is used for an explanatory or persuasive purpose. Analogy appeals to reason and understanding. For example, if you throw a rock into a pond and cry out with delight, "Look, I made circus rings in the water!" you have created a *metaphor* by comparing circus rings and water rings. In contrast, *analogy* develops slowly and fully, explaining that the ripples created in the water are like a radio station sending radio waves through the air. Then the analogous features—transmission, wave movement, reception, and so forth—can be developed to demonstrate the comparison more fully.

A PATTERN OF ANALOGY WILL CLARIFY BUT NOT PROVE

Although analogy adds richness to your writing, its primary purpose is to illustrate and clarify. A simple analogy is like a series of examples—interesting, illustrative, but not conclusive. To say that your enrollment in college is like a legal contract is an interesting comparison, but it's doubtful you could sustain the analogy. In similar fashion, Holmes's tree/animal analogy does not *prove* that a tree's trunk and branches are minor appendages, but it does educate and delight us with its comparison.

Because it explains how one thing is like another, analogy can imply that the two are similar in many ways. Reasonable people know, however, that analogy enlightens but does not authenticate, corroborate, or substantiate. Therefore, arguing from analogy is generally discouraged, yet later in this chapter Dick Gregory and Tom Wolfe use analogy to enforce their persuasive themes.

AVOID FALSE AND OVERUSED ANALOGY

You might compare a disease like cancer with a swarm of termites attacking a house, or compare life to a game, or nature to a mother. However, it is best to avoid such obvious analogies, so timeworn as to be offensive to the reader. A few trite analogies are: life is a game, nature is a gentle mother, life is a prison, a bridge is the passageway to life, a fork in the road is a moment of decision. In the very near future the analogy of computers to the human brain will be worn by usage and, accordingly, the better writers avoid it.

ORDER YOUR ANALOGY ESSAY BY A LOGICAL SEQUENCE

Use one of the following approaches for maintaining a sequence in the paper:

A central-subject focus, with analogous elements added as descriptive elements

A two-subject focus, which develops one topic in full and then discusses its similarities to another

A point-by-point approach, which provides in sequence the analogous features

A process-order approach, which compares a series of stages or timed events

A past-to-present or present-to-future approach, which spreads the analogy over a two-part time period

(See Chapter 4 for a discussion of these methods.)

To review: Your essay developed by the pattern of analogy will require

1. An extended figurative comparison
2. An interest in illustrating a point, not in proving an argument
3. A fresh, new comparison that avoids worn, trite analogies
4. A logical sequence that keeps the focus on key elements of the comparison

Virginia Woolf (1882–1941), the daughter of the scholar Sir Leslie Stephen, was born in London. Although she suffered a mental breakdown in 1916, she recovered to write such novels as Mrs. Dalloway *(1925) and* To the Lighthouse *(1927). Interested in psychology and mental processes, she attempted to reveal the inner essence of her characters.*

The following passage by Virginia Woolf describes a fluttering moth captured inside a windowpane. The moth represents all who live and die, especially mortals like all of us. Woolf says, "Watching him, it seemed as if a fiber, very thin but pure, of the enormous energy of the world had been thrust into his frail and diminutive body." Throughout the essay she extends her comparison of the moth to the energy of all living things. Yet the moth grows weak, flutters, and finally dies. Thus Woolf uses the frantic efforts of "a tiny bead of pure life" to serve as an analogy of human existence. Her analogy also reveals her own feelings, as she responds subjectively to the vibrant energy of life set in opposition to the great mystery of death.

As you read the essay, note passages that compare the moth and its flurry of activities to human endeavors.

"The Death of a Moth" is reprinted from Woolf's The Death of the Moth and Other Essays *(1942).*

VIRGINIA WOOLF

🔲 The Death of the Moth

Moths that fly by day are not properly to be called moths; they do not   1
excite that pleasant sense of dark autumn nights and ivy-blossom which
the commonest yellow underwing asleep in the shadow of the curtain
never fails to rouse in us. They are hybrid creatures, neither gay like
butterflies nor sombre like their own species. Nevertheless the present
specimen, with his narrow hay-colored wings, fringed with a tassel of
the same color, seemed to be content with life. It was a pleasant morning, mid-September, mild, benignant, yet with a keener breath than that
of the summer months. The plough was already scoring the field opposite the window, and where the share had been, the earth was
pressed flat and gleamed with moisture. Such vigor came rolling in
from the fields and the down beyond that it was difficult to keep the
eyes strictly turned upon the book. The rooks too were keeping one of
their annual festivities; soaring round the treetops until it looked as if a
vast net with thousands of black knots in it has been cast up into the air;

which, after a few moments sank slowly down upon the trees until every twig seemed to have a knot at the end of it. Then, suddenly, the net would be thrown into the air again in a wider circle this time, with the utmost clamor and vociferation, as though to be thrown into the air and settle slowly down upon the treetops were a tremendously exciting experience.

The same energy which inspired the rooks, the ploughmen, the 2 horses, and even, it seemed, the lean bare-backed downs, sent the moth fluttering from side to side of his square of the windowpane. One could not help watching him. One was, indeed, conscious of a queer feeling of pity for him. The possibilities of pleasure seemed that morning so enormous and so various that to have only a moth's part in life, and a day moth's at that, appeared a hard fate, and his zest in enjoying his meager opportunities to the full, pathetic. He flew vigorously to one corner of his compartment, and, after waiting there a second, flew across to the other. What remained for him but to fly to a third corner and then to a fourth? That was all he could do, in spite of the size of the downs, the width of the sky, the far-off smoke of houses, and the romantic voice, now and then, of a steamer out at sea. What he could do he did. Watching him, it seemed as if a fiber, very thin but pure, of the enormous energy of the world had been thrust into his frail and diminutive body. As often as he crossed the pane, I could fancy that a thread of vital light became visible. He was little or nothing but life.

Yet, because he was so small, and so simple a form of the energy 3 that was rolling in at the open window and driving its way through so many narrow and intricate corridors in my own brain and in those of other human beings, there was something marvelous as well as pathetic about him. It was as if someone had taken a tiny bead of pure life and decking it as lightly as possible with down and feathers, had set it dancing and zigzagging to show us the true nature of life. Thus displayed one could not get over the strangeness of it. One is apt to forget all about life, seeing it humped and bossed and garnished and cumbered so that it has to move with the greatest circumspection and dignity. Again, the thought of all that life might have been had he been born in any other shape caused one to view his simple activities with a kind of pity.

After a time, tired by his dancing apparently, he settled on the win- 4 dow ledge in the sun, and the queer spectacle being at an end, I forgot about him. Then, looking up, my eye was caught by him. He was trying to resume his dancing, but seemed either so stiff or so awkward that he could only flutter to the bottom of the windowpane; and when he tried to fly across it he failed. Being intent on other matters I watched these futile attempts for a time without thinking, unconsciously waiting for him to resume his flight, as one waits for a machine, that has stopped momentarily, to start again without considering the reason for its failure. After perhaps a seventh attempt he slipped from the wooden ledge and fell, fluttering his wings, on to his back on the windowsill. The helplessness of his attitude roused me. It flashed upon me that he was in difficulties; he could no longer raise himself; his legs struggled vainly. But, as I stretched out a pencil, meaning to help him to right himself, it came over me that the failure and awkwardness were the approach of death. I laid the pencil down again.

The legs agitated themselves once more. I looked as if for the enemy 5
against which he struggled. I looked out of doors. What had happened there? Presumably it was midday, and work in the fields had stopped. Stillness and quiet had replaced the previous animation. The birds had taken themselves off to feed in the brooks. The horses stood still. Yet the power was there all the same, massed outside indifferent, impersonal, not attending to anything in particular. Somehow it was opposed to the little hay-colored moth. It was useless to try to do anything. One could only watch the extraordinary efforts made by those tiny legs against an oncoming doom which could, had it chosen, have submerged an entire city, not merely a city, but masses of human beings; nothing, I knew, had any chance against death. Nevertheless after a pause of exhaustion the legs fluttered again. It was superb this last protest, and so frantic that he succeeded at last in righting himself. One's sympathies, of course, were all on the side of life. Also, when there was nobody to care or to know, this gigantic effort on the part of an insignificant little moth, against a power of such magnitude, to retain what no one else valued or desired to keep, moved one strangely. Again, somehow, one saw life, a pure bead. I lifted the pencil again, useless though I knew it to be. But even as I did so, the unmistakable tokens of death showed themselves. The body relaxed, and instantly grew stiff. The struggle was over. The insignificant little creature now knew death. As I looked at the dead moth, this minute wayside triumph of so great a force over so mean an antagonist filled me with wonder. Just as life had been strange a few minutes before, so death was now as strange. The moth having righted himself now lay most decently and uncomplainingly composed. O yes, he seemed to say, death is stronger than I am.

AIMS AND STRATEGIES OF THE WRITER

Comment. A reflective essay like Woolf's will show a writer who pauses briefly in the hurly-burly pace of life, meditates quietly on the forces that affect humans, and shares those fleeting thoughts. The attitude is quiet and compassionate, for reflection recalls the pain as well as the joy of living. Woolf demonstrates this reflective mood. The fact that she later committed suicide as a release from periods of insanity adds a poignant dimension to this essay.

Assignment 1. Search for a topic for which you can use analogy. Start by meditating reflectively about your past. What was your mother like? A fragile china dish? A fortress of strength? A mysterious river flowing quietly but with underlying strength? And your house: Was it a sanctuary and safe harbor? A crowded ship tossing on tumultuous waves?

Comment. Woolf has no intention of describing the moth in scientific terms. Nor does she define death. Her aim is to portray for us the life force. "It was as if someone had taken a tiny bead of pure life and decking it as lightly as possible with down and feathers, had set it dancing and zigzagging to show us the true nature of life."

Assignment 2. Make notes for an essay that uses an analogy. You might start with a general idea—such as isolation, insanity, creation, beauty, or suicide—and compare these complex items with something familiar, such as a rose, a book, or a mountain stream. Put the analogy into a brief statement: Silence is like death; self-imposed isolation is like suicide; the earth is like a fragile egg.

Comment. Woolf takes a well-known fact, that death is stronger than any of us, and portrays it with "a pure bead" of life, the moth. She touches on elements that extend the comparison through several paragraphs.

Assignment 3. Make a list of similarities between your main subject and the one used for analogy. Note everything that comes to mind, group the items, and eliminate unwarranted comparisons.

Comment. Woolf uses analogy to clarify a difficult concept. The tiny moth, pitted against a mighty enemy, provides a lesson in energy and determination. Woolf probably considered life superior to death, yet the battle appears unfair and unequal in favor of the powers of darkness.

Assignment 4. Develop a brief writing situation that explains the purpose of your analogy, your role as speaker, your main subject, the analogous subject, and how you plan to extend the comparison throughout the essay.

THE WRITING PROCESS

Comment. Woolf uses a minor analogy in her description of the rooks in the first paragraph.

Assignment 5. Explain Woolf's rook analogy and how this analogy contributes to the essay as a whole.

Comment. In paragraph 3 Woolf uses a metaphor of the moth as a dancer. The energy of the moth's dance relates to the frantic movements of the rooks.

Assignment 6. Write a paragraph that builds the dance metaphor into a full-blown analogy showing how dance and dancer are like the life force.

Comment. Woolf does not use the first-person voice until the end of the second paragraph, saying "I could fancy that a thread of vital light became visible." Thereafter she participates with personal feelings.

Assignment 7. Consider again the voice needed for your essay. Should you employ subjective description and enter the essay with the first-person voice? If so, write passages that uncover your own thinking as well as describe a physical scene. Should you remain objective? If so, write with a focus on the subject, not yourself, to keep your emotions and personal voice removed from the essay.

Comment. Woolf uses more than analogy as a pattern of development. She *describes* the fragile down and feathers of the moth. She *narrates* the story of its death. *Examples* throughout help to detail the energy of the moth. Her *comparison* between the moth and the rooks implies the connection between the moth and all living things.

Assignment 8. You will probably need a blend of patterns for your analogy essay. Examine your plans and build paragraphs, as appropriate, using the following patterns: *description, narration, example, comparison/contrast.*

The next two essays develop analogies between the human brain and the computer. Isaac Asimov draws parallels between the two to advance futuristic and controversial conclusions. He suggests that we may be unable to create a computer as complex as the human brain, but he adds that we can probably build a computer that is complex enough to design another computer. The computers themselves could then create more complex computers until, on their own, they would surpass the human brain.

In contrast, Lewis Thomas in "Why Can't Computers Be More Like Us?" approaches the same analogy differently, suggesting that "mistakes are at the very base of human thought," so computers should be programmed, like humans, with the potential for error.

Isaac Asimov is a noted scientific writer who was born in Russia but came to the United States at three years of age. He has served as professor of biochemistry at Boston University and has written numerous scholarly texts, such as Chemistry and Human Health *and* Understanding Physics. *Yet he is also a writer of science fiction books, with such titles as* Lucky Starr and the Pirates of the Asteroids. *"The Difference Between a Brain and a Computer" is from his book* Please Explain *(1973).*

Lewis Thomas is a medical doctor who serves as chancellor of the Memorial Sloan-Kettering Cancer Center in New York. He began writing essays for the New England Journal of Medicine. *His columns display his talent for writing about a diverse set of topics. "Why Can't Computers Be More Like Us?" is from* The Saturday Evening Post *(1976).*

As you read and compare the two essays, list the various analogous features of the brain and computer as advanced by these two scientists. You might wish to add some comparisons of your own. The purpose? To discover that analogy draws many parallels, not just one or two.

ISAAC ASIMOV

 ## The Difference between a Brain and a Computer

The difference between a brain and a computer can be expressed in a single word: complexity.

The large mammalian brain is the most complicated thing, for its size, known to us. The human brain weighs three pounds, but in that three pounds are ten billion neurons and a hundred billion smaller cells. These many billions of cells are interconnected in a vastly complicated network that we can't begin to unravel as yet.

Even the most complicated computer man has yet built can't com- 3
pare in intricacy with the brain. Computer switches and components
number in the thousands rather than in the billions. What's more, the
computer switch is just an on-off device, whereas the brain cell is itself
possessed of a tremendously complex inner structure.

Can a computer think? That depends on what you mean by "think." 4
If solving a mathematical problem is "thinking," then a computer can
"think" and do so much faster than a man. Of course, most mathematical problems can be solved quite mechanically by repeating certain
straightforward processes over and over again. Even the simple computers of today can be geared for that.

It is frequently said that computers solve problems only because 5
they are "programmed" to do so. They can only do what men have them
do. One must remember that human beings also can only do what they
are "programmed" to do. Our genes "program" us the instant the
fertilized ovum is formed, and our potentialities are limited by that
"program."

Our "program" is so much more enormously complex, though, that 6
we might like to define "thinking" in terms of the creativity that goes
into writing a great play or composing a great symphony, in conceiving
a brilliant scientific theory or a profound ethical judgment. In that sense,
computers certainly can't think and neither can most humans.

Surely, though, if a computer can be made complex enough, it can 7
be as creative as we. If it could be made as complex as a human brain,
it could be the equivalent of a human brain and do whatever a human
brain can do.

To suppose anything else is to suppose that there is more to the 8
human brain than the matter that composes it. The brain is made up of
cells in a certain arrangement and the cells are made up of atoms and
molecules in certain arrangements. If anything else is there, no signs of
it have ever been detected. To duplicate the material complexity of the
brain is therefore to duplicate everything about it.

But how long will it take to build a computer complex enough to 9
duplicate the human brain? Perhaps not as long as some think. Long
before we approach a computer as complex as our brain, we will
perhaps build a computer that is at least complex enough to design
another computer more complex than itself. This more complex
computer could design one still more complex and so on and so on
and so on.

In other words, once we pass a certain critical point, the computers 10
take over and there is a "complexity explosion." In a very short time
thereafter, computers may exist that not only duplicate the human
brain—but far surpass it.

Then what? Well mankind is not doing a very good job of running 11
the earth right now. Maybe, when the time comes, we ought to step
gracefully aside and hand over the job to someone who can do it better.
And if we don't step aside, perhaps Supercomputer will simply move
in and push us aside.

LEWIS THOMAS

Why Can't Computers Be More Like Us?

Everyone must have had at least one personal experience with a com- 1
puter error by this time. Bank balances are suddenly reported to have
jumped from 379 dollars into the millions, appeals for charitable con-
tributions are mailed over and over to people with crazy-sounding
names at your address, utility companies write that they're turning
everything off—that sort of thing. If you manage to get in touch with
someone and complain, you then get instantaneously typed, guilty letters from the same computer, saying, "Our computer was in error, and
an adjustment is being made in your account."

These are supposed to be the sheerest, blindest accidents. Mistakes 2
are not believed to be part of the normal behavior of a good machine.
If things go wrong, it must be a personal, human error, the result of
fingering, tampering, a button getting stuck. The computer, at its normal best, is infallible.

I wonder whether this can be true. After all, the whole point of 3
computers is that they represent an extension of the human brain, vastly
improved upon but nonetheless human, superhuman maybe. A good
computer can think clearly and quickly enough to beat you at chess,
and some of them have even been programmed to write obscure verse.
They can do anything we can do, and more besides.

It is not yet known whether a computer has its own consciousness, 4
and it would be hard to find out about this. When you walk into one of
those great halls now built for the huge machines, and stand listening,
it is easy to imagine that the faint, distant noises are the sound of
thinking, and the turning of the spools gives them the look of wild
creatures rolling their eyes in the effort to concentrate, choking with
information. But real thinking, and dreaming, are other matters.

On the other hand, the evidences of something like an *unconscious*, 5
equivalent to ours, are all around, in every mail. As extensions of the
human brain, they have been constructed with the same property of
error, spontaneous, uncontrolled, and rich in possibilities.

Mistakes are at the very base of human thought, embedded there,   6
feeding the structure like root nodules. If we were not provided with
the knack of being wrong, we could never get anything useful done.
We think our way along by choosing between right and wrong alternatives, and the wrong choices have to be made as frequently as the right
ones. We get along in life this way. We are built to make mistakes, coded
for error.

We learn, as we say, by "trial and error." Why do we always say that?   7
Why not "trial and rightness," or "trial and triumph"? The old phrase
puts it that way because that is, in real life, the way it is done.

A good laboratory, like a good bank, or a corporation or a govern-   8
ment, has to run like a computer. Almost everything is done flawlessly,
by the book, and all the numbers add up to the predicted sums. The
days go by. And then, if it is a lucky day, and a lucky laboratory, somebody makes a mistake: the wrong buffer, something in one of the
blanks, a decimal misplaced in reading counts, the warm room off by a
degree and a half, a mouse out of his box, or just a misreading of the
day's protocol. Whatever, when the results come in, something is obviously screwed up, and then the action can begin.

The misreading is not the important error; it opens the way. The   9
next step is the crucial one. If the investigator can bring himself to say,
"But even so, look at that!" the new finding, whatever it is, is ready for
snatching. What is needed, for progress to be made, is the move based
on the error.

Whenever new kinds of thinking are about to be accomplished, or   10
new varieties of music, there has to be an argument beforehand. With
two sides debating in the same mind, haranguing, there is an amiable
understanding that one is right and the other wrong. Sooner or later
the thing is settled, but there can be no action at all if there are not the
two sides, and the argument. The hope is in the faculty of wrongness,
the tendency toward error. The capacity to leap across mountains of
information to land lightly on the wrong side represents the highest of
human endowments.

We are at our human finest, dancing with our minds, when there   11
are more choices than two. This process is called exploration and is
based on human fallibility. If we had only a single center in our brains,
capable of responding only when a correct decision was to be made,
instead of the jumble of different, credulous, easily conned clusters of
neurons that provide for being flung off into blind alleys, up wrong
trees, down dead ends, out into blue sky, along wrong turnings, around
bends, we could only stay the way we are today, stuck fast.

The lower animals do not have this splendid freedom. They are   12
limited, most of them, to absolute infallibility. Fish are flawless in every-

thing they do. Individual cells in a tissue are mindless machines, perfect in their performance, as absolutely inhuman as bees.

We should have this in mind as we become dependent on more   13
complex computers for the arrangement of our affairs. Give the computers their heads, I say; let them go their way. Your average good computer can make calculations in an instant that would take a lifetime of slide rules for any of us. Think of what we could gain from the near infinity of precise, machine-made miscomputation that is now so easily within grasp. We could begin the solving of some of our hardest problems. What we need for moving ahead is a set of wrong alternatives much longer and more interesting than the short list of mistaken courses that any of us can think up right now. We need, in fact, an infinite list, and when it is printed out we need the computer to turn on itself and select, at random, the next way to go. If it is a big enough mistake, we could find ourselves on a new level, out in the clear, ready to move again.

AIMS AND STRATEGIES OF THE WRITERS

Comment. Asimov promotes the computer as potentially superior to the human brain, but Thomas would program computers like humans—with the potential for mistakes.

Assignment 1. Draft a paper that compares the theories advanced by Thomas and Asimov. At this point you need not choose one theory over another, for you may find them compatible in various ways.

Comment. We know that Asimov writes serious scientific works as well as science fiction. We also know that Thomas is a medical doctor.

Assignment 2. Write paragraphs (1) to evaluate Asimov's determination to examine and question present versus future developments in computer science, and (2) to explore Thomas's recognition that a bold move based on error or miscalculation helps advance human civilization.

Comment. Both writers examine a relatively new science. Such exploratory writing differs from simple explanation because it asks more questions and explores the options. Exploratory writers look for answers but do not always find them. Consequently, they do not presume to know the correct answers. They raise the problem, explore it, and leave the reader to reason about it.

Assignment 3. Draft a dialectical essay, one that explores connections between divergent ideas while searching for valid answers. The essay will have a built-in analogy. You can develop your own topic, or you can choose to explore

Sports violence in terms of childhood temper tantrums

Fraternity parties in comparison with Dionysian rituals of ancient Greece

Chemical technology as a poison to the environment

THE WRITING PROCESS

Comment. By its very nature, exploratory discourse provokes questions, both in prewriting stages and in the finished essay. Asimov asks more questions than Thomas.

Assignment 4. Examine the question/answer technique of Asimov. What questions frame his discourse? Does he answer each one? Make notes for a question/answer sequence for your paper.

Comment. Both writers employ analogy and use it to extoll the virtues of computers as well as of the human brain. In their own ways, they both say that computers can serve the needs of humanity.

Assignment 5. Write a brief paragraph that explains the use of analogy of Asimov's essay in contrast with that of Thomas's essay. Include an answer to this question: Does either writer prove his point?

Comment. Analogy, in general, requires a point-by-point order for sequencing the items of comparison. If you have kept reading notes, look again at your list of analogous features in the two essays.

Assignment 6. Make an outline or list that will show the sequence of comparisons for your paper.

Comment. Both Thomas and Asimov depend on the present-to-future pattern to structure their essays. Asimov suggests a supercomputer of the future, and Thomas suggests an infinite list of alternatives that might someday be programmed into the computer.

Assignment 7. Begin writing your essay, as begun in assignment 3. Choose an effective order. Point-by-point might work best if you wish to prove that chemical technology acts as a poison to the environment, but the past-to-present pattern would serve for a paper on fraternity parties; a process analysis might prove best for the sports violence topic.

Dick Gregory *is a political activist, so expect from him a persuasive appeal, one that tugs at your emotions and intellect. He makes a pitch for each of his three favorite causes—a literal reading of the Bible, vegetarianism, and social justice for his fellow blacks and other minorities. In particular, he uses vegetarianism as his vehicle of analogy, pointing out that people who eat a steak without recognizing the painful slaughter of the animal are like the rich upper classes who profit from but are protected from the horrors of ghetto life.*

Gregory has long been a man of convictions, enduring civil rights violence, suffering through long periods of fasting for special causes, and responding verbally at political forums across the nation. Yet he has a sense of humor; he started in show business as a stand-up comic in small nightclubs.

As you read his essay, carefully note the repetition of his comparison. Where does he argue from analogy? Does he extend his analogy to levels he cannot prove? Does this really matter? Explore your answers to these questions.

This essay is reprinted from Gregory's book The Shadow That Scares Me *(1971), which expresses his views on American life-styles and political foibles. He received the presidential nomination in 1968 from the Peace and Freedom Party. Some of his other books are* Nigger *(1964),* Dick Gregory's Political Primer *(1971),* Dick Gregory's Natural Diet for Folks Who Eat *(1973),* Up from Nigger *(1976), and* Code Name Zorro *(1977).*

DICK GREGORY

If You Had to Kill Your Own Hog

My momma could never understand how white folks could twist the words of the Bible around to justify racial segregation. Yet she could read the Ten Commandments, which clearly say, "Thou shalt not kill," and still justify eating meat. Momma couldn't read the newspaper very well, but she sure could interpret the Word of God. "God meant you shouldn't kill people," she used to say. But I insisted, "Momma, He didn't say that. He said, 'Thou shalt not kill.' If you leave that statement alone, a whole lot of things would be safe from killing. But if you are going to twist the words about killing to mean what you want them to mean, then let white folks do the same thing with justifying racial segregation."

"You can't live without eating meat," Momma would persist. "You'd   2
starve." I couldn't buy that either. You get milk from a cow without
killing it. You do not have to kill an animal to get what you need from
it. You get wool from the sheep without killing it. Two of the strongest
animals in the jungle are vegetarians—the elephant and the gorilla.
The first two years are the most important years of a man's life, and
during that period he is not involved with eating meat. If you suddenly
become very ill, there is a good chance you will be taken off a meat
diet. So it is a myth that killing is necessary for survival. The day I decide
that I must have a piece of steak to nourish my body, I will also give the
cow the same right to nourish herself on human beings.

There is so little basic difference between animals and humans. The   3
process of reproduction is the same for chickens, cattle, and humans.
If suddenly the air stopped circulating on the earth, or the sun collided
with the earth, animals and humans would die alike. A nuclear holocaust will wipe out all life. Life in the created order is basically the same
and should be respected as such. It seems to me the Bible says it is
wrong to kill—period.

If we can justify *any* kind of killing in the name of religion, the door   4
is opened for all kinds of other justifications. The fact of killing animals
is not as frightening as our human tendency to justify it—to kill and not
even be aware that we are taking life. It is sobering to realize that when
you misuse one of the least of Nature's creatures, like the chicken, you
are sowing the seed for misusing the highest of Nature's creatures, man.

Animals and humans suffer and die alike. If you had to kill your own   5
hog before you ate it, most likely you would not be able to do it. To
hear the hog scream, to see the blood spill, to see the baby being taken
away from its momma, and to see the look of death in the animal's eye
would turn your stomach. So you get the man at the packing house to
do the killing for you. In like manner, if the wealthy aristocrats who are
perpetrating conditions in the ghetto actually heard the screams of
ghetto suffering, or saw the slow death of hungry little kids, or witnessed the strangulation of manhood and dignity, they could not continue the killing. But the wealthy are protected from such horror. They
have people to do the killing for them. The wealthy profit from the daily
murders of ghetto life but they do not see them. Those who immerse
themselves in the daily life of the ghetto see the suffering—the social
workers, the police, the local merchants, and the bill collectors. But the
people on top never really see.

By the time you see a piece of meat in the butcher shop window, all   6
the blood and suffering have been washed away. When you order a
steak in a restaurant, the misery has been forgotten and you see the
finished product. You see a steak with butter and parsley on it. It looks

appetizing and appealing and you are pleased enough to eat it. You never even consider the suffering which produced your meal or the other animals killed that day in the slaughterhouse. In the same way, all the wealthy aristocrats ever see of the black community is the finished product, the window dressing, the steak on the platter—Ralph Bunche and Thurgood Marshall.[1] The United Nations or the Supreme Court bench is the restaurant and the ghetto street corner is the slaughterhouse.

Life under ghetto conditions cuts short life expectancy. The Negro's   7
life expectancy is shorter than the white man's. The oppressor benefits from continued oppression financially; he makes more money so that he can eat a little better. I see no difference between a man killing a chicken and a man killing a human being, by overwork and forcing ghetto conditions upon him, both so that he can eat a little better. If you can justify killing to eat meat, you can justify the conditions of the ghetto. I cannot justify either one.

Every time the white folks made my momma mad, she would grab   8
the Bible and find something bitter in it. She would come home from the rich white folks' house, after they had just called her "nigger" or patted her on the rump or caught her stealing some steaks, open her Bible and read aloud, "It is easier for a camel to pass through the eye of a needle than for a rich man to get into Heaven." When you get involved with distorting the words of the Bible, you don't have to be bitter. The same tongue can be used to bless and curse men.

AIMS AND STRATEGIES OF THE WRITER

Comment. Dick Gregory feels strongly about vegetarianism, about literal readings of scripture, and about social injustice. He speaks out with conviction on these issues.

Assignment 1. List a few topics that you feel strongly about. Every writer must speak from personal emotions. Possible topics might include birth control, seat-belt laws, unethical advertising, political gamesmanship, or exploitation of sex by advertisers.

Comment. Gregory hammers home his point. If you justify killing one thing, you can justify other killings. If you kill a hog yourself, you won't be able to eat it. If wealthy landlords go to the ghetto and see the pain

[1]Bunche (1904–1971) was a black diplomat and undersecretary of the United Nations who was awarded the Nobel Peace Prize in 1950; Marshall is the first black to be appointed to the Supreme Court.—ED.

of the poor, they will understand the stark reality of their source of monetary gain.

Assignment 2. Search out analogies for your topics to see if one works well. Compare your subject to something your reader will understand. You could argue, for instance, that rules of the game govern most political activities, even on campus. Or that the star wars program is just a bigger *gun*. Or that seat-belt laws and speed limits represent an *invisible net* for governmental control. Your comparative thinking should result in ideas that you can transcribe into notes and preliminary paragraphs.

Comment. Persuasive essays like Gregory's require confident and impassioned attitudes. Seldom does an aggressive, angry voice serve a serious writer, because it alienates the audience. Gregory's anger is controlled and therefore he uses it effectively.

Assignment 3. Determine how aggressive you need to be in writing and defending your position. Do you feel strongly enough about the subject to speak with the passion that comes from deep commitment and personal involvement? After you determine this need, develop it with emotional appeals. Then, for balance, check that you have sufficient knowledge of the issue to speak with bold confidence and factual details. If not, research the topic to build support for your position.

THE WRITING PROCESS

Comment. Gregory uses numerous comparisons in his essay: Suffering in the ghettos is window dressed and removed from the view of the rich, just as the suffering of a steer, who provides a good steak, is hidden from diners. Gregory says there's little difference between killing a chicken and killing a human being.

Assignment 4. Explain Gregory's fundamental analogy. First, what is his primary subject? Is it social injustice, vegetarianism, or biblical interpretation? Second, with what is the primary subject compared?

Comment. Gregory opens the essay with images of his mother and closes with additional descriptions of her. However, she is not his primary subject. She adds a personal touch to the essay that mutes the hard-driving persuasion. Thus the main issues are sandwiched between moments of fond irritation with "Momma."

Assignment 5. A circular pattern might serve your writing. That is, use a personal experience to open and later to close your serious essay. You could, for example, provide a brief personal anecdote, then examine sex education for grade school students, and then finish with another personal reminiscence.

Comment. Gregory's persuasive appeal is addressed to a general audience. He addresses the audience as "you," which seems to include all those who require a message about social injustice.

Assignment 6. Identify your audience: Are you addressing a general audience or a specific group? Next develop your writing situation; for example, "I want to address those athletes who use steroids. I'll warn them with this analogy: Their actions are like those of any greedy person who seeks immediate gratification with little regard for long-term consequences."

Comment. Gregory demonstrates the basic ingredients for a persuasive essay. He advances a *proposition* about social injustice. He *assumes* that men everywhere want justice and freedom. He speaks with the *credibility* of one who knows social injustice. He provides explicit examples for *evidence*. And he uses appeals to *reason, ethics,* and *emotion*.

Assignment 7. Begin writing your persuasive essay that features analogy. Your writing process should control the elements mentioned above: a proposition that is based on reasonable assumptions, a voice of credibility as developed by research or personal experience, specific evidence, and an appeal to your reader's sense of justice and honorable behavior.

T*om Wolfe gained recognition in the 1960s and 1970s for his New Journalism style, a style that reports general news as though it were a short story or novel. He creates a persona, a speaker who gets inside the story and participates with an active voice, that affects long lists, nonsense words, interjections, dashes, dots, italics, and various sorts of typographic gymnastics. He adds plenty of dialogue and paints descriptive scenes. Yet the fundamental key to his writing remains his sense of journalism and his desire to report facts of the feature article. He does it his way, imaginatively, like a good story, not just news.*

This essay employs an analogy that compares human behavior in New York City with the frenzy that overtakes animals who become overcrowded in a maze. As he puts it, "sheer overcrowding is converting New Yorkers into animals in a sink pen." So after a fiction-like description of scurrying New Yorkers, he gets down to reporting the nature of a "behavioral sink" among a group of Norway rats confined within a four-part maze, much as New Yorkers are confined to narrow spaces in Manhattan.

On one level Wolfe reports social behavior and scientific findings. On another level he creates a story with actors, dialogue, description, and a plot—or at least a semiplot—in which some rats gain power, private space, and harems but other rats sink, slide downward into the muck of the middle, fall into degenerate behavior, get zapped into homosexuality . . . die.

As you read, note features of New Yorkers that Wolfe ignores. That is, people in a crowded city may sometimes act like animals, but they also are humans with social and cultural qualities.

"O Rotten Gotham—Sliding Down into the Behavioral Sink" is an excerpt from his book The Pump House Gang *(1968).*

TOM WOLFE

O Rotten Gotham—Sliding Down into the Behavioral Sink

I just spent two days with Edward T. Hall, an anthropologist, watching 1
thousands of my fellow New Yorkers short-circuiting themselves into
hot little twitching death balls with jolts of their own adrenalin. Dr. Hall
says it is overcrowding that does it. Overcrowding gets the adrenalin
going, and the adrenalin gets them queer, autistic, sadistic, barren, batty,
sloppy, hot-in-the-pants, chancred-on-the-flankers, leering, puling,

numb—the usual in New York, in other words, and God knows what else. Dr. Hall has the theory that overcrowding has already thrown New York into a state of behavioral sink. Behavioral sink is a term from ethology, which is the study of how animals relate to their environment. Among animals, the sink winds up with a "population collapse" or "massive die-off." O rotten Gotham.

It got to be easy to look at New Yorkers as animals, especially look- 2 ing down from some place like a balcony at Grand Central at the rush hour Friday afternoon. The floor was filled with the poor white hu-mans, running around, dodging, blinking their eyes, making a sound like a pen full of starlings or rats or something.

"Listen to them skid," says Dr. Hall. 3

He was right. The poor old etiolate animals were out there skidding 4 on their rubber soles. You could hear it once he pointed it out. They stop short to keep from hitting somebody or because they are disori-ented and they suddenly stop and look around, and they skid on their rubber-soled shoes, and a screech goes up. They pour out onto the floor down the escalators from the Pan-Am Building, from 42nd Street, from Lexington Avenue, up out of subways, down into subways, railroad trains, up into helicopters—

"You can also hear the helicopters all the way down here," says Dr. 5 Hall. The sound of the helicopters using the roof of the Pan-Am Building nearly fifty stories up beats right through. "If it weren't for this ceil-ing"—he is referring to the very high ceiling in Grand Central— "this place would be unbearable with this kind of crowding. And yet they'll probably never 'waste' space like this again."

They screech! And the adrenal glands in all those poor white ani- 6 mals enlarge, micrometer by micrometer, to the size of cantaloupes. Dr. Hall pulls a Minox camera out of a holster he has on his belt and starts shooting away at the human scurry. The Sink!

Dr. Hall has the Minox up to his eye—he is a slender man, calm, 7 fifty-two years old, young-looking, an anthropologist who has worked with Navajos, Hopis, Spanish-Americans, Negroes, Trukese. He was the most important anthropologist in the government during the crucial years of the foreign aid program, the 1950s. He directed both the Point Four training program and the Human Relations Area Files. He wrote *The Silent Language* and *The Hidden Dimension*, two books that are picking up the kind of "underground" following his friend Marshall McLuhan started picking up about five years ago. He teaches at the Illinois Institute of Technology, lives with his wife, Mildred, in a high-ceilinged town house on one of the last great residential streets in downtown Chicago, Astor Street; he has a grown son and daughter, loves good food, good wine, the relaxed, civilized life—but comes to New York with a Minox at his eye to record!—perfect—The Sink.

We really got down in there by walking down into the Lexington   8
Avenue line subway stop under Grand Central. We inhaled those nice big fluffy fumes of human sweat, urine, effluvia, and sebaceous secretions. One old female human was already stroked out on the upper level, on a stretcher, with two policemen standing by. They other humans barely looked at her. They rushed into line. They bellied each other, haunch to paunch, down the stairs. Human heads shone through the gratings. The species North European tried to create bubbles of space around themselves, about a foot and a half in diameter—

"See, he's reacting against the line," says Dr. Hall.   9

—but the species Mediterranean presses on in. The hell with bub-   10
bles of space. The species North European resents that, this male human behind him presses forward toward the booth ... *breathing* on him, he's disgusted, he pulls out of the line entirely, the species Mediterranean resents him for resenting it, and neither of them realizes what the hell they are getting irritable about exactly. And in all of them the old adrenals grow another micrometer.

Dr. Hall whips out the Minox. Too perfect! The bottom of The Sink.   11

It is the sheer overcrowding, such as occurs in the business sections   12
of Manhattan five days a week and in Harlem, Bedford-Stuyvesant, southeast Bronx every day—sheer overcrowding is converting New Yorkers into animals in a sink pen. Dr. Hall's argument runs as follows: all animals, including birds, seem to have a built-in inherited requirement to have a certain amount of territory, space, to lead their lives in. Even if they have all the food they need, and there are no predatory animals threatening them, they cannot tolerate crowding beyond a certain point. No more than two hundred wild Norway rats can survive on a quarter acre of ground, for example, even when they are given all the food they can eat. They just die off.

But why? To find out, ethologists have run experiments on all sorts   13
of animals, from stickleback crabs to Sika deer. In one major experiment, an ethologist named John Calhoun put some domesticated white Norway rats in a pen with four sections to it, connected by ramps. Calhoun knew from previous experiments that the rats tend to split up into groups of ten to twelve and that the pen, therefore, would hold forty to forty-eight rats comfortably, assuming they formed four equal groups. He allowed them to reproduce until there were eighty rats, balanced between male and female, but did not let it get any more crowded. He kept them supplied with plenty of food, water, and nesting materials. In other words, all their more obvious needs were taken care of. A less obvious need—space—was not. To the human eye, the pen

did not even look especially crowded. But to the rats, it was crowded beyond endurance.

The entire colony was soon plunged into a profound behavioral sink. "The sink," said Calhoun, "is the outcome of any behavioral process that collects animals together in unusually great numbers. The unhealthy connotations of the term are not accidental: a behavioral sink does act to aggravate all forms of pathology that can be found within a group." 14

For a start, long before the rat population reached eighty, a status hierarchy had developed in the pen. Two dominant male rats took over the two end sections, acquired harems of eight to ten females each, and forced the rest of the rats into the two middle pens. All the overcrowding took place in the middle pens. That was where the "sink" hit. The aristocrat rats at the end grew bigger, sleeker, healthier, and more secure the whole time. 15

In The Sink, meanwhile, nest building, courting, sex behavior, reproduction, social organization, health—all of it went to pieces. Normally, Norway rats have a mating ritual in which the male chases the female, the female ducks down into a burrow and sticks her head up to watch the male. He performs a little dance outside the burrow, then she comes out, and he mounts her, usually for a few seconds. When The Sink set in, however, no more than three males—the dominant males in the middle sections—kept up the old customs. The rest tried everything from satyrism to homosexuality or else gave up on sex altogether. Some of the subordinate males spent all their time chasing females. Three or four might chase one female at the same time, and instead of stopping at the burrow entrance for the ritual, they would charge right in. Once mounted, they would hold on for minutes instead of the usual seconds. 16

Homosexuality rose sharply. So did bisexuality. Some males would mount anything—males, females, babies, senescent rats, anything. Still other males dropped sexual activity altogether, wouldn't fight and, in fact, would hardly move except when the other rats slept. Occasionally a female from the aristocrat rats' harems would come over the ramps and into the middle sections to sample life in The Sink. When she had had enough, she would run back up the ramp. Sink males would give chase up to the top of the ramp, which is to say, to the very edge of the aristocratic preserve. But one glance from one of the king rats would stop them cold and they would return to The Sink. 17

The slumming females from the harems had their adventures and then returned to a placid, healthy life. Females in The Sink, however, were ravaged, physically and psychologically. Pregnant rats had trouble continuing pregnancy. The rate of miscarriages increased significantly, 18

198   *Analogy*

and females started dying from tumors and other disorders of the mammary glands, sex organs, uterus, ovaries, and Fallopian tubes. Typically, their kidneys, livers, and adrenals were also enlarged or diseased or showed other signs associated with stress.

Child-rearing became totally disorganized. The females lost the interest or the stamina to build nests and did not keep them up if they did build them. In the general filth and confusion, they would not put themselves out to save offspring they were momentarily separated from. Frantic, even sadistic competition among the males was going on all around them and rendering their lives chaotic. The males began unprovoked and senseless assaults upon one another, often in the form of tail-biting. Ordinarily, rats will suppress this kind of behavior when it crops up. In The Sink, male rats gave up all policing and just looked out for themselves. The "pecking order" among males in The Sink was never stable. Normally, male rats set up a three-class structure. Under the pressure of overcrowding, however, they broke up into all sorts of unstable subclasses, cliques, packs—and constantly pushed, probed, explored, tested one another's power. Anyone was fair game, except for the aristocrats in the end pens.

Calhoun kept the population down to eighty, so that the next stage, "population collapse" or "massive die-off," did not occur. But the autopsies showed that the pattern—as in the diseases among the female rats—was already there.

The classic study of die-off was John J. Christian's study of Sika deer on James Island in the Chesapeake Bay, west of Cambridge, Maryland. Four or five of the deer had been released on the island, which was 280 acres and uninhabited, in 1916. By 1955 they had bred freely into a herd of 280 to 300. The population density was only about one deer per acre at this point, but Christian knew that this was already too high for the Sikas' inborn space requirements, and something would give before long. For two years the number of deer remained 280 to 300. But suddenly, in 1958, over half the deer died; 161 carcasses were recovered. In 1959 more deer died and the population steadied at about 80.

In two years, two-thirds of the herd had died. Why? It was not starvation. In fact, all the deer collected were in excellent condition, with well-developed muscles, shining coats, and fat deposits between the muscles. In practically all the deer, however, the adrenal glands had enlarged by 50 percent. Christian concluded that the die-off was due to "shock following severe metabolic disturbance, probably as a result of prolonged adrenocortical hyperactivity.... There was no evidence of infection, starvation, or other obvious cause to explain the mass mortality." In other words, the constant stress of overpopulation, plus the normal stress of the cold of the winter, had kept the adrenalin flowing so constantly in the deer that their systems were depleted of blood sugar and they died of shock.

Well, the white humans are still skidding and darting across the floor of Grand Central. Dr. Hall listens a moment longer to the skidding and the darting noises, and then says, "You know, I've been on commuter trains here after everyone has been through one of these rushes, and I'll tell you, there is enough acid flowing in the stomachs in every car to dissolve the rails underneath." 23

Just a little invisible acid bath for the linings to round off the day. The ulcers the acids cause, of course, are the one disease people have already been taught to associate with the stress of city life. But overcrowding, as Dr. Hall sees it, raises a lot more hell with the body than just ulcers. In everyday life in New York—just the usual, getting to work, working in massively congested areas like 42nd Street between Fifth Avenue and Lexington, especially now that the Pan-Am Building is set in there, working in cubicles such as those in the editorial offices at Time-Life, Inc., which Dr. Hall cites as typical of New York's poor handling of space, working in cubicles with low ceilings and, often, no access to a window, while construction crews all over Manhattan drive everybody up the Masonite wall with air-pressure generators with noises up to the boil-a-brain decibel level, then rushing to get home, piling into subways and trains, fighting for time and for space, the usual day in New York—the whole now-normal thing keeps shooting jolts of adrenalin into the body, breaking down the body's defenses and winding up with the work-a-daddy human animal stroked out at the breakfast table with his head apoplexed like a cauliflower out of his $6.95 semi-spread Pima-cotton shirt, and nosed over into a plate of No-Kloresto egg substitute, signing off with the black thrombosis, cancer, kidney, liver, or stomach failure, and the adrenals ooze to a halt, the size of eggplants in July. 24

One of the people whose work Dr. Hall is interested in on this score is Rene Dubos at the Rockefeller Institute. Dubos's work indicates that specific organisms, such as the tuberculosis bacillus or a pneumonia virus, can seldom be considered "the cause" of a disease. The germ or virus, apparently, has to work in combination with other things that have already broken the body down in some way—such as the old adrenal hyperactivity. Dr. Hall would like to see some autopsy studies made to record the size of adrenal glands in New York, especially of people crowded into slums and people who go through the full rush-hour-work-rush-hour cycle every day. He is afraid that until there is some clinical, statistical data on how overcrowding actually ravages the human body, no one will be willing to do anything about it. Even in so 25 obvious a thing as air pollution, the pattern is familiar. Until people can actually see the smoke or smell the sulphur or feel the sting in their eyes, politicians will not get excited about it, even though it is well known that many of the lethal substances polluting the air are invisible and odorless. For one thing, most politicians are like the aristocrat rats. They are insulated from The Sink by practically sultanic buffers—limousines, chauffeurs, secretaries, aides-de-camp, doormen, shuttered houses, high-floor apartments. They almost never ride subways, fight rush hours, much less live in the slums or work in the Pan-Am Building.

AIMS AND STRATEGIES OF THE WRITER

Comment. Wolfe is a social critic as well as a journalist. He looks around, seizes on foolish behavior by one group of people or another, then exposes it with his special blend of humor, irony, exaggeration, linguistic gymnastics, and satire. He ridicules his fellow man for petty, foolish behavior, but he does so with love and affection, not rancor, bitterness, or sarcasm.

Assignment 1. List subjects that might lend themselves to satiric treatment; that is, humorously ridicule some kind of social activity, such as the clustering of small groups in the student center, drivers who fail to use turn signals, the behavior of fans before a big game.

Comment. Wolfe has a serious purpose: He wants to report that overcrowding affects human behavior and personal health. He raises this issue: Increases of adrenalin in humans cause nervous breakdowns and premature death.

Assignment 2. Narrow your topic selection from assignment 1 to a single subject worthy of attention. What serious matter can you raise, for example, about people who refuse to use their turn signals? Look at both positive and negative issues and then exaggerate the negatives for effect. Remember, the purpose of satire is not sarcasm that merely attacks; satire should educate, offer insights, and enlighten the reader. Refer to your reading notes in which you were asked to balance positive features of humans against Wolfe's negative exaggerations. This sense of balance is the reconciliation Wolfe wants, not a gullible acceptance of his analogy that humans, when crowded, become animals.

Comment. Wolfe writes with a free-wheeling style that sometimes baffles but always delights readers. Note his second sentence: "Overcrowding gets the adrenalin going, and the adrenalin gets them queer, autistic, sadistic, barren, batty, sloppy, hot-in-the-pants, chancred-on-the-flankers, leering, puling, numb—the usual in New York, in other words, and God knows what else." Speaking about his style, Wolfe comments,

> I had the feeling, rightly or wrongly, that I was doing things no one had ever done before in journalism. I used to try to imagine the feeling readers must have had upon finding all this carrying on and cutting up in a Sunday supplement. I like that idea. . . . Only through the most searching forms of reporting was it possible, in nonfiction, to use whole scenes, extended dialogue, point-of-view, and interior monologue. Eventually I, and others, would be accused of "entering people's minds" . . . But exactly! I figured that was one more doorbell a reporter had to push.*

Assignment 3. Basing your ideas on Wolfe's preceding comment and on his essay, write a brief description of this new literary genre that Wolfe initiated, known now as New Journalism. In particular, how does his form differ from a traditional news story?

THE WRITING PROCESS

Comment. Like other writers in this chapter, Wolfe uses analogy as a fundamental technique. His primary subject is overcrowding, especially its effects on people in New York. He compares their behavior to Dr. Hall's Norway rats, which, when overcrowded, became physically and psychologically ravaged.

Assignment 4. Use an analogy as a key ingredient for your satiric essay. For instance, you could compare insensitive drivers (who fail to use turn signals) with children who refuse to obey their parents. Can you build an analogy between courtship and gamesmanship?

Comment. In addition to writing news stories as fiction, Wolfe also affects certain stylistic mannerisms: a lavish use of dots, dashes, exclamation marks, italics, unusual words, nonsense words, and strange typography. Yet he controls his medium. For instance, the word "puling" in sentence 2 looks at first to be a misspelling for "pulling," but "puling" is correct, meaning "crying in a high thin voice."

Assignment 5. Trace through the essay and list Wolfe's writing mannerisms that catch your eye. What makes them unusual? What is their effect on you as a reader? What do they contribute to the essay as a whole? What effect is gained by words such as "autistic," "etiolate," or "sebaceous"?

*Tom Wolfe, *The New Journalism* (New York: Harper & Row, 1973) 20.

Comment. Wolfe has a personal involvement in the essay. He refers in the opening sentence to "my fellow New Yorkers."

Assignment 6.   Consider your voice and role in your essay. Should you enter the piece and speak in the first-person "I"? If so, you will join the reader as participant in the human folly that you satirize. With a third-person voice, on the other hand, you will appear distant and authoritarian.

Comment. Wolfe uses a minor analogy with his story of the Sika deer, further reinforcing his thesis. Obviously, Wolfe's process has included careful research. However, arguing from analogy does not prove anything.

Assignment 7.   Begin writing your satiric essay, using analogy to reinforce your ideas and to create an effect. Don't use analogy as proof. Like Wolfe, you might want to employ the circular pattern by beginning with your subject, shifting into analogy, and returning at the end to your subject.

Bernice Cook writes from her perspective on racial relations. As a black woman, she faces discrimination in general, but as a black woman dating and planning to marry a white man, she confronts outright hostility at various times and in many places. Therefore, she writes from a deep personal commitment, and she uses the pattern of analogy to clarify not just her emotions but also the nonbiased nature of love.

The fundamental analogy of her essay, love is color blind, uses personification with ironic implications. Personification normally gives human characteristics to nonhuman items. While some humans can be physically color blind, most persons, she says, are not blind to color in mixed relationships.

As you read the essay, note how Cook expands her figurative comparison across the breadth of the essay. In addition, make marginal notes to record her point-by-point sequence of ideas. Mark the arguments that she advances to defend her thesis that love is color blind.

BERNICE COOK, STUDENT

Love Is Color Blind

What color is love? Black, white, yellow? It has no color, at least in my   1
opinion. I asked an admitted racist that question. His answer was a long
pause, dropped jaw, and the typical expression of one who hates because of race. He didn't answer me.

The racist does not believe in interracial relationships. Larry King,   2
in *Confessions of a White Racist*, states, "Inside my white boy's craw I
was resentful, fearful, perhaps a little sickened . . . not for some time
would the sight of a black man with his white woman fail to stir some
deeply rooted old deposit of poisons in my soul."

I have neither heard nor read any logical reasons why love must be   3
based on race and the color of one's skin. Certainly Larry King has
failed to supply the logic.

Harold, my fiancé, happens to be white. Neither of us is to blame   4
for that. We did not have a hand in planning our races, so we don't give
it much attention. Obviously, King is less discomforted by white men
with their black women, so we're fairly safe, and since love has no color,
no one will notice. (Hurumph!)

When love happens there is no red light to pop up, "Stop—Off   5
Limits"; instead the light reads, "All Systems Go!" For us, it was too good

to give up, so we started an elaborate campaign to take it to the limit. We loved through our eyes and touch, our voices and smiles. It was fantastic. I wonder, which of us is black?

So we mutually agreed that any problems with our racial difference   6 belonged to the racist. We have the advantage; we understand "them," and we won't allow "them" to hamper our relationship.

The most ridiculous characteristic of people who are preoccupied   7 with insignificant things is loneliness and unfulfillment in their own lives. They appear everywhere, in restaurants, movie houses, dinner parties, grocery stores. They want to stare and point at others rather than enjoy their own lives.

Happy people will not share precious time with racial ugliness.   8 "Make love, not hate" are the words carved into a plain piece of wood in my apartment. Being compatible racially offers no guarantees for bliss. All of us women take chances when we invite a man into our arms. Nevertheless, racial differences can cause problems between the partners only when the importance of the differences outweighs the love.

While adversity weakens some interracial couples; it strengthens   9 us. We developed tough skins over the year, so by the time we met we were ready for something "real." The color of the package was irrelevant.

Coincidence was the culprit of our meeting. Coordination is our joy,   10 for two cultures and two backgrounds provide the best of both. We do not advocate interracial relationships; we *do* advocate happiness. This one works for us, and if it works why fix it? Besides, what color would we paint it?

BERNICE COOK TALKS ABOUT HER AIMS AND STRATEGIES

Mainly, I needed a positive, upbeat approach to this somewhat touchy subject. I had been too emotional in my original version, reacting not only to King's book but also to a group of bigots at a restaurant who were obviously miserable in their marriages and wanted to make Harold and me uncomfortable in our partnership. So I threw out the first draft and approached the subject honestly, as I truly felt, not as a knee-jerk reaction to others. After I listed the benefits of a racially mixed relationship, I saw that only one fact mattered—our love for one another. The blending of two cultures and two backgrounds is just an added plus.

Comment. Cook takes a metaphor, some might say it's a cliché. She does something special with it, however, by expanding it into an analogy and using it as the organizing principle for her essay.

Assignment 1. List possible topics for your analogy paper. You should work with subjects that touch you emotionally, such as Cook does. For example, one group of students focused on the football stadium in order to see it in various ways. A football player built his description around the analogy of Roman gladiators. A band member, whirling and dodging trombones and tubas, called it "a jungle out there." A hell-raising fraternity member saw it all as one giant saloon with dancing girls and plenty of booze. A person's perspective can motivate or provoke the idea for an analogy.

Comment. Cook maintains her analogy throughout the essay, and her final sentence gives the idea reinforcement.

Assignment 2. Consider the circular or echo pattern for your essay. That is, open with the analogy, develop your major issues and ideas, and return to the analogy at the end of the essay.

Comment. Cook does not attempt to argue from analogy, but she does want readers to see beyond color differences to matters of more importance. Her topic, aim, sense of audience, and pattern all merge for effective communication.

Assignment 3. Like Cook, you must consider a proper mix of these four ingredients. You may need a first draft that you can revise. Or you may start by jotting down your writing situation (see pages 4–5 for details and examples). In every case, justify your topic and your approach to it. After all, the fraternity member who sees the stadium as just another saloon must carefully identify his audience and his aim, otherwise he will come across as juvenile or insensitive.

CHAPTER SIX

Classification and Analysis

Classification means arranging the subject into separate categories, sections, or groups. Analysis examines one thing in depth, subdividing it as necessary to look at parts and issues. In the following brief example, Bertrand Russell discusses three different passions that governed his life and examines each one in depth.

Three passions, simple but overwhelmingly strong, have governed my life: the longing for love, the search for knowledge, and unbearable pity for the suffering of mankind. These passions, like great winds, have blown me hither and thither, in a wayward course, over a deep ocean of anguish, reaching to the very verge of despair.

I have sought love, first, because it brings ecstasy—ecstasy so great that I would often have sacrificed all the rest of life for a few hours of this joy. I have sought it, next, because it relieves loneliness—that terrible loneliness in which one shivering consciousness looks over the rim of the world into the cold unfathomable lifeless abyss. I have sought it, finally, because in the union of love I have seen, in a mystic miniature, the prefiguring vision of the heaven that saints and poets have imagined. This is what I sought, and though it might seem too good for human life, this is what—at last—I have found.

With equal passion I have sought knowledge. I have wished to understand the hearts of men. I have wished to know why the stars shine. And I have tried to apprehend the Pythagorean power by which number holds sway above the flux. A little of this, but not much, I have achieved.

Love and knowledge, so far as they were possible, led upward toward the heavens. But always pity brought me back to earth. Echoes of cries of pain reverberate in my heart. Children in famine, victims tortured by oppressors, helpless old people a hated burden to their sons, and the whole world of loneliness, poverty, and pain make a mockery of what human life should be. I long to alleviate the evil, but I cannot, and I too suffer.

This has been my life. I have found it worth living, and would gladly live it again if the chance were offered me.*

*Bertrand Russell, *The Autobiography of Bertrand Russell* (London: Allen & Unwin, 1968) 3–4.

Russell's basic categories provide an organizing principle for his essay. He does not divide love or knowledge or pity into subclasses, but he does relate them to his personal experiences.

USE CLASSIFICATION TO ESTABLISH MAJOR CATEGORIES OF THE TOPIC

Arrange your general subject into a sequence of balanced items. For instance, you might choose a couple of items for a two-part arrangement of knowledge and wisdom, love and *agape*, or pain and gain. Such arrangements generally become comparison/contrast discussions (see Chapter 4). Or you might select three or more categories, as with an examination of youth, middle age, and old age.

USE ANALYSIS TO EXAMINE EACH CATEGORY IN DEPTH

Subdivide each major category to provide all relevant details. For example, you might classify youth into three parts—infancy, preteen, and teen years. Your analysis could then examine part by part the stages of development for physical and mental growth, with a special look at speech development. When you carry such an examination of parts to the finite details through several subdivisions, you will have made an analysis of the subject.

USE LOGICAL DIVISION FOR ANALYSIS AND DEFINITION

Analysis, like definition, answers the question: What is the essence of this subject? By classifying the subject into broad categories and dividing each category into fundamental parts, you achieve understanding by analytical reasoning. The goal of analysis is explanation, definition, and interpretation of the subject. The naming of parts helps you accomplish this task.

OBSERVE TWO RULES FOR FORMAL ANALYSIS

First, the division must be complete. Second, the division must follow one consistent principle of classification. You can't write about automobiles of America, Germany, Japan, and the subcompacts. The fourth item breaks the consistency. Likewise, you can't limit the discussion, without a disclaimer, to automobiles of three countries, especially since Yugoslavia and Korea have entered the marketplace, not to mention Italy, Sweden, and France.

USE INFORMAL ANALYSIS FOR EXPRESSIVE EXPLORATION OF A SUBJECT

As the name implies, informal analysis relaxes the rules and does not examine all classes or study all divisions. For example, a sociologist's formal analysis of child abuse in one city must cover every claim with enormous amounts of data. However, your personal, informal essay on the subject could focus on a narrow issue, such as spanking as a discipline measure and severe spanking as an abuse to the child. However, this informal analysis requires consistency and completeness within the narrow boundaries of your classification.

ORDER THE ESSAY BY MAJOR CLASSIFICATIONS

Some writers number their major divisions. Thomas Boswell numbers from one to eight his rules for watching a baseball game (pages 268–270). Other writers categorize the stages of personal involvement, as shown in Russell's three passions of life in the example that opened this chapter. Other writers reduce a problem to manageable categories for a problem-solving discussion, as shown by L. S. Stavrianos (pages 233–235), who examines the myths that cause apprehension about the future. Such problem-solving essays require separation of relevant materials from the irrelevant, the important from the unimportant, and the timely from the obsolete. Use process analysis for classifying and dividing your materials by progression. Arrange items step-by-step, event-to-event, item-to-item, or part-to-part, with all items building toward a whole. (See Chapter 7 for a detailed discussion of process analysis.) Finally, scientific order arranges by class, genus, species, and so forth. You will encounter this type of classification and division in your various scientific textbooks.

To review: Build essays with the pattern of classification by conforming to the following general guidelines:

1. Use classification to isolate major issues, categories, or types.

2. Use a naming of parts for in-depth analysis of each major class and its important subdivisions.

3. Use informal analysis that focuses on a narrow issue, rather than formal analysis that will demand complete and wholly consistent principles of classification.

Helen Keller, a small, somewhat frail child, lost both her sight and hearing when she was only nineteen months old. She lived from 1880 to 1968, and in her lifetime she became a symbol of those who conquer physical handicaps, for she learned to speak, to write on a typewriter, to listen by touching another's lips and larynx, and to live a full life. She worked ceaselessly to improve conditions for the blind and handicapped.

In her essay "Three Days to See" Keller writes expressively about the things she would crowd into three days of sight. She presents her personal preferences, moreover, as guidelines for her audience, for she encourages her readers to imagine the things they would wish to see under similar circumstances. Then she reminds readers to hear, see, taste, touch, and smell with new awareness.

Keller uses a three-part structure as a technique for categorizing the major segments of her essay. She uses three days for three classifications: to see friends, art, and contemporary life. Within each classification, she subdivides the anticipated objects awaiting her limited period of sight. She thereby structures and controls the numerous details that she probably would wish to see.

As you read, make notes about your own ability to really see. That is, respond to Keller's first paragraph by imagining that this lecture is, indeed, a "compulsory course in 'How to Use Your Eyes.'"

Keller is the author of several books, including The Story of My Life *(1903),* Out of the Dark *(1913), and* Teacher *(1955). The latter book tells the story of her mentor Anne Sullivan Macy.*

HELEN KELLER

❖ Three Days to See

If I were the president of a university I should establish a compulsory 1
course in "How to Use Your Eyes." The professor would try to show his
pupils how they could add joy to their lives by really seeing what passes
unnoticed before them. He would try to awake their dormant and
sluggish faculties.

Perhaps I can best illustrate my imagining what I should most like 2
to see if I were given the use of my eyes, say, for just three days. And
while I am imagining, suppose you, too, set your mind to work on the
problem of how you would use your own eyes if you had only three
more days to see. If with the oncoming darkness of the third night you

knew that the sun would never rise for you again, how would you spend those three precious intervening days? What would you most want to let your gaze rest upon?

I, naturally, should want most to see the things which have become   3
dear to me through my years of darkness. You, too, would want to let your eyes rest long on the things that have become dear to you so that you could take the memory of them with you into the night that loomed before you.

If, by some miracle, I were granted three seeing days, to be followed   4
by a relapse into darkness, I should divide the period into three parts.

On the first day, I should want to see the people whose kindness   5
and gentleness and companionship have made my life worth living. First I should like to gaze long upon the face of my dear teacher, Mrs. Anne Sullivan Macy, who came to me when I was a child and opened the outer world to me. I should want not merely to see the outline of her face, so that I could cherish it in my memory, but to study that face and find in it the living evidence of the sympathetic tenderness and patience with which she accomplished the difficult task of my education. I should like to see in her eyes that strength of character which has enabled her to stand firm in the face of difficulties, and that compassion for all humanity which she has revealed to me so often.

I do not know what it is to see into the heart of a friend through that   6
"window of the soul," the eye. I can only "see" through my fingertips the outline of a face. I can detect laughter, sorrow, and many other obvious emotions. I know my friends from the feel of their faces. But I cannot really picture their personalities by touch. I know their personalities, of course, through other means, through the thoughts they express to me, through whatever of their actions are revealed to me. But I am denied that deeper understanding of them which I am sure would come through sight of them, through watching their reactions to various expressed thoughts and circumstances, through noting the immediate and fleeting reactions of their eyes and countenance.

Friends who are near to me I know well, because through the   7
months and years they reveal themselves to me in all their phases; but of casual friends I have only an incomplete impression, an impression gained from a handclasp, from spoken words which I take from their lips with my fingertips, or which they tap into the palm of my hand.

How much easier, how much more satisfying it is for you who can   8
see to grasp quickly the essential qualities of another person by watching the subtleties of expression, the quiver of a muscle, the flutter of a hand. But does it ever occur to you to use your sight to see into the inner nature of a friend or acquaintance? Do not most of you seeing people grasp casually the outward features of a face and let it go at that?

For instance, can you describe accurately the faces of five good   9
friends? Some of you can, but many cannot. As an experiment, I have
questioned husbands of long standing about the color of their wives'
eyes, and often they express embarrassed confusion and admit that they
do not know. And, incidentally, it is a chronic complaint of wives that
their husbands do not notice new dresses, new hats, and changes in
household arrangements.

The eyes of seeing persons soon become accustomed to the routine   10
of their surroundings, and they actually see only the startling and spectacular. But even in viewing the most spectacular sights the eyes are
lazy. Court records reveal every day how inaccurately "eyewitnesses"
see. A given event will be "seen" in several different ways by as many
witnesses. Some see more than others, but few see everything that is
within the range of their vision.

Oh, the things that I should see if I had the power of sight for just   11
three days!

The first day would be a busy one. I should call to me all my dear   12
friends and look long into their faces, imprinting upon my mind the
outward evidences of the beauty that is within them. I should let my
eyes rest, too, on the face of a baby, so that I could catch a vision of the
eager, innocent beauty which precedes the individual's consciousness
of the conflicts which life develops.

And I should like to look into the loyal, trusting eyes of my dogs—   13
the grave, canny little Scottie, Darkie, and the stalwart, understanding
Great Dane, Helga, whose warm, tender, and playful friendships are so
comforting to me.

On that busy first day I should also view the small simple things of   14
my home. I want to see the warm colors in the rugs under my feet, the
pictures on the walls, the intimate trifles that transform a house into
home. My eyes would rest respectfully on the books in raised type
which I have read, but they would be more eagerly interested in the
printed books which seeing people can read, for during the long night
of my life the books I have read and those which have been read to me
have built themselves into a great shining lighthouse, revealing to me
the deepest channels of human life and the human spirit.

In the afternoon of that first seeing day, I should take a long walk in   15
the woods and intoxicate my eyes on the beauties of the world of
Nature, trying desperately to absorb in a few hours the vast splendor
which is constantly unfolding itself to those who can see. On the way
home from my woodland jaunt my path would lie near a farm so that I
might see the patient horses plowing in the field (perhaps I should see
only a tractor!) and the serene content of men living close to the soil.
And I should pray for the glory of a colorful sunset.

When dusk had fallen, I should experience the double delight of being able to see by artificial light, which the genius of man has created to extend the power of his sight when Nature decrees darkness. 16

In the night of that first day of sight, I should not be able to sleep, so full would be my mind of the memories of the day. 17

The next day—the second day of sight—I should arise with the dawn and see the thrilling miracle by which night is transformed into day. I should behold with awe the magnificent panorama of light with which the sun awakens the sleeping earth. 18

This day I should devote to a hasty glimpse of the world, past and present. I should want to see the pageant of man's progress, the kaleidoscope of the ages. How can so much be compressed into one day? Through the museums, of course. Often I have visited the New York Museum of Natural History to touch with my hands many of the objects there exhibited, but I have longed to see with my eyes the condensed history of the earth and its inhabitants displayed there—animals and the races of men pictured in their native environment; gigantic carcasses of dinosaurs and mastodons which roamed the earth long before man appeared, with his tiny stature and powerful brain, to conquer the animal kingdom; realistic presentations of the processes of evolution in animals, in man, and in the implements which man has used to fashion for himself a secure home on this planet; and a thousand and one other aspects of natural history. 19

I wonder how many readers of this article have viewed this panorama of the face of living things as pictured in that inspiring museum. Many, of course, have not had the opportunity, but I am sure that many who *have* had the opportunity have not made use of it. There, indeed, is a place to use your eyes. You who see can spend many fruitful days there, but I, with my imaginary three days of sight, could only take a hasty glimpse, and pass on. 20

My next stop would be the Metropolitan Museum of Art, for just as the Museum of Natural History reveals the material aspects of the world, so does the Metropolitan show the myriad facets of the human spirit. Throughout the history of humanity the urge to artistic expression has been almost as powerful as the urge for food, shelter, and procreation. And here, in the vast chambers of the Metropolitan Museum, is unfolded before me the spirit of Egypt, Greece, and Rome, as expressed in their art. I know well through my hands the sculptured gods and goddesses of the ancient Nile-land. I have felt copies of Parthenon friezes, and I have sensed the rhythmic beauty of charging Athenian warriors. Apollos and Venuses and the Winged Victory of Samothrace are friends of my fingertips. The gnarled, bearded features of Homer are dear to me, for he, too, knew blindness. 21

My hands have lingered upon the living marble of Roman sculpture 22
as well as that of later generations. I have passed my hands over a plaster
cast of Michelangelo's inspiring and heroic Moses; I have sensed the
power of Rodin; I have been awed by the devoted spirit of Gothic wood
carving. These arts which can be touched have meaning for me, but
even they were meant to be seen rather than felt, and I can only guess
at the beauty which remains hidden from me. I can admire the simple
lines of a Greek vase, but its figured decorations are lost to me.

So on this, my second day of sight, I should try to probe into the 23
soul of man through his art. The things I knew through touch I should
now see. More splendid still, the whole magnificent world of painting
would be opened to me, from the Italian Primitives, with their serene
religious devotion, to the Moderns, with their feverish visions. I should
look deep into the canvases of Raphael, Leonardo da Vinci, Titian,
Rembrandt. I should want to feast my eyes upon the warm colors of
Veronese, study the mysteries of El Greco, catch a new vision of Nature
from Corot. Oh, there is so much rich meaning and beauty in the art of
the ages for you who have eyes to see!

Upon my short visit to this temple of art I should not be able to 24
review a fraction of that great world of art which is open to you. I
should be able to get only a superficial impression. Artists tell me that
for a deep and true appreciation of art one must educate the eye. One
must learn through experience to weigh the merits of line, of composition, of form and color. If I had eyes, how happily would I em-
bark upon so fascinating a study! Yet I am told that, to many of you
who have eyes to see, the world of art is a dark night, unexplored and
unilluminated.

It would be with extreme reluctance that I should leave the Metro- 25
politan Museum, which contains the key to beauty—a beauty so neglected. Seeing persons, however, do not need a Metropolitan to find
this key to beauty. The same key lies waiting in smaller museums, and
in books on the shelves of even small libraries. But naturally, in my
limited time of imaginary sight, I should choose the place where the
key unlocks the greatest treasures in the shortest time.

The evening of my second day of sight I should spend at a theater or 26
at the movies. Even now I often attend theatrical performances of all
sorts, but the action of the play must be spelled into my hand by a
companion. But how I should like to see with my own eyes the fascinating figure of Hamlet, or the gusty Falstaff amid colorful Elizabethan
trappings! How I should like to follow each movement of the graceful
Hamlet, each strut of the hearty Falstaff! And since I could see only one
play, I should be confronted by the many-horned dilemma, for there
are scores of plays I should want to see. You who have eyes can see any

you like. How many of you, I wonder, when you gaze at a play, a movie, or any spectacle, realize and give thanks for the miracle of sight which enables you to enjoy its color, grace, and movement?

I cannot enjoy the beauty of rhythmic movement except in a sphere 27 restricted to the touch of my hands. I can vision only dimly the grace of a Pavlova, although I know something of the delight of rhythm, for often I can sense the beat of music as it vibrates through the floor. I can well imagine that cadenced motion must be one of the most pleasing sights in the world. I have been able to gather something of this by tracing with my fingers the lines in sculptured marble; if this static grace can be so lovely, how much more acute must be the thrill of seeing grace in motion.

One of my dearest memories is of the time when Joseph Jefferson 28 allowed me to touch his face and hands as he went through some of the gestures and speeches of his beloved Rip Van Winkle. I was able to catch thus a meager glimpse of the world of drama, and I shall never forget the delight of that moment. But, oh, how much I must miss, and how much pleasure you seeing ones can derive from watching and hearing the interplay of speech and movement in the unfolding of a dramatic performance! If I could see only one play, I should know how to picture in my mind the action of a hundred plays which I have read or had transferred to me through the medium of the manual alphabet.

So, through the evening of my second imaginary day of sight, the 29 great figures of dramatic literature would crowd sleep from my eyes.

The following morning, I should again greet the dawn, anxious to 30 discover new delights, for I am sure that, for those who have eyes which really see, the dawn of each day must be a perpetually new revelation of beauty.

This, according to the terms of my imagined miracle, is to be my 31 third and last day of sight. I shall have no time to waste in regrets or longings; there is too much to see. The first day I devoted to my friends, animate and inanimate. The second revealed to me the history of man and Nature. Today I shall spend in the workaday world of the present, amid the haunts of men going about the business of life. And where can one find so many activities and conditions of men as in New York? So the city becomes my destination.

I start from my home in the quite little suburb of Forest Hills, Long 32 Island. Here, surrounded by green lawns, tree, and flowers, are neat little houses, happy with the voices and movements of wives and children, havens of peaceful rest for men who toil in the city. I drive across the lacy structure of steel which spans the East River, and I get a new and startling vision of the power and ingenuity of the mind of man.

Busy boats chug and scurry about the river—racy speedboats, stolid, snorting tugs. If I had long days of sight ahead, I should spend many of them watching the delightful activity upon the river.

I look ahead, and before me rise the fantastic towers of New York, a 33 city that seems to have stepped from the pages of a fairy story. What an awe-inspiring sight, these glittering spires, these vast banks of stone and steel—structures such as the gods might build for themselves! This animated picture is a part of the lives of millions of people every day. How many, I wonder, give it so much as a second glance? Very few, I fear. Their eyes are blind to this magnificent sight because it is so familiar to them.

I hurry to the top of one of those gigantic structures, the Empire 34 State Building, for there, a short time ago, I "saw" the city below through the eyes of my secretary. I am anxious to compare my fancy with reality. I am sure I should not be disappointed in the panorama spread out before me, for to me it would be a vision of another world.

Now I begin my rounds of the city. First, I stand at a busy corner, 35 merely looking at people, trying by sight of them to understand something of their lives. I see smiles, and I am happy. I see determination, and I am proud. I see suffering, and I am compassionate.

I stroll down Fifth Avenue. I throw my eyes out of focus so that I see 36 no particular object but only a seething kaleidoscope of color. I am certain that the colors of women's dresses moving in a throng must be a gorgeous spectacle of which I should never tire. But perhaps if I had sight I should be like most other women—too interested in styles and the cut of individual dresses to give much attention to the splendor of color in the mass. And I am convinced, too, that I should become an inveterate window shopper, for it must be a delight to the eye to view the myriad articles of beauty on display.

From Fifth Avenue I make a tour of the city—to Park Avenue, to the 37 slums, to factories, to parks where children play. I take a stay-at-home trip abroad by visiting the foreign quarters. Always my eyes are open wide to all the sights of both happiness and misery so that I may probe deep and add to my understanding of how people work and live. My heart is full of the images of people and things. My eye passes lightly over no single trifle; it strives to touch and hold closely each thing its gaze rests upon. Some sights are pleasant, filling the heart with happiness; but some are miserably pathetic. To these latter I do not shut my eyes, for they, too, are part of life. To close the eyes on them is to close the heart and mind.

My third day of sight is drawing to an end. Perhaps there are many 38 serious pursuits to which I should devote the few remaining hours, but

I am afraid that on the evening of that last day I should again run away to the theater, to a hilariously funny play, so that I might appreciate the overtones of comedy in the human spirit.

At midnight my temporary respite from blindness would cease, and permanent night would close in on me again. Naturally in those three short days I should not have seen all I wanted to see. Only when darkness had again descended upon me should I realize how much I had left unseen. But my mind would be so crowded with glorious memories that I should have little time for regrets. Thereafter the touch of every object would bring a glowing memory of how that object looked.   39

Perhaps this short outline of how I should spend three days of sight does not agree with the program you would set for yourself if you knew that you were about to be stricken blind. I am, however, sure that if you actually faced that fate your eyes would open to things you had never seen before, storing up memories for the long night ahead. You would use your eyes as never before. Everything you saw would become dear to you. Your eyes would touch and embrace every object that came within your range of vision. Then, at last, you would really see, and a new world of beauty would open itself before you.   40

I who am blind can give one hint to those who see—one admonition to those who would make full use of the gift of sight: Use your eyes as if tomorrow you would be stricken blind. And the same method can be applied to the other senses. Hear the music of voices, the song of a bird, the mighty strains of an orchestra, as if you would be stricken deaf tomorrow. Touch each object you want to touch as if tomorrow your tactile sense would fail. Smell the perfume of flowers, taste with relish each morsel, as if tomorrow you could never smell and taste again. Make the most of every sense; glory in all the facets of pleasure and beauty which the world reveals to you through the several means of contact which Nature provides. But of all the senses; I am sure that sight must be the most delightful.   41

AIMS AND STRATEGIES OF THE WRITER

Comment. Keller proposes a renewed awareness of life for all her readers. She would awaken our "dormant and sluggish faculties."

Assignment 1. List the activities that might need renewed appreciation in your life and in the lives of your readers. For example, look with new eyes at sports activities, television, automobiles, contemporary art, and so forth. (Your marginal reading notes should suffice for this assignment.)

Comment. An expressive writer will discuss personal matters and preferences. Keller details what she would accomplish during three days of sight, yet she draws her readers into the essay by suggesting renewed attention to the use of sight, hearing, touch, smell, and taste.

Assignment 2. Examine the details of Keller's essay for their universal appeal. Make a list of her planned sightseeing trip that would be applicable to all people. That list should remind you that personal examples should be representative so that all readers can participate in the essay.

Comment. Keller walks a delicate line between heartfelt advice to her readers and didacticism (*didacticism* means to preach and lecture). However, she avoids sermonizing by inviting her readers to participate in her sightless world and her dreams.

Assignment 3. Suppose you have decided to write an essay on what you would say to a friend or relative, now dead, who could return for thirty minutes. How can you avoid excessive pathos and sentimentality? Will categories of universal values serve you as they do Keller? Will focus on concrete scenes and images avoid the mundane? Consider the difference between "I miss you so much" and "I miss the vigorous energy I felt on my sixth birthday when you placed me on your feet and danced me around and around the room." Write a paragraph and practice controlling pathos and sentimentality.

THE WRITING PROCESS

Comment. Keller uses a fundamental classification for her essay—three days of sight. She then devotes the days to friends, art and world history, and contemporary affairs.

Assignment 4. Plan an essay that you can arrange by large categories, such as "Three Kinds of Parental Love" or "Four Types of Aggressive Behavior." Remember, if you plan an expressive essay, the details should grow out of personal experiences.

Comment. Keller uses the technique of analysis within each category to break down into smaller segments her proposed activities for each day. For example, she subdivides the first day for viewing loved ones and intimate things in and near her home.

Assignment 5. Use analysis with your subject by partitioning one category. If writing an expressive essay, list items that affect you and reflect your attitudes. For example, subdivide parental "tough" love, which means that parents should set standards and stick with them even when they cause disharmony.

Comment. Keller's essay demonstrates that most essays require a blending of several patterns. She *describes* with graphic detail, provides numerous *examples*, *compares* and analyzes the various things she would view, and provides a brief chronological *narration* of each day's activities.

Assignment 6. Chart a blending of patterns for your essay. For example, if it features types (types of work ethics, types of marriage), consider how you might compare and contrast, use examples, specify with description, or use narrative episodes.

Comment. By classifying her subject with a three-day limitation and by dividing each day into fundamental elements, Keller achieves her goal: analysis that explains the value of sight.

Assignment 7. Develop a brief one-paragraph writing situation that establishes the issue you want to analyze. Do you have a thesis sentence? To whom are you speaking? What major categories will you employ? How will a naming of parts help you analyze the issue?

Comment. Keller's informal analysis permits an expressive exploration of her subject. She does not attempt a scientific analysis of all classes nor does she establish all divisions. Yet she maintains consistency and completeness by her focus on a narrow issue.

Assignment 8. Examine your notes and preliminary paragraphs (see assignment 4) for consistency and completeness within the boundaries of your limited, expressive focus. Be sure that you have a grasp of the whole aspect of the subject and its universal values, not merely a personal, biased view. Look to the Keller essay for guidance.

In his book Body Language *(1970), Julius Fast captured the imagina-tions of readers from all walks of life. He advanced the theory, now widely accepted, that people signal their feelings and emotions by phys-ical mannerisms.*

In "Winking, Blinking and Nods," a chapter from Body Language, *Fast explores the role of eyes in transmitting information to friends and enemies alike, especially the subtle timing involved in looking at somebody and then looking away while speaking and listening. A knowledge of these signals, suggests Fast, can help one understand the hidden attitudes of our associates. His aim is to explain social interac-tion, yet his style avoids the directness of a textbook discourse because he enlivens it with plenty of examples and anecdotes.*

The author establishes clear categories of classification, examining stares, glances, awkward eyes, bedroom eyes, and so on. He subdivides each topic to analyze the variations in eye signals. In addition, Fast demonstrates the value of blending various patterns of comparison, example, description, and narration. By such blending of patterns, he builds fully developed sections that have length and substance.

As you read, make marginal notes of the many examples Fast pro-vides for each classification. The exercise will help you recognize the value of full development for each category.

JULIUS FAST

 Winking, Blinking and Nods

The Stare That Dehumanizes

The cowpuncher sat his horse loosely and his fingers hovered above his   1
gun while his eyes, ice cold, sent chills down the rustler's back.

A familiar situation? It happens in every western novel, just as in   2
every love story the heroine's eyes *melt* while the hero's eyes *burn* into
hers. In literature, even the best literature, eyes are *steely, knowing,*
mocking, piercing, glowing and so on.

Are they really? Are they ever? Is there such a thing as a burning   3
glance, or a cold glance or a hurt glance? In truth there isn't. Far from
being windows of the soul, the eyes are physiological dead ends, simply

organs of sight and no more, differently colored in different people to be sure, but never really capable of expressing emotion in themselves.

And yet again and again we read and hear and even tell of the eyes   4
being wise, knowing, good, bad, indifferent. Why is there such confusion? Can so many people be wrong? If the eyes do not show emotion, then why the vast literature, the stories and legends about them?

Of all parts of the human body that are used to transmit information,   5
the eyes are the most important and can transmit the most subtle nuances. Does this contradict the fact that the eyes do not show emotion? Not really. While the eyeball itself shows nothing, the emotional impact of the eyes occurs because of their use and the use of the face around them. The reason they have so confounded observers is because by length of glance, by opening of eyelids, by squinting and by a dozen little manipulations of the skin and eyes, almost any meaning can be sent out.

But the most important technique of eye management is the look,   6
or the stare. With it we can often make or break another person. How? By giving him human or nonhuman status.

Simply, eye management in our society boils down to two facts.   7
One, we do not stare at another human being. Two, staring is reserved for a non-person. We stare at art, at sculpture, at scenery. We go to the zoo and stare at the animals, the lions, the monkeys, the gorillas. We stare at them for as long as we please, as intimately as we please, but we do not stare at humans if we want to accord them human treatment.

We may use the same stare for the side-show freak, but we do not   8
really consider him a human being. He is an object at which we have paid money to stare, and in the same way we may stare at an actor on a stage. The real man is masked too deeply behind his role for our stare to bother either him or us. However, the new theater that brings the actor down into the audience often gives us an uncomfortable feeling. By virtue of involving us, the audience, the actor suddenly loses his non-person status and staring at him becomes embarrassing to us.

As I said before, a southern white may stare at a black in the same   9
way, making him, by the stare, into an object rather than a person. If we wish pointedly to ignore someone, to treat him with an element of contempt, we can give him the same stare, the slightly unfocused look that does not really see him, the cutting stare of the socially elite.

Servants are often treated this way as are waiters, waitresses and   10
children. However, this may be a mutually protective device. It allows the servants to function efficiently in their overlapping universe without too much interference from us, and it allows us to function comfortably without acknowledging the servant as a fellow human. The

same is true of children and waiters. It would be an uncomfortable world if each time we were served by a waiter we had to introduce ourselves and indulge in social amenities.

A Time for Looking

With unfamiliar human beings, when we acknowledge their human- 11 ness, we must avoid staring at them, and yet we must also avoid ignoring them. To make them into people rather than objects, we use a deliberate and polite inattention. We look at them long enough to make it quite clear that we see them, and then we immediately look away. We are saying, in body language, "I know you are there," and a moment later we add, "But I would not dream of intruding on your privacy."

The important thing in such an exchange is that we do not catch the 12 eye of the one whom we are recognizing as a person. We look at him without locking glances, and then we immediately look away. Recognition is not permitted.

There are different formulas for the exchange of glances depending 13 on where the meeting takes place. If you pass someone in the street you may eye the oncoming person till you are about eight feet apart, then you must look away as you pass. Before the eight-foot distance is reached, each will signal in which direction he will pass. This is done with a brief look in that direction. Each will veer slightly, and the passing is done smoothly.

For this passing encounter Dr. Erving Goffman in *Behavior in Pub-* 14 *lic Places* says that the quick look and the lowering of the eyes is body language for, "I trust you. I am not afraid of you."

To strengthen this signal, you look directly at the other's face before 15 looking away.

Sometimes the rules are hard to follow, particularly if one of the 16 two people wears dark glasses. It becomes impossible to discover just what they are doing. Are they looking at you too long, too intently? Are they looking at you at all? The person wearing the glasses feels protected and assumes that he can stare without being noticed in his staring. However, this is a self-deception. To the other person, dark glasses seem to indicate that the wearer is always staring at him.

We often use this look-and-away technique when we meet famous 17 people. We want to assure them that we are respecting their privacy, that we would not dream of staring at them. The same is true of the crippled or physically handicapped. We look briefly and then look away before the stare can be said to be a stare. It is the technique we use for any unusual situation where too long a stare would be embarrassing.

When we see an interracial couple we use this technique. We might use it when we see a man with an unusual beard, with extra long hair, with outlandish clothes, or a girl with a minimal mini-skirt may attract this look-and-away.

Of course the opposite is also true. If we wish to put a person down 18 we may do so by staring longer than is acceptably polite. Instead of dropping our gazes when we lock glances, we continue to stare. The person who disapproves of interracial marriage or dating will stare rudely at the interracial couple. If he dislikes long hair, short dresses or beards he may show it with a longer-than-acceptable stare.

The Awkward Eyes

The look-and-away stare is reminiscent of the problem we face in ado- 19 lescence in terms of our hands. What do we do with them? Where do we hold them? Amateur actors are also made conscious of this. They are suddenly aware of their hands as awkward appendages that must somehow be used gracefully and naturally.

In the same way, in certain circumstances, we become aware of our 20 glances as awkward appendages. Where shall we look? What shall we do with our eyes?

Two strangers seated across from each other in a railway dining car 21 have the option of introducing themselves and facing a meal of inconsequential and perhaps boring talk, or ignoring each other and desperately trying to avoid each other's glance. Cornelia Otis Skinner, describing such a situation in an essay, wrote, "They re-read the menu, they fool with the cutlery, they inspect their own fingernails as if seeing them for the first time. Comes the inevitable moment when glances meet, but they meet only to shoot instantly away and out the window for an intent view of the passing scene."

This same awkward eye dictates our looking behavior in elevators 22 and crowded buses and subway trains. When we get on an elevator or train with a crowd we look briefly and then look away at once without locking glances. We say, with our look, "I see you. I do not know you, but you are a human and I will not stare at you."

In the subway or bus where long rides in very close circumstances 23 are a necessity, we may be hard put to find some way of not staring. We sneak glances, but look away before our eyes can lock. Or we look with an unfocused glance that misses the eyes and settles on the head, the mouth, the body—for any place but the eyes is an acceptable looking spot for the unfocused glance.

If our eyes do meet we can sometimes mitigate the message with a 24 brief smile. The smile must not be too long or too obvious. It must say, "I am sorry we have looked, but we both know it was an accident."

Bedroom Eyes

The awkward eye is a common enough occurrence for all of us to have 25 experienced it at one time or another. Almost all actions and interactions between humans depend on mutual glances. The late Spanish philosopher José Ortega y Gasset, in his book *Man and People*, spoke of "the look" as something that comes directly from within a man "with the straight-line accuracy of a bullet." He felt that the eye, with its lids and socket, its iris and pupil, was equivalent to a "whole theater with its stage and actors."

The eye muscles, Ortega said, are marvelously subtle and because 26 of this every glance is minutely differentiated from every other glance. There are so many different looks that it is nearly impossible to name them, but he cited, "the look that lasts but an instant and the insistent look; the look that slips over the surface of the thing looked at and the look that grips it like a hook; the direct look and the oblique look whose extreme form has its own name, 'looking out of the corner of one's eye.'"

He also listed the "sideways glance" which differs from any other 27 oblique look although its axis is still on the bias.

Every look, Ortega said, tells us what goes on inside the person 28 who gives it, and the intent to communicate with a look is more genuinely revealing when the sender of the look is unaware of just how he sends it.

Like other researchers into body language Ortega warned that a 29 look in itself does not give the entire story, even though it has a meaning. A word in a sentence has a meaning too, but only in the context of the sentence can we learn the complete meaning of the word. So too with a look. Only in the context of an entire situation is a look entirely meaningful.

There are also looks that want to see but not be seen. These the 30 Spanish philosopher called sideways glances. In any situation we may study someone and look as long as we wish, providing the other person is not aware that we are looking, providing our look is hidden. The moment his eyes move to lock with ours, our glance must slide away. The more skilled the person, the better he is at stealing these sideways glances.

In a charming description Ortega labels one look "the most effec- 31 tive, the most suggestive, the most delicious and enchanting." He called it the most complicated because it is not only furtive, but it is also the very opposite of furtive, because it makes it obvious that it is looking. This is the look given with lidded eyes, the sleepy look or calculating look or appraising look, the look a painter gives his canvas as he steps back from it, what the French call *les yeux en coulisse*.

Describing this look, Ortega said the lids are almost three-quarters   32 closed and it appears to be hiding itself, but in fact the lids compress the look and "shoot it out like an arrow."

"It is the look of eyes that are, as it were, asleep but which behind   33 the cloud of sweet drowsiness are utterly awake. Anyone who has such a look possesses a treasure."

Ortega said that Paris throws itself at the feet of anyone with this   34 look. Louis XV's DuBarry was supposed to have had it, and so was Lucien Guitry. In our own Hollywood, Robert Mitchum certainly had it and it set him up for years as a masculine sex symbol. Mae West copied it and the French actress Simone Signoret has it so perfectly controlled that even in middle age she comes across as a very sexy and attractive woman.

Other Cultures, Other Looks

The recognition of the eye as a means of communication, or of a look   35 as having special significance is nothing new. Looking is something that has always had strong emotions attached to it and has been forbidden, under certain circumstances, in prehistory and legend. Lot's wife was turned to a pillar of salt for looking back, and Orpheus lost Eurydice by looking at her. Adam, when he tasted the fruit of knowledge, was afraid to look at God.

The significance of looking is universal, but usually we are not sure   36 of just how we look or how we are looked at. Honesty demands, in our culture, that we look someone straight in the eye. Other cultures have other rules, as a principal in a New York City high school recently discovered.

A young girl at the high school, a fifteen-year-old Puerto Rican, had   37 been caught in the washroom with a group of girls suspected of smoking. Most of the group were known troublemakers, and while this young girl, Livia, had no record, the principal after a brief interview was convinced of her guilt and decided to suspend her with the others.

"It wasn't what she said," he reported later. "It was simply her atti-   38 tude. There was something sly and suspicious about her. She just wouldn't meet my eye. She wouldn't look at me."

It was true. Livia at her interview with the principal stared down 39
at the floor in what was a clear-cut guilty attitude and refused to meet
his eyes.

"But she's a good girl," Livia's mother insisted. Not to the school, for 40
she was too much of a "troublemaker" the principal felt, to come to
the authorities with her protest. Instead, she turned to her neighbors
and friends. As a result there was a demonstration of Puerto Rican parents at the school the next morning and the ugly stirrings of a threatened riot.

Fortunately, John Flores taught Spanish literature at the school, and 41
John lived only a few doors from Livia and her family. Summoning his
own courage, John asked for an interview with the principal.

"I know Livia and her parents," he told the principal. "And she's a 42
good girl. I am sure there has been some mistake in this whole matter."

"If there was a mistake," the principal said uneasily, "I'll be glad to 43
rectify it. There are thirty mothers outside yelling for my blood. But I
questioned the child myself, and if ever I saw guilt written on a face—
she wouldn't even meet my eyes!"

John drew a sigh of relief, and then very carefully, for he was too 44
new in the school to want to tread on toes, he explained some basic
facts of Puerto Rican culture to the principal.

"In Puerto Rico a nice girl, a good girl," he explained, "does not 45
meet the eyes of an adult. Refusing to do so is a sign of respect and
obedience. It would be as difficult for Livia to look you in the eye as it
would be for her to misbehave, or for her mother to come to you with
a complaint. In our culture, this is just not accepted behavior for a
respectable family."

Fortunately the principal was a man who knew how to admit that he 46
was wrong. He called Livia and her parents and the most vocal neighbors in and once again discussed the problem. In the light of John
Flores' explanation it became obvious to him that Livia was not avoiding
his eyes out of defiance, but out of a basic demureness. Her slyness,
he now saw, was shyness. In fact, as the conference progressed and
the parents relaxed, he realized that Livia was indeed a gentle and
sweet girl.

The outcome of the entire incident was a deeper, more meaningful 47
relationship between the school and the community—but that of
course is another story. What is of particular interest in this story is the
strange confusion of the principal. How did he so obviously misinter-
pret all the signals of Livia's behavior?

Livia was using body language to say, "I am a good girl. I respect 48
you and the school. I respect you too much to answer your questions,

too much to meet your eyes with shameless boldness, too much to defend myself. But surely my very attitude tells you all this."

How could such a clear-cut message be interpreted as, "I defy you. 49 I will not answer your questions. I will not look you in the eyes because I am a deceitful child. I will evade your questions slyly—"

The answer of course is a cultural one. Different cultures have dif- 50 ferent customs and, of course, different body language. They also have different looks and different meanings to the same looks.

In America, for instance, a man is not supposed to look at a woman 51 for any length of time unless she gives him her permission with a body language signal, a smile, a backward glance, a direct meeting of his eye. In other countries different rules apply.

In America, if a woman looks at a man for too long a period of time, 52 she commits herself to a verbal approach. Her signal says, "I am interested. You can approach me." In Latin countries, though freer body movements are permissible, such a look might be a direct invitation to a physical "pass." It becomes obvious then why a girl like Livia would not look the principal in the eye.

Again, in our country, two men are not allowed to stare at each other 53 for more than a brief period of time unless they intend to fight or to become intimate. Any man who looks at another man for too long embarrasses and annoys him and the other man begins to wonder just what he wants.

This is another example of the rigidity of the rules of looking. If 54 someone stares at us and we meet his eye and catch him staring, it is his duty to look away first. If he does not look away as we engage his eye, then we become uncomfortable and aware that something is wrong. Again we become embarrassed and annoyed.

A Long Look at Oneself

In an attempt to discover just how some of these rules for visual com- 55 munication work, Dr. Gerhard Neilson of Copenhagen analyzed the "looks" of the subjects in his self-confrontation studies. To discover just how long, and when, the people being interviewed looked at the interviewer, he filmed interviews and replayed them a number of times in slow motion.

While he started with no clear-cut idea of how long one man would 56 look at another during an interview, he was surprised to find how little looking there actually was. The man who looked at his interviewer the most, still looked away 27 percent of the time. The man who looked at his interviewer the least looked away 92 percent of the time. Half of the people interviewed looked away for half of the time they were being interviewed.

Dr. Neilson found that when people spoke a lot they looked at their partners very little; when they listened a lot they also looked a lot. He reports that he expected people to look at each other more when they listened more, but he was surprised to find them looking less when they spoke more.   57

He found that when people start to speak, they look away from their partners at first. There is a subtle timing, he explains, in speaking, listening, looking and looking away. Most people look away either immediately before or after the beginning of one out of every four speeches they make. A few look away at the beginning of half their speeches. As they finish speaking, half the people look at their partners.   58

As to why so many people refuse to meet the eyes of their partners during a conversation, Dr. Neilson believes this is a way of avoiding distraction.   59

How Long Is a Glance?

Another study, carried out by Dr. Ralph V. Exline at the University of Delaware, involved forty men and forty women, all freshmen and sophomores. In the study a man interviewed twenty men and twenty women and a woman interviewed the other twenty of each sex. Half the students were questioned by both interviewers about intimate subjects, their plans, desires, needs and fears. The other half were asked about recreational interests, reading, movies, sports.   60

Dr. Exline found that when the students were interviewed about personal subjects, they didn't look at the interviewer as often as they did when they were interviewed about recreational subjects. Women, however, in both types of interview, looked at the interviewers more frequently than men did.   61

What seems to come across from both these studies, and others of a similar nature, is that when someone looks away while he's speaking, it generally means he's still explaining himself and doesn't want to be interrupted.   62

A locking of his gaze with his partner's at this point would be a signal to interrupt when he paused. If he pauses and is not looking at his conversational partner, it means he hasn't yet finished. He is signaling, "This is what I want to say. What is your answer?"   63

If you look away from the person who is speaking to you while you are listening, it is a signal, "I am not completely satisfied with what you are saying. I have some qualifications."   64

If you look away while you are speaking it may mean, "I am not   65
certain of what I am saying."

If while you are listening, you look at the speaker, you signal, "I   66
agree with you," or "I am interested in what you are saying."

If while you are speaking, you look at the listener, you may be   67
signaling, "I am certain of what I am saying."

There are also elements of concealment in looking away from your   68
partner. If you look away while he is speaking, you signal, "I don't want
you to know what I feel." This is particularly true if the partner is critical
or insulting. It is something like an ostrich burying his head in the sand.
"If I cannot see you, you cannot hurt me." This is the reason children
will often refuse to look at you when you are scolding them.

However, there are more complexities here than meet the eye . . . or   69
the glance. Looking away during a conversation may be a means of
concealing something. Therefore when someone else looks away, we
may think he is concealing something. To practice deceit we may sometimes deliberately look at our partner instead of refusing to meet his
glance.

In addition to length and direction of glances, there is a good deal   70
of signaling involved in the act of closing the lid. In addition to the half-
lidded look Ortega described, Birdwhistell states that five young
nurses, in a series of tests, reported twenty-three different positions of
lid closure that they could distinguish.

But they all agreed that only four out of the twenty-three "meant   71
anything." Retesting allowed Dr. Birdwhistell to label these four positions, "open-eyed, droopy-lidded, squinting, eyes-closed tight."

Working from the opposite end, trying to get the girls to reproduce   72
the lid positions, was not so successful. All could reproduce five of the
twenty-three positions, but only one could reproduce more than five.

Using a group of men in the same type of experiment, he found that   73
all could reproduce at least ten positions. Unexpectedly men were
more facile at winking. Some of the men could reproduce fifteen different positions, and one—fantastically eloquent in body language—
came up with thirty-five different eyelid positions.

Branching out into cultural comparisons Dr. Birdwhistell found that   74
among the Japanese both sexes were similar in the number of eyelid
positions they could reproduce. But even the Japanese could recognize,
in others, more positions than they could assume themselves.

When movement of the eyebrows is added to movement of the lids,   75
many more recognizable signals are produced. Some scientists have
found as many as forty different positions of the brows alone, though
most agree that less than half of them are significant. It is only when the

significant eyebrow movements are combined with the significant lid movements and we add forehead creases that the permutations and combinations are endless.

If each combination has a different implication, then there is no end 76 to the number of signals we can transmit with our eyes and the skin around them.

AIMS AND STRATEGIES OF THE WRITER

Comment. Fast, a sociologist, explores variations in human interaction, especially the role of body movements and eye contact for communicating our feelings toward others. He would educate us so that, armed with his special knowledge, we might communicate more effectively.

Assignment 1. As a thinking and prewriting activity, examine your behavior and that of your friends within the boundaries of Fast's thesis. Are you shy, aggressive, friendly? Does your body language communicate that personality? After observation of a friend's body language, write a paragraph describing this person, especially his or her attitude toward you as evidenced by body language.

Comment. One aim of discourse, explanation, examines a subject for educational purposes. It enlightens the reader with analysis that explores divisions of the subject and provides plenty of specific details.

Assignment 2. Make two lists that categorize looks by others: ones that you enjoy and ones that annoy you. As an adjunct to this assignment, you might also categorize another element of interpersonal relations, such as greetings, kisses, touches and hugs, ways of walking, and so forth.

Comment. Although the informative writer must concentrate on explanation, many writers, including Fast, recognize the value of entertainment. Expository prose need not be dull. To that end, sociologists like Fast employ plenty of descriptive, narrative, and comparative elements. The exposition of the topic thereby comes alive.

Assignment 3. Begin the preliminary draft of several paragraphs to explore your response to body language. For example, draft a paragraph describing the types of hugging and touching that attract or repel you. Or develop a paragraph that explores mannerisms of "moving or positioning the head." (Include plenty of descriptive examples and narrative episodes to bring scenes to life.)

THE WRITING PROCESS

Comment. Fast classifies his essay according to types of eye movement. He introduces the subject (paragraphs 1 through 5), moves to stares (6 through 10), then to glances (11 through 18), and so on.

Assignment 4. Carefully plan the categories for your essay on body language. For example, if you focus on walking, establish specific types that you can explore. In effect, you are building an outline for your paper.

Comment. Fast uses analysis to examine each of his categories in depth. For example, his discussion of glances in paragraphs 11 through 18 explores the look-and-away technique used by passing strangers.

Assignment 5. Begin drafting your paper. Look for methods that help you examine fully each category—by stages, types, processes, examples, and so forth. Share your draft with a friend or fellow student for help in discovering any weaknesses or omissions.

Comment. By classifying looks into broad categories and by examining each in great detail, Fast achieves explanation by analytical reasoning.

Assignment 6. Consider the role of analysis in your preliminary draft. You must break down the subject into its component parts and examine each for significance and meaning. For example, an affectionate kiss features several stages: the meeting of the eyes, forward movement, positioning of the heads, contact of the lips, duration of the kiss, backward movement, eye contact. Your paragraph should analyze these stages for significance. The essay as a whole could explore several types of kisses.

*S*ome writers employ classification for persuasive purposes in order to solve problems, explore issues, and argue the fine points. L. S. Stavrianos uses a three-part division for his examination of contemporary myths about human nature, population, and technology, analyzing each to demonstrate its negative influence. He then offers solutions and answers. Thereby, he not only explains his subject but also persuasively defends his answers.

Stavrianos structures the elements of his essay to stress his own optimism. Between his optimistic statements in the opening and the closing, he inserts an analysis of what he calls a paradox: Many Americans look to the future with apprehension at a time of great potential and worldwide power.

He argues that human beings are not aggressive by nature, that population growth is not out of control, and that technological growth brings new levels of human participation rather than mass surrender to machines. His detailed analysis of each classification serves his persuasive purpose: to enunciate a message of optimism, hope, and faith about the future.

As you read, make marginal notes of Stavrianos's three categories, and then list each myth and the words and phrases that Stavrianos uses to disprove the myth. Employing specific words and jargon of the field is useful in the defense of a thesis.

"Myths of Our Time" was written by Stavrianos for The New York Times *(8 May 1976).*

L. S. STAVRIANOS

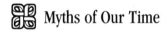 Myths of Our Time

"I am just as convinced as can be," states the geochemist Harrison   1
Brown of the California Institute of Technology, "that man has it within his power today to create a world in which people the world over can lead free and abundant and even creative lives. . . . I am convinced that we can create a world which will pale the Golden Age of Pericles into nothingness."

Very few Americans share this optimism. Unlike our forefathers, we   2
look to the future with apprehension rather than expectation—and this at a time when, as Harrison Brown correctly notes, the human race enjoys unprecedented power and potentiality.

233

One reason for this paradox is that we have become the prisoners 3
of paralyzing myths. These myths depict various problems as being
inherently insoluble, whereas actually they are basically socio-political
in nature, and their solutions can and are being found.

Three of the most basic and widespread of these myths have to do 4
with allegedly perverse human nature, allegedly uncontrollable population increase, allegedly malignant technological growth.

Let us take a look at each of these in turn. 5

The "human nature" myth holds that *Homo sapiens* is a singularly 6
disagreeable creature—selfish, covetous and bellicose. But when we
examine the record of our paleolithic ancestors, whose history com-
prises some 80 percent of total human experience, we find that they
were the precise opposite of this "human nature" stereotype. The proof
of this is the dramatic discovery in 1971 of the Tasaday—a tribe of
twenty-seven Stone Age tribesmen who had been living in complete
isolation in southern Mindanao Island of the Philippines for at least six
centuries.

Their outstanding characteristic is a complete lack of aggressive- 7
ness. They have no words for weapons, hostility, anger or war. They
have eagerly adopted the long Filipino knife, the bolo, as it is much
superior to their stone tools for gathering food, chopping wood
and slashing through jungle growth. But they have rejected the spear
and the bow and arrow as inefficient tools for gathering food. And all
the food they collect (yams, fruit, berries, flowers, fish, crabs, frogs)
they divide equally with scrupulous care among all members of
the band.

We may conclude, then, that human beings are not born with an 8
inherited instinct for aggression and selfishness. "Human nature" concludes Professor Albert Bandura of Stanford University, a psychologist,
"is a vast potentiality that can be fashioned by social influences into a
variety of forms ... aggression is not an inevitable or unchangeable
aspect of man but a product of aggression-promoting conditions within
society."

The second great myth of our times is that population growth is 9
uncontrollable and that the human race is doomed to decimation by
mass starvation or war. But again this is a case of perceiving an insoluble Malthusian predicament in a soluble socio-political problem.

In demographic matters, as in others, people act according to their 10
best interests as they perceive them. In societies with gross inequities
in income distribution and with little opportunity for social mobility
and economic security, parents naturally resort to the only available
insurance: a large number of children. Conversely, in more egalitarian
societies that offer mass education, social mobility and employment

opportunities to women, the number of children per family tends to fall.

Hence the substantial decline of birth rates in Taiwan, Sri Lanka and China, as against the soaring rates in India, Indonesia and South America. Dissemination of birth-control information and devices is not enough. Families must be provided with the *motivation* as well as the *means* to limit births. As soon as this has been done, birth rates in country after country have slowed down and populations have stabilized at manageable levels. 11

The third myth concerns technology, which is considered a Frankenstein monster that forces human beings to be the servants of soulless machines. But the historical record shows that this simply is not so. Each major technological breakthrough in the past has been accompanied by a corresponding breakthrough in mass assertiveness and participation rather than in mass subjugation and submissiveness. 12

Aristotle perceived this fact when he stated: "There is only one condition in which we can imagine managers not needing subordinates, and masters not needing slaves. This condition would be that each [inanimate] instrument could do its own work ... as if a shuttle should weave of itself." 13

Aristotle's observation points up the trap in which all pre-modern civilizations were caught: Technological backwardness promoted slavery, and slavery perpetuated technological backwardness by reducing incentive for experimentation and invention. The great historic contribution of the West was to spring this trap. 14

The first Industrial Revolution (a labor-*saving* revolution with its machines and steam power) and the second Industrial Revolution (a labor-*replacing* revolution with its computers and automation) have opened new horizons for mankind everywhere. 15

They are primarily responsible for the pervasive demand for self-management, as expressed by the movements for women's lib, minority rights, student activism and worker control. The current technological revolution, like the earlier ones, is leading not to a new age of the pharaohs but to a new level of humanity—to the transcendence of *Homo sapiens* to *Homo humanus*. 16

The problems of humankind, despite our popular myths, are not insoluble. They can, and are, being solved by peoples capable of social innovation. Those who oppose such innovation view the future with foreboding, but those who welcome it share the buoyancy of Harrison Brown, and also of Cesar Chavez, leader of the United Farm Workers, who declares: "You know what I really think? I really think that one day the world will be great. I really believe the world gonna be great one day." 17

AIMS AND STRATEGIES OF THE WRITER

Comment. Stavrianos wishes to explain certain myths that affect the behavior of some Americans. In addition, he argues several underlying issues to convince readers that these myths have little basis in fact.

Assignment 1. Begin preliminary thinking and perhaps some prewriting activities about a subject that concerns you deeply. For example, you may wish to preserve wilderness areas or defend freedom of expression by student journalists. You might wish to frame your topic in terms of "mythic" considerations, such as, "Three Myths of Our Time about X."

Comment. Stavrianos narrows the distance between himself and his reader so that his writing becomes a form of recommendation. Put another way, he expresses his position, develops ways to defend it, and attempts to convince the reader of his reasonableness.

Assignment 2. In planning your own persuasive appeal, consider carefully your target. Whom will you reach with the message? You may want to direct an essay on wilderness preservation to the state legislature, or you may want to address your peers with a paper on social elitism. Remember that persuasion will quietly but effectively convince others, not in a polemical sense of opposites but in synthesis that brings new insights to the reader.

Comment. A writer's underlying attitude will affect the reader. Stavrianos, for example, exhibits confidence in his position, so his authority remains unchallenged. He maintains consistency within the three balanced elements of his essay. He cites plenty of evidence, including quotations from other authorities. He also appears reasonable and unbiased.

Assignment 3. Consider your choice of voice carefully in drafting a persuasive paper. Your credibility, like that of Stavrianos, will depend on (1) your knowledge of the subject, (2) your consideration of all sides of the issue, and (3) your supply of examples and other evidence. If necessary, research the subject in the library and use quotations from experts in the field.

THE WRITING PROCESS

Comment. Stavrianos uses classification to establish the major categories of his topic. He admits, however, that his three-part development includes only "the most basic and widespread of these myths." For that reason we must label his essay as *informal analysis*.

Assignment 4. Determine the nature of your essay. A *formal analysis*, which requires complete and consistent divisions, may seem beyond reach due to limitations of time, space, and research, but *informal analysis* is attainable in short papers. Therefore, qualify the nature of your work by saying "three important factors" or "four major considerations." In that way you can avoid challenges by readers who might raise questions about additional categories.

Comment. Stavrianos examines only three myths that cause apprehension about the future, yet each one represents a large category. His three-part classification allows him to explore various issues.

Assignment 5. Review the categories for your essay. Do your categories represent large, general issues? For example, a paper on the freedom of student journalists might focus on three items: access to newsmakers, confidentiality of sources, and freedom of expression. You could then analyze specific details within each category by division, examples, comparison, and other techniques.

Comment. Stavrianos structures his essay with a clear, effective plan: an introduction in five short paragraphs, a body that provides equal attention to each of his three classifications, and a short closing paragraph.

Assignment 6. Finalize your own outline. See if the Stavrianos outline will suit your essay, yet keep in mind that every essay must find its own path of development.

Comment. Persuasive writing requires a reasonable foundation that will be acceptable to the reader. Stavrianos uses a quotation to launch the essay and establishes his thesis in the next three paragraphs.

Assignment 7. If you have been building an essay in the pattern of "Myths of Our Time," you have probably done some *prethinking* and plenty of *thinking* and *drafting*, so now you can enter the *rethinking* stage, which has importance for any essay and especially for persuasive discourse. The *rethinking* stage requires that you reconsider your position, reformulate your thesis, and reaffirm the validity of your ideas. Consider peer review as one method for reexamining the paper.

Judy Syfers takes an imaginative approach to her role as a wife. She creates a persona that speaks with an ironic voice about the duties of any wife. She argues that she too would enjoy having a wife. The premise requires that she classify the roles played by a wife to support a husband and raise a family. She establishes five broad categories of roles and subdivides each into numerous duties and responsibilities of the typical wife.

Judy Syfers was born in 1937 in San Francisco. In 1962 she earned a BFA in painting from the University of Iowa and later specialized in social studies. She is currently a writer on social issues such as abortion and union organizing. Syfers has actively supported the feminist movement. Her essay "I Want a Wife" appeared in the first issue of Ms *magazine in December 1971. Since that time the piece has become a minor feminist classic.*

While reading this piece, mark the divisions of the essay and write a brief summary to describe the issue of each one.

JUDY SYFERS

I Want a Wife

I belong to that classification of people known as wives. I am a Wife. 1
And, not altogether incidentally, I am a mother.

Not too long ago a male friend of mine appeared on the scene fresh 2
from a recent divorce. He had one child, who is, of course, with his ex-
wife. He is obviously looking for another wife. As I thought about him
while I was ironing one evening, it suddenly occurred to me that I, too,
would like to have a wife. Why do I want a wife?

I would like to go back to school so that I can become economically 3
independent, support myself, and, if need be, support those dependent
on me. I want a wife who will work and send me to school. And while I
am going to school I want a wife to take care of my children. I want a
wife to keep track of the children's doctor and dentist appointments.
And to keep track of mine, too. I want a wife to make sure that my
children eat properly and are kept clean. I want a wife who will wash
the children's clothes and keep them mended. I want a wife who is a
good nurturant attendant to my children, who arranges for their
schooling, makes sure they have an adequate social life with their peers,
takes them to the park, the zoo, etc. I want a wife who takes care of the
children when they are sick, a wife who arranges to be around when
the children need special care, because, of course, I cannot miss classes

at school. My wife must arrange to lose time at work and not lose the job. It may mean a small cut in my wife's income from time to time, but I guess I can tolerate that. Needless to say, my wife will arrange and pay for the care of the children while my wife is working.

I want a wife who will take care of *my* physical needs. I want a wife   4
who will keep the house clean. A wife who will pick up after me. I want a wife who will keep my clothes clean, ironed, mended, replaced when need be, and who will see to it that my personal things are kept in their proper place so that I can find what I need the minute I need it. I want a wife who cooks the meals, a wife who is a *good* cook. I want a wife who will plan the menus, do the necessary shopping, prepare the meals, serve them pleasantly, and then do the cleaning up while I do my studying. I want a wife who will care for me when I am sick and sympathize with my pain and loss of time from school. I want a wife to go along when our family takes a vacation so that someone can continue to care for me and my children when I need a rest and change of scene.

I want a wife who will not bother me with rambling complaints   5
about a wife's duties. But I want a wife who will listen to me when I feel the need to explain a rather difficult point I have come across in my course of studies. And I want a wife who will type my papers for me when I have written them.

I want a wife who will take care of the details of my social life. When   6
my wife and I are invited out by my friends, I want a wife who will take care of the babysitting arrangements. When I meet people at school that I like and want to entertain, I want a wife who will have the house clean, prepare a special meal, serve it to me and my friends, and not interrupt when I talk about the things that interest me and my friends. I want a wife who will have arranged that the children are fed and ready for bed before my guests arrive so that the children do not bother us. I want a wife who takes care of the needs of my guests so that they feel comfortable, who makes sure that they have an ashtray, that they are passed the hors d'oeuvres, that they are offered a second helping of the food, that their wine glasses are replenished when necessary, that their coffee is served to them as they like it.

And I want a wife who knows that sometimes I need a night out by   7
myself.

I want a wife who is sensitive to my sexual needs, a wife who makes   8
love passionately and eagerly when I feel like it, a wife who makes sure that I am satisfied. And, of course, I want a wife who will not demand sexual attention when I am not in the mood for it. I want a wife who assumes the complete responsibility for birth control, because I do not want more children. I want a wife who will remain sexually faithful to me so that I do not have to clutter up my intellectual life with jealousies.

And I want a wife who understands that *my* sexual needs may entail more than strict adherence to monogamy. I must, after all, be able to relate to people as fully as possible.

If, by chance, I find another person more suitable as a wife than the   9
wife I already have, I want the liberty to replace my present wife with another one. Naturally, I will expect a fresh, new life; my wife will take the children and be solely responsible for them so that I am left free.

When I am through with school and have a job, I want my wife to   10
quit working and remain at home so that my wife can more fully and completely take care of a wife's duties.

My God, who *wouldn't* want a wife?   11

AIMS AND STRATEGIES OF THE WRITER

Comment.   Syfers chooses a distinctive, satiric voice for her essay, one that engages the reader with a persona who imagines a different scenario—a woman who wants a wife. The creative nature of the scene evokes both a humorous response and a serious understanding of many women's situation.

Assignment 1.   Begin preliminary thinking and prewriting for a paper that features a distinctive voice. Create a persona that speaks out on an issue that you feel strongly about. Perhaps you can turn the irony on yourself by saying, "I didn't want to be a teenager." You can then lampoon your own eccentric behavior during your high school days.

Comment.   Satire features penetrating commentary to awaken readers to social imbalances and injustices. Syfers wishes to awaken readers to a clear understanding of the many supporting roles played by a wife.

Assignment 2.   During the planning stages of your first draft, consider carefully the satiric thrust that will expose the folly of some human behavior. Remember that satire ridicules *for a purpose*; it does not merely hurt or demean.

Comment.   The tone of voice in an essay of this type is crucial to its success. If the speaker withdraws toward an objective stance, the writing becomes explanatory. If the speaker tilts toward an emotional, strident voice, the writing may become too impassioned. Syfers balances her piece between the two extremes.

Assignment 3.   Use irony and exaggeration to dull the sharp edges of your discourse and to elicit a smile from the reader. Keep your voice under control with *verbal irony* (saying the opposite of what is meant), *dramatic irony* (speaking with a voice other than your own), *irony of situation* (emphasizing the strangeness of some life situations), and *hyperbole* (exaggerating for humorous effect).

THE WRITING PROCESS

Comment. Syfers uses a five-part division for her essay to portray the support, care, companionship, social planning, and sexual attention a "typical" wife should provide her husband.

Assignment 4. Plan the major classifications of your draft and then begin building evidence for each one. Syfers, for instance, uses many examples to build each paragraph. In addition to examples, you may need other patterns of development, such as narrative episodes, description, and comparison. Share your outline with a friend or fellow student to determine if your classifications are complete, uniform, and valid.

Comment. Syfer's technique features the assumptions of a persona speaking out about a real-world issue in hopes of awakening the audience to the plight of women.

Assignment 5. Develop a writing situation for your paper by listing the biases and special points of view of your persona/speaker. Explain the issue under consideration and the message you plan to send to the reader. Will the reader understand any irony in the speaker's voice? (See pages 4–5 for details about developing a writing situation.)

Comment. One technique that Syfers demonstrates with excellent results is that precise details will *show* a reader and carry more weight than many words of *telling*.

Assignment 6. Review each division of your essay to determine if you have employed enough concrete images. Let the details develop and carry the point. Emotion, for example, can be shown by one image far more effectively than by abstract discussion.

Comment. Syfer's process includes a delicate balance of the comic and tragic, for many traditional roles of a wife can demean and destroy. Syfers blunts her bitter edges with irony.

Assignment 7. Consider using a serious tone of voice for your emotional statements and then consider methods for developing humor. Try to mute a harsh truth with an exaggerated tone and a lively voice that remains triumphant, confident, and energetic, not moody, defeated, and tired.

Rachel Thomas writes an interpretation of a poem by Thomas Kinsella that represents the explanatory aim of discourse for literary interpretation. She addresses a body of knowledgeable readers who enjoy poetry, have probably read Kinsella's poem, and who want more insight into its meaning.

On one level this essay explores as well as explains, for Thomas uses the evidence she has before her to move into unknown territory. However, she stays on the trail, using Kinsella's words and phrasing, and does not wander into dead ends or pointless side trips.

Thomas uses classification to examine the progressive structure of Kinsella's poem, its imagery, its metaphorical language, and the child's unendurable dream, which she proclaims as the key to the poem.

Interpretation of this sort requires careful classification of the poem's major sections, examples of lines and images from the poem, an analysis of each section, and some inductive leaps to conclusions about the poem's message. The blending of patterns helps Thomas reach one interpretation of Kinsella's poem.

As you read the essay, make marginal notes that devote special attention to each category of Thomas's analysis.

RACHEL THOMAS, STUDENT

Figurative Language in "First Light"

Thomas Kinsella's poem, "First Light," captures that usually hard to describe time of daybreak most vividly through the use of several images and devices of figurative language. The poem reads as follows: 1

First Light

A prone couple still sleeps.   2
Light ascends like a pale gas   3
out of the sea: dawn—   4
Light, reaching across the hill   5
To the dark garden. The grass   6
Emerges, soaking with gray dew.   7

Inside, in silence, an empty   8
Kitchen takes form, tidied and swept,   9
Blank with marriage—where shrill   10
Lover and beloved have kept   11
Another vigil far   12
Into the night, and raved and wept.   13

Upstairs a whimper or sigh   14
Comes from an open bedroom door   15
And lengthens to an ugly wail   16
—A child enduring a dream   17
That grows, at the first touch of day,   18
Unendurable.   19

First, Kinsella divides the poem into three different sections, start-   20
ing outside with the beginning of dawn, moving inside a house, and
finally ending with the specific upstairs portion of a house. The reader
can easily follow the progression, since it is logically arrived at through
consideration of natural order.

Second, Kinsella makes use of images with much success. Sight   21
imagery is seen in the opening line of the poem with the "prone
couple." After that, "The grass / Emerges, soaking with gray dew." The
grass emerges only after being bathed in sunlight after the light "ascends like a pale gas." The tidy and empty kitchen provides the audience
with a picture, but the silent kitchen even touches on a sound image,
or a lack-of-sound image. The use of the kitchen by Kinsella helps the
reader to understand exactly the time of morning written about because most readers can remember a quiet kitchen in the morning from
personal experiences. In the third stanza, sound imagery is prevalent
with the child's early morning "whimper or sigh" and "ugly wail,"
which are indicative of the groans of awakening children.

Next, "First Light" contains metaphorical language with the first   22
stanza's light ascending like a pale gas, making use of both personification and simile. Personification is also used with "light reaching" and,
later, with the kitchen taking form and the dream that grows unendurable. The second stanza's contrast in the kitchen between late night and
early morning is interesting to indicate how the room has settled down
after "another vigil" which indicates other arguments have taken place
there. The substitution of "lover and beloved" for man and wife is
effective when one examines the poem further and finds "raved and
wept" to follow respectively. The man or lover raves, perhaps, and the
beloved wife weeps.

Finally, to end the poem Kinsella utilizes a child's dream. As the   23
child's dream becomes unendurable, the dream of night is unendurable also and has to give way to morning. One cannot keep a dream in
the morning after sunlight has chased away the magic of evening. This
helps put the final touch on the work and gives the reader a clearer
understanding of its meaning. The special time of the world's awakening is delicately handled through the use of familiarity of the reader
with dawn and the first light of day. The child's morning wail echoes
the night cries of the parents.

RACHEL THOMAS TALKS ABOUT
HER AIMS AND STRATEGIES

I'll be honest. I didn't understand this poem at first, and I still wonder how close I am to a good, scholarly reading. But my professor liked it. He said my interpretation is valid because it stayed within the boundaries of the poem. One guy in class argued that the couple was getting a divorce and that's why the child cried, but we all agreed that divorce is never mentioned in the poem and, besides, the child might be too young to know all that anyway. The poem is about darkness of night and evidently the bitterness of marriage, but it also gives us two images of a new start—a child at the first light of day. That's what I depended on. The move from darkness to daylight. Ugly dreams cannot endure into the new day.

As far as my writing process is concerned, I just picked out the images and drafted a paragraph. Then I did the same with figurative language. Then I wrote the introduction and copied the poem. I added the section on structure, I guess, because the poem faced me there in three parts. I saved the sunrise business for the ending.

Comment. The aim of Thomas is interpretation of a poem, which requires her to select criteria by which to judge the work. She classifies four areas for explanation: structure, imagery, figurative language, and, finally, the dream imagery.

Assignment 1. Select a poem of your own or use the short one that follows and begin making notes on crucial areas, such as theme, imagery, figurative language, structure, voice and tone of the speaker, and so forth.

Fire and Ice

Some say the world will end in fire,
Some say ice.
From what I've tasted of desire
I hold with those who favor fire.
But if I had to perish twice,
I think I know enough of hate
To say that for destruction ice
Is also great
And would suffice.

Robert Frost (1923)

Comment. Thomas explains Kinsella's poem within the scope of the poet's language. She avoids applying meaning or symbolism that would extend the boundaries of the poem.

Assignment 2. In the interpretation of your poem, classify and then analyze the parts with good reason and judiciousness. Most poems mean what they say. Seldom will poets insert secret or bizarre meanings. To give yourself an overview, write into your notes a brief paraphrase of the poem.

Comment. One feature of Thomas's style is her willingness to cite examples and quotations from the poem to support each of her topic sentences. The poem is her evidence.

Assignment 3. List the major classifications of your study, such as imagery, voice, or language, and under each one begin a list of specific items from the poem that will support your analysis.

Comment. Although Thomas follows the order of the poem in the progression of her essay, she does not merely paraphrase the poem or write a long summary.

Assignment 4. Write an analysis of your selected poem. Avoid merely summarizing the poem; establish clear criteria of judgment that will serve to classify and order your paper. Focus especially on the poet in the opening and closing, but focus on the poem itself in the body.

CHAPTER SEVEN

Process Analysis

Process analysis explains an action or series of actions. In the following paragraph Peter Elbow explains the process of freewriting:

> The most effective way I know to improve your writing is to do freewriting exercises regularly. At least three times a week. They are sometimes called "automatic writing," "babbling," or "jabbering" exercises. The idea is simply to write for ten minutes (later on, perhaps fifteen or twenty). Don't stop for anything. Go quickly without rushing. Never stop to look back, to cross something out, to wonder how to spell something, to wonder what word or thought to use, or to think about what you are doing. If you can't think of a word or a spelling, just use a squiggle or else write, "I can't think of it." Just put down something. The easiest thing is just to put down whatever is in your mind. If you get stuck it's fine to write "I can't think what to say, I can't think what to say" as many times as you want; or repeat the last word you wrote over and over again; or anything else. The only requirement is that you *never* stop.*

Elbow's paragraph demonstrates the process analysis procedure, presenting "how-to" instructions for freewriting. Writing a process analysis essay can be relatively simple, such as explaining the steps for baking cookies, or it can be complicated, such as explaining the human circulatory system.

As a pattern of development, process analysis can be used for topics of discourse. The essays that follow in this chapter use the technique for an expressive discourse on oranges, an explanation of the snapping turtle, a persuasive discourse on schooling, an imaginative approach to watching the game of baseball, and an account of the complex emotional adjustment of organ transplant recipients.

*Peter Elbow, *Writing without Teachers* (New York: Oxford UP, 1973).

BLEND PROCESS ANALYSIS WITH
OTHER RHETORICAL PATTERNS

Narration is closely linked with process analysis because both patterns employ chronological order. However, narration relates a one-time fictional or historic event that happens in a random, unpredictable manner, while process analysis relates a sequence of steps or events that can be repeated. For example, a story about the origins of Toll House cookies is different from the recipe; one is historical narration and the other is a process. In another example, a writer used a blend of patterns to develop a paper on fruit trees. He employed process analysis to explain general growing procedures and specific processes for cross-pollination. He used historic narration to describe the development of hybrid varieties from native root stock. He also classified the types of trees in a typical orchard, used division and partition to explain the basic structure of dwarf and semi-dwarf trees, gave examples, described the trees, and used contrast to highlight differences in types. Each rhetorical pattern served a particular purpose, but he used process analysis prominently to demonstrate stages of development and steps of procedure.

USE A DIRECTIVE PROCESS FOR "HOW TO" TOPICS

The "how to" essay is a step-by-step explanation of the necessary procedures for doing something—how to walk for exercise, how to raise bees, how to lose weight, and so forth. You will need to break down the tasks into clear, logical steps and provide plenty of detailed descriptions and examples to make the processes clear. Two essays in this chapter feature the directive process. Larry Woiwode's expressive essay, "Wanting an Orange," offers tempting instructions for enjoying the juicy taste of oranges, and Thomas Boswell's explanatory essay, "The View from the Dugout," offers insightful instructions for watching a baseball game. This type of essay appears in instructional textbooks and workbooks in many fields, especially in the applied sciences and education. A key to success in writing "how to" essays is the attention given to the needs of the audience so that sufficient details, steps, and examples are supplied. Also, your voice should reveal your familiarity with this activity, even to the extent of mentioning your own errors and dead ends.

USE INFORMATIVE PROCESS ESSAYS
TO TELL ABOUT A NATURAL PROCESS

Such an essay does not explain how to make something happen; rather, it explains natural processes, such as the growth and development of snapping turtles, as in the essay by Alan Devoe later in this chapter. McPhee's essay "Grizzly" (see Chapter 1) examines another natural phenomenon of the wild, and Julius Fast's essay (Chapter 6) studies the process of human eye contact. This type of essay is most familiar in textbooks in the natural and physical sciences. Research is the key to successful process writing, for you need authoritative details about your topic, such as the life cycle of the grey squirrel, which is not the type of paper you can write off the top of your head.

USE INFORMATIVE PROCESS ESSAYS TO EXAMINE HISTORICAL AND SOCIAL PROCESSES

Later in this chapter, Ellen Goodman in "The Long Transition to Adulthood" studies the social forces that affect a child's transition into the adult world. Catton (Chapter 4) traces the social backgrounds of Generals Lee and Grant. Jefferson in "The Declaration of Independence" (Chapter 3) demonstrates with precise examples the process by which the British government caused harm to the colonies. These types of essays appear regularly in history and social science textbooks. A key to writing this type of process analysis is your ability to locate and isolate a social problem or issue.

USE INFORMATIVE PROCESS ESSAYS TO EXPLORE INTELLECTUAL AND CREATIVE PROCESSES

The essay on freewriting by Elbow that opened this chapter demonstrates an intellectual exercise that can aid a writer's creativity. Elbow's process essay programs a mental activity for the reader. Boswell demonstrates an intellectual approach with his instructions for watching a baseball game. The key to writing this type of process analysis is to keep your attention focused on mental, not physical or natural, processes, so that you can explore such topics as "thinking your way through an essay examination," "enjoying classical music," or "mental conditioning for long distance running."

To review: Your essay of process analysis should conform to these guidelines.

1. Use process analysis to explain an action or series of actions.
2. Use process analysis to give depth and texture to the essay; also use other patterns of development, especially narration, example, and classification.

3. Use the "how to" process essay to explain step-by-step procedures.

4. Use the informative process essay to explain a natural process or to explain historical and social developments.

Larry Woiwode recalls with explicit details the savory, lip-smacking joy of eating an orange during the icy North Dakota winters of the 1940s. One of the simple delights of his youth has provoked him into writing an essay that combines nostalgic reminiscence with a familiar process.

His process analysis includes directives in the "how to" pattern; he tells readers how to peel and eat an orange. However, he uses this expressive discourse primarily to explore his feelings about oranges, especially the way an orange tasted to him in the dead of winter when he divided it into sections, when he sliced it in half, or when he ate it whole.

Woiwode was born in 1941 in Carrington, North Dakota, a small farming community near the center of the state. His recollections reflect his rural midwest heritage, for he invests the arrival of oranges in North Dakota with a mythic quality. He attended the University of Illinois in 1959–1964 and has since worked full time as a free-lance writer. His works have won several awards, including the National Book Award and Critic's Circle Award. Most notable are his two novels, What I'm Going to Do, I Think *(1969) and* Beyond the Bedroom Wall: A Family Album *(1975), and a book of poetry* Even Tide *(1975). "Wanting an Orange" appeared originally in the winter issue of* Paris Review *(1984) and was reprinted as "Ode to an Orange" in* Harper's *(January 1986).*

While reading this essay, note Woiwode's two techniques: (1) use of dialogue and personal reminiscense to open and close the essay and (2) a detailed process that appeals to taste sensations.

LARRY WOIWODE

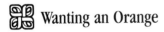 Wanting an Orange

Oh, those oranges arriving in the midst of the North Dakota winters of 1 the forties—the mere color of them, carried through the door in a net bag or a crate from out of the white winter landscape. Their appearance was enough to set my brother and me to thinking that it might be about time to develop an illness, which was the surest way of receiving a steady supply of them.

"Mom, we think we're getting a cold." 2

"*We?* You mean, you two want an orange?" 3

This was difficult for us to answer or dispute; the matter seemed 4 moved beyond our mere wanting.

"If you want an orange," she would say, "why don't you ask for one?" 5

251

"We want an orange."   6

"'We' again. '*We want an orange.*'"   7

"May we have an orange, please."   8

"That's the way you know I like you to ask for one. Now, why don't   9
each of you ask for one in that same way, but separately?"

"Mom . . ." And so on. There was no depth of degradation that we   10
wouldn't descend to in order to get one. If the oranges hadn't wended
their way northward by Thanksgiving, they were sure to arrive before
the Christmas season, stacked first in crates at the depot, filling that
musty place, where pews sat back to back, with a springtime acidity, as
if the building had been rinsed with a renewing elixir that set it right
for yet another year. Then the crates would appear at the local grocery
store, often with the top slats pried back on a few of them, so that we
were aware of a resinous smell of fresh wood in addition to the already
orangy atmosphere that foretold the season more explicitly than any
calendar.

And in the broken-open crates (as if burst by the power of the   11
oranges themselves), one or two of the lovely spheres would lie free of
the tissue they came wrapped in—always purple tissue, as if that were
the only color that could contain the populations of them in their
nestled positions. The crates bore paper labels at one end—of an orange against a blue background, or of a blue goose against an orange
background—signifying the colorful otherworld (unlike our wintry
one) that these phenomena had arisen from. Each orange, stripped of
its protective wrapping, as vivid in your vision as a pebbled sun, encouraged you to picture a whole pyramid of them in a bowl on your
dining room table, glowing in the light, as if giving off the warmth that
came through the windows from the real winter sun. And all of them
came stamped with a blue-purple name as foreign as the otherworld
that you might imagine as their place of origin, so that on Christmas
day you would find yourself digging past everything else in your Christmas stocking, as if tunneling down to the country of China, in order to
reach the rounded bulge at the tip of the toe which meant that you had
received a personal reminder of another state of existence, wholly
separate from your own.

The packed heft and texture, finally, of an orange in your hand—   12
this is it!—and the eruption of smell and the watery fireworks as a
knife, in the hand of someone skilled, like our mother, goes slicing
through the skin so perfect for slicing. This gaseous spray can form a
mist like smoke, which can then be lit with a match to create actual
fireworks if there is a chance to hide alone with a match (matches being
forbidden) and the peel from one. Sputtery ignitions can also be produced by squeezing a peel near a candle (at least one candle is generally

always going at Christmastime), and the leftover peels are set on the stove top to scent the house.

And the ingenious way in which oranges come packed into their 13 globes! The green nib at the top, like a detonator, can be bitten off, as if disarming the orange, in order to clear a place for you to sink a tooth under the peel. This is the best way to start. If you bite at the peel too much, your front teeth will feel scraped, like dry bone, and your lips will begin to burn from the bitter oil. Better to sink a tooth into this greenish or creamy depression, and then pick at that point with the nail of your thumb, removing a little piece of the peel at a time. Later, you might want to practice to see how large a piece you can remove intact. The peel can also be undone in one continuous ribbon, a feat which maybe your father is able to perform, so that after the orange is freed, looking yellowish, the peel, rewound, will stand in its original shape, although empty.

The yellowish whole of the orange can now be divided into sections, 14 usually about a dozen, by beginning with a division down the middle; after this, each section, enclosed in its papery skin, will be able to be lifted and torn loose more easily. There is a stem up the center of the sections like a mushroom stalk, but tougher; this can be eaten. A special variety of orange, without any pits, has an extra growth, or nubbin, like half of a tiny orange, tucked into its bottom. This nubbin is nearly as bitter as the peel, but it can be eaten, too; don't worry. Some of the sections will have miniature sections embedded in them and clinging as if for life, giving the impression that babies are being hatched, and should you happen to find some of these you've found the sweetest morsels of any.

If you prefer to have your orange sliced in half, as some people do, 15 the edges of the peel will abrade the corners of your mouth, making them feel raw, as you eat down into the white of the rind (which is the only way to do it) until you can see daylight through the orangy bubbles composing its outside. Your eyes might burn; there is no proper way to eat an orange. If there are pits, they can get in the way, and the slower you eat an orange, the more you'll find your fingers sticking together. And no matter how carefully you eat one, or bite into a quarter, juice can always fly or slip from a corner of your mouth; this happens to everyone. Close your eyes to be on the safe side, and for the eruption in your mouth of the slivers of watery meat, which should be broken and rolled fine over your tongue for the essence of orange. And if indeed you have sensed yourself coming down with a cold, there is a chance that you will feel it driven from your head—your nose and sinuses suddenly opening—in the midst of the scent of a peel and eating an orange.

And oranges can also be eaten whole—rolled into a spongy mass 16
and punctured with a pencil (if you don't find this offensive) or a knife,
and then sucked upon. Then, once the juice is gone, you can disem-
bowel the orange as you wish and eat away its pulpy remains, and eat
once more into the whitish interior of the peel, which scours the coat-
ing from your teeth and makes your numbing lips and the tip of your
tongue start to tingle and swell up from behind, until, in the light from
the windows (shining through an empty glass bowl), you see orange
again from the inside. Oh, oranges, solid *o*'s, light from afar in the
midst of the freeze, and not unlike that unspherical fruit which first
went from Eve to Adam and from there (to abbreviate matters) to my
brother and me.

"Mom, we think we're getting a cold." 17

"You mean, you want an orange?" 18

This is difficult to answer or dispute or even to acknowledge, finally, 19
with the fullness that the subject deserves, and that each orange bears,
within its own makeup, into this hard-edged yet insubstantial, incomplete, cold, wintry world.

AIMS AND STRATEGIES OF THE WRITER

Comment. Larry Woiwode divides his focus and therefore his aim of
discourse. He first takes a nostalgic trip into his youth for expressive
reminiscence about the cold North Dakota winters that were brightened by the arrival of oranges. Second, he provides precise information
on the process of eating an orange.

Assignment 1. Plan an essay that, like Woiwode's essay, will dip into
your remembrances and describe a particular process from your past.
One student writer, for example, recalled his childhood passion for
racing big wheels. He later graduated to minibikes, three-wheelers, and
finally dirt bikes. He described and contrasted the processes for racing
each vehicle but at the same time kept the focus on his infatuation with
racing, not just the process of riding.

Comment. Woiwode wishes to recapture the atmosphere and flavor of
those early days. His strategy includes blending family activities into
the essay on oranges. Thus he describes his and his brother's efforts to
get oranges from his mother.

Assignment 2. Consider ways to build into your essay the local atmosphere of your homeplace. For example, describe your mother's

kitchen and your mother at the same time you provide details for making popcorn balls at Halloween. You can even include a detailed recipe. Your essay in the Woiwode tradition will do two things: invite readers into your life and give them a process analysis.

Comment. Woiwode's personal attitudes point the direction for his thesis—that oranges always brought warmth to North Dakota in the cold of winter.

Assignment 3. When planning your paper, keep in mind that you may need an expressed or implied thesis to explain your reasons for writing the essay. Give the reader a recipe, a set of actions, or a plan to follow, and also suggest reasons why it is important to you.

THE WRITING PROCESS

Comment. Note how Woiwode arranged his essay: He opens with personal elements, provides background information on the subject, describes three methods of eating an orange, and closes with a return to personal elements.

Assignment 4. Preplan the arrangement of your process analysis essay. For example, one student discussed his joy with his new computer, established its role in his life, explained his techniques for writing computer software programs, and closed with an example of his new graphics design along with the actual program.

Comment. Process analysis requires careful attention to details. Woiwode describes with great precision.

> If you prefer to have your orange sliced in half, as some people do, the edges of the peel will abrade the corners of your mouth, making them feel raw, as you eat down into the white of the rind (which is the only way to do it) until you can see daylight through the orangy bubbles composing its outside.

Assignment 5. When writing the process section of your essay, pay careful attention to detail. Imagine a recipe needing one teaspoon of salt (tsp) listed as needing one *tablespoon* (tbs) or, worse, one *cup*! Double-check all details if it's possible that readers will follow your directions.

Comment. Woiwode writes with a pleasant, friendly voice. We recognize a person who has lived this process. Also, he speaks to his readers ("if you don't find this offensive" or "if you prefer to have your orange sliced in half").

Assignment 6. Use Woiwode's essay as a model and write your process paper in a personal voice. Draw your readers into the piece by addressing them with the second-person "you" or "your." Even though you should generally avoid the second-person "you," process analysis is a pattern that often requires this voice.

Comment. Woiwode blends several patterns into his essay. He uses narration to build episodes with his mother, uses description for the arrival of orange crates at the railroad station, gives numerous examples that appeal to all our senses, and classifies and compares the three methods for eating oranges.

Assignment 7. Make a mental or written checklist for your process essay. Do you need examples? Can you relate a narrative episode from the past to highlight your feelings about the subject? Do your descriptive elements bring the subject into sharp focus for your readers? Should you compare this subject with one that is similar? Can you contrast your attitudes today with those of your childhood?

Alan *Devoe (1909–1955) displays a gift for discovering the essential nature of animals of all kinds and for reporting his findings with detailed and informative precision. A zoologist and dedicated naturalist, he was a prolific writer on animals of all types. His informative essays educate readers about natural processes, in this case the nature of the snapping turtle. His careful research, including personal observation, gives authenticity to his writing. He seems to know well the beast of which he writes, saying, "A snapping turtle makes its biological success by the gifts of size, inconspicuousness, and a sluggish, reptile-witted savagery."*

Devoe combines a storyteller's art with informative discourse so that his relaxed prose style blends with biological accuracy to make scientific writing accessible to most readers. He accomplishes this style by avoiding formal, scientific jargon in favor of descriptive and narrative elements that illustrate the subject for general readers, not just scientists. Along the way, he shares with readers the secret, rhythmic lessons of nature that most will never experience.

"Snapping Turtle" is from Devoe's book Speaking of Animals *(1947), which features the life cycles of many natural animals, as based on his lifetime of study in the wilds and hidden sanctuaries around the world.*

As you read, make marginal notes to record instances where Devoe defends his thesis that nature's principle of compensation may give the snapping turtle some virtues but also brings with it some limitations.

ALAN DEVOE

🔲 Snapping Turtle

There is a rule of economy in the endowments with which nature 1
equips her creatures. For each one, there is the gift of this or that kind
of competence to achieve living effectiveness; but, such competence
being assured, there are not commonly given gifts beyond that necessary measure. Each possession of an endowment implies, so to speak,
the sacrifice—or at any rate the lack—of others. It is given to a rat to
be canny and quick; and a rat's body, compensatingly, is vulnerable. A
porcupine is dim and slow; it has the gift of a protecting armament.
A hare can outrun its foes; it has not the genius of outfighting them. A
mole can outburrow its enemies; it has not the gift of outthinking them.
Natural economy disallows that any creature shall have at once agility,
armor, fighting tools, keen senses, and shrewd wits.

The principle of compensation is evident in the case of the turtles. 2
A common box turtle, that amiable wanderer of the moist woods and

swamp margins, is conspicuous, extremely slow, and incapable of making—with its harmless little jaws designed for nibbling at insects and berries—even the feeblest defense against attack by any sizable enemy. Predators are constantly coming upon box turtles; and the lumbering race of *Terrapene* must long ago have gone down to defeat were it not for their one great gift: the gift, of course, of armor. An attacked box turtle can quickly pull its head, legs, and tail completely inside its shell, and can then draw the plastron so tightly closed that there is not a chink in the armor which will give admission to so much as a fox's whisker. The box turtles enjoy a success by insulation. To the tribe of turtles called *Chelydra*, there is given no such extensive and close-fitting plastron. Even when most fully withdrawn into their shells, the legs and heads and long fleshy tails of this family are considerably exposed. Their gift for survival is of a different order. They are the snapping turtles. A snapping turtle makes its biological success by the gifts of size, inconspicuousness, and a sluggish, reptile-witted savagery.

Snapping turtles are the biggest fresh-water turtles in the country. 3 The hugest of them, the alligator snapping turtles of the Mississippi and the Gulf, attain to 140 pounds. Even a specimen of the common species, found everywhere east of the Rockies, may attain in old age to seventy or eighty pounds or more, and almost any grown individual will weigh twenty. Squat, chunky, massive, the snapping turtle has a dull-colored carapace, roughened and ridged, with a series of broken, saw-toothed indentations at the rear of the shell. Past these projects a long, heavy-fleshed tail, scaly and serrated, like a dragon's. From the sides of the shell protrude the powerful legs, with great, broad feet, heavily webbed, bearing strong, coarse nails. From under the fore edge of the carapace is perpetually extruded the snapper's oversized snake-necked head, too big ever to be withdrawn inside the inadequate shell. The reptilian eyes are tiny, but the power of vision in them is exceptionally keen. The jaws of the great head are heavy and hooked, and in both upper and lower are bony cutting edges that make the snapper's beak an instrument comparable to a pair of powerful shears with jagged blades.

If there is little other evident beauty in a snapping turtle, there is at 4 least that beauty which attaches to all kinds of natural efficiency: the animal-in-itself, the success-as-such. Snapping turtles companioned the dinosaur. They continue to companion us. A snapping turtle has not the ingenious and entrancing shell of other turtles. It has small gifts of speed or grace or mind. But it is still effectively alive, and for its own good reasons. It has its gifts. It can hide in the dim ooze of the bottom of a pond. It can amputate a man's hand.

Many turtles frequently go land-wandering. Pond turtles like to 5 clamber from the water and bask on a sun-warmed log, and a box turtle may live its whole lifetime terrestrially. The snapper is nearly inalienable from the murky water. The only regular venture ashore is the expedition of the female in the early summer to make her deposit of eggs. Laboriously then she hauls herself up the pond bank and goes creeping and rasping overland on her slow webbed feet until she has come to the nearest place where there is soft, loose earth. If possible, her site-selection is likeliest to be a sandbank. Clawing, scraping, turning her heavy body ponderously around, she begins to scoop out a hollow in the ground. She digs with her strong hind feet, thrusting them backward in a gesture like slow swimming. Gradually the cavity deepens until there is a hollow which will admit her body. She slithers into it, twisting and turning in a sluggish, reptilian version of the way a bird shapes the interior of the nest's cup. Loose soil settles and falls back over her. She sets about the voiding of her eggs, perhaps eighteen or twenty of them: spherical, white, with thin, tough shells. Finished, she rears up cumbrously and clambers out of the cavity. Loose soil settles over the clutch. She wheels and goes lurching away. She is filled with an urgent drive to get back to the dim, cool world of underwater, away from the air and the light. When the young turtles shall have hatched, under the agency of time and the heat of the sun, they too will urgently and instantly feel in them that drive. Fresh from the egg, obeying the pull of their turtle nature, they will make for the pond.

Much of the time a snapper lies motionless in the mud of the pond 6 bottom. Early in its sluggish life its dull brown carapace becomes still duller and less conspicuous by the growth on it of water vegetations. It becomes nearly indistinguishable from the surrounding ooze. Motionless, seeming only a part of mud and rocks, the snapper lies and waits. It is waiting for fish, frogs, snails—for almost any item of carnivorous diet. As the unsuspecting prey approaches, there is no stir of the lethargic, scaly hunter; but the tiny eyes are watchful, the muscles of the reptilian neck are tensed. Abruptly, the prey is gone. A human eye can hardly see the motion of a striking snapping turtle's head. It is as fast as the lunge of a snake's strike. The neck is so long, so lithely muscled, that it can be thrown far back over the snapper's shell, or whipped in a darting jab far to either side. Before it seems possible that the snapper can have moved at all, the lashing strike has been made, the bony jaws that can sever a broom handle have clashed together. The snapper, fed, is again motionless, or has perhaps gone creeping slowly off through the mud to take up a new waiting place.

Now and again the snapper leaves its embedment in the bottom- 7 mud and floats at the surface, its hooked snout barely visible above the surface scum as it breathes. With good luck, a bird may skim down to drink. The snapper, so ponderous and awkward of body, is amply agile to catch it. With specially good luck, perhaps ducks may light on the pond. The snapper, reptile-slow, withdraws its head unobtrusively beneath the water. The heavy body submerges in the murk; the webbed feet paddle gently; and the turtle glides unnoticeably and silently as a shadow underneath the ducks. Slowly, like an unwieldy, maneuvering submarine, the turtle turns, tilts, and then slips upward through the water. There is the snap of bony jaws. Before it has had a chance even to cry out, a duck has been yanked down. The snapper bears it to the dark depths of the pool and devours it at leisure, tearing the warm body to pieces with its hooked jaws, eating it gulpingly, morsel by morsel.

A snapping turtle is little beset by enemies. Snappers' eggs are 8 sometimes discovered and eaten by skunks and raccoons and other shore prowlers, and it may happen that a young snapping turtle is attacked in the water by an otter. An otter is just swift enough and subtle enough sometimes to be able to strike before the snapper can. It lunges unexpectedly and bites off the reptilian head. But in maturity a snapping turtle's two chief equipments for biological success—near-invisibility in the mud and murk, and power and fury of jaw—give it an almost unassailable security. As is always the case in the natural economy, however, the particular gifts entail particular limitations. The snapper, fitted to its pond life and its environment of mud and water as rightly as lock fits with key, is disqualified from ever going far from that environment. Not that it cannot and does not sometimes creep ashore, or that it is there vulnerable to enemies. On land, as in the pond, a snapper is formidably effective: it strikes and lashes out with such fury that its whole heavy body may leap in the air. But on land it cannot eat. Whatever prey it may seize ashore it must drag back to the pond. Unless its snaky head is under water, plunged in the element to which its slow, cold life is triumphantly adjusted, a snapping turtle cannot swallow.

AIMS AND STRATEGIES OF THE WRITER

Comment. "Snapping Turtle" demonstrates a scientific writer's primary aim: to relate information

Assignment 1. List topics for your own scientific explanatory discourse. You might select a topic from your studies of natural science, such as the role and function of pine needles, or choose one from your personal experience, such as the physical effects of participating in a sport such as weight lifting, jogging, or swimming.

Comment. Devoe suggests a secondary, implied purpose with his essay: to reestablish the link between his readers and natural processes. He regrets our contemporary isolation from the mysteries and wonders of nature.

Assignment 2. Note any secondary purpose for writing your informative process analysis. For example, an explanation of the Heimlich maneuver to save someone from choking to death might include an expressed appeal or an unspoken desire to your readers to take life-saving classes.

Comment. Devoe aims for scientific accuracy. He wishes to provide a precise, well-researched report on the snapping turtle.

Assignment 3. Consider the necessity of research for your topic. You may have a considerable amount of personal knowledge about jogging or running or body building, but consultation with others and the reading of source materials can help augment your ideas and add authority to your essay.

THE WRITING PROCESS

Comment. Devoe writes an analysis about a natural process: the role of snapping turtles in the natural order.

Assignment 4. Be certain that your topic develops a series of naturally occurring events, not merely a set of "how to" instructions. For example, your paper on a runner might focus primarily on muscle stress and fatigue due to exercise. Then you might offer a "how to" program for controlling fatigue.

Comment. Devoe blends into the essay several patterns of development. He uses comparison and contrast to show distinctions between the snapping and box turtles. He examines one classification of turtles and uses division to explore it in depth. He also uses detailed description and pertinent examples.

Assignment 5. Develop your essay with patterns that add detail and substance. Should you use description, narration, example, comparison? Should you classify and divide?

Comment. Devoe opens his essay with a special rhetorical scheme: antithesis. This technique requires a statement (thesis) and a contradictory comment (antithesis). It has a positive-negative flow to it, as with, "While a rat is canny and quick, a rat's body, in compensation, is vulnerable." Devoe uses this device in his opening to establish a thesis about nature's principle of compensation.

Assignment 6. Try writing a similar block of sentences for your essay. It may appear anywhere in the essay, but openings and closings benefit by such techniques.

Comment. Examine the order of Devoe's essay, which opens with his thesis on nature's principle of compensation. He then compares the box and snapping turtles, describes the snapping turtle, explains the process of the female laying eggs, and relates the turtle's role as underwater predator and surface scavenger. Then he returns in circular fashion to his thesis—the snapping turtle, like all things of nature, has its limitations.

Assignment 7. Preplan your essay in order to stress a thesis. Your examination of a natural process will produce a report, *but not an essay*, unless you make a point with your thesis. Devoe states his thesis early and returns to it late in the essay. If your topic is "jogging for exercise," express a thesis: jogging demands a professional attitude, jogging benefits the heart muscles as much as the leg muscles, jogging represents only one part of a weight-loss program, and so forth.

Ellen Goodman, a nationally syndicated newspaper columnist, earned a Pulitzer Prize in 1980 for distinguished commentary. One of her goals is "tracking some sane path through a thicket of confusion" about human values.

In this essay she examines the changing nature of a child's education where "school is what young people do for a living." Saying that schools now bear the burden of producing adults, she reaches a somewhat shocking conclusion: "But schools are where the young are kept, not where they grow up."

By examining the process by which society produces adults, Goodman persuades her readers that youths have few alternatives for "adulthood training"; thus they use driving, drinking, and sex as rites of passage.

Goodman does more than describe a process. She argues a point about society's insistence that schools house and train all children. Therefore, her aim of discourse is persuasion rather than explanatory analysis. She wishes to awaken readers to a fact of life to promote better understanding of the behavior of the young.

As you read, make notes about your feelings and memories of school days. Where do you agree with Goodman? Where do you disagree?

Some of Goodman's essays have been collected into Close at Home *(1979) and* At Large *(1981), from which "The Long Transition to Adulthood" is reprinted.*

ELLEN GOODMAN

The Long Transition to Adulthood

"When I was a child, I spake as a child, I understood as a child, I thought 1
as a child: but when I became a man, I put away childish things."
(I Corinthians 13:11)

What about the years in between childhood and adulthood? How 2
do we speak then? How do we think? How do we become men and
women?

For most of history there was no in-between, no adolescence as we 3
know it. There was no such lengthy period of semi-autonomy, economic
"uselessness," when the only occupation of a son or daughter was
learning.

In the eighteenth century, Americans weren't legally adults until they 4
turned twenty-one, but they did important work on farms by seven or

eight. When they were physically grown, at only thirteen or sixteen, they had virtually the same jobs as any other adult.

In those days, education was irregular at best, but each child had his or her own vocational guidance teacher: the family. So the transition to adulthood was handled—though not always easily or without tension—through a long apprenticeship, on the farm or in a craft, by people who could point out a direct social path to adulthood.

It was industrialization that changed all that. In the nineteenth century, mills and factories replaced farms, and cities replaced the countryside. Children didn't automatically follow their parents' occupations and so family relations became less important for job training than something called school.

In that century, the need for child labor on farms diminished and the horrors of industrial child labor became widespread. So we passed laws against child labor and in favor of mandatory education. Decade by decade we have raised both ages.

School has replaced work not just out of our benevolence. There are also deep economic reasons. In 1933, at the height of the Depression, the National Child Labor Committee put it as baldly as this: "It is now generally accepted that the exploitation of children, indefensible on humanitarian grounds, has become a genuine economic menace. Children should be in school and adults should have whatever worthwhile jobs there are."

School became the place of reading and writing and certification. It provided the necessary paper for employment. School not only kept young people out of the marketplace but promised "better" jobs if they stayed and studied.

The result of all this is clear: Today, school is what young people do for a living.

In 1870, less than 5 percent of the high school age group were in high school. In 1976, 86.1 percent of those fourteen to seventeen were in school. In 1977, nearly one-third of the eighteen to twenty-one-year-olds were in college.

There has been a 129 percent increase in college enrollment in this country since 1960. In many places today, community colleges are entered as routinely as high schools.

While a high school diploma or a college degree no longer guarantees a job, there are more and more jobs you can't even apply for without them. So the payoff is less certain, but the pressure is even greater to go to school longer and longer, to extend the state of semi-autonomy further and further.

The irony is that society worries more when the young try to grasp at adult "privileges" than when they remain in the passive fraternity-house state of mind. We worry about teenage drinking and driving and pregnancy—all perhaps misguided attempts at "grown-up behavior." Yet we offer few alternatives, few meaningful opportunities for adulthood training. We have virtually allowed sex, drinking and driving to become rites of passage.

School just isn't enough. It demands only one skill, tests only one   15 kind of performance. From a pre-med dorm to an Animal House, it is a youth ghetto where adults are only authority figures, where students don't get the chance to test their own identities, their own authority, their own responsibility to others.

Without enough alternatives, we have left schools the job of produc-   16 ing adults. But schools are where the young are kept, not where they grow up.

Adolescence isn't a training ground for adulthood now. It is a hold-   17 ing pattern for aging youth.

AIMS AND STRATEGIES OF THE WRITER

Comment. Goodman proposes social awareness that might produce changes. When challenged by an interviewer that her topics were too "cozy," she responded: "It is certainly not cozy to be talking about abortion, the vast social changes in the way men and women lead their lives and deal with each other, about children, about the whole category of subjects I deal with. Those subjects are certainly not cozy; they are pretty uncomfortable."*

Assignment 1. Select a problem appropriate for public debate. Consider two possibilities: (1) a subject that causes you personal irritation (for example, companies that invade your privacy by promoting products over the telephone) or (2) a subject that has far-reaching social impact (such as the franchising of national retail chain stores and fast food outlets, which threatens to destroy the local flavor of hometown shopping and dining).

Comment. Goodman's persuasive aim of discourse exposes a problem, but she does not offer a program for reform. Rather, she addresses the issues to create awareness. Later essays by others might introduce reform programs.

Assignment 2. Adjust your persuasive essay to your expectations. Do you wish to bring awareness to your readers? Do you want to convince

---

*From "CA Interview," in *Contemporary Authors* 104 (Detroit: Gale, 1982).

them? Do you want readers to take action? Your answer will affect your voice and the organization of the essay. To firm up your plans, develop a writing situation (see pages 4–5).

Comment. Goodman, like most social commentators, maintains a focus on a social issue: the development of children into adults.

Assignment 3. You may wish to expose social problems, such as public disregard for human decency in the prison systems, or to examine environmental consequences, such as an untimely or unfortunate dumping of chemical wastes. If a thesis statement is not expressed in your writing situation (see assignment 2), write one now.

THE WRITING PROCESS

Comment. Goodman maintains a focus on the historical processes of child education from early frontier days, through industrialization, and into modern times. This past-to-present pattern is common in commentaries on social issues.

Assignment 4. Keep the content of your own essay focused on analysis of a process. In your notes or first draft examine a series of actions that have resulted in consequences that concern you. One student writer, for example, analyzed the springtime rituals of college students who flock to the nation's beaches to frolic in the sun. Consider also the use of a past-to-present pattern. For example, one student examined the demise of downtown shopping in correlation with the growth of contemporary mall shopping.

Comment. Goodman opens her essay with a quotation. Many essayists employ this technique.

Assignment 5. Find a quotation that would be appropriate for your topic. You may need to consult the index to a book of quotations. If you find a timely saying, consider placing it in your opening or your conclusion.

Comment. Statistics are useful in many persuasive essays. The evidence of facts and figures helps convince the reader. Goodman employs this technique in paragraphs 11 and 12.

Assignment 6. If your topic lends itself to statistical evidence, use it. For example, your research may uncover interesting figures. One student interviewed fifty of his peers on their use of turn signals. The results of his survey became a valuable addition to his essay.

Comment. Persuasive writers usually advance one side of an issue. In Goodman's view, the youth of America exist in a "state of semi-autonomy."

Assignment 7. Consider briefly the opposite side of this argument, one that might feel that semi-autonomy produces young people who have initiative, creativity, and more liberal views than past generations. Write a response to Goodman by developing persuasive discourse in opposition to her views. Note a few basic ideas of this argument and then develop a complete essay on the subject.

Thomas Boswell is a sportswriter for the Washington Post. *In 1984 he published a book of twenty essays on baseball entitled* Why Time Begins on Opening Day, *which both praises and critically analyzes his favorite game and its role in America's sport culture.*

His essay "The View from the Dugout" is taken from this book and presents an imaginative and enlightening set of instructions for viewing the game. In particular, Boswell lists eight insightful suggestions, with special commentary. He features an intellectual process on how to enjoy and how to judge the quality of a game and its players and blends his technical knowledge with a human touch that enables readers to perceive a complete picture of baseball theory.

Boswell functions much like a teacher. He tells readers how to approach the subject, how to digest the fundamental processes, and how to arrive at final judgments about the merits of a baseball game. Like a good teacher, he loves his subject and wishes to share with others his special insights.

As you read, note that Boswell has provided numbers and italicized headings so that marginal notes are not essential. However, you might wish to summarize each rule with a marginal note in order to get it firmly in mind.

THOMAS BOSWELL

 The View from the Dugout

What is the big-league point of view?   1

In many ways, the pros watch a baseball game, a season, just as we   2
do; when a fly ball is heading for the fence, they root exactly like the
folks in the bleachers. However, more often than not, the ballplayer
sees things much differently from the rest of us. If we want to taste the
facts of the game, get the flavors right, then we must add this insider's
perspective to our own. Let's have a preliminary Eight Commandments
of the Dugout:

1. Judge Slowly.

No, even more slowly than that.   3

Never judge a player over a unit of time shorter than a month. A   4
game or even a week is nothing; you must see a player hot, cold, and in
between before you can put the whole package together.

2. Assume Everybody Is Trying Reasonably Hard.

Of all the facets at work in baseball, effort is the last to consider. In the   5
majors, players seldom try their hardest; giving 110 percent, as a general
mode of operation, would be counterproductive for most players. The
issue is finding the proper balance between the effort and relaxation.
Usually, something on the order of 80 percent effort is about right.

3. Forgive Even the Most Grotesque Physical Errors.

On good teams, the physical limitations of players are nearly always   6
ignored. The short hop that eats an infielder alive, the ball in the dirt
that goes to the screen, the hitter who is hopelessly overpowered by a
pitcher—all these hideous phenomena are treated as though they never
happened. "Forget it," players say to each other, reflexively. It's assumed
that every player is physically capable of performing every task asked
of him. If he doesn't, it's never his fault. His mistake is simply regarded
as part of a professional's natural margin of error.

4. Judge Mental Errors Harshly.

The distinction as to whether a mistake has been made "from the neck   7
up or the neck down" is always drawn. As an extreme example, a pitcher
who walks home the winning run is guilty of a grievous mental error,
because a major league pitcher is assumed to be able to throw a strike
whenever he absolutely must.

5. Pay More Attention to the Mundane
Than to the Spectacular.

Baseball is a game of huge samplings. The necessity for consistency   8
usually outweighs the need for the inspired. Never judge any player by
his greatest catch, his longest home run, his best pitched game. That is
the exception; baseball is a game of the rule.

6. Pay More Attention to the Theory of the Game Than to the
Outcome of the Game. Don't Let Your Evaluations Be Swayed
Too Greatly by the Final Score.

Don't ask, "Did that pinch hitter get a hit?" In a sense, that's a matter of   9
chance. The worst hitter will succeed one time in five, while the best

hitter will fail two times in three. Instead, ask, "Given all the factors in play at that moment, was he the correct man to use?"

Only then will you begin to sense the game as a team does. If a team   10
loses a game but has used its resources properly—relieved its starting pitcher at a sensible juncture, had the proper pinch hitters at the plate with the game on the line in the late innings—then that team is often able to ignore defeat utterly. Players say, "We did everything right but win."

If you do everything right every day, you'll still lose 40 percent of   11
your games—but you'll end up in the World Series. Nowhere is defeat so meaningless as in baseball. And nowhere are the theories and broad tactics that run the game so important.

7. Keep in Mind That Players Always Know Best How They're Playing.

At the technical level, they seldom fool themselves—the stakes are too   12
high. Self-criticism is ingrained. If a player on a ten-game hitting streak says that he's in a slump, then he is; if a player who's one for fifteen says he's "on" every pitch but that he's hitting a lot of "atom" balls ("right at 'em"), then assume he's about to go on a tear.

8. Stay Ahead of the Action, Not behind It or Even Neck and Neck with It.

Remember, the immediate past is almost always prelude. Ask hurlers   13
how they go about selecting their pitches and they invariably say, "By watching the previous pitch." The thrower plans his game in advance; the pitcher creates it as he goes. A veteran pitcher usually doesn't know what he'll throw on his second pitch until he sees what happened to the first.

Was that batter taking or swinging? Was he ahead of the curveball or   14
behind the fastball? Was he trying to pull, to go to the opposite field, or simply "go with the pitch"? Was he trying for power or contact? And just as important, how has he reacted to these factors in the past? Does he tend to adjust from pitch to pitch (which is unusual)? From at-bat to at-bat (which is more common)? Or is he so stubborn that he has a plan for the whole game and will "sit on a fastball" or "wait for the change-up all night" in hopes of seeing one pitch that he can poleaxe?

That's how baseball has been watched in every respectable dugout   15
for as long as the oldest hand can remember.

AIMS AND STRATEGIES OF THE WRITER

Comment. Boswell's purpose is to provide an insider's perspective on the game. Thereby he explores an intellectual process. He explains how readers can creatively think their way through a baseball game.

Assignment 1. List possible topics for an essay that will explore a mental activity. Use the paragraph on freewriting by Peter Elbow that introduced this chapter to motivate your creativity. Consider such topics as *concentration* for tennis or golf, the *techniques* of speed reading, *methods* for enjoying a rock concert, *planning* a political campaign, or some other activity that requires mental gymnastics.

Comment. In an unexpressed manner, Boswell wishes to share his love for the game of baseball. He wants to draw readers to the ballpark where, armed with his insight, they can share his delight with obvious big plays, such as a grand slam home run, and also the less noticeable elements, such as "Don't let your evaluation be swayed too greatly by the final score."

Assignment 2. As you develop your own process analysis of a mental activity, remember the unspoken Boswell principle: Inspire the reader. Your voice must carry a subtle, unspoken affection for the set of actions. Your voice needs an appreciative tone to accompany its informative purpose.

Comment. Writers must always remember the needs of their audience. Boswell offers a penetrating, knowledgeable analysis of the game for dedicated baseball fans.

Assignment 3. Identify and address an audience as you develop the draft of your essay. If your views are too simplistic for your audience, then you will offend a reader's intelligence, so write from a foundation of your experience and the reader's probable knowledge.

THE WRITING PROCESS

Comment. Boswell blends other patterns of rhetoric into his process essay. He classifies the rules, provides numerous examples, indirectly defines the game, describes it, narrates brief episodes, and compares types of errors.

Assignment 4. If you have planned an essay that explores a mental activity, select patterns that add specific detail to your writing, especially descriptive examples and comparisons. Write one paragraph of your process analysis and embellish it with at least three examples.

Comment. Boswell employs a numerical classification for his eight rules.

Assignment 5. Consider a method for listing the steps of your process. Is chronology important? Does one activity depend on the completion of another? For example, writing computer software requires a sequence of steps that must be followed in a set order. Interrupt the program's sequence and it will "crash." Make an outline of steps, numerical items, or a time sequence that will govern your writing.

Comment. In paragraph 14 Boswell uses a series of eight rhetorical questions. He does not ask them directly of the reader but poses them as questions a pitcher might consider during the course of a game.

Assignment 6. Rhetorical questions stimulate the reader if the reader is *not* challenged to answer them. You might develop a set of rhetorical questions for your essay, as in this example from one student's paper.

> The successful tennis player must respond creatively to the game as it unfolds. He can't allow his left brain, his reasoning side, to interfere with play: Is my grip correct? Am I ready to receive? Can I reach a serve to my backhand? Will this guy try to fool me with an off-speed serve? Obviously, such a baffling array of questions may well freeze the player's instinctive reactions.

Use this sample and the one by Boswell as models for writing a paragraph that features a set of rhetorical questions about your topic.

Comment. Boswell provides a set of instructions, but it differs from a "how to" process in that each person will respond in a different way. Since he cannot control the reaction of readers, he offers commentary that explains and defends his rules.

Assignment 7. As you develop your essay, keep in mind that mental processes will differ from one person to another. Therefore, offer advice in general terms and justify it as Boswell has. Also, look again at the freewriting instructions.

Susan Noe writes an explanatory paper about organ transplants, especially about the process of psychological adjustment necessary for recipients. Although she has not personally experienced such an event, Noe confronts her readers with this possibility, saying, "The statistics are beginning to stack the odds so that young persons especially can expect in their lifetimes to be recipients of a transplanted organ."

Noe blends several patterns into her explanation. She explains psychological processes, gives numerous examples, compares the reactions of various organ recipients, and conducts causal analysis to discuss the consequences for her readers.

Most effectively, she addresses the issue of organ transplants to herself and her readers, saying, "One of us may be next—as donor or recipient." She relates what she herself has done about this possibility and thereby suggests what actions the reader might take.

As you read the essay, make marginal notes to record each stage of the process. Also write a brief summary of Noe's closing three paragraphs to understand how she applies the scientific process to herself and her readers, thereby giving it relevance. Study also her use of MLA style in the citations of her sources.

SUSAN NOE, STUDENT

 A Stranger Lives within Me

For a person with a chronic or terminal illness such as kidney failure, cirrhosis of the liver, or blockage of the arteries, replacement of the diseased organ with a healthy one is becoming an increasingly popular method of treatment. Receiving someone else's organ is a drastic alteration of the physical body and the person's mental condition. Thus, after a transplant, the patient has physical pain and also a difficult psychological adjustment.

Whether the transplanted organ is a cornea or a heart, the process of psychological adjustment is similar in most recipients. Immediately after a successful operation, the recipient experiences feelings of renewed life and heightened self-confidence. Helen Michalisko, a Johns Hopkins University social worker, observes, "There's a sense of rebirth and renewal; like a newborn child, they think everything they see and touch is sensational" (qtd. in Rodgers 63). These feelings result not only from the recipient's exhilaration at being physically "well," but also from the euphoria induced by routine medications (Rodgers 63).

After a short period of time, however, indications of physical rejec- 3
tion or other postoperative complications revive the worries and concerns that the recipient experienced before the transplant. As a result,
the patient again becomes frightened, yet at the same time tries to deny
any fears of possible death (Rodgers 63).

Later, after release from the hospital, the recipient recognizes the 4
realities of organ transplant, with depressing effects. "If I had known
then what I know now, I probably would have declined the surgery,"
revealed a young man after a heart transplant (Rodgers 60–61). Although he had been cautioned prior to his operation, this patient became depressed by the pain, diet limitations, and constant fear that still
remained with him.

The recipient, in effect, experiences stages of acceptance to this new 5
life, including uncertainty, apprehension, and even denial of the alien
organ. Like the stages of grief, the recipient must adjust the mental
image of the body to include a transplanted organ.

Some recipients, however, cannot learn to accept the alien organ. 6
The self-image and personality of these people are often altered because they feel that another person is living inside them, to the point
that some attempt to assume characteristics of the donor. For example,
Dr. Donald T. Lunde, a psychiatrist at Stanford University Medical Center, reports a patient who, upon receiving the heart of a prominent
citizen, felt a compelling urge to change his life-style and "become
more like the donor" (qtd. in *Newsweek*, 118).

What does all this medical trauma have to do with me? With you? 7
One of us may be next—as donor or recipient. The statistics are beginning to stack the odds so that young persons especially can expect in
their lifetimes to be recipients of a transplanted organ. And why not? If
medical science continues its phenomenal success, I see no reason why
transplants of arms and legs can't occur to join transplants of eyes,
hearts, kidneys, and livers.

I look forward to such medical breakthroughs. Therefore, I have 8
filled out my donor card. If I die, at least a part of me lives on. In the
same manner, I would accept a donor organ. Granted, I would surely
experience the various stages of coping as described above, but I would
be alive, thanks to medical science.

Any recipient who can successfully meet the physical and the mental 9
challenges will be able to take full advantage of this miraculous medical
achievement and enjoy a greatly improved life.

Works Cited

Rodgers, Joann. "Life on the Cutting Edge." *Psychology Today* Oct. 1984: 58–67.
"Transplant Psychosis." *Newsweek* 19 May 1969: 118.

SUSAN NOE TALKS ABOUT HER AIMS AND STRATEGIES

I wrote the first draft after reading a *Newsweek* article. But my peer reviewer on that draft asked me bluntly, "So what? You report on organ transplants, but you don't make a point. I can't find a thesis."

That's when I developed the ending. For the first time, I confronted the issue myself and addressed the reader more realistically. My whole purpose changed with this new mission of action. I signed a donor card and called on my readers to do the same.

However, my instructor, after looking at the second draft, said I needed some examples or quotations of persons who had experienced donor transplants. I went back to *Newsweek* to cite some material from that article. While in the library I found another reference in *Readers' Guide to Periodical Literature*. It turned out to be the good article by Joann Rodgers in *Psychology Today*. Those two articles gave me the voice of authority on the subject and also provided my answer to the instructor's challenge: to find examples and quotations of people involved.

I had to write this paper three times to get it right, if it really is. My research paper manual helped me write correct citations and a bibliography. I had never realized that little papers like this would require such formal handling. I made an A on it, but I think it needs more development, yet that would make it into a research paper rather than a short essay of explanation.

So that's it. I drafted a report. Then I changed it into a thesis essay. On third draft I added the sources to make it into a little research paper.

Comment. As she explained in her comments above, Noe did not write this essay off the top of her head. She read an article in *Newsweek* and used its idea to launch her first draft. At the urging of her instructor, she went back to the library and cited two sources.

Assignment 1. Begin the note-taking and preliminary drafting of a paper in the manner of Noe. That is, go to the library and read a few magazines. After you find one article that explores a social or scientific process, use an index to find another on the same topic. Then use these in your paper.

Comment. Noe admits that her first draft was a report of facts, not an essay that explores an issue and defends a thesis.

Assignment 2. After you have selected a topic (as suggested in assignment 1), describe your audience. Why are you addressing these readers with this particular subject?

Comment. Although process analysis serves as her primary pattern of development, Noe carefully blends additional patterns into the paper, especially the patterns of example, comparison, and cause and effect.

Assignment 3. Every paper must find its own path of development, but your thoughtful consideration of special patterns of development will give your paper substance. If you employ process analysis as your basic pattern, also look for others to provide descriptive detail, comparison, and causal relationships.

Comment. Noe uses the names of authorities in her paper and quotes from their articles. That bit of scholarship adds a distinguishing touch to the essay, raising its validity and her rating as a writer.

Assignment 4. Search out two or three quotations from your library reading on the topic and use them to support your ideas. The quotation should be pertinent and well worded and should not seem artificial or forced; it should grow naturally out of your reading. If you change the quotation into a paraphrase, you should cite the source in the same manner as Noe (see the final sentence of paragraph 2).

 Definition

Definition essays require exact statements about the meaning of a term, phrase, or nature of a thing. The need for definition as a writing pattern develops from a writer's aims and purposes. Most writers desire to explain using precise meaning and exact wording. Some writers present their personal definition of a subject; others use definition to argue a point. For example, Peter Farb (see his essay later in this chapter) wrote an entire book to explain words and word play; his aim is the explanation of a term (such as "black English"), his approach is judicious and critical, his primary pattern of development is definition, and his secondary pattern is example. In contrast, Rachel Jones writes an essay (which follows in this chapter) not only to define but also argue about the term "black English." She defines it, in part, as a language that isolates and separates black youth from the mainstream of American society.

USE PERSONAL DEFINITION TO EXPLAIN YOUR ATTITUDE

Sometimes a writer's purpose and attitude appear less formal and judicious and thus more relaxed, ironic, and humorous. The writer, in effect, says "Let me define this concept in my own way, not by dictionary methodology." The writer then stipulates the conditions under which the term applies.

For example, in the following quote Sidney Harris offers a personal definition of the word "jerk." He constructs an insightful, although not a dictionary, definition of the word.

A jerk, then, is a man (or woman) who is utterly unable to see himself as he appears to others. He has no grace, he is tactless without meaning to be, he is a bore even to his best friends, he is an egotist without charm. All of us are egotists to some extent, but most of us—unlike the jerk—are perfectly and horribly aware of it when we make asses of ourselves. The jerk never knows.*

The writer shares a personal response to a topic. The definition grows expressively from that base. In similar fashion, William Zinsser (pages 282–283) offers his personal definition of "clutter" in the English language.

USE LEXICAL DEFINITION FOR PRECISION AND EXACTNESS

A lexical definition names an item, the class to which it belongs, and the way it differs from others in that class (for instance, "man is a reasoning animal," or "an acorn is the fruit of an oak tree"). Such formal definition establishes validity of meaning and attempts to avoid ambiguity. For this reason, Farb (pages 286–295) uses lexical definition to explain black English and its distinctive place in linguistic history. In similar fashion, Peter Elbow (page 280) explains that freewriting belongs to the class of writing but differs from most writing by being automatic and spontaneous.

Word selection becomes crucial when defining terms. An abstract word such as "freedom" may mean liberty, permission, or immunity; your aim and writing form will dictate the meaning. To say "Every person needs elbow room" signals a relaxed, colloquial approach directed at a general audience. To say "Every person needs autonomy" indicates a formal, judicious viewpoint directed at an educated audience. In general, explanatory writing uses longer, more precise words and avoids slang and colloquial expressions, yet all writers must choose words from their own vocabularies. Padding an essay with big words usually leads to confusion rather than precision of meaning.

The etymology of a word, as set forth in a good dictionary, can serve your definition. A brief definition of "university," as explored by Isaac Asimov, demonstrates the value of researching a word's history.

"Universe" and "University"

A group of individuals acting, in combination, toward a single goal under a single direction, behaves as though it were one person. In the Middle Ages, such a group was called a "universitas," from the Latin "unum" (one) and "vertere" (to turn); a group, in other words, had "turned into one" person. In the most general sense, this came to mean the group of everything in existence considered as a unit; that is, the *universe*.

It also came to be used in a more restricted sense. In the early Middle

---

*Sidney J. Harris, "What Makes a 'Jerk' a Jerk?" in *Last Things First* (Boston: Houghton Mifflin, 1957).

Ages, for instance, a school of higher learning was called a "studium," from the Latin "studere," meaning "to be zealous" or "to strive after." From this, come our words *study* and *student*. The Italian version of "studium" is *studio*, which has come into English as a place where the fine arts, particularly, are studied or practiced (a memorial to the fact that in Renaissance times, Italy was the center of the world of fine art).

A group of students at such a school would refer to themselves (with the usual good opinion of themselves that students always have) as "universitas magistrorum et scholarium"—a "group of masters and scholars." They were a "universitas," you see, because they were all pursuing the single goal of learning. And gradually the name of the group became, in shortened form, the name of the schools which, around 1300, began to be known as *universities*.

Meanwhile, within the university, groups of students following a particular specialty, as, for instance, law, would band together for mutual aid. They were a group of *colleagues* (Latin, "collegae") from the Latin "com-" (together) and "ligare" (to bind). They were bound together for a common purpose. Such a group of colleagues formed a *college* (Latin, "collegium") a word now used to denote a particular school within a university.

The older meaning as simply "a group of colleagues" persists today in the College of Cardinals of the Roman Catholic Church, and in America's own electoral college which meets every four years to elect a president.*

WRITE EXTENDED DEFINITION BY BLENDING SEVERAL PATTERNS

You can compress a lexical definition into one sentence. However, when writers have additional aims, such as capturing the essence of the American dream or explaining black English, they need a combination of techniques—comparison, classification and division, process analysis, and others. Zinsser, who defines "clutter" in the English language, uses several patterns: He names parts, gives different meanings, provides examples, narrates personal experiences, quotes other sources, compares and contrasts, and in general blends together almost all rhetorical patterns into a master essay.

USE NEGATION TO EXPLAIN WHAT SOMETHING IS NOT

Sometimes you will need to tell your readers what the subject is *not*. Negation denies the existence or validity of something. For example, Elbow tells what freewriting is not in the following passage:

*Isaac Asimov, *Words of Science and the History behind Them* (Boston: Houghton Mifflin, 1959).

The main thing about freewriting is that it is *nonediting*. It is an exercise in bringing together the process of producing words and putting them down on the page. Practiced regularly, it undoes the ingrained habit of editing at the same time you are trying to produce. It will make writing less blocked because words will come more easily. You will use up more paper, but chew up fewer pencils.

This passage demonstrates another element of definition: Writers often counterbalance negative elements against positive ones. The negative side makes more evident the positive stance of the writer.

USE EXPERT TESTIMONY TO ADD AUTHORITY

Expert testimony from other sources can lend substance and authority to a pattern of definition. Quotations and paraphrases reinforce both lexical definitions and personal opinions. Student writer Theresa Kleynhans defines "reincarnation" and willingly cites her sources to reinforce her meaning.

One observer notes, "The theosophical conception of the soul is that it is literally a fragment of the one supreme life, or God—an individualized portion of the cosmic mind—and that an immense period of time is required for its evolution" (Montgomery 210). The major part of the long evolutionary journey is spent in nonphysical realms. Periodically the soul—the center of consciousness that is the real man—presses itself on this material plane because there are lessons to be learned here that cannot elsewhere be acquired. Montgomery explains that this soul gradually "takes possession of a nascent human organism" some months before birth and is born within the infant body (82). It grows from youth to old age and finally dies, a death which destroys that which is no longer useful. The released consciousness passes tranquilly back into the invisible world from which it came. "There the experience which he [it] gained while on earth is transmuted into skill, wisdom and power," says Hodson (79).

Kleynhans does two important things: (1) She uses quoted material to reinforce the aim and purpose of the essay (see pages 318–322 for the manner in which the material fits the context of the whole paper), and (2) she recognizes all borrowed materials with in-text citations to name and page and later, at the end of the paper, provides a "Works Cited" page.

To review: Conform to these guidelines when writing an essay of definition.

1. Allow definition to grow logically out of your aims and attitudes

about a subject. The definition may be central to an entire essay or it may only occupy one paragraph.

2. Use lexical definition that expresses your concepts and meanings.

3. To avoid ambiguity, use lexical definition in the form of an exact, three-part structure: the *subject*, the *class* to which it belongs, and its *difference* from others in the class.

4. To build an extended definition, use a blending of several patterns of development, such as example, comparison, classification with analysis, and description.

5. Use negation to show what the subject is not and to develop a negative-positive sequence.

6. Use expert testimony properly and as necessary to support and defend your ideas.

William Zinsser defines "clutter" in his own terms. As a professional writer he finds offensive clutter in everyday language. "Are you experiencing any pain?" asks the dentist, when in truth he means, "Does it hurt?" Such clutter, says Zinsser, is a "drag on energy and momentum."

He defines clutter as those words and phrases that have replaced short, effective words that mean the same thing, such as "at the present time we are experiencing precipitation" rather than "it is raining." His definition is a personal one. The language, according to Zinsser, becomes untidy when people use it carelessly. A word that clutters the language is similar to a euphemism, which is a pleasant-sounding term substituted for a short, blunt one, such as "to pass away" for "to die."

Zinsser has had a long career as journalist and teacher of writing. Thus his subjective definition of clutter will help any writer who needs a strong statement on untidy language, especially one that goes beyond a dictionary meaning. Zinsser's work has appeared in the New York Herald Tribune, Life *magazine,* The New York Times, *several books of essays, and his recent book* On Writing Well *(1976) in which he explores his theories and attitudes about the English language and from which "Clutter" is excerpted.*

Perform two activities as you read the essay: First, note Zinsser's various definitions of clutter, realizing that writers may provide more than one view of a term. Second, mark or number his numerous examples, noting the importance of example as a method of development for definition essays.

WILLIAM K. ZINSSER

 Clutter

Clutter is the laborious phrase which has pushed out the short word   1
that means the same thing. These locutions are a drag on energy and
momentum. Even before John Dean gave us "at this point in time,"
people had stopped saying "now." They were saying "at the present
time," or "currently," or "presently" (which means "soon"). Yet the idea
can always be expressed by "now" to mean the immediate moment
("now I can see him"), or by "today" to mean the historical present
("today prices are high"), or simply by the verb "to be" ("it is raining").
There is no need to say "at the present time we are experiencing
precipitation."

Speaking of which, we are experiencing considerable difficulty get-   2
ting *that* word out of the language now that it has lumbered in. Even
your dentist will ask if you are experiencing any pain. If he were asking
one of his own children he would say, "Does it hurt?" He would, in
short, be himself. By using a more pompous phrase in his professional
role he not only sounds more important; he blunts the painful edge of
truth. It is the language of the airline stewardess demonstrating the
oxygen mask that will drop down if the plane should somehow run out
of air. "In the extremely unlikely possibility that the aircraft should
experience such an eventuality," she begins—a phrase so oxygen-
depriving in itself that we are prepared for any disaster, and even gasp-
ing death shall lose its sting.

Clutter is the ponderous euphemism that turns a slum into a de-   3
pressed socioeconomic area, a salesman into a marketing representative, a dumb kid into an underachiever and a bad kid into a pre-
delinquent. (The Albuquerque public schools announced a program
for "delinquent and pre-delinquent boys.")

Clutter is the official language used by the American corporation—   4
in the news release and the annual report—to hide its mistakes. When
a big company recently announced that it was "decentralizing its
organizational structure into major profit-centered businesses" and
that "corporate staff services will be aligned under two senior vice-
presidents" it meant that it had had a lousy year.

Clutter is the language of the interoffice memo ("the trend to mosaic   5
communication is reducing the meaningfulness of concern about
whether or not demographic segments differ in their tolerance of pe-
riodicity") and the language of computers ("we are offering functional
digital programming options that have built-in parallel reciprocal
capabilities with compatible third-generation contingencies and
hardware").

AIMS AND STRATEGIES OF THE WRITER

Comment. This writer develops a personal, special meaning for the
word "clutter" to make a point about language usage. He decries the
use of a laborious phrase to replace a short, more effective word.

Assignment 1. Consider your own language usage. You might focus
on unusual verb usage, such as "Let's do lunch" or "Let's catch a movie."
Or you might examine slang expressions, such as "jock," "fox," "smack,"
and "crack." You might also explore the jargon of a trade or profession,
such as "byte," "bit," "chip," and "loop" in the computer field.

Comment. Zinsser supplies a series of definitions for his special usage of "clutter." He calls clutter a "laborious phrase" and a "ponderous euphemism," and he labels it "the official language used by the American corporation."

Assignment 2. Levels of meaning serve the devotees of slang language. "Smack" may mean "to hit," "to kiss," or "heroin." Slang can disguise the meaning of a word and at the same time enrich it with new metaphoric levels. Write a paragraph on a familiar word that is "cluttered" by euphemistic expressions. (Consider such words as "sex," "love," "death," or "illegal drugs.")

Comment. Zinsser's ultimate aim, which is also the purpose of his book *On Writing Well*, is to improve language usage by his readers. Therefore, his personal definition of *clutter* is not like a dictionary entry because he narrows his focus.

Assignment 3. Write an experimental paragraph in which you have a dual purpose. For example, define and give examples of the language of print media advertising but at the same time endorse or condemn it. Make your personal response apparent to the reader.

THE WRITING PROCESS

Comment. On a general level, clutter means "things lying about in untidy order." Zinsser narrows his meaning to mean language clutter. To do so, he redefines the word in his own terms: "Clutter is the laborious phrase which has pushed out the short word that means the same thing."

Assignment 4. Write a paragraph or two that defines in a personal way a word or phrase. That is, take a word that has a dictionary meaning, such as "alcohol," "frisk," or "insane," and approach it in the Zinsser style.

Comment. Zinsser supplies several definitions, not just the one in the first sentence. Because he knows that a word can have several connotations, he names it at the beginnings of paragraphs 3, 4, and 5.

Assignment 5. Write a brief paragraph that explores the multiple meanings of a common word. For example, *mushroom* as noun means an "edible fungus," as a verb it means "growing rapidly," and as an adjective it means "shaped like a mushroom."

Comment. Zinsser loads every paragraph with detailed examples that illustrate his meaning.

Assignment 6. In order to appreciate the value and importance of examples in developing a definition, go through the Zinsser essay and lightly cross through all examples. How much remains?

Comment. Zinsser divides clutter into several categories: the laborious phrase, the ponderous euphemism, the official language of corporations, and the language of interoffice memos.

Assignment 7. Select a word that has emotional connotations, such as "love," "affection," or "hate," and classify it into types. Write a definition essay that uses each type as the topic sentence for paragraph development.

The following selection defines "black English" with an expansive, thorough look at a linguistic dialect "that has a strikingly different grammar and sound system." Farb argues that black English may sound like an inferior kind of standard English, but in truth "it is no more different from Standard English than is any other dialect."

To build his case, Farb must abandon any personal definition of black English and write an extended definition that interacts with several patterns of development, especially example, comparison, and causal analysis.

The order of his essay is worth studying: He introduces his subject, dismisses narrow and biased views of the issue, and examines the historical and causal influences. He then compares black English with standard English on several levels. He closes with an assessment of schooling and the role of bilingualism.

As you read, make marginal notes that endorse or disagree with Farb's pronouncements, for he does more than merely define a linguistic concept: He builds the essay on a controversial social and political foundation. See, for instance, the essay by Rachel Jones which follows this one and read also the essay by Richard Rodriguez on pages 86–96. Both are vigorous advocates for teaching standard English to minority students.

Farb is a respected linguist who has degrees from Vanderbilt University and Columbia University. He has published one book on the language of American Indians. "Linguistic Chauvinism" appeared originally in his book Word Play: What Happens When People Talk *(1973).*

PETER FARB

🔲 Linguistic Chauvinism

Very few white Americans are aware of the extent to which the great 1
majority of black Americans suffer from linguistic schizophrenia—of a
unique sort. The diglossia problem of the lower-class black is unusual
because he does not speak a colloquial or "incorrect" form of Standard
English. Instead, he speaks a dialect that has a strikingly different grammar and sound system, even though to white ears the black appears to
be trying to speak Standard English. Anyone who speaks Black English
is likely to find himself stigmatized as a user of an inferior kind of
Standard English, whereas actually he is speaking a radically different
dialect that is as consistent and elegant as whites consider their Stan-

dard English to be. (I must emphasize that my discussion of the history of Black English is both hypothetical and controversial. At least three major points of view exist: that Black English is a completely different language despite its apparent similarity to Standard English, that it is a radically different dialect, and that it is no more different from Standard English than is any other dialect. The position taken in this book is the second one because I feel that linguistic research now being carried on will ultimately prove it correct.)

The whole subject of Black English is so tied up with both racism   2 and good intentions that it rarely is discussed calmly, even by specialists in the field. At one extreme is the racist, conscious or unconscious, who attributes black speech to some physical characteristic like thick lips or a large tongue; he is certain that it is inferior speech and that it must be eradicated. At the other extreme is the well-intentioned liberal who denies that he detects much of a departure from white speech; he regards Black English as simply a southern United States dialect, and he is likely to attribute any departure from white speech to the black's educational deprivation. Both views are wrong. Black English's radical departure from Standard English has nothing to do with the anatomy of race or with educational deprivation. The history of the English spoken by New World blacks shows that it has been different from the very beginning, and that it is more different the farther back in time one goes. Of course, some blacks speak exactly like whites, but these cases are both recent and exceptional; the overwhelming majority speak Black English some or all of the time.

By "Black English" I do not mean the spirited vocabulary whose   3 adoption by some whites gives them the mistaken impression that they are talking real soul to their black brothers. These rich and metaphoric words are much less important than grammar for a description of Black English. They originated by the same processes that gave rise to the slang, jargon, and argot words of Standard English, and, like the Standard words, they have seeped out to become part of the general vocabulary. Many words that were once the exclusive property of speakers of Black English—*groovy, square, jive, rap, cool, chick, dig, rip off*, and so on—are now commonly used by speakers of the white Standard. When I say that Black English is different from Standard English, I do not refer to the superficial vocabulary which changes from year to year, but to its largely different history, sound system, and basic structure.

What we hear today as Black English is probably the result of five   4 major influences: African languages; West African pidgin; a Plantation Creole once spoken by slaves in the southern United States as well as by blacks as far north as Canada; Standard English; and, finally, urbanization in the northern ghettos. The influence of African languages on black speech was long denied, until in 1949 Lorenzo Dow Turner published the results of his fifteen-year study of Gullah, a black dialect spoken in the coastal region around Charleston, South Carolina, and Savannah, Georgia. Gullah is important in the history of Black English because this region continued to receive slaves direct from Africa as late as 1858—and so any influence from Africa would be expected to survive there longer. Turner accumulated compelling evidence of resemblances in pronunciation, vocabulary, and grammar between Gullah and various West African languages. He listed some 4,000 Gullah words for personal names, numbers, and objects that are derived directly from African languages. Some of these words—such as *tote, chigger, yam,* and *tater* ("potato")—eventually entered Standard English.

The second influence, pidginization, is more apparent because the languages spoken today by the descendants of slaves almost everywhere in the New World—regardless of whether these languages were based on English, French, Dutch, Spanish, or Portuguese—share similarities in sound patterns and in grammar. For example, the common Black English construction *He done close the door* has no direct equivalent in Standard English, but it is similar to structures found in Portuguese Pidgin, Weskos of West Africa, French Creole of Haiti, the Shanan Creole of Surinam, and so on. An analysis of the speech of slaves—as recorded in eighteenth-century letters, histories, and books of travel—indicates that the great majority of them in the continental United States spoke pidgin English, as much in the North as in the South. This was to be expected since blacks speaking many languages were thrown together in the West African slave factories and they had to develop some means of communication. No matter what their mother tongues were, they had been forced to learn a second language, an African Pidgin English that at least as early as 1719 had been spread around the world by the slave trade. We can be certain of that year because it marked the publication of Daniel Defoe's *Robinson Crusoe,* which contains numerous examples of this pidgin and also uses, in the character Friday, the West African and slave tradition of bestowing personal names based on the days of the week.

Therefore most slaves must have arrived in the New World speaking a pidgin that enabled them to communicate with each other and eventually also with their overseers. In the succeeding generations a small number of blacks were taught Standard English. But the great majority apparently expanded their pidgin into a creole language—called Plantation Creole by some linguists even though it was also spoken in the North—by grafting an English vocabulary onto the structures of their native languages and pidgins. This creole probably began to develop as soon as the first generation of slaves was born in the New World. Cotton Mather and other writers record its use in Massachusetts; the writings of T. C. Haliburton (creator of the humorous Yankee character Sam Slick) show that it reached as far north as Halifax, Nova Scotia; Harriet Beecher Stowe attests to its use in New York and Benjamin Franklin to its presence in Philadelphia. Emancipation did not do away with Plantation Creole. In fact, it spread its use to the offspring of the former house slaves who had been taught Standard English. That is because segregated schools and racial isolation after the Civil War caused the great number of speakers of Plantation Creole to linguistically overwhelm the small number of black speakers of Standard English. Nevertheless, the fourth step—a process known as decreolization—has been constantly at work as blacks tend to move closer in speech to the Standard English they hear all around them. The final step in the creation of the Black English known today was the surge of blacks into northern ghettos. The ghetto experience placed the final stamp on Black English by mixing various kinds of Plantation Creole, filtering out some features and emphasizing others. Variations are apparent in the Black English spoken locally in such cities as Baltimore, New York, Detroit, Chicago, and Los Angeles, but these variations are minor in comparison to the major differences between Black English in general and Standard English.

I would need an entire volume to discuss these differences adequately, but let me at least point out a few of them. Black English does not sound like Standard English because it often uses different sounds. In the case of vowels, groups of words like *find-found-fond* and *pen-pin* are pronounced almost exactly alike. The distinctive sounds of Black English, though, result more from the pronunciation of the consonants. *Th* at the beginning of a word is often pronounced either *d*, as in *dey*, or *t*, as in *tink*; in the middle of a word or at the end, *th* often becomes *v* or *f*, with the result that *father* is pronounced *faver* and *mouth* is pronounced *mouf*. Black English dispenses with *r* to an even greater extent than the Standard speech heard along the eastern coast of North America. It not only loses the *r* after vowels and at the end of words, as do some Standard dialects which pronounce *sore* and *saw* in the same way, but in addition it dispenses with *r* between vowels, thus making *Paris* and *pass* sound alike. *L* also is almost completely lost except when it begins a word, with the result that no distinction is made between such pairs of words as *help-hep* and *toll-toe*. Final clusters of consonants are nearly always simplified by the loss of one of the consonants, usually *t* or *d* but often *s* or *z* as well, with the result that *meant-mend-men, start-started*, and *give-gives* are pronounced in the same way.

Some linguists have stated that Black English grammar resulted   8
simply from the loss of the consonant sounds that carry much of the
burden of forming suffixes in Standard English. The absence of verb
tenses, for example, was attributed to the loss of *d* (as when *burned*
becomes *burn*') or *l* (as when *I'll go* becomes *I go*). The statement in
Black English *He workin'* was long thought to be the same as the
Standard *He's working*, except that black pronunciation dropped the *s*
in the contraction of the verb *is*. But it now appears that the structure
of Black English is much more complicated than the mere loss of suffixes due to a failure to pronounce them.

The black speaker is apparently using a different grammar, which   9
disregards *is* in the Standard *He's working* and instead chooses to
emphasize the auxiliary verb *be*. *He be workin'* means that the person
referred to has been working continuously for a long time; but *He
workin'*, without the *be*, means that the person is working now, at this
very moment. A speaker of Black English would no more say *He be
workin' right now* (that is, use the habitual *be* to tell about something
happening only at this moment) than a speaker of Standard English
would say *He is sleeping tomorrow* (that is, ignore the tense of the
verb). The use and non-use of the auxiliary *be* is clearly seen in the
Black English sentence *You makin' sense, but you don't be makin'
sense*—which in Standard English means "You just said something
smart, but you don't habitually say anything smart." The speaker of
Black English, therefore, is obliged by his language to mark certain
kinds of verbs as describing either momentary action or habitual action. In contrast, the speaker of Standard English is not obliged to make
this distinction—although he must make others which speakers of
Black English ignore, such as the tense of the verb.

Black English also differs considerably from Standard English in the   10
various ways in which negative statements are structured. The Black
English *He ain't go* is not simply the equivalent of the Standard *He
didn't go*. The speaker of Black English is not using *ain't* as a past tense,
but rather to express the negative for the momentary act of going,
whether it happened in the past or is happening right now. If the Black
English speaker, on the other hand, wants to speak of someone who is
habitually the kind of person who does not go, he would say *He ain't
goin'*. *Ain't* also serves several other functions in Black English. *Dey
ain't like dat* might be thought by speakers of Standard to mean "They
aren't like that"—but it actually means "They didn't like that," because
in this usage *ain't* is the negative of the auxiliary verb to do. *Ain't* can
also emphasize a negation by doubling it, as in *He ain't no rich*. And in
what would be a negative *if*-clause in Standard English, the rules of

Black English eliminate the *if* and invert the verb—with the result that the equivalent of the Standard *He doesn't know if she can go* is the Black English *He don't know can she go.*

I have touched on merely a few of the obvious differences between   11 the rules of Black English and the rules of Standard English in regard to verbs. Numerous other aspects of Black English verbs could be discussed—such as *I done go, I done gone, I been done gone,* and *I done been gone.* Or I could mention other constructions, such as the possessive case, in which I could demonstrate that *John book* in Black English is a different kind of possessive than *John's book* is in Standard English. But by now it should be apparent that important differences exist between the two dialects.

The wonder is that it took people so long to realize that Black   12 English is neither a mispronunciation of Standard English nor an accumulation of random errors made in the grammar of Standard. Utterances in Black English are grammatically consistent and they are generated by rules in the same way that utterances in Standard English are generated by rules. Miss Fidditch may not regard utterances in Black English to be "good English"—but that is beside the point, because Black English is using a different set of rules than those of Standard English.

In addition to pronunciation and grammatical distinctions, Black   13 English differs from Standard in the way language is used in the speech community. Black speakers generally place much more emphasis on effective talking than do white speakers, and they are immersed in verbal stimulation throughout the day to a considerably greater extent than middle-class whites. Playing the dozens is only one of the numerous speech events which depend upon the competitive exhibition of verbal skills in the ghetto. Rapping, jiving, rifting, louding, and toasting are other verbal ways in which the black achieves status in his community. Whereas a white is apt to feel embarrassed when he repeats himself, a black feels he has the license to repeat whatever he is saying, sometimes from the very beginning. And he expects to evoke a feedback from his audience that not only permits him to continue talking but also urges him to do so by such expressions of audience approval as *right on* or *amen.* Status within the black community is sometimes determined by one's material or spiritual attributes, but it is almost always determined by a speaker's ability to demonstrate his command over the different uses of language. Speech is, in fact, regarded as a performance in which the speaker is continually on stage. His verbal behavior is appraised by the standards of performance as being either *cool* or *lame*—and not by the white standards of tactful conversation.

The sharing of much the same vocabulary camouflages basic differ-   14
ences between Black and Standard English. And that is why most school
systems are unaware that lower-class black children enter the first grade
speaking a mother dialect that is not Standard English. The exasperated
white teacher, who knows little about Black English, usually concludes
that the black child is unteachable because he refuses to learn to read
the simple English of his mother tongue. The teacher reprimands the
black child for saying *they toys* and *He work* when he clearly sees
printed in his reader *their toys* and *He's working*. Actually, the black
child should be commended for his quickness in translating Standard
English symbols on the printed page into his own dialect, Black
English.

The black child's ability to read Black English, even though he may   15
fail in reading Standard, is supported by an incident that happened to
William A. Stewart, of the Center for Applied Linguistics in Washington,
D.C. He was in the process of translating "The Night Before Christmas"
into Black English, ignoring Black English pronunciation but otherwise
using Black English grammar:

> It's the night before Christmas, and all through the house   16
> Ain't nobody moving, not even a mouse.   17
> There go them stocking, hanging up on the wall.   18
> So Santa Claus can full them up, if he pay our house a call.   19

While he was working on the translation, a ten-year-old black girl,
who was regarded in her school as having a reading problem, glanced
over his shoulder. With great speed and accuracy, she read aloud what
Stewart had written. But when he asked her to read the same lines in
the original Standard English form, she failed miserably. Clearly, the
girl could read perfectly well—not Standard English, but the language
of her mother dialect, Black English.

Experiences such as this one have led some linguists to advocate   20
teaching ghetto children the rules of Standard English as if they were
learning a foreign language. But Stewart would go even further. He
wants black children to be taught to read Black English first, so that the
words and structures they see on the printed page would correspond
directly to the daily speech they hear in their community. He argues
that once the child has mastered the principle of reading the tongue in
which he is fluent, he will find it comparatively easy to make the transition to the Standard. To that end he has produced several readers in
parallel Black and Standard versions, one of which, *Ollie*, contains such
sentences as:

> Ollie big sister, she name La Verne. La Verne grown up now, and she ain't   21
> scared of nobody. But that don't mean she don't never be scared. The other

day when she in the house, La Verne she start to screaming and hollering. Didn't nobody know what was the matter.

If the black child survives the trauma of school—and most black children do not, because of the problem in the early years of learning to read that strange dialect, Standard English—he will have become, in effect, bilingual in two dialects that use English words. And, like most bilinguals, he will have to employ the strategy of language-switching. But whereas someone in Paraguay has to know only when to speak either Spanish or Guarani, the black must know the two extremes of Black English and Standard English, as well as the many gradations in between. The expert dialect-switcher can quickly place his speech somewhere along the spectrum ranging from Black English to Standard English, depending upon whom he is talking to: upper-class white, lower-class white, educated black, lower-class black, recent black migrant from the South, family and close friends, and so on. It is a formidable linguistic accomplishment. 22

The problems faced by the bilingual black speaker are the same as those faced by American-born children of immigrant parents who enter school knowing Spanish, Italian, Greek, Yiddish, Polish, Hungarian, or other foreign languages—with one important difference. Teachers feel that the white children speak real languages, languages with their own dictionaries and literature, and therefore the teachers are likely to be patient in starting at the beginning when teaching these children English. But few teachers display the same sympathy toward the black child who speaks a language that they believe is the same as their own, the only difference being that the black child speaks it carelessly and stubbornly refuses to be grammatical. Often black teachers themselves are the worst offenders in stigmatizing Black English. They struggled for an education and put tremendous effort into learning to speak Standard English. Obviously, they view as inferior that speech which they worked so hard to unlearn in themselves. 23

The native languages of Africa were suppressed long ago, in the slave factories and on the plantations, but pressure against the numerous foreign languages spoken by immigrants to the United States did not begin until after the First World War. That was when many native-born Americans considered "Americanization" and "the melting-pot philosophy" to be the alchemy that would transmute the "baser" languages of immigrants into the golden American tongue. Americanization placed a special emphasis on extirpating the languages of the immigrants, for the obvious reason that language carries the culture of its speakers. Get rid of the language—and the nation has also rid itself of the alien's instrument of perception, his means of expressing foreign 24 values, his maintenance of a culture transported from another continent. Theodore Roosevelt's statement in 1919 is typical of the Americanization position:

> We have room for but one language here and that is the English language, 25
> for we intend to see that the crucible turns our people out as Americans
> and not as dwellers in a polyglot boarding house.

The Americanization movement reached its height in the 1930s, but its effects continue to be felt. Every census since then has revealed that fewer Americans claim a non-English mother tongue. And even those who acknowledge their bilingualism do so with a feeling that they have traitorously maintained an alien way of life. The crime of Americanization is that it convinced those whose tongues were stigmatized that they were deserving of the stigma.

Other people, though, regard the maintenance of a diversity of 26 languages as a source of strength for the nation. They recall that English is not an indigenous language of America, that it was merely one of the languages exported to the New World by colonial powers. Opponents of Americanization also point out that no nation in the world speaks only one language. Even France, which comes closest to the uniformity of a single national language, has German speakers in Alsace-Lorraine, Breton speakers in Brittany, Basque speakers in the Pyrenees, and Provençal speakers in the south.

The simple truth is that a culturally diversified society is a vital one 27 and affords maximum freedom for creativity and achievement. But if a practical benefit of linguistic diversity is needed, then it can be found in the fact that non–English speakers in America provide a natural resource that both in war and in peace has met national needs. Millions of Americans were shamed into losing their foreign-language competence at the very time that the federal and local governments spent vast amounts of money to increase the teaching of foreign languages in schools.

It is as dispiriting to hear a language die as it is to stand idly by and 28 watch the bald eagle, the whooping crane, or any other form of life disappear from the face of the earth. The supporters of linguistic diversity do not propose a return to the curse of Babel; they do not urge a world fragmented into groups that are unable to communicate. Instead, linguistic sciences can possibly achieve the best of two worlds. . . . Some linguists are searching for language universals, the common denominators of all languages, in the hope that the damage done at Babel can be repaired. And some applied linguists, who find great value in the diversity of the thousands of tongues spoken on the planet today, seek to preserve minority languages from being swamped by dominant languages. Since more than half of the world's speakers have shown that the strategy of bilingualism is workable, common sense dictates that the search for universals and the maintenance of a rich diversity of languages go hand in hand.

AIMS AND STRATEGIES OF THE WRITER

Comment. Farb's aim is to dispel confusion about black English. Therefore, he must use a full range of definition methods, from technical discussion to the negation of biased points of view.

Assignment 1. Identify a topic that has been misunderstood or improperly defined. Look especially for a term or phrase that brands one group of people, such as "handicapped," "manic depressive," "housewives," "frat rats," or "jocks."

Comment. Farb titles his essay "Linguistic Chauvinism" for a purpose. He desires to focus on the misunderstanding of some people and the prejudiced devotion of others to racial superiority.

Assignment 2. Begin making notes and a few preliminary paragraphs about a topic you wish to define, defend, and free from misconceptions. Keep in mind your aim of discourse: to explain a subject in order to bring the reader new understanding.

Comment. One of Farb's aims in this essay is to defend blacks' distinctive dialect. If blacks' language is legitimate, he implies, then denouncing it as inferior is wrong and labeling it educational deprivation is equally erroneous.

Assignment 3. Carefully consider biased points of view of your subject and begin making notes to address them. You must defend your definition against critics who have already established opinions about, for instance, fraternities or about mental illness.

THE WRITING PROCESS

Comment. In many cases, defining a subject requires the writer to explain what he does not mean. In his second paragraph Farb takes a negative view of both the racist approach to black English and the equally distorted view of the liberal. In his third paragraph Farb explains that black English, for his purposes, does not mean soul language or slang.

Assignment 4. Write a paragraph that uses negation. That is, tell the reader what you do not mean, what the subject is not, or how some approaches or views of the subject are not correct.

Comment. In paragraphs 4 through 6 Farb sketches the history of black English so that he can examine influences and the causal forces behind the dialect.

Assignment 5. Examine Farb's development of historical influences, then look at your subject to determine if a past-to-present approach will benefit your development of the essay. For example, how did fraternities begin, what was their original purpose, how have definitions or purposes changed?

Comment. In paragraphs 8 through 12 Farb launches a technical discussion, using the pattern of comparison/contrast to show differences between black dialect and standard English. In paragraph 13 he compares the social uses of language and examines the verbal stimulation among black speakers.

Assignment 6. Draft a comparison/contrast paragraph about your subject. Compare college fraternities to other fraternal organizations or compare manic depression with everyday depression.

Comment. In paragraphs 14 through 15 Farb cites an authority on the subject to advance additional evidence for his point.

Assignment 7. Before finishing the rough draft of your definition essay, consult a couple of sources in the library. Look for innovative ideas, wording of excellent quality, and speakers with credentials. (Farb explains clearly that Stewart is associated with the Center for Applied Linguistics.)

Comment. Farb's conclusion, paragraphs 16 through 21, represents his answer to the problem. He does not imply that speakers of black English need not learn standard English, but he certainly advocates preserving the minority language.

Assignment 8. Offer your reader a comprehensive conclusion for your draft. Suggest a course of action, an answer, or a set of guidelines. Be thorough at this point. Avoid giving a quick summary that would appear to dismiss what should be a serious issue.

As a college sophomore at Southern Illinois University, Rachel Jones wrote this article and submitted it to Newsweek (27 December 1982), whose editors published it in the column "My Turn." Jones is a black who has developed skills with standard English only to find that some people condemn her for talking "proper."

She channeled her reaction to this "white pipes" problem into an essay of persuasive discourse in which she defends her use of standard English rather than black dialect. Like Richard Rodriguez, who abandoned his native Spanish language in favor of English (see pages 86–96), Jones would abandon bilingualism if it keeps some blacks from economic opportunities. While recognizing her affinity to the linguistic rhythms of her people, she nevertheless chooses the language that will open channels of opportunity. As she puts it, "I don't think I talk white, I think I talk right."

In the course of the essay she defines black English and compares it with standard English. She blends other rhetorical patterns into the piece, providing examples, narrative episodes, descriptive phrases, and process analysis that explains how she developed her skills with the language.

During your reading of Jones's essay, make marginal notes that compare and contrast her positions with those of Farb's, whose preceding essay also considers the topic of black English. In particular, write a brief summary of Jones's view on black dialect.

RACHEL L. JONES

 ## What's Wrong with Black English

William Labov, a noted linguist, once said about the use of black English, "It is the goal of most black Americans to acquire full control of the standard language without giving up their own culture." He also suggested that there are certain advantages to having two ways to express one's feelings. I wonder if the good doctor might also consider the goals of those black Americans who have full control of standard English but who are every now and then troubled by that colorful, grammar-to-the-winds patois that is black English. Case in point—me. 1

I'm a twenty-one-year-old black born to a family that would probably be considered lower-middle class—which in my mind is a polite way of describing a condition only slightly better than poverty. Let's just say we rarely if ever did the winter-vacation thing in the Caribbean. I've often had to defend my humble beginnings to a most unlikely group of 2

people for an even less likely reason. Because of the way I talk, some of
my black peers look at me sideways and ask, "Why do you talk like
you're white?"

The first time it happened to me I was nine years old. Cornered in   3
the school bathroom by the class bully and her sidekick, I was offered
the opportunity to swallow a few of my teeth unless I satisfactorily
explained why I always got good grades, why I talked "proper" or
"white." I had no ready answer for her, save the fact that my mother had
from the time I was old enough to talk stressed the importance of
reading and learning, or that L. Frank Baum and Ray Bradbury were my
closest companions. I read all my older brothers' and sisters' literature
textbooks more faithfully than they did, and even lightweights like the
Bobbsey Twins and Trixie Belden were allowed into my bookish inner
circle. I don't remember exactly what I told those girls, but I somehow
talked my way out of a beating.

"White Pipes"

I was reminded once again of my "white pipes" problem while apart-   4
ment hunting in Evanston, Illinois, last winter. I doggedly made out lists
of available places and called all around. I would immediately be invited over—and immediately turned down. The thinly concealed looks
of shock when the front door opened clued me in, along with the
flustered instances of "just getting off the phone with the girl who was
ahead of you and she wants the rooms." When I finally found a place to
live, my roommate stirred up old memories when she remarked a few
months later, "You know, I was surprised when I first saw you. You
sounded white over the phone." Tell me another one, sister.

I should've asked her a question I've wanted an answer to for years: 5
how does one "talk white"? The silly side of me pictures a rabid white
foam spewing forth when I speak. I don't use Valley Girl jargon, so
that's not what's meant in my case. Actually, I've pretty much deduced
what people mean when they say that to me, and the implications are
really frightening.

It means that I'm articulate and well-versed. It means that I can talk   6
as freely about John Steinbeck as I can about Rick James. It means that
"ain't" and "he be" are not staples of my vocabulary and are only used
around family and friends. (It is almost Jekyll and Hyde-ish the way I
can slip out of academic abstractions into a long, lean, double-negative-
filled dialogue, but I've come to terms with that aspect of my personality.) As a child, I found it hard to believe that's what people meant by
"talking proper"; that would've meant that good grades and standard
English were equated with white skin, and that went against everything

I'd ever been taught. Running into the same type of mentality as an adult has confirmed the depressing reality that for many blacks, standard English is not only unfamiliar, it is socially unacceptable.

James Baldwin once defended black English by saying it had added 7 "vitality to the language," and even went so far as to label it a language in its own right, saying, "Language [black English] is a political instrument" and a "vivid and crucial key to identity." But did Malcolm X urge blacks to take power in this country "any way y'all can"? Did Martin Luther King Jr. say to blacks, "I has been to the mountaintop, and I done seed the Promised Land"? Toni Morrison, Alice Walker and James Baldwin did not achieve their eloquence, grace and stature by using only black English in their writing. Andrew Young, Tom Bradley and Barbara Jordan did not acquire political power by saying, "Y'all crazy if you ain't gon vote for me." They all have full command of standard English, and I don't think that knowledge takes away from their blackness or commitment to black people.

Soulful

I know from experience that it's important for black people, stripped 8 of culture and heritage, to have something they can point to and say, "This is ours, *we* can comprehend it, *we* alone can speak it with a soulful flourish." I'd be lying if I said that the rhythms of my people caught up in "some serious rap" don't sound natural and right to me sometimes. But how heartwarming is it for those same brothers when they hit the pavement searching for employment? Studies have proven that the use of ethnic dialects decreases power in the marketplace. "I be" is acceptable on the corner, but not with the boss.

Am I letting capitalistic, European-oriented thinking fog the issue? 9 Am I selling out blacks to an ideal of assimilating, being as much like whites as possible? I have not formed a personal political ideology, but I do know this: It hurts me to hear black children use black English, knowing that they will be at yet another disadvantage in an educational system already full of stumbling blocks. It hurts me to sit in lecture halls and hear fellow black students complain that the professor "be tripping dem out using big words dey can't understand." And what hurts most is to be stripped of my own blackness simply because I know my way around the English language.

I would have to disagree with Labov in one respect. My goal is not 10 so much to acquire full control of both standard and black English, but to one day see more black people less dependent on a dialect that excludes them from full participation in the world we live in. I don't think I talk white, I think I talk right.

AIMS AND STRATEGIES OF THE WRITER

Comment. Jones draws on personal experience for the subject of her essay. She has been hurt by condemnation from her peers for talking "proper" or "white." Now she speaks out strongly in defense of her linguistic talents.

Assignment 1. List similar topics that you feel strongly about, especially injustices you've experienced. How have you, like Jones, been the victim of prejudice or mistreatment? Do you have a friend who has experienced physical and/or mental suffering?

Comment. Jones has a persuasive aim of discourse, not only to defend her "white pipes" but also to argue that her fellow blacks can only enter the marketplace successfully using standard English. Her aim is similar to that of Rodriguez (pages 86–96), who argues that his reluctant abandoning of the Spanish language and his eventual acceptance of the English language enabled him to gain recognition as an "American."

Assignment 2. Compare the essays of Jones and Rodriguez in considering this concept: Can members of a minority maintain their ethnic identity and also move into the mainstream of American culture? Find statements by Jones and Rodriguez that support your answer.

Comment. The aim of the persuasive writer should be to reach and motivate a specific audience. In the case of Jones, the audience would be her fellow blacks rather than Caucasians, whom she wishes to encourage rather than upbraid.

Assignment 3. As you develop a persuasive essay in the pattern of Jones, pinpoint your audience: Whom do you wish to reach, inform, and motivate? Narrow the distance between yourself and the reader. Clarify your purpose; one student did this using this preliminary statement: "I plan to urge my fellow sorority members to join the whole university community rather than retreat into private and somewhat petty cliques." Approach the assignment with the attitude that you *want* people to read your words and react to them.

Comment. Remember one point about persuasive writing: The views you advance can be challenged by others who have a different understanding of the issue and its implications. Jones accepts the polarity of the topic and argues within this framework. A comparison of her essay with the one by Farb (pages 286–295) demonstrates the wide range of possible viewpoints.

Assignment 4. Develop a writing situation for your topic, especially to consider others' opposing viewpoints. (See pages 4–5 for tips on developing a writing situation.) How can you address their complaints? Are you willing to recognize their positions? Don't ignore the opposition. Your voice will have more authority if it embraces all sides with understanding and if it then stresses one aspect of the subject on logical, moral, and emotional grounds. (See the next comment.)

THE WRITING PROCESS

Comment. As a mode of discourse, persuasion serves to convince readers with logical, emotional, and ethical appeals. Jones includes all three types of appeals. Emotionally, she suffers condemnation by her fellow blacks and wishes to defend her position. Then, while defending the ethics and moral basis of black culture, she nevertheless argues the logical and economic validity of her cause. In contrast to Jones's essay, Farb's essay is based almost entirely on logical considerations.

Assignment 5. As you develop ideas for your essay, consider the rationale of your argument. Write a sentence to answer these questions: Is it logical, reasonable, and natural? Is it morally correct and honorable? Is it emotionally intense and likely to arouse strong feelings in readers? If you can satisfactorily answer these questions, you probably have a provocative topic worthy of persuasive discourse.

Comment. Jones does not attempt a scholarly definition of black English, as does Farb, because her goal is persuasion, not explanation. Yet she provides enough evidence, including examples, to explain black English and its differences from white English.

Assignment 6. Use definition as a primary pattern of your persuasive essay. For example, one writer found it necessary to answer these questions: What is the meaning of sorority? What role should sororities play in the academic community? Another writer found it necessary to define "amateur" when arguing about eligibility of Olympic athletes. Understanding key terms can help you win the argument.

Comment. Jones blends several rhetorical patterns into her essay. She defines, uses examples, provides personal narration, compares and contrasts, and describes.

Assignment 7. Consider the patterns that may contribute to your persuasive essay. Define your key terminology. Provide examples. Compare and contrast the differences of opinion. Include process analysis, classification, description, causal analysis, and other techniques as necessary to build a complete statement.

Comment. Jones uses a circular pattern for opening and closing her essay. She opens with a quotation by William Labov and then develops her thesis. At the end of the essay she again mentions Labov and expresses her position in opposition to his statement.

Assignment 8. Use the circular pattern as a technique in your paper. Take a statement by somebody with whom you disagree and use it to launch your argument. After exploring the issues that demonstrate the logic and ethics of your thesis, you can return to the original quotation to attack it a final time.

Studs Terkel has gained fame as an author and an interviewer on radio and television. In the following interviews, Terkel listens with a fine ear and allows the interviewees to disclose their particular definitions of the American dream.

Terkel thereby defines the concept of the American dream in a new and creative way: He lets the words of these people define it. He does not write an essay as such but reproduces several monologues that, when combined, form a powerful statement on the dreams of a good life.

"American Dreams" is taken from Terkel's book American Dreams: Lost and Found *(1980), which sets forth the commentary of ninety-eight persons from various walks of life; each one provides a special, private understanding of the search for happiness in America. This book is a sequel to an earlier book of interviews by Terkel entitled* Working: People Talk About What They Do All Day and How They Feel About What They Do *(1972). The first statement features Terkel's interview with Sharon Fox, a messenger at the Chicago Board of Trade; the second comes from Carey Edwards, a former child actor; the third is spoken by Ted Turner, a famous sportsman and business entrepreneur; the fourth records the thoughts of John Fielding, a college professor.*

Terkel's technique demonstrates that definition appears in a variety of forms—lecture, poem, essay, journal entry, interview, and so forth. The dictionary may serve as the logical place for definitions, but the creative person observes, listens, and learns from others.

During your reading of these interviews, watch for and make marginal notes of the speakers' various definitions of the American dream.

STUDS TERKEL

 American Dreams

Sharon Fox

She is one of Chicago's most assiduous collectors of autographs. She earns her daily bread as a messenger at the Board of Trade. 1

"It's very prestigious to work there, even if you're a messenger, 'cause it's the largest commodity house in the world. There are a lot of rich people who work there, and it's respected. Not everybody can get a job there. You have to know somebody. Not everybody can walk through the door. So when I do, I feel kind of proud, even though I'm just a messenger. 2

303

"My father and mother are both retired. My father just worked in a 3
factory. My mother worked years ago for Pepsodent Tooth Company.
They're just laborers." (She pauses, then softly) "I shouldn't put it down."

She carries an impressively thick leather-bound book of signatures 4
and photographs; there are scrawled phrases: "Best wishes" and "God
bless" are among the most frequent.

I'm just one of millions. A hundred years from now, I'll be just a 5
name on a gravestone and that will be it, I won't be in libraries or
records or movies that they watch on TV. It's kind of nice to stand out in
a crowd and be remembered rather than being just a face in the crowd.

Someone famous, they're important. That's why you want to see 6
them and get their autograph. It means that you may never see them
again, but you've shared a few minutes. We're rather quiet, dull people,
and anything that has a little shine to it is exciting.

I met Prince Charles, and he kissed me for my birthday. He's impor- 7
tant and he's also famous. When he came to the Board of Trade, everything just stopped. We were told not to even approach him, but it got
so crowded, it was his idea to just come out and shake hands.

I happened to be there. He shook my hand and I said: "Today's my 8
birthday." Which it was, it's no lie. I said: "Can I have a kiss?" He thought
about it for a second and he said: "Why not?" He kissed me on the
cheek, and I kissed him. Everybody at the Board saw it. I don't think
my feet were on the ground.

I may never see him again and never have that opportunity, and he 9
may be king of England some day. I wish I could get to know him. He
seemed like he could be nice. It was just a few minutes between us, and
there we were. . . . I wrote him a letter and sent him a picture that I had
taken. I said, "It's not every girl who can be kissed by a prince," and I
wanted to thank him.

That keeps me happy. I'm not happy all the time at the Board of 10
Trade, so I have this side project, which keeps me going: meeting
celebrated people and getting autographs. (She opens her book of
treasures.) Barbra Streisand, Presley, a lot of people in here. There's
Sylvester Stallone, there is Jack Nicholson and Louise Fletcher. There's
Jack Ford. The son of the president.

More pages of the book are turned; familiar faces appear and all 11
manner of signatures. Let us now praise famous men: Tony Bennett,
Yul Brynner, George Burns, Buster Crabbe.

I've grown up with these people, watching them on TV. I never had 12
many friends, so it was a substitute. I decided to go one step further
and meet these people instead of admiring them from afar. My mother
has an autographed picture of Jean Harlow. So maybe it's in the genes
somewhere. (Laughs.)

I live at home. I never liked hanging out on street corners or going 13
to parties. I don't drink or smoke. We're a churchgoing family, Baptist.
My parents are all I've got, and I'm all they've got. They never had any
hobbies. They have no real outside interest, outside of me. They want
to see me happy, and they're interested in what I'm doing. Whatever I
do reflects on them. They're like living through me. This is one country
where you can do anything, and they prove it every day.

Are you familiar with Brenda Starr? I can identify with her. She's 14
glamorous, not what I am. She's got this great love in her life, Basil St.
John, which I don't have yet. She goes on all these exciting capers.
(Laughs.) Dale Messick, the lady who draws her, drew me into Brenda's
wedding a couple of years ago. She hardly knew me. I took pictures of
her and looked her up. She said: "Brenda's getting married. Would you
like to be at the wedding?" I said: "Sure." So she drew me while I was
at her office. I would have to point out to people it was me 'cause there's
an awful lot of people in the strip.

I keep up by following the gossip columns: Kup, Gold, Maggie Daly.* 15
I know them and they know me. Kup has mentioned me once or twice.
So has Aaron. So has Maggie. In my own little group, I became a
celebrity. People I work with and the brokers at the Board of Trade,
even though they make more money than I do, respect me more because I got my name in the paper.

I put out my magazine on Elvis Presley. It was after he died. It cost 16
almost my whole bank account, but I wanted to do it. I put in the article
"He Touched My Life." It was one of Presley's hymns I played all the
time. People wanted *my* autograph. They asked me to sign the article
that I didn't even write. My pastor asked me to sign the article. My
pastor! (Laughs.) He was impressed that I get around and meet people,
'cause I look like a wallflower. They don't think I have it in me. They
put it in the church bulletin, too.

My parents have everything they worked for. They have a house, they 17
go to church. Whatever dreams they have now are through me. They
can say: "My daughter got her name in the paper." Not every mother
can say that. "Here's my daughter with Elvis Presley."

Her magazine lies open on the table. There are photographs of Elvis 18
Presley. There is writing. She reads: "*Elvis was a gift from God. How
else could you explain the sudden rise from humble beginning to
becoming a national star? It would be best if we remembered his religious songs. He was, after all, a being with human frailties. Thank you,
Elvis, for touching my life. Love, Sharon Fox.*'" *(She adds softly)* "*Adios,
I'll see you again.*"

---

*Three Chicago columnists who chronicle the comings and goings of the celebrated.

Do you believe in the hereafter?   19

Yes. Because there has to be more to it than autographs. (Laughs.)   20
There's just so many people and so many planets, and this is only one
little step. If I can leave something behind creative, that I've done,
maybe I'll be important to somebody.

What would happen if you lost your autograph book?   21

There are worse things that could happen. *C'est la vie.*   22

Carey Edwards, 25

Bearded, skinny, freckled, red-headed.   23

My mother came from a poor family. When she was growin' up, she   24
always wanted to be an actress. She took tap-dancing lessons. We all did
a little bit of show business. My older brother was on the cover of
Liberty magazine. It was during the war, had something to do with
being bandaged up. Ansel Adams took pictures of him and my sister.
I became a model when I was three. Modeling clothes and stuff
for catalogs, billboards, and magazines. A freckle-faced little red-
headed kid.

He shows me a photograph of himself at ten. He bears a startling   25
resemblance to Wesley Barry, the All-American country-boy hero of
silent films.

I did about a hundred TV commercials. My younger brother and I   26
were the "Look, Mom, no cavities" kids. We each did three Crest commercials. They showed 'em a lot and were much quoted. (Laughs.) Of
course, they don't do that any more. Now they say: "Look, I only got one
or two cavities." The announcer comes in and says: "Even Colgate or
whatever cannot guarantee you'll get only two cavities per checkup."

My brother and I were flown to New York, along with my mother, to   27
do a Crest commercial live. Just this one-minute commercial. They
interviewed us. I had three cavities at the time. I told the director that.
He said: "Just go ahead and say you don't have any." In other words, lie
to these millions of people who were watching and believing everything you say. I did what he said, and it really left a deep impression
with me, about the power of the media and how it's abused.

I had to do it because it was my job. I didn't feel quite right about it.   28
It's different when they give you a script and you're playing a part, a
character, but they were interviewing me. They were saying: Here's
Carey Edwards.

They were interviewing us with our mother. They asked her: "Do   29
you always use Crest?" "Yes." Even though sometimes we used Colgate
or Ipana. The whole thing rubbed me the wrong way.

I didn't want to get out of the business. It was a very enjoyable way   30 to grow up. I remember the TV shows better than the commercials. I did a lot of westerns. I was very good at learning my lines. I was on *The Virginian* three times, once in a major role.

When I was twelve, I decided to get out of it. I wanted to be a normal 31 teenager. Growing up as a child actor has certain disadvantages. We went on interviews after school, four, sometimes five times a week. We were in an adult world. We were workers. At first, I liked it very much. I got a lot of attention. It was like being a grownup. We had to go up to these producers and directors by ourselves and convince them we were right for the part. We'd introduce ourselves, shake hands, selling ourselves. . . .

They were interviewing other freckle-faced red-headed kids. They'd 32 ask me what I had done, credits and stuff like that. They'd rarely ask what your interests were. I'd have to read a script, which I was pretty good at. It all seemed perfectly normal and natural to me, because I'd started so young. I didn't have any inhibitions.

Television affected my life not only just by being on it but by watch- 33 ing. It was like an electronic parent. I spent a lot of time with it, and I learned a lot from it. You pick up things about what's going on in the world. It helped me get involved in what I'm doing. My brother and I used to sit around making up new lyrics to TV commercials, the jingles and all that. It was a fairly new medium, and I grew up with it. It came like right after the Milton Berle era. Being born and raised in Holly-wood, it was all around us anyway.

I could still get back into show business if I really wanted to. If I had 34 the chance to do the types Dustin Hoffman does—but I did not enjoy doing TV commercials. When I was eighteen, I went to a meeting of the Screen Actors Guild, I gave a short talk in favor of truth in advertising. The president pounded his gavel. He didn't like what I was saying. Since then, I've seen him on Bank of America commercials. (Laughs.)

I guess I'm still looking for the American Dream. To me, it's people 35 having control over their lives. I feel like I have a hell of a lot of control over my own life, but I know that's not true for a lot of people. The real dream to me—I don't know whether it's a fantasy—is the attitude you see in the movies of the thirties and forties. Where people don't even have to lock their doors, you know all the neighbors and the milkman, friendly. That's not the way it is in the seventies at all. Maybe the image I have is just a Hollywood image and is not real after all.

We observe the photograph once more: Carey Edwards at ten: 36 *freckles.*

I was on the Hennessey show with Jackie Cooper. (Wistfully, softly) 37 After the show was over, he bought me an ice cream cone for each hand. A chocolate one and a vanilla one. He raised me up on his shoulders, and the crew all gave me three cheers. He'd been a child star himself, so I guess he knew how it felt. It was a small triumph.

Oh, I've had my moments of glory. (Laughs.) 38

Ted Turner

He owns the Atlanta Braves, a baseball team; the Atlanta Hawks, a 39
basketball team; the Atlanta Chiefs, a soccer team; Channel 17, a tele-
vision station; and is a celebrated yachtsman.

Though his day may be somewhat planned, there is an improvised, 40
jazz-like, high-spirited tempo to it. Our conversation came about acci-
dentally, suddenly, whimsically. A phone call, a request, his response:
"Whatcha doin' now?" "Nothin'." "Hop over."

There was a silly little thing that inspired me when I first saw *Gone* 41
with the Wind. I've always been kind of a romantic. I featured myself as
maybe a modern-day Rhett Butler. I thought he was a dashing figure.
Everybody should see themselves as a dashing figure. Don't you see
yourself as a dashing figure? He came to Atlanta. So did I. So I got a
little mustache and everything. I was one of the first people to grow
one, when I was twenty-five. Nobody had 'em fifteen years ago. I'll be
forty next week. Looks like I've made it, if I don't crash tomorrow on
my trip to Alabama.

I always wanted to win. I didn't win at that many things. I eventually 42
found sailing and business. It's not the actual winning. Something's
over, it's done with. It's *trying* to win. Whether it's the World Series or
a boat race, getting there is half the fun. Then I think about what I'm
going to do next.

I'd say I'm from the upper middle class, but I don't like to use the 43
word "class." In certain ways, my father was real low class. He was a
wild man. He used to drink a lot and got in barroom fights. He was one
of those rugged individualists. He was fifteen, sixteen when the depression hit.

My grandfather lost everything in the depression. It took him the 44
rest of his life to pay off his debts. He didn't declare personal bank-
ruptcy. He washed out with debts of forty thousand dollars, which was
a lot of money in '31. It would be like three, four hundred thousand
today. It took him another twenty years to pay it all off. He paid off every
penny before he passed away.

My father had to drop out of college and go to work, but that didn't 45
bother him. He went into business for himself, outdoor advertising.
Small, but it got pretty big before he passed away.

My father was bitter about the fact that they were dirt poor. He 46 decided, when he was about seventeen, that he was going to be a millionaire when he was thirty. He didn't accomplish it until he was fifty. When he achieved his dream, he was dead by his own hand, two years later. He told me, when I was twenty-four: "Don't ever set your goal. Don't let your dream be something you can accomplish in your lifetime."

If I made one mistake—I wanted to be a millionaire so bad that I 47 missed out on a lot by doing it. Set your goal so high that you can never reach it, so you'll always have something to look forward to when you get old.

I would like to have lived a whole bunch of lives. I would like to 48 have gone to West Point or Annapolis and had a military career, I would like to have been a fireman, I would like to have been a state trooper, I would like to have been an explorer, I would like to have been a concert pianist, an Ernest Hemingway, an F. Scott Fitzgerald, a movie star, a big league ballplayer, Joe Namath. (He pauses to catch his breath.) I like it all. (As he resumes, the tempo builds.) I would like to have been a fighter pilot, a mountain climber, go to the Olympics and run the marathon, a general on a white horse. (His guest's laughter appears to encourage him.) A sea captain, back in the days of sailing ships, sailed with Horatio Nelson. I would like to have gone with Captain Cook to find the Spice Islands, with Columbus, with Sir Francis Drake. I would like to have been a pilot, a privateer, a knight in shining armor, gone on the Crusades. Wouldn't you? I'd like to have gone looking for Dr. Livingston, right? In the heart of darkest Africa. I woud like to have discovered the headwaters of the Nile and the Amazon River.

(Philosophically) When I lay my baseball bat in the rack for the final 49 game, I'd like to have people look back and just gasp at what I did in my lifetime. In my time, I think maybe I can do it. When Columbus sailed, discovering the New World was the thing to do. The territories have been pretty well discovered. I'm blazing a new frontier. I'm a pioneer in this satellite technology. I'm building a fourth network. It won't be as big as CBS or ABC or NBC, but it's gonna be big.

I would like to think I'm a very humble person because of the things 50 I haven't done. I consider my limited ability, but I'm proud of myself because I got the most out of it. I worked really hard in school, and the most I could get was ninety-five percent. I never was valedictorian. I couldn't make the football team, I couldn't make the baseball team, I couldn't make the track team. That's kinda how I got into sailing.

I've won the America's Cup. It's considered the Holy Grail of yacht- 51 ing. I've won the yachtsman of the year award three times. No one else has ever won it that many times. It's like the most valuable player award.

Our attention is turned toward the plaques on the wall. "You've   52
been a cover boy of Time, *I see." "No, not* Time. *That's* Sports Illustrated. *Burt Lance knocked me off* Time. *There's all sorts of ways of
becomin' a cover boy."*

I want to win the World Series. I want to set up a dynasty in baseball.   53
I want to win the NBA Championship and set up a dynasty in basketball.
I'm running so fast, I'm gonna burn myself out. So I'm taking up pho-
tography. I'm gonna become a wildlife and nature photographer. Hey,
that's not competitive, is it?

Money is nothing. In America, anybody can be a billionaire, if they   54
put their mind to it. Look at Ray Kroc, started McDonald's when he was
fifty. Between fifty and seventy he made, I don't know, a billion or two.
Seven years ago, I was almost broke. Today, I'm well-off. On paper. It
could all go tomorrow. I've been broke before. Easy come, easy go. You
never know whether a depression's coming. Money is something you
can lose real easy.

Being something big to yourself, that's important. Being a star.   55
Everybody's a star in the movie of their life. It was a pretty big deal
when I had lunch with Muhammad Ali and Henry Aaron at the same
time. Not many people have done that. Everybody wants to have lunch
with a star, but if they could have both at the same time, wow.

John Fielding

A professor of American history at the University of Kentucky. A few   56
*days before this conversation, he had been denied tenure. "I'll be thirty-
three next Monday. Happy birthday to me."*

I remember growing up in a small Texas town, with all the red dirt,   57
sandstorms, and cotton farmers, the isolation, the whole bit. Post, Texas.
There wasn't a whole lot to do, other than play baseball, go to school,
and watch the cowboys. Except, perhaps, movies and listening to Baptist
preachers. If you've seen *The Last Picture Show*, you've seen my town.

You were given a sense that every American had a personal mission: 58
the idea of personal destiny. Texas, in the fifties, was a special state: it
was the growingest, the biggest.

The images you'd get on the movie screen in the fifties were differ-   59
ent from what you get today. There were no Dustin Hoffmans, no Robert
Redfords. There were none of these antiheroes. The heroes were not
confused. They knew what they had to do. Randolph Scott, remember him?

You walk into the movies, you sit down, the lights go down, and   60
suddenly you're in this fantasy world where the guy comes riding up

on his horse. It's very real to an eight-year-old, young and blubbering. He lives his fantasies out in that dark theater, eating that popcorn, drinking that cherry Coke. Randolph Scott would come riding up and always save something, the man on the shining white horse. The ladies would look up to him, the townfolk, always muddled and confused, had no idea what to do until this one guy'd come along.

Fundamentalist religion is very big out there, and getting bigger. You have to do things and do them right, and if you don't, you're gonna suffer terrible consequences. If you do them right, you're gonna enter Emerald City. You'll be Dorothy and Toto running down the yellow brick road to Oz. Doing something important was always the big thing. It's hard to live this out in a little red-dirt Texas town. All the movies are set in Los Angeles or New York or Chicago or someplace like that. 61

All my friends had the same kind of feelings. You had to be number one on the baseball team, you had to be the best in class. When we got older, we had to have the best hot rod. A lot of it was success. That was the recurrent theme. You can't buy anything cheap. 62

I think there's more to the American Dream than that. I don't find a great many people happy with just a big income. I think they want something more. For the most bitter people I've met, it ends up being that bank account. For some of the others, the seekers, it becomes a sense of self-worth. For me, it became that sort of thing: patriotism. This idea that we're important to ourselves as individuals and collectively as a nation. There's a lot of that running around in Texas. It took on a kind of mindless chauvinism, as I look back on it. 63

For my generation, it took on an added dimension with the civil rights movement and with folk music as the expression. We'd see Peter, Paul and Mary, we'd see Bob Dylan up there, crooning away about missions. It gave you a warm, inspirational feeling. 64

"My father worked as a traveling salesman for International Harvester during the recession and spent most of his weeks on the road. He didn't have a big expense account, but it was enough. He had no place to spend it because he'd go to such great cities as Haskell, Laredo, Taboka, and other such exciting urban centers. 65

"My mother would sit at home, taking care of the kids. I was the youngest of three boys. My oldest brother was married when I was eight. He's always been a distant figure. He's a very successful insurance salesman, working on an early death. In the meantime, he's making sixty, seventy thousand a year. 66

"My second brother was artistic, a musician. He made culture respectable for me, a hard thing to do in Post, Texas. One of my first memories is of this huge bookcase my brother built, filled with probably 67

six hundred volumes, most of which we got from the Book-of-the-Month Club. I was the brightest kid in class, and also athletic. I had the best of both worlds. It was a happy childhood.

"*We always had a new car every year, because my father sold Pon-* 68 *tiacs as a sideline. He owned a farm implement store, sold tractors, pickups, trucks. He was good at his game, worked hard, and made money. For about ten years he was riding at the top of the wave—'47 to '57 were expanding years, particularly for farmers. About 1956, the weather turned very bad. They had a three-year drought and, on top of that, the recession. It wiped him out.*

"*He was fifty years old in 1960 and did a courageous thing. He* 69 *moved to a city about forty miles north, Lubbock, and started all over again. Just about starved. He became an insurance salesman. Lubbock's about 275,000, a huge place. And I got a chance to go to a good high school.*"

That was a very special time, 1960 to 1964, okay? They still talk about 70 my graduating class of '64. It was scholastically one of the best. We were caught up in politics, music, struggle, mission. We all wore button-down madras shirts, 1¼-inch leather belts, white Levis, and black loafers. We were stamped out of a mold, but it was a pretty good one because it went beyond self.

In September of '63, a friend of mine was standing in the cafeteria 71 line with a Yale catalog. I said: "Only diplomats' kids and the very rich can get into Yale." He said: "No, no, no, they got this thing called geographical distribution, with token Texans and Idaho people, to give it spice. Why don't you apply? You're smart enough." Yale intimidated me, but when a Columbia representative came along with a spiel, I thought: Hell, why not? Goddamn it, I'll never know unless I give it a try. March of '64, I got in.

My parents were scared. I was the first kid they'd ever known to get 72 into an Ivy League school. And they were proud, man. Scared and proud. September 18, 1964, we all three rolled into New York. My mother, my father, and me. Drove all the way in. I was gonna take the bus, but my dad said: "I'm gonna take you, that's it."

It was a clear day, kind of hazy. We pulled over there into College 73 Walk, and I looked at the library, a massive structure. It's got this frieze work: Homer, Herodotus, Plato, Demosthenes, and on and on and on. I thought this is it: I've arrived. Big city, big culture, I made it. That's where my life broke in two.

I was impressed, scared, intimidated, and really excited. It was more 74 than just being an Ivy Leaguer. I'd have to go to Harvard or Princeton to really have that feeling. I was in New York! I had made the big jump.

My roommate and I hit the subway, we went downtown. We were look-ing for the Empire State Building, we had to find that thing.

'64 to '68 was when Vietnam set in. The bombing started when I 75
was a freshman at the time. I thought it'd be a quick war. I said: "Okay, just go ahead and bomb 'em." It was part of this whole patriotism: bringing democracy to the whole world. It was exactly what Kennedy was telling us in his inaugural speech. I believed that crap.

For the first year, I was for it. It kept going on and on. All the horror 76
stories started coming out. I began to think: This isn't what we're fight-ing for.

I remember a dramatic scene. I was Paul on the road to Damascus. 77
In April '67, I had to do an art paper on two Monets. I was walking toward the museum along Fifth Avenue, thirty blocks, because there was a victory parade. I saw this guy in a convertible with three little kids dressed up in Uncle Sam costumes. On the side of the car was a sign: *Bomb 'em back into the Stone Age.* I thought: Do these kids know what death is about?

I kept walking, and there was a long-haired kid, near the bleachers, 78
being assailed by this guy. The guy was yelling from the top of the bleachers: "You guys ought to be eliminated. In a democracy like this, you're not fit." I stopped and thought: If this is what Vietnam is doing to us, it's time it was over. I was antiwar from that day on.

"The next year, when the marine recruiters came on the Columbia 79
campus, the SDS didn't want them there. I said: "If they want to come
on the campus, it's their right. This is a pluralistic society." When SDS
took over one of the buildings and the riots began, I was caught in the
middle.

"During the next six weeks, arguing days and nights with people 80
who had wildly differing ideas, I learned more than I had in three and
one half years. I was also 1-A at the time. I got out of it medically. I
wasn't going anyway, but it was fortunate I got out the easy way,
without going to jail or Canada."

During the summer of '68, I drove a taxicab. Again, I learned some- 81
thing about people. They're not really committed pro and con on is-sues. If they are, it's because they don't really know what other way to go. They're scared. They agreed Vietnam was a mess. They all had a sense that it would make or break the American Dream. For some, winning was as bad as losing. For others, we had to win, because if we didn't, we'd be the lesser for it. If the nation was demeaned, you person-ally were demeaned. They didn't know what the hell to do. There was such a void. Randolph Scott had not ridden up on the white horse. He wasn't there to save the struggling community.

What about the American promise and me? I'd come out of a small 82
Texas town. I'd gone to one of the best colleges in the country and done
well. Now I was accepted into another, Johns Hopkins. There I learned
that success is a two-edged sword. There's a cost. It never dawned on
the college student and it never dawned on the kid, sitting there in the
dark movie house, watching Randolph Scott.

You start out in the Texas town, with the Protestant ethic that you've 83
got to work hard and do well; and if you succeed, God will pat you on
the back and send you into heaven. It was the same thing at school.

The universities are corporations first, educational institutions sec- 84
ond. Education is what they market. They're also in a prestige race.
Boeing wants the biggest jet. Universities want the most prestigious
faculty. They do this through the tenure system. They give you six years,
and then they review you. If you've taught well and done your committee work well and published the right things in the right places, they
pat you on the head again and hand you this lifetime contract. Nirvana.
The golden dream.

There are three buttons. I pushed all three. I taught well, I was 85
reasonably liked by my colleagues, and I've published. I had more than
fulfilled everything, right? Wrong.

The variable I hadn't counted on was the prestige race. The univer- 86
sities are committed to building up their faculty by hiring superstars.
They're like the Yankees buying their ball club. They end up by firing
untenured professors or denying them tenure. All of a sudden, what
was acceptable a few years ago is no longer so.

I was recommended for tenure by the faculty, overwhelmingly. But 87
the administration decided there was no room for another assistant
professor in the history department. So I'm in my final year now.

This came as a total shock. I had no idea I was doing the wrong 88
thing, nobody ever told me. They can change the rules at will. The
administration has the power, the faculty doesn't. The faculty's ass is on
the line, too.

They thought they ran their own department. Now they realize that 89
they don't. I'm taking it hardest because I'm out of a job, with very little
chance of getting another.

I'm almost middle-aged, but I feel like a kid. When I was eleven 90
years old, Elvis made his first record. I kept wondering: What's gonna
happen to poor old Elvis when he turns thirty? When the Beatles
and Bob Dylan turned thirty, we kept thinking: What's gonna happen
to them?

There are a whole lot of us over thirty: artists, failed historians, 91
philosophers, mathematicians, overqualified and underemployed. Unemployed humanists. What's gonna happen ten years from now when

they start turning gray? What's gonna happen when the bitterness sets in? They'll be unemployed, but will they be humanists?

I discovered in the hardest way possible that I had let other people   92
tell me what my values were. I was not Randolph Scott. I was the blithering town mayor who didn't know what he had to do, even though I thought of myself as Randolph Scott. What ever happened to Randolph Scott? (Laughs.)

AIMS AND STRATEGIES OF THE WRITER

Comment. Terkel wishes to examine the role of American dreams in shaping the lives of people. However, he has no intention of making the definition himself. Instead, he allows others to speak and thereby builds a composite view of the concept.

Assignment 1. Develop a list of possible topics that you might explore by the Terkel method of interviewing. Consider your audience and the circle of acquaintances available to you for interviews. Select topics that will give you and your readers new insight into the meaning of certain terms, such as "date rape," "parental responsibility," "snobbery," "nuclear winter," and so on.

Comment. In his introduction to this book of interviews, Terkel says, "In this book are a hundred American voices, captured by hunch, circumstance, and a rough idea. There is no pretense at statistical 'truth,' no consensus. There is, in the manner of a jazz work, an attempt, of theme and improvisation, to recount dreams, lost and found, and a recognition of possibility."

Assignment 2. Establish a theme that will control the general subject of your interview sessions. You need some limiting guidelines for interviewees. Framing several questions on a focused topic will probably serve your needs. You can adjust and expand as necessary during the interviews. For example: How would you define boredom? Can you give me some examples of boredom? Can you describe some boring persons? Can you narrate the most boring period of time in your life?

Comment. Terkel aims for a broad-based definition of the American dream. He selected representatives from all walks of life and interviewed hundreds of different persons. He then selected portions of these interviews for inclusion in his book.

Assignment 3. As you plan the subject and nature of your interview sessions, consider carefully the nature of your audience. Be sure that you seek out persons of different sexes, races, and backgrounds so that points of view contrast.

THE WRITING PROCESS

Comment. Terkel allows his interviewees to speak for themselves in the first-person voice. He keeps introductory matter and interruptions to a minimum and distinguishes them with italic lettering. He does not mark a monologue with quotation marks because only one person speaks.

Assignment 4. Begin your interview sessions and keep accurate records, using a notepad or tape recorder. Remember, you may not use everything a person says, but words reproduced in your paper must be an accurate rendering. One tip: Allow persons to answer your questions at their own pace, to pause for short periods, and to continue on their own. The special personality of the speaker will emerge if you reproduce long blocks of uninterrupted discourse.

Comment. Terkel uses an interesting form of the comparison/contrast pattern. He allows the voices and personalities of the interviewees to establish differences. For example, he sets the highly successful Ted Turner beside a frustrated college professor who has been denied tenure.

Assignment 5. As you assemble your interview notes and plan an order, consider the value of contrast in personality, voice, style, and so forth. Balance a quiet speaker against an angry one or place a negative voice next to a positive voice.

Comment. Although not reproduced above, Terkel does feature an introduction to his book of essays. However, it does not define his version of the American dream; he wants his various speakers to accomplish that task.

Assignment 6. Prepare a brief introduction for your collection of interviews. It should establish the subject and the general nature of your methods. Later, if necessary, you can write a conclusion that pulls together the ideas of your interviewees.

Comment. Terkel has carefully edited the words of each person. He hasn't altered what is said, he just cuts to the good parts; that is, he employs foreshortening, which is skipping the dull comments and jumping forward to the good parts.

Assignment 7.   Examine your interviews and consider carefully the task of editng. You can leave an interview whole and untouched or you can cut nonrelevant matter. Maintain the person's style so that each voice has its distinctive sound and rhythm.

Theresa Jane Kleynhans is an undergraduate student who faced a writing assignment on a contemporary mythic issue. She chose the topic "Myths of Reincarnation." Her task then took her to the library for research, which ultimately opened her mind to serious religious ideas, including a few issues that affected her personally.

Kleynhans provides informative discourse on a real-world subject for fellow scholars. Her expression reflects a judicious, explanatory attitude balanced with exploratory discourse. Her principal pattern of development is definition. In addition, she provides examples, comparison, and classification for analysis of key issues.

The essay is longer than the average theme, but it comprehensively surveys a complex subject, one that demands length as well as careful research and use of documented sources.

As you read the essay, make marginal notes of this writer's various methods for building an extended definition and analysis of the subject. In particular, mark the major classifications, such as paragraphs 6 through 9, where she examines four mythic considerations about reincarnation.

THERESA JANE KLEYNHANS, STUDENT

🎴 Reincarnation

The belief of "life after death" is older than recorded history, having 1 been handed down by word of mouth until man learned to write his thoughts down on parchment or the walls of caves. Since time began one comes into the world, one lives, loves, parts, and then, standing in agony beside the silent grave, are those remaining persons who search their hearts and intellects anew for some explanation of life's purpose. Some have found a suitable answer in reincarnation.

Those who accept reincarnation as a reality believe that man evolves 2 spiritually to perfection by means of successive lives on earth. To understand human evolution, we must escape the notion that the body is the self and grasp the fact that the life evolves through changing forms, which give the life varied experiences. The butterfly is an excellent analogy of the folly of identifying the life with the form it wears. We see the one life of the butterfly first in the caterpillar, then in the chrysalis, and finally in the butterfly. Yet each form is the same individual life. In the same respect, the true self of a person is distinct from the physical body; it is an eternal, immortal spiritual being, and, being immortal, it does not and cannot die.

One observer notes, "The theosophical conception of the soul is ₃ that it is literally a fragment of the one supreme life, or God—an individualized portion of the cosmic mind—and that an immense period of time is required for its evolution" (Montgomery 210). The major part of the long evolutionary journey is spent in nonphysical realms. Periodically the soul—the center of consciousness that is the real man—presses itself on this material plane because there are lessons to be learned here that cannot elsewhere be acquired. Montgomery explains that this soul gradually "takes possession of a nascent human organism" some months before birth and is born within the infant body (82). It grows from youth to old age and finally dies, a death that destroys that which is no longer useful. The released consciousness passes tranquilly back into the invisible world from which it came. "There the experience which he [it] gained while on earth is transmuted into skill, wisdom and power," says Hodson (79). "When that work of digestion and assimilation is over, the desire for sentient expression awakens, and the attraction of the material world once more draws the soul back into physical existence" (79). Rebirth again starts the soul on another period of experiences at a higher point in evolution than it has yet attained.

In other words, the Christian soul dies and joins God. The nonsaved ₄ soul discovers Hell. The reincarnated soul passes into a tranquil, invisible state for a period of, let's say, attitude adjustment.

To convince those who consider reincarnation as merely a myth, ₅ some scientists have studied the laws of evolution and found them in perfect harmony with the hypothesis of reincarnation (see Head and Cranston). This hypothesis regards the soul as making a great cyclic journey toward its goal in the infinite, yet this one vast journey requires a series of smaller cyclic trips into the physical life and back again. The laws of evolution operate in periods of alternating activity and rest, as with daily work and nightly rest or the bounty of summer followed by the dormancy of winter. This evolutionary cycle coincides with reincarnation where the activity of life and the passivity of death follow each other in orderly succession. Another characteristic of the laws of evolution is that all movements are in cycles—especially the rotation of the earth on its axis and the revolution of the earth about the sun. Reincarnation also has cycles, like the successive return to physical life from the invisible world. Additionally, evolution exhibits constant progress; cycle follows cycle, but always with the upward movement of a spiral, like running the fingers over the keyboard of a piano from A to G and on up, each octave being a cycle, continually returning to A but on a higher key. Similarly, reincarnation shows the soul returning again and again to this physical life but at a higher point in evolution than in the preceding life.

Three other mythic considerations emerge. First, the myth of trans- 6 migration of the human soul into animal forms is often associated with reincarnation. This myth is not accepted by theorists of reincarnation, for once the soul in any form of life has reached a certain level of unfoldment, no real retrogression can occur (see Rogers 82).

Second, many myths are associated with the existence of child prod- 7 igies who very early in life display remarkable natural faculties enabling them to excel in mathematics, literature, or music. They present unexplainable problems—unless one accepts them as reincarnations of people who, having achieved mastery in former lives, have brought over their acquired faculties as so-called natural gifts.

Third, in contrast to this gifted idea is the injustice of the world. If 8 all persons came into the world with identical mental and moral features and during life faced the same conditions, life would be identical for all. However, one is born in a mansion and one in the slums, one is born a genius and the other stupid, one has the advantages of wealth and the other the handicaps of poverty. If they come with such inequality from the Creator, as many believe, there is really no justice in the original endowment of these souls. Why should one be overwhelmed with wealth all his life and the other with poverty, one be a genius and the other stupid, one be naive about the crimes in the slums and ghettos and the other forced to learn the ways of life among such surroundings in order to survive—and then be judged, and consequently rewarded or punished, for their earthly behavior on judgment day by the Creator himself? When we see such inequalities among human beings at the very beginning of this life, we feel there must be a reason for it; the hypothesis of reincarnation makes inequality clear without charging God with cruel injustice. When we remember that two souls have come to their present condition of development through thousands of years of evolution and that the genius of the one is the result of striving through many lives, while the stupidity of the other is either the result of negligence and indifference through the equivalent period or the soul is younger and therefore morally and mentally deficient in comparison, we can establish a theory that we ourselves are responsible for our destiny, not the Creator.

Another issue that causes people to dismiss reincarnation is mem- 9 ory. If we have lived previous lives, why do we not remember them? A little reflection, however, will show that recollection of the process of education is in no sense essential to possession of the acquired knowledge and faculty. We don't need to remember the process of learning to walk and talk and so on. Similarly, the absence of memory of incidents and experiences in past lives doesn't prevent the use of the resultant power in later incarnations. Furthermore, just as remembrances of childish struggles when learning to walk and talk are rarely retained in adult life, so recollection of experiences in past lives does not descend into the new, conscious mind, thereby leaving it free to investigate and assimilate new ideas.

Proven cases of accurate memory of former lives have been recorded and constitute strong additional evidence to support the doctrine of reincarnation. While the only final proof lies in the direct knowledge of one's own past life, there have been convincing results from experiments done with hypnosis. A young servant girl was chosen for one such experiment (see Stevenson 92–110). She had little or no education, and her knowledge of history was minimal. When taken back to her preceding life by the hypnotist, she described in great detail certain events, little incidents, ancient customs, and other matters of which she was completely ignorant in her conscious mind. Other persons remember while fully conscious. For example, a lady experienced visions of an old house from an early childhood and pictured herself walking up and down the terrace, being sad, dejected, and suffering from ill health (Stevenson 21–15). She also remembered that she had died of consumption in her twenty-fifth year almost one hundred years ago. Later she visited Genoa, Italy, the place of her former incarnation, and there the house of her visions existed in reality. Her inquiries of the residing family confirmed that a former lady of the house did in fact die of consumption in her twenty-fifth year. **10**

People also shrink from acceptance of reincarnation on the grounds that rebirth will separate loved ones and no future reunion will be possible. However, Montgomery stipulates that neither rebirth nor death can ever completely or finally separate those who form deep spiritual, intellectual, and physical bonds (115). In their spiritual selves they are forever one, for separation is impossible and parting is unknown to the spiritual self in its union with a soul mate. The existence of this close bond causes them repeatedly to descend into incarnation at about the same time and under conditions in which they are likely to meet. In each new association, love deepens, grows more unselfish, more noble, until at last the state is reached of love perfected, which is life perfected (Montgomery 116). **11**

Reincarnation is considered a myth by many Christians because to accept it violates Christian doctrine. Yet the Bible gives evidence to a **12** belief in rebirth. Matthew says: "When Jesus came into the coasts of Caesarea Phillippi, he asked his disciples, saying, 'Whom do men say that I the son of man am?' And they said, 'Some say that thou art John the Baptist; some Elias; and others, Jeremias, or one of the prophets'" (Matthew 16: 13–14). The ancient Jews continually expected the reincarnation of their great prophets. Moses was in their opinion Abel, the son of Adam, and their messiah was to be the reincarnation of Adam himself who had already come a second time as David.

In conclusion, the hypothesis of reincarnation can be accepted by 13 everyone because it provides solutions to many problems. The scientist can accept it because it is in harmony with all of nature's laws and presents a coherent plan of evolution that includes the physical as well as the spiritual. The Christian can accept it because it is in perfect harmony with the Christian principles—exact justice, highest love, widest wisdom—and is therefore consistent with the highest conception of God. It can be accepted by those of no particular faith who might see that nothing is better calculated to promote general morality than a plan of evolution that brings people back for life after life in close association with others, to work out and adjust with them the evil they have done. Even the materialist must admit that if reincarnation is not a fact, then in the interest of justice, progress, and the common welfare of the race, it ought to be. If we do return to earth, growing a little and advancing a few steps toward the goal of perfection on each occasion, we face a future that is full of light and of the promise of spiritual victory.

The fulfillment of becoming perfect physically, intellectually, and 14 spiritually is impossible in one brief lifetime, so a person cannot succeed in developing to the point of genius in every human faculty, mastering every weakness, or making manifest every God-like power. It is therefore not difficult to understand that reincarnation—the spiritual evolution through successive lives on earth—can inspire hope and give confidence and courage to those for whom it is acceptable.

Works Cited

Head, Joseph, and S. L. Cranston. *Reincarnation*. New York: Julian Press, 1961.

Hodson, Geoffrey. *Reincarnation: Fact or Fallacy?* Adyai, India: Theosophical Publishing House, 1956.

Montgomery, Ruth. *Here and Hereafter*. Greenwich: Fawcett, 1968.

Rogers, L. W. *Reincarnation and Other Lectures*. Wheaton, Ill.: Theosophical Press, n.d.

Stevenson, Ian. *Twenty Cases Suggestive of Reincarnation*. New York: American Society for Psychical Research, 1966.

THERESA KLEYNHANS TALKS ABOUT
HER AIMS AND STRATEGIES

My paper on reincarnation took me rather deeply into a subject that I had often wondered about but had never really investigated and, consequently, never believed. However, after researching the matter, I have much more difficulty in deciding whether it is indeed fact or fallacy. Compounding the problem is my discovery that mythology is a contemporary matter, not some belief of pagans long ago in the past.

Forced to confront mythology in our celebrations of Christmas, Halloween, or Easter (bunnies and colored eggs, indeed!), I began to realize that mythmakers had a hand in manipulating religion as well as in dictating social customs and other mores of civilized society. Always a solid Christian, I began to realize that my sleepy acquiescence to church doctrine had drawn me into ignorance of other ideas. Like a babe in the woods, I was reluctantly shocked by how much sense this business of reincarnation really made. And how attractive it could be! After all, who could resist a few repetitive ventures into human form, especially when returning on higher levels at each stage of development?

In practical aspects, I divided the project into three basic stages: library research, preparation of notes and rough drafts on fragments of the paper, and writing the formal report for submission. I was developing a definition of a concept or theory, so my instructor warned me to maintain awareness of my audience, who would require detailed explanation and plenty of examples. Then a peer reviewer of my first draft asked me to define and explain all concepts, most of which were new to him. My recognition of a student audience caused me to search always for precise methods of expression with plenty of examples, comparison, and clear classification of the issues. The peer reviewer forced me to defend the point of every paragraph. I could not merely present theory; I needed to *explain* it.

I soon discovered, however, that explaining reincarnation doesn't dissolve one's doubts about it in any way. I considered reincarnation as merely a myth, yet scientific writers kept trying to convince me (or so it seemed at the time) that the hypothesis of reincarnation was a harmonious balance of universal laws.

To avoid confusion, I laid out a chart of the major arguments. In that way I could handle each one separately and work to control the whole project. I isolated these items.

theosophical conception of the soul

laws of evolution

rectification and transmigration to animal forms

child prodigies

memory of a previous life

affinity of souls that move toward love perfected

In effect, that list became the master plan for the paper. I developed an opening that defined the concept. I then struggled to form a conclusion, which did not jell until I remembered the three parts of any dialectic: thesis, antithesis, and synthesis. My conclusion was built by synthesis— reincarnation is basically in harmony with all laws and offers a coherent plan for evolutionist, Christian, agnostic, and even the materialist.

In the end I could not condemn it nor deny its universal appeal. From the heart I admitted that spiritual evolution through successive lives on earth inspires hope and gives confidence and courage to those for whom it is acceptable, even to me, a devout Christian who considers herself part of the one supreme God and only a small individualized portion of the immense cosmic mind.

Comment. Kleynhans selected a topic that she knew little about. Her task was therefore twofold: She must learn the subject and then explain it to others.

Assignment 1. Select a topic that will challenge you in a similar fashion. Create your own subject or choose from this list: inductive logic, symbolism, existentialism, agnosticism, genetic engineering, terrorism, polytheism.

Comment. Kleynhans describes above her problems with creating the essay. In particular, her third and fourth paragraphs chart organizational issues, both the stages of discovering her subject and also the classification of the paper's content.

Assignment 2. Begin research that will help you discover the major issues of your chosen subject (see assignment 1). You might start at the card catalog or with one of these indexes:

Social science topic: *Social Sciences Index*

Applied science topic: *Applied Sciences and Technology Index*

Literary or humanities topic: *Humanities Index*

Business topic: *Business Periodicals Index*

Natural science topic: *Biological Abstracts*

Reading an article or two will add substance to your thinking. If you find quotable materials or want to paraphrase somebody's original thinking, be certain to note the source for your citations in the text and the "Works Cited" page.

Comment. Kleynhans started this assignment with thoughts of writing a short paper. Her diligence, however, provided a momentum that carried her from a typical short theme to a major essay with sources. We might label it a miniresearch paper.

Assignment 3. Begin drafting notes and paragraphs of your definition. Use Kleynhans as a model; this means carefully reading a limited number of sources and thoughtfully blending your ideas with those of the sources.

CHAPTER NINE

Cause and Effect

Causal analysis generally does one of three things: (1) It classifies and examines the causes for a given situation, (2) it categorizes the known effects, or (3) it forecasts possible consequences. Causal analysis answers why and therefore differs from process analysis, which answers how. Let's look at a very brief essay by James Jeans that explains "Why the Sky Is Blue."

> Imagine that we stand on any ordinary seaside pier, and watch the waves rolling in and striking against the iron columns of the pier. Large waves pay very little attention to the columns—they divide right and left and reunite after passing each column, much as a regiment of soldiers would if a tree stood in their road; it is almost as though the columns had not been there. But the short waves and ripples find the columns of the pier a much more formidable obstacle. When the short waves impinge on the columns, they are reflected back and spread as new ripples in all directions. To use the technical term, they are "scattered." The obstacle provided by the iron columns hardly affects the long waves at all, but scatters the short ripples.
>
> We have been watching a sort of working model of the way in which sunlight struggles through the earth's atmosphere. Between us on earth and outer space the atmosphere interposes innumerable obstacles in the form of molecules of air, tiny droplets of water, and small particles of dust. These are represented by the columns of the pier.
>
> The waves of the sea represent the sunlight. We know that sunlight is a blend of lights of many colors—as we can prove for ourselves by passing it through a prism, or even through a jug of water, or as Nature demonstrates to us when she passes it through the raindrops of a summer shower and produces a rainbow. We also know that light consists of waves, and that the different colors of light are produced by waves of different lengths, red light by long waves and blue light by short waves. The mixture of waves which constitutes sunlight has to struggle through the obstacles it meets in the atmosphere, just as the mixture of waves at the seaside has to struggle past the columns of the pier. And these obstacles treat the light waves much as

327

the columns of the pier treat the sea waves. The long waves which constitute red light are hardly affected, but the short waves which constitute blue light are scattered in all directions.

Thus, the different constituents of sunlight are treated in different ways as they struggle through the earth's atmosphere. A wave of blue light may be scattered by a dust particle, and turned out of its course. After a time a second dust particle again turns it out of its course, and so on, until finally it enters our eyes by a path as zigzag as that of a flash of lightning. Consequently the blue waves of the sunlight enter our eyes from all directions. And that is why the sky looks blue.*

Jeans uses causal analysis to explain both the cause (light waves) and the effect (our eyes see blue as the dominating color). (Keep this explanation of the atmosphere in mind for later when you read Carl Sagan's essay entitled "The Nuclear Winter" on pages 345–351.)

TRACE CAUSES TO EXPLAIN WHY A CONDITION EXISTS

If you develop an essay in the style of Jeans, you will need to identify an existing condition (such as water pollution, half-finished but abandoned nuclear power plants, overcrowded prisons) and then trace the causes for it. This approach answers the basic question of Why. For instance, you might ask, "How did our country (or our college or our fraternity) get into this mess?" Your answer will be causal analysis. Quite often causal analysis serves as the basis for momentous decisions, as shown by Jefferson's "Declaration of Independence" (pages 133–136). an essay that provides a long list of causes for why the colonies sought separation from Britain. Sometimes an essay will explain reasons for private decisions in one's life. For example, Jones (pages 297–299) uses her personal experience in listing causes for her discontent with black English. Similarly, Muhammad Ali (pages 333–336) lists causes as defenses of personal decisions and to clarify existing conditions.

USE CAUSAL ANALYSIS TO CATEGORIZE AND DISCUSS KNOWN EFFECTS

Writers often use the best available evidence to explain prevailing theories. Jeans explains why the sky looks blue. Other writers explain why the sky is dark at night, why our eyes move during sleep, or why

*James Jeans. *The Stars in Their Courses* (Cambridge, Mass.: Cambridge UP, 1982).

hurricanes develop in the warm Carribbean waters. An essay that categorizes the "known effects" will avoid speculation and be based on the evidence. In an essay that follows later entitled "Fitness Fallacies," two writers examine known conditions and conclude that "there is no evidence that running five miles a day, for instance, improves life expectancy or even appreciably enhances health." You too can write such essays by examining prevailing conditions (such as driving drunk despite DUI laws or drivers speeding despite the sixty-five-mile-per-hour speed limit).

USE CAUSAL ANALYSIS TO FORECAST POSSIBLE CONSEQUENCES

Carl Sagan, writing on nuclear winter (see later in this chapter), says, "Nobody knows, of course, how many megatons would be exploded in a real nuclear war." There you are: Nobody knows. Yet Sagan and other writers like him, including you and me, are willing to step into the breach to predict certain possibilities. The essay that forecasts consequences usually depends on an if-clause to clarify the writer's explanation: "If the sun were to diminish in its production of heat"; "If polar ice were to melt"; "If there should be a stoppage of Middle East oil." These if-clauses lead the writer to the possible effects of a given condition. Writers can speculate about probable happenings or predict the future. For example, the legislature may enact a new law and your essay could predict and analyze possible results. You would thus focus your discussion on the consequences of the legislation rather than on the reasons for its passage.

IF NECESSARY, SHOW BOTH CAUSES AND EFFECTS

Sometimes causal analysis will require you to cite causes for an existing condition and then to examine the possible and predictable consequences. This type of essay will, for instance, not only examine how society got itself into a particular situation but will also warn about the consequences if society fails to enact solutions. The essay by Sagan fits this pattern, as he examines humanity's misuse of the environment and warns about impending consequences. Similarly, Jonathan Schell's description of the bombing of New York (pages 46–53) paints an awesome scene of nuclear destruction (the cause) and forecasts the inanimate darkness to follow (the effects).

COMBINE CAUSAL ANALYSIS WITH OTHER PATTERNS TO EXPAND AND CLARIFY

Description, examples, and *narrative episodes* can bring vivid images of your subject to the reader. *Comparison* and *contrast* will balance the past with the present, compare the present with the future, or show positive-negative aspects of your subject. *Analogy* can explain a difficult idea in terms of something fairly simple (see the preceding Jeans essay). *Classifying* the various causes and/or effects will be elementary preparation for the essay. In order to explain *how* causal forces are at work, you may need *process analysis.* (See especially the essays that follow later by Joseph and Richard Wassersug and by Carl Sagan.) Inevitably, you will *define* and explain key terminology. (Jeans defines sunlight, the Wassersugs define fitness, and Sagan defines nuclear winter.)

CONFORM TO THE STANDARD CONVENTIONS OF CAUSAL ANALYSIS

Uniformity in causal analysis means balance and equality. If you have more than one reason, each should have equal force. The political arguments of Jefferson have uniformity. Sometimes uniform laws govern, but just as often they do not, especially in human affairs. For example, busing to achieve racial integration did not achieve uniformity in the nation's schools, and federal appropriations to education have not provided a balanced quality of education.

In other situations your reasons should have *logical sequence*, which means that one cause logically follows the preceding. This logical sequence is featured in the essays of Schell (pages 46–53) and Sagan (pages 345–351). However, a predicted sequence of results will seldom occur exactly as anticipated; for example, harsh drunk driving laws to diminish accidental highway deaths have unexpectedly caused severe overcrowding of the municipal jails.

In addition, you should determine the *sufficiency* of motivating factors. What look like multiple reasons may in truth be reduced to one fundamental reason. Ask yourself a few questions: How many reasons exist? Are the causes equal? Should I rank the motivating factors into a sequence of minor ones to important ones? Am I dealing with a major cause or a minor one? For this latter question, you need to understand types of causes, as explained below.

A *necessary cause* must be present for the event to occur, but it cannot alone cause the final consequence. For example, good study habits are necessary for achieving good grades, but they cannot ensure that you will get an A for every examination. As the essay "Fitness Fallacies" points out (see pages 338–342), exercise alone will not bring about physical fitness. In fact, a good diet may contribute more to good health than will exercise.

A *contributory cause* may serve to produce an effect but cannot do so by itself. Thus, exercise and diet contribute to your good health, but they do not ensure a long life.

A *sufficient cause* can produce the effect by itself. For example, a severe heart attack is sufficient to kill you no matter how fit you are. Jogging daily may contribute to your good health, but it is not sufficient to guarantee a few extra days in your life.

A *main cause* is similar to a sufficient one, but it often requires contributory causes. For example, conditioning might contribute to your winning a five-kilometer run, but the main cause would be your physical speed and stamina on that particular day.

A *remote cause*, one that takes place in the distance, and an *immediate* cause, which closely precedes an effect, may both play important roles. For example, some persons die while exercising. The immediate cause may be the strenuous running, but a preexisting heart condition may be the remote (as well as the main) cause.

A *causal chain* requires that A cause B, B cause C, C cause D, and so forth. For example, some persons think in this pattern: "Exercise will make me fit, which means I will look and feel better, which means I will be more attractive to members of the opposite sex, which means I will enjoy a more active sex life." The essay by the Wassersugs touches on this causal chain.

Finally, keep your essay as honest, objective, and logical as possible. Readers react negatively to misappropriation of causes and effects. In particular, be conscious of the following mistakes: (1) failure to consider all relevant causes and to keep the sequence of causes accurate and complete by mentioning *all* links in the causal chain; (2) the writing of mere generalization without in-depth exploration of causes or consequences; (3) the failure to provide the concrete evidence of facts, quotations, statistics, expert testimony, charts, and graphs; (4) the tendency to rely on mere linear sequence, which is argument by *post hoc ergo propter hoc* ("after this, therefore because of this"), which is a fallacious means of argument (for example, the heart attack occurred after vigorous exercise, so the exercise caused the heart attack).

USE A SET OF PENETRATING QUESTIONS
ABOUT THE TOPIC

Ask five basic questions as you conduct causal analysis.

1. What? Explain the act, which may occur or has already occurred. Sagan warns us about a nuclear winter that looms on the horizon.

2. Who? Name the personality or mental condition that prevails. Sagan worries that warmongers or madmen could trigger a nuclear war.

3. Where? Set the scene, the place, the circumstances. Sagan describes the United States, primarily, but he suggests that a nuclear winter would cast its cold darkness over the entire world.

4. Why? The main cause, as discussed above, can be difficult to nail down. Sagan says, for example, that even a limited nuclear war would be sufficient to cause a nuclear winter. But for what purpose? Sagan cannot answer the basic question, but some writers on other subjects can. Jones, for example, says that black children need standard English, not black dialect, in order to succeed in the modern culture.

5. How? The stages of action in the whole process may need explanation. Sagan, for example, spends much of his essay explaining step by step the damaging consequences of nuclear explosions to our atmosphere and ultimately to the planet itself.

To review: Conform to these guidelines when writing with a cause-and-effect pattern.

1. Classify, examine, and trace the known causes for a given situation.

2. Categorize the known effects as based on scientific evidence.

3. Forecast probable consequences with essays of speculation.

4. Combine both cause and effect, if necessary, and blend additional patterns of development into your essay to expand and clarify your explanation.

5. Use standard conventions of causal analysis.

   Uniformity to give items balance and equality

   Logical sequence to show that one cause precedes and, perhaps, precipitates the next, especially when causal chains are operative

   Sufficiency of causal forces and motivating factors

In 1965 in a heavyweight boxing match in Las Vegas, Muhammad Ali knocked out Floyd Patterson, who had been champion during 1956 through 1959 and 1960 through 1961. In this essay Ali explains the reasons for his tenacious physical and verbal attacks on Patterson.

Ali combines expressive discourse with causal analysis that explores several motivating factors for his actions on the night of the fight. He ignores the contributory causes (pride in the title, monetary rewards, and love for the sport) in order to focus on personal reasons that have universal meaning. In truth, Ali admits that the strongest cause was racially motivated. He saw Patterson as a puppet of the white reporters and white celebrities. Ali's essay demonstrates that causal forces function in our personal lives.

As you read, note especially the use of the first-person "I" voice and the role of dialogue in the essay. The voice of the boxer reveals the causal forces at work in the strained relationship of the two men.

Ali's essay appeared in The New York Times *(18 September 1975) and is from* The Greatest—My Own Story *(1975) by Muhammad Ali with Richard Durham.*

MUHAMMAD ALI

Why Ali Whipped Patterson

I had not seen Floyd Patterson[1] since our fight in Las Vegas, but when I 1 came across an article he'd written for a national magazine, saying some honest things about the "loser," the admiration I'd had for him during my amateur days returned and I accepted an invitation to go out to his farm.

"The losing fighter loses more than just his pride in the fight," 2 Patterson had said in the article. "He loses part of his future. He's a step closer to the slum he came from." Then, turning his attention to me, "I'm sure that before each fight Cassius Clay also goes through the mental torture and doubt. He knows how happy thousands of Americans would be if he got beaten bad, and maybe that's why Clay has to say, 'I'm the greatest. I'm the greatest.' He wants people to say, 'You're not,' and then he's forced to meet the challenge. Put himself in a do-or-die frame of mind. Go a little crazy, maybe, crazy with some ferocious fear. So far it has worked for him. What he will be like if he loses, I do not know."

---

[1]Floyd Patterson (1935–   ) was heavyweight champion in 1956–59 and 1960–61. Ali knocked out Patterson in Las Vegas in 1965.

So Floyd wants to know how I'd take a loss, I thought, as I flew out   3
to his place in New York. He greeted me warmly and introduced me to
his family. It had been a long time since I had been with a competitor,
free from the artificial "hate" promoters and the press use to divide two
opponents, and we began to discover and like each other.

We lounged around, talking about the future—his fight plans, my   4
possible jail sentence[2]—and I told him I'd read what he'd written about
"losers." "I know the feeling," I said.

He surprised me with his sudden coldness. "You don't know what   5
you're talking about."

"I do," I told him.   6

But he turned away. "You've been lucky. You've never lost," he said   7
with what I thought was a touch of regret.

His chilliness caught me by surprise. Plainly, the bitterness of our   8
fight in Vegas had not been washed far enough down the drain so that
we could become buddies. "I've been on the brink," I said. "Man, I've
looked down in that pit. I know."

"But as an amateur," he said spitefully. "You don't know until some-   9
one knocks you down from the top."

For a quick second I had the impression he was still in that ring in   10
Las Vegas. How could I explain to him what drove me on to whip him
so thoroughly and totally? What I was doing in the ring with Patterson
that night in Vegas was directly related to what had been going on
outside the ring. The rage and uproar over me becoming a Muslim was
still at a fever pitch.

Looking at Floyd now, quiet and happy here at home with his wife   11
and children, I felt he still didn't understand what happened that night
and I wanted to tell him. I wanted to say, "Floyd, when I became a
Muslim, you announced in all the papers you were out to 'bring the
title back to America.' You said this was the main reason you wanted to
beat me. It was then that I said, 'What do you mean, bring it back to
America? It's already in America!' Floyd, I'm the Heavyweight Champion
of the World, and I'm an American. I stand for the people, the black
people, the poor people, the poor people in ghettos, both black and
white.

"When you were Champion, Floyd, whenever you took a picture   12
you'd either be picking up a little white boy or hugging a little white
girl, which was all right, but I never saw you pick up little black children
and pose with them. You came from the black, the poor, the oppressed,
the denied, but you always catered to the whites, the privileged. Even
then, I kept my peace until you made the statement that you wanted to

[2]Banned by the World Boxing Association for draft evasion in 1967, Ali was cleared
by the Supreme Court in 1970.

bring the title back to America. You let the whites goad you into attacking me because I'd become a follower of the Honorable Elijah Muhammad,[3] this black man who preached unity and progress, who had taken thousands of hopeless dope addicts off the streets and changed their lives, gave them purpose and programs. What he wanted was freedom, justice and equality for black people. You told the white press you'd never call me by my Muslim name, Muhammad Ali. You said, 'I'm gonna call him Cassius Clay, because that's the way he was born.'

"Then I said I was gonna give you a whipping. I said, 'I'm gonna give you a whipping until you call me Muhammad Ali'. I challenged you. I said, 'If you whip me, I'll go and join the Catholic Church, and if I whip you, you come and join the Honorable Elijah Muhammad and be a Muslim.' You never answered me on that. All the white press was backing you, all the Catholics, all the white Protestants. And even though Sonny Liston[4] had destroyed you twice, they revived you just so you could get to me. The only reason they gave you a chance at a title fight was they wanted to see you perform a miracle. They wanted to see a nice Catholic boy defeat a Black Muslim.   13

"You told them Elijah Muhammad was taking all my money, which was untrue, because actually I was borrowing money from the Nation of Islam. They hadn't taken a quarter from me. You said when I lost the title the Muslims would drop me like a hot potato, so I wanted to take all this out on you, but not really on you—on your white supporters.   14

"And when the fight was on, whenever you'd get in a blow the crowd would roar: 'Ooooooohhh! Aaaaaaahhh!' But whenever I'd throw blows on you, things were quiet. So for thirteen rounds, things were mostly very quiet, because I was doing the whipping. I didn't see myself fighting you, Floyd. I didn't see myself hitting Floyd Patterson. I was fighting the white reporters behind you, the Jimmy Cannons, and the white celebrities, the Frank Sinatras, the Jim Bishops, the Arch Wards, the Dick Youngs, and when it was over they talked about how cruel I was. I don't regret what I did. The trouble was, they wanted to see something cruel happen to me.   15

"But it's not true when they say I carried you, that I could have knocked you out, gotten you out of your misery. That's not true. Although I didn't really press the fight until after the eighth round, I never saw a time when I felt you were going to fall. I hit you so many times my hands were in pain and I could hardly move them, but you wouldn't fall. You kept taking it. You stood in there and kept taking it. You took everything I threw and you still had punches to throw back at me. You   16

---

[3] Elijah Muhammad (1897–1975) was leader of the Black Muslims.

[4] Sonny Liston (c. 1932–1970) knocked out Patterson in 1962 and again in a rematch.

were good. You had guts and heart. You were greater than those egg-
ing me on.

"Like the next morning when you went to see Frank Sinatra, what   17
did he do? When you went to see him to apologize for the poor showing? You went up to his room and he turned his back on you and hardly
spoke to you, and you came out with tears in your eyes. But it was not
you that I was trying to beat and knock out. It was those backing you. I
was talking back to them. I was saying, 'I am America. Only I'm the part
you won't recognize. But get used to me. Black, confident, cocky; my
name, not yours; my religion, not yours; my goals my own—get used
to me! I can make it without your approval! I won't let you beat me and
I won't let your Negro beat me!'"

AIMS AND STRATEGIES OF THE WRITER

Comment. Ali uses the title of his essay to make clear his primary aim:
to explain the reasons for his defeat of the former champion, Floyd
Patterson.

Assignment 1. Begin a list of "why" topics of your own to defend your
position on major issues in your life, such as "why I am majoring in
commercial art," "why school dominates my life," or "why part-time
work is necessary for me."

Comment. Ali had many reasons for winning the professional boxing
match—money, the title, fame, and so forth—yet he focuses on one
main reason. He admits that he was motivated by his own black pride
in conflict with the white supporters of Patterson. His prejudice sur-
faces as the main cause; all others become merely contributory.

Assignment 2. Expressive discourse should feature your personal
voice in a moment of self-examination. You need to probe your mind
for sufficient reasons, for main and contributory causes, and for remote
and repressed reasons. Begin writing notes, journal entries, or preliminary paragraphs for your causal essay. A topic such as "Why My Parents Abused Me" would be an emotionally wrenching subject for any
writer. Remember: The risk of expressive writing is exposure of your
inner self.

Comment. Obviously stung by the barbs of some fight critics, Ali also
aims to defend his actions in the fight. He says, "But it's not true when
they say I carried you, that I could have knocked you out, gotten you
out of your misery. That's not true." In this way he also defends Patterson
as a worthy opponent.

Assignment 3. Assess the nature of your topic selection. Are you defending yourself against criticism by explaining *why* you did it your way or against future criticism by providing reasons why you *will* do it your way? If so, work to control your bias and to recognize other positions. Develop a writing situation (see page 4) in order to recognize the needs of your readers, who will expect you to address their points of view as well as your own.

THE WRITING PROCESS

Comment. Ali uses a basic formula for causal analysis: He names a specific effect (his defeat of Patterson) and traces the causes for it.

Assignment 4. Plan your paper according to the Ali formula. That is, name a condition that now exists and analyze its causes. You will need to establish the subject (for instance, why your team won the high school championship) and examine the causes (players, coaches, support, luck, and so forth).

Comment. Ali's voice appears prominently throughout the essay. Dialogue therefore plays an important role, for it establishes the mood, tone, and general character of the essay.

Assignment 5. Consider the role that dialogue might play in your essay. Would a conversation with your mother or teacher or employer add to the development of the paper? If so, add it as a block of material to the essay but remember to use quotation marks and new paragraphs for each person's comments.

Comment. Ali blends several patterns into this essay. He describes, narrates, gives examples, and explains the process by which he won the match. In addition, he carefully establishes a distinct contrast between himself and Patterson.

Assignment 6. Make a checklist of patterns that may serve your needs. Define the act or issue under consideration so that readers know *what* subject you wish to examine. Describe the scene to answer *where* events occur. Use process analysis to explain *how* events occur. Classify causes and consequences that explain *why* these things occur. Name the actors involved and give examples and comparisons of their attitudes and purposes. You can blend these elements into your master plan or, in some cases, write the patterns as blocks of material to be inserted into the main text at key points.

Joseph Wassersug, a physician of internal medicine, has authored seven health books. His son, Richard Wassersug, is an associate professor of anatomy and an expert in evolutionary biology. Together they form an authoritative team on health and physical fitness.

They use causal analysis in this essay to categorize and discuss known effects, and in the process they refute certain myths about exercise and fitness. They address the fallacy that hard exercise improves life expectancy. The authors explain that such cause-and-effect thinking by fitness advocates has no basis in scientific evidence.

While exposing the faulty reasoning of fitness advocates, the Wassersugs also forecast consequences that have scientific validity. For example, rather than increase life expectancy, vigorous exercise may contribute to early death and disability.

In effect, the writers investigate the evidence for sufficient causes *and* main causes. *Although they say that exercise is sufficient for improving "one's sense of well-being," they dismiss it as a* necessary cause *for increased life expectancy.*

As you read, make marginal notes to record the essential point of each paragraph. The first paragraph, for example, defines fitness, the second establishes the thesis, the third names one positive consequence, and so forth.

"Fitness Fallacies" appeared in Natural History *(March 1986).*

JOSEPH D. WASSERSUG AND RICHARD J. WASSERSUG

Fitness Fallacies

The current pervasive push toward the body perfect is based on some 1 semantic misunderstandings that sorely need clarification. Much of the problem, we think, lies with popular understanding of the term "fitness." Many of the ardent joggers we know seem to think that with the achievement of "fitness," they will not only be healthier but also live longer. For others, if we are to judge by the most-advertised exercise programs, fitness is simply the attainment of the body beautiful, a state that has a lot more to do with physique than physiology.

While there is no denying that vigorous exercise may improve one's 2 sense of well-being (comparable, say, to Zen meditation or vegetarianism), there is no evidence that running five miles a day, for instance, improves life expectancy or even appreciably enhances health. A long-term epidemiologic study of nearly 17,000 Harvard University graduates (published in 1984 in the *Journal of the American Medical Associa-*

tion) found that the risk of coronary heart disease was lower in people who claimed to exercise enough to burn off the equivalent of 2,000 kilocalories (kcal.) a week than in those who claimed that they exercised less. But while this may sound like a lot of energy, it doesn't amount to a lot of exercise. A normal 165-pound man, for example, can easily use up that many calories through three to five hours a week of routine walking on level ground.

Carefully prescribed exercises may increase the chances of survival   3
in some people—primarily those who have had heart attacks or coronary surgery. Because walking pumps blood back to the heart, it reduces ankle edema and often improves breathing in patients with congestive heart failure; regulated exercise may also help those who suffer attacks of angina pectoris. But the physical fitness that daily rigorous exercise is supposed to produce does little to prevent heart disease in otherwise healthy people. And there is no evidence at all that physical fitness protects against the other maladies that are common causes of human mortality. Cancer of the breast, lungs, or bowel; Alzheimer's and Parkinson's disease; and a great variety of anemias and dystrophies kill the fit and the unfit with equal ruthlessness.

If one is in generally good health (at the right weight for one's height   4
and age, not smoking, not eating a lot of foods rich in saturated fats), then excessive physical exertion, that is, much beyond what is needed to maintain ideal weight, does nothing to improve life expectancy. Regrettably, few physical-fitness fanatics seem willing to accept this. Heavy-duty iron pumpers and triathalon trekkies will argue forcefully that they are *sure* that there *must* be many medical studies to show that heavy exercise (for example, burning off more than 2,000 kcal. a day above basal consumption levels) increases life expectancy. But if such a single, controlled study exists, it would be known, cited, and re-cited in the medical literature. There is no such study.

On the other hand, there is some evidence that the opposite is true.   5
Since vigorous exercise initially increases heart rate and output, raises blood pressure, and, to some extent, deprives the heart of oxygen, it may contribute to early death and disability. Exercise guru James Fixx died at fifty-two and Olympic oarsman John B. Kelly, Jr., clad in his running clothes, died at fifty-eight. While many runners who die suddenly had preexisting heart disease (and may have been aware of it), other deaths while running happen to those with no known earlier heart impairment and no significant myocardial or coronary artery disease detectable at autopsy. These deaths have been attributed to occult biochemical or electrophysiological derangements.

Writing recently in *Cardiovascular Reviews and Reports*, Drs. A.   6
Sadaniantz and P. D. Thompson have suggested that coronary spasm

may also play a role. Reviewing the literature, these authors found that the hourly death rate while jogging was about seven times that of those engaged in more sedentary activities. The death rate was particularly high in men unaccustomed to physical activity. They conclude: "Exercise and fitness may help prevent, but do not guarantee protection against, an exercise death. Other risk factors such as hyperlipidemia [too much fat in the blood], cigarette smoking, and hypertension are more powerful predictors of CAD [coronary artery disease] than sedentary behavior."

We don't at present have all the answers to longevity—there may be 7 as-yet unexplored factors of climate, nutrition, and heredity. Geographically, greatest longevity is achieved by the mountain dwellers of Turkestan and the farmers of Vermont. Among professions, orchestra conductors and concert musicians—not athletes or heavy laborers— live the longest.

The myth of workout longevity may stem from confusion about the 8 definitions of fitness. Biologists use the term in several different ways. In the field of physiology—the field that pertains to joggers—the definition of fitness is "increased capacity for work." What this means is that a person who regularly runs five miles each day will be more capable of running five miles the next day *if* he is alive the next day. The fit person can do more work in a single day than the person who is not fit. This, of course, is a good enough reason to get some exercise now and then. It does not follow, however, that the fit person who jogs five miles a day will have more days in his life in which to jog than a person who runs, say, only a half mile three times a week. The older person can do as much as a younger person but needs more time to do it. Age slows down even the fittest.

The latest scientific work on the relationship between exercise and 9 heart attack suggests that three brief bouts (fifteen to twenty minutes) a week of extremely brisk exercise are all one needs to give one the same statistical probability of living to an old age as sweating up a storm for thirty or fifty minutes a day.

At the other extreme, there is considerable data to show that over- 10 exertion can kill at a young age. While regularly increasing the heart rate for *short* periods by exercise may enhance coronary circulation, prolonged episodes of tachycardia (a racing heart) are definitely damaging. We don't know exactly where the curve for the risk of coronary heart disease versus calories consumed in exercise per week turns upward, but researchers studying the relationship between health and exercise acknowledge that at some point the curve must turn upward. For all individuals there is a point where they are burning off too many calories and increasing the risk of injury and death. If you need a long time to recover from your workout, you might do well to discuss your exercise program with your doctor.

The myth that exercise and longevity are linked is based on two 11 misconceptions. The first is the old idea that helps keep over-the-counter vitamin sales so high, namely, "if a little is good for you, then a lot is much better." Yet high doses of the fat-soluble vitamins, such as A and D, are definitely toxic; the B and C vitamins are readily excreted by the kidneys and thus an excess provides no more health benefits than the minimum daily requirement. The more-is-not-better principle also applies to physical exercise. We may live longer if we have a certain, minimal amount of exercise. We will not necesarily live longer if we have ten times that amount.

Perhaps a second source of the myth about exercise and longevity 12 stems from a misunderstanding of the phrase "survival of the fittest," which is associated with Darwin's *Origin of Species*. Actually, it wasn't Charles Darwin who coined the phrase, but the social philosopher Herbert Spencer. Darwin liked the one-liner enough at the time to adapt it for use in his book. But Darwin's own definition of fitness did not directly concern individual survival. There are thus really two definitions of fitness in the Darwinian literature—Darwin's and Spencer's; but both are quite independent of the physiologists' definition. To Darwin, and to all evolutionary biologists working today, increased fitness means increased fecundity. In plain English, fitter organisms leave more offspring than less fit organisms. According to Darwin's definition, a man who died young, but left more children (and potential grandchildren) than other people, would be more "fit."

Both the physiological and the Darwinian definitions of fitness may 13 concurrently apply to many organisms. During the rutting season, a male moose that can last the longest in a duel with another moose will probably increase his access to a female moose at the height of her reproductive cycle (more sex, more offspring; *ergo*, increased Darwinian fitness). But only in a fairy-tale world—where kings give away daughters to knights who win athletic events against other knights— does the increased physiological fitness necessary to win the contest also mean increased Darwinian fitness for the victor.

Perhaps what attracts people today to physical fitness programs is 14 an unconscious wish to improve their fitness in the Darwinian sense. If one jogs and pumps iron to attract members of the opposite sex, then increased physiological fitness could lead to increased Darwinian fitness. There are, however, two caveats here. First, attracting sexual partners does not in itself lead to increased Darwinian fitness. Attraction must lead to increased fecundity: there must be more offspring for there to be an increase in evolutionary fitness. The skinny, unathletic

Harvard M.B.A. who earns $300,000 a year may be as likely to attract compliant females as the high-school football coach who earns $30,000. But neither is guaranteed a houseful of grandchildren. For modern man, neither fiscal nor physical fitness forecasts fecundity.

Second, rigorous programs of physical exertion can actually inter-   15 fere with the organisms's ability to reproduce. A study published last year in the *New England Journal of Medicine* documented that women athletes on a rigorous training regime ceased to menstruate and, presumably, to ovulate. Women who continually push themselves to their physical limits are on a course leading to the extinction of their family line. Surely, the sacrifice of evolutionary fitness for a hypothetical increase in physical fitness carries the more-is-better idea to its absurd conclusion.

AIMS AND STRATEGIES OF THE WRITERS

Comment. As scholars, the Wassersugs approach their subject with scientific inquiry for accuracy in causal analysis. They design the essay to refute privately held myths and fallacies about fitness and health.

Assignment 1. Begin your search for a topic in the Wassersug manner. That is, list subjects that interest you, that you can research readily, and that need the exposure of causal analysis. For example, you could examine the amateur status of college athletes (what causes one to lose amateur status?) or examine charity fund-raisers (what consequences might result from a donation?).

Comment. The primary aim of the Wassersugs, to search out sufficient causes and isolate them from contributory and remote causes, directs them to a conclusion that "excessive physical exertion . . . does nothing to improve life expectancy." Such exertion is not a sufficient cause.

Assignment 2. After you select a topic, begin your examination of causes. (If necessary, review again the types of causes on pages 330–331.) Write a list of *sufficient* causes and *main* causes. For example, would an athlete selling his complimentary football tickets for $100 each be sufficient cause to ruin his amateur standing?

Comment. The underlying idea and probably the main cause for this essay on fitness is the Wassersugs' concern for public health. They want to destroy the myth that "more is better" when it comes to jogging, running, weight lifting, or aerobics.

Assignment 3. As you develop your essay of causal analysis, consider the primary cause for your inquiry. Do you want to dispel misconceptions about the term "amateur" or do you want to go further and argue a few points? Consider the needs of your audience in this matter: Should you inform or convince them? The latter will demand more investigation and the citation of sources and other evidence. Now is the time to develop a writing situation for your essay.

THE WRITING PROCESS

Comment. The Wassersugs use causal analysis as their basic pattern of writing; they present a prevailing theory (that exercise can increase life expectancy) and disprove its causal force. In addition, they forecast the most likely consequences.

Assignment 4. Does your subject lend itself to causal analysis? Can you trace both contributory and main causes? Can you predict consequences? List them to see if they fall into a pattern that fits your paper's outline.

Comment. The Wassersugs use comparison and contrast effectively throughout the essay to weigh relative merits of myth and scientific evidence. For example, they cite weight lifters who maintain that heavy exercise will increase life expectancy and then, in contrast, cite evidence that the opposite is true.

Assignment 5. Consider the value of comparison and contrast as a pattern for your essay. For example, interview a few people on their definitions of "amateur" and compare those statements with your carefully researched evidence.

Comment. The Wassersugs increase the credibility of their essay by citing expert testimony resulting from their investigation (see especially paragraphs 2, 6, and 15).

Assignment 6. If you have researched your topic in the library or conducted interviews, consider using this evidence in your paper; it will add authority to the piece. (You will be expected to provide scholarly citation of your sources in the form of proper in-text citations and a "Works Cited" page; accurate records of names, titles, and page numbers are important.)

Comment. In paragraphs 12 through 14 the authors use the pattern of historical narration to explain the phrase "survival of the fittest," which is associated with Darwin's research. Historical narration, in brief, chronicles events of the past or the achievements of a notable person.

Assignment 7. You will probably need to study the history of your subject. As you examine the past for causal forces, you will also discover historic patterns, events, and characters. For example, a paper on the amateur athlete would benefit by an exploration of the term's history, its etymology as explained in a good dictionary, and perhaps its precise meaning according to the National Collegiate Athletic Association.

Comment. The authors close the essay using the technique of *paradox*; they say that fitness fanatics who sacrifice their ability to reproduce carry "the more-is-better idea to its absurd conclusion." (*Paradox* is a statement that conflicts with a general belief but one that nevertheless contains a truth.)

Assignment 8. Consider the limits of your topic. Can you add a satiric, ironic touch in the manner of the Wassersugs? Reading Jonathan Swift's "A Modest Proposal" (pages 354–361) might provide additional insights into the use of an ironic and satiric point of view.

C*arl Sagan ranks as one of the most notable and visible contemporary space scientists. Through his television commentaries, essays in popular magazines, and best-selling books, Sagan has introduced concepts of modern space technology to laymen throughout the nation. His credentials include several degrees in astronomy as well as a number of medals from the National Aeronautics and Space Administration for his pioneer work in the space program.*

In cooperation with other scientists, he prepared a scientific paper, "Global Atmospheric Consequences of Nuclear War." From that study he developed this article, "The Nuclear Winter," for publication in Parade (30 October 1983), a popular newspaper supplement. Thereby, he brought his chilling, frightening message to millions of Americans, rather than just a narrow group of scholars, in order to make a political statement and win a following of antinuclear advocates.

The essay combines scientific analysis with persuasive discourse. It serves as a classic study of cause and effect to show how a nuclear war might affect the earth and its population. Although unstated, Sagan issues an implicit call to action. He motivates readers to support nuclear control that would set stringent limits on stockpiled weapons.

Read the essay with an eye for its three-part structure. Paragraphs 1 through 13 establish the prevailing scientific wisdom and the causal forces at work; paragraphs 14 through 22 explain the consequences of a nuclear explosion; and paragraphs 23 through 27 discuss humanity's role in safeguarding civilization.

CARL SAGAN

 The Nuclear Winter

> Into the eternal darkness, into fire, into ice.
> Dante, *The Inferno*

Except for fools and madmen, everyone knows that nuclear war would be an unprecedented human catastrophe. A more or less typical strategic warhead has a yield of two megatons, the explosive equivalent of two million tons of TNT. But two million tons of TNT is about the same as all the bombs exploded in World War II—a single bomb with the explosive power of the entire Second World War but compressed into a few seconds of time and an area thirty or forty miles across. . . . 1

In a two-megaton explosion over a fairly large city, buildings would be vaporized, people reduced to atoms and shadows, outlying structures blown down like matchsticks and raging fires ignited. And if the 2 bomb were exploded on the ground, an enormous crater, like those that can be seen through a telescope on the surface of the moon, would be all that remained where midtown once had been. There are now more than 50,000 nuclear weapons, more than 13,000 megatons of yield, deployed in the arsenals of the United States and the Soviet Union—enough to obliterate a million Hiroshimas.

But there are fewer than 3,000 cities on the Earth with populations   3 of 100,000 or more. You cannot find anything like a million Hiroshimas to obliterate. Prime military and industrial targets that are far from cities are comparatively rare. Thus, there are vastly more nuclear weapons than are needed for any plausible deterrence of a potential adversary.

Nobody knows, of course, how many megatons would be exploded   4 in a real nuclear war. There are some who think that a nuclear war can be "contained," bottled up before it runs away to involve many of the world's arsenals. But a number of detailed analyses, war games run by the U.S. Department of Defense and official Soviet pronouncements, all indicate that this containment may be too much to hope for: Once the bombs begin exploding, communications failures, disorganization, fear, the necessity of making in minutes decisions affecting the fates of millions and the immense psychological burden of knowing that your own loved ones may already have been destroyed are likely to result in a nuclear paroxysm. Many investigations, including a number of studies for the U.S. government, envision the explosion of 5,000 to 10,000 megatons—the detonation of tens of thousands of nuclear weapons that now sit quietly, inconspicuously, in missile silos, submarines and long-range bombers, faithful servants awaiting orders.

The World Health Organization, in a recent detailed study chaired   5 by Sune K. Bergstrom (the 1982 Nobel laureate in physiology and medicine), concludes that 1.1 billion people would be killed outright in such a nuclear war, mainly in the United States, the Soviet Union, Europe, China and Japan. An additional 1.1 billion people would suffer serious injuries and radiation sickness, for which medical help would be unavailable. It thus seems possible that more than 2 billion people— almost half of all the humans on Earth—would be destroyed in the immediate aftermath of a global thermonuclear war. This would rep- resent by far the greatest disaster in the history of the human species and, with no other adverse effects, would probably be enough to re- duce at least the Northern Hemisphere to a state of prolonged agony and barbarism. Unfortunately, the real situation would be much worse.

In technical studies of the consequences of nuclear weapons explo-   6 sions, there has been a dangerous tendency to underestimate the results. This is partly due to a tradition of conservatism, which generally works well in science but which is of more dubious applicability when the lives of billions of people are at stake. In the Bravo test of March 1, 1954, a fifteen-megaton thermonuclear bomb was exploded on Bikini Atoll. It had about double the yield expected, and there was an unanticipated last-minute shift in the wind direction. As a result, deadly radioactive fallout came down on Rongelap in the Marshall Islands, more than 200 kilometers away. Almost all the children on Rongelap subsequently developed thyroid nodules and lesions, and other long-term medical problems, due to the radioactive fallout.

Likewise, in 1973, it was discovered that high-yield airbursts will 7 chemically burn the nitrogen in the upper air, converting it into oxides of nitrogen; these, in turn, combine with and destroy the protective ozone in the Earth's stratosphere. The surface of the Earth is shielded from deadly solar ultraviolet radiation by a layer of ozone so tenuous that, were it brought down to sea level, it would be only three millimeters thick. Partial destruction of this ozone layer can have serious consequences for the biology of the entire planet.

These discoveries, and others like them, were made by chance. They 8 were largely unexpected. And now another consequence—by far the most dire—has been uncovered, again more or less by accident.

The U.S. Mariner 9 spacecraft, the first vehicle to orbit another 9 planet, arrived at Mars in late 1971. The planet was enveloped in a global dust storm. As the fine particles slowly fell out, we were able to measure temperature changes in the atmosphere and on the surface. Soon it became clear what had happened:

The dust, lofted by high winds off the desert into the upper Martian 10 atmosphere, had absorbed the incoming sunlight and prevented much of it from reaching the ground. Heated by the sunlight, the dust warmed the adjacent air. But the surface, enveloped in partial darkness, became much chillier than usual. Months later, after the dust fell out of the atmosphere, the upper air cooled and the surface warmed, both returning to their normal conditions. We were able to calculate accurately, from how much dust there was in the atmosphere, how cool the Martian surface ought to have been.

Afterwards, I and my colleagues, James B. Pollack and Brian Toon 11 of NASA's Ames Research Center, were eager to apply these insights to the Earth. In a volcanic explosion, dust aerosols are lofted into the high atmosphere. We calculated by how much the Earth's global temperature should decline after a major volcanic explosion and found that our results (generally a fraction of a degree) were in good accord with actual measurements. Joining forces with Richard Turco, who has

studied the effects of nuclear weapons for many years, we then began
to turn our attention to the climatic effects of nuclear war.*

We knew that nuclear explosions, particularly groundbursts, would   12
lift an enormous quantity of fine soil particles into the atmosphere
(more than 100,000 tons of fine dust for every megaton exploded in a
surface burst). Our work was further spurred by Paul Crutzen of the
Max Planck Institute for Chemistry in Mainz, West Germany, and by
John Birks of the University of Colorado, who pointed out that huge
quantities of smoke would be generated in the burning of cities and
forests following a nuclear war.

Groundbursts—at hardened missile silos, for example—generate   13
fine dust. Airbursts—over cities and unhardened military installa-
tions—make fires and therefore smoke. The amount of dust and soot
generated depends on the conduct of the war, the yields of the weapons
employed and the ratio of groundbursts to airbursts. So we ran computer models for several dozen different nuclear war scenarios. Our
baseline case, as in many other studies, was a 5,000-megaton war with
only a modest fraction of the yield (20 percent) expended on urban or
industrial targets. Our job, for each case, was to follow the dust and
smoke generated, see how much sunlight was absorbed and by how
much the temperatures changed, figure out how the particles spread in
longitude and latitude, and calculate how long before it all fell out of
the air back onto the surface. Since the radioactivity would be attached
to these same fine particles, our calculations also revealed the extent
and timing of the subsequent radioactive fallout.

Some of what I am about to describe is horrifying. I know, because   14
it horrifies me. There is a tendency—psychiatrists call it "denial"—to
put it out of our minds, not to think about it. But if we are to deal
intelligently, wisely, with the nuclear arms race, then we must steel
ourselves to contemplate the horrors of nuclear war.

The results of our calculations astonished us. In the baseline case,   15
the amount of sunlight at the ground was reduced to a few percent of
normal—much darker, in daylight, than in a heavy overcast and too
dark for plants to make a living from photosynthesis. At least in the
Northern Hemisphere, where the great preponderance of strategic targets lies, an unbroken and deadly gloom would persist for weeks.

Even more unexpected were the temperatures calculated. In the   16
baseline case, land temperatures, except for narrow strips of coastline,
dropped to minus 25° Celsius (minus 13° Fahrenheit) and stayed below

*The scientific paper, "Global Atmospheric Consequences of Nuclear War," is written
by R. P. Turco, O. B. Toon, T. P. Ackerman, J. B. Pollack and Carl Sagan. From the last
names of the authors, this work is generally referred to as "TTAPS."

freezing for months—even for a summer war. (Because the atmospheric structure becomes much more stable as the upper atmosphere is heated and the lower air is cooled, we may have severely *under*estimated how long the cold and the dark would last.) The oceans, a significant heat reservoir, would not freeze, however, and a major ice age would probably not be triggered. But because the temperatures would drop so catastrophically, virtually all crops and farm animals, at least in the Northern Hemisphere, would be destroyed, as would most varieties of uncultivated or undomesticated food supplies. Most of the human survivors would starve.

In addition, the amount of radioactive fallout is much more than 17 expected. Many previous calculations simply ignored the intermediate time-scale fallout. That is, calculations were made for the prompt fallout—the plumes of radioactive debris blown downwind from each target—and for the long-term fallout, the fine radioactive particles lofted into the stratosphere that would descend about a year later, after most of the radioactivity had decayed. However, the radioactivity carried into the upper atmosphere (but not as high as the stratosphere) seems to have been largely forgotten. We found for the baseline case that roughly 30 percent of the land at northern midlatitudes could receive a radioactive dose greater than 250 rads, and that about 50 percent of northern midlatitudes could receive a dose greater than 100 rads. A 100-rad dose is the equivalent of about 1,000 medical X-rays. A 400-rad dose will, more likely than not, kill you.

The cold, the dark and the intense radioactivity, together lasting for 18 months, represent a severe assault on our civilization and our species. Civil and sanitary services would be wiped out. Medical facilities, drugs, the most rudimentary means for relieving the vast human suffering, would be unavailable. Any but the most elaborate shelters would be useless, quite apart from the question of what good it might be to emerge a few months later. Synthetics burned in the destruction of the cities would produce a wide variety of toxic gases, including carbon monoxide, cyanides, dioxins and furans. After the dust and soot settled out, the solar ultraviolet flux would be much larger than its present value. Immunity to disease would decline. Epidemics and pandemics would be rampant, especially after the billion or so unburied bodies began to thaw. Moreover, the combined influence of these severe and simultaneous stresses on life are likely to produce even more adverse consequences—biologists call them synergisms—that we are not yet wise enough to foresee.

So far, we have talked only of the Northern Hemisphere. But it now 19 seems—unlike the case of a single nuclear weapons test—that in a real nuclear war, the heating of the vast quantities of atmospheric dust and soot in northern midlatitudes will transport these fine particles toward and across the equator. We see just this happening in Martian dust storms. The Southern Hemisphere would experience effects that, while less severe than in the Northern Hemisphere, are nevertheless extremely ominous. The illusion with which some people in the Northern Hemisphere reassure themselves—catching an Air New Zealand flight in a time of serious international crisis, or the like—is now much less tenable, even on the narrow issue of personal survival for those with the price of a ticket.

But what if nuclear wars *can* be contained, and much less than   20
5,000 megatons is detonated? Perhaps the greatest surprise in our work was that even small nuclear wars can have devastating climatic effects. We considered a war in which a mere 100 megatons were exploded, less than one percent of the world arsenals, and only in low-yield airbursts over cities. This scenario, we found, would ignite thousands of fires, and the smoke from these fires alone would be enough to generate an epoch of cold and dark almost as severe as in the 5,000-megaton case. The threshold for what Richard Turco has called the "nuclear winter" is very low.

Could we have overlooked some important effect? The carrying of   21
dust and soot from the Northern to the Southern Hemisphere (as well as more local atmospheric circulation) will certainly thin the clouds out over the Northern Hemisphere. But, in many cases, this thinning would be insufficient to render the climatic consequences tolerable—and every time it got better in the Northern Hemisphere, it would get worse in the Southern.

Our results have been carefully scrutinized by more than one   22
hundred scientists in the United States, Europe and the Soviet Union. There are still arguments on points of detail. But the overall conclusion seems to be agreed upon: There are severe and previously unanticipated global consequences of nuclear war—subfreezing temperatures in a twilit radioactive gloom lasting for months or longer.

Scientists initially underestimated the effects of fallout, were amazed   23
that nuclear explosions in space disabled distant satellites, had no idea that the fireballs from high-yield thermonuclear explosions could deplete the ozone layer and missed altogether the possible climatic effects of nuclear dust and smoke. What else have we overlooked?

Nuclear war is a problem that can be treated only theoretically. It is   24
not amenable to experimentation. Conceivably, we have left something important out of our analysis, and the effects are more modest than we calculate. On the other hand, it is also possible—and, from previous

experience, even likely—that there are further adverse effects that no one has yet been wise enough to recognize. With billions of lives at stake, where does conservatism lie—in assuming that the results will be better than we calculate, or worse?

Many biologists, considering the nuclear winter that these calcula- 25 tions describe, believe they carry somber implications for life on Earth. Many species of plants and animals would become extinct. Vast numbers of surviving humans would starve to death. The delicate ecological relations that bind together organisms on Earth in a fabric of mutual dependency would be torn, perhaps irreparably. There is little question that our global civilization would be destroyed. The human population would be reduced to prehistoric levels, or less. Life for any survivors would be extremely hard. And there seems to be a real possibility of the extinction of the human species.

It is now almost forty years since the invention of nuclear weapons. 26 We have not yet experienced a global thermonuclear war—although on more than one occasion we have come tremulously close. I do not think our luck can hold forever. Men and machines are fallible, as recent events remind us. Fools and madmen do exist, and sometimes rise to power. Concentrating always on the near future, we have ignored the long-term consequences of our actions. We have placed our civilization and our species in jeopardy.

Fortunately, it is not yet too late. We can safeguard the planetary 27 civilization and the human family if we so choose. There is no more important or more urgent issue.

AIMS AND STRATEGIES OF THE WRITER

Comment. The introduction to the essay discusses the strategy of Sagan. He published the essay in *Parade*, a popular Sunday newspaper supplement, to reach a mass audience of Americans. Thereby, he brings his warning about nuclear destruction to the public, not to a handful of scientific specialists or a specific group of politicians.

Assignment 1. Design a paper that will warn readers about a current condition that could have far-reaching consequences. Begin with a list of regional topics—water pollution at a local stream, a hazardous waste disposal site in your county, drug testing for scholarship athletes, or mandatory sex education in local schools. Remember, the consequences might be positive rather than negative.

Comment. A persuasive writer like Sagan tries to convince readers about the truth of a proposition. Sagan does this by referring to technical studies by the World Health Organization, the U.S. Mariner 9 space project, NASA's Ames Research Center, and others.

Assignment 2. As you narrow your choices for a persuasive cause-and-effect essay, consider carefully the sources that might be available to support your contentions. Library references will inform you of material on, for instance, hazardous waste disposal. In addition, you may wish to interview key individuals (in person or by phone) and use their comments. Like Sagan, complete your research before writing on complex and controversial issues.

Comment. Persuasive writers often urge their readers into action. Perhaps more than anything else, Sagan wants to awaken Americans to the consequences of nuclear war. In addition, he would seemingly welcome a national outcry against nuclear tests and against the continued buildup and stockpiling of nuclear weapons.

Assignment 3. After choosing your topic, develop a writing situation. Carefully consider the effect of your essay. Should you issue a call for action or can you quietly convince others, not in a polemical sense of opposites (you against the reader) but with a sense of synthesis that brings insight and supporting evidence to the reader? Your best approach might be a paper in the style of Sagan. Invite your readers into a discussion of the subject, present your evidence in support of your thesis, and allow readers to draw their own conclusions.

THE WRITING PROCESS

Comment. Sagan cites evidence from the Bravo test in 1954, the 1973 discovery on high-yield airbursts, and the evidence from a Martian dust storm. He uses these events to develop, with others, a paper grimly referred to as TTAPS (see the footnote to paragraph 11). Based on that evidence, Sagan discusses the consequences of a nuclear war.

Assignment 4. Outline your cause-and-effect paper to provide evidence before offering any conclusions on the subject. Allow readers to grasp the facts and figures; this will help win their confidence.

Comment. Sagan provides a persuasive discourse that demonstrates the absolute necessity for evidence. Anybody can argue points on an issue, but only certain persons have the weight of evidence to convince the listener or reader.

Assignment 5. Develop your rough draft and advance and defend your fundamental proposition with sound reasons and evidence. Your persuasive writing must advance a thesis and then provide logical reasoning drawn from evidence in the form of examples, expert testimony, statistics, and so forth. Your authoritative grasp of all issues should be apparent to the reader.

Comment. Sagan answers the fundamental questions of causal analysis (as set forth in the beginning of this chapter). He names *what* (nuclear winter that will destroy whatever life remains after the nuclear explosion), *who* (human beings), *where* (the Northern Hemisphere but probably the entire Earth), *why* and *to what purpose* (nuclear war started by fools and madmen in quest of power), and *how* (nuclear winter will be caused by dust particles blocking out necessary sunlight).

Assignment 6. Use the basic questions for developing your causal analysis. Note this example.

What: drug use

Who: scholarship athletes

Where: training rooms

Why: to gain a higher level of physical and mental preparation

How: use of steriods or stimulants

Comment. Consider Sagan's use of the various causal types. A nuclear war would probably be a *sufficient* cause to destroy life on earth, there would be several *contributory* causes for a nuclear winter, and the *main* cause would be darkness and cold caused by particles in the atmosphere. The explosions would set off a *causal chain* of effects that could neither be stopped nor escaped.

Assignment 7. List or outline relevant causes, causal chains, and a reasonable sequence of consequences for your topic. As you develop your essay, keep it honest, objective, and logical. Readers will react negatively to any misappropriation of causes and effects.

In A Modest Proposal *(1729) Jonathan Swift takes an imaginative approach to causal analysis, applying it with deft, satiric strokes to the abominable conditions of his native country, Ireland, during the late 1600s when Ireland was harshly ruled by the British. Noticing the excessive number of women and children begging on the streets, Swift considers the problem and offers an absurd solution, but his contemporaries in Ireland and England were shocked by the piece. Those who misunderstood and took him seriously were ready to burn him at the stake. Swift, however, intended the piece as irony and as a gross exaggeration; he lashed out with this satiric essay to condemn both England's exploitation of Ireland and the meek acquiescence of the Irish citizenry.*

Swift does introduce (in paragraph 29) a reasonable program of behavior: taxing the British, curing pride and vanity, learning to love Ireland, and ending all internal animosities. He had little hope that reasonableness would prevail, but he did manage to shock readers into recognizing Ireland's condition.

Swift ranks as the foremost satirist of the English language. Although his great work, Gulliver's Travels, *has become, in a brief expurgated form, a popular children's story, it remains in the original a fierce attack on the petty, gross, and greedy.*

JONATHAN SWIFT

A Modest Proposal

It is a melancholy object to those who walk through this great town or 1
travel in the country, when they see the streets, the roads, and cabin doors, crowded with beggars of the female sex, followed by three, four, or six children, all in rags and importuning every passenger for an alms. These mothers, instead of being able to work for their honest livelihood, are forced to employ all their time in strolling to beg sustenance for their helpless infants: who as they grow up either turn thieves for want of work, or leave their dear native country to fight for the pretender in Spain, or sell themselves to the Barbadoes.

I think it is agreed by all parties that this prodigious number of 2
children in the arms, or on the backs, or at the heels of their mothers, and frequently of their fathers, is in the present deplorable state of the kingdom a very great additional grievance; and, therefore, whoever could find out a fair, cheap, and easy method of making these children

sound, useful members of the commonwealth, would deserve so well of the public as to have his statue set up for a preserver of the nation.

But my intention is very far from being confined to provide only for the children of professed beggars; it is of a much greater extent, and shall take in the whole number of infants at a certain age who are born of parents in effect as little able to support them as those who demand our charity in the streets.

As to my own part, having turned my thoughts for many years upon this important subject, and maturely weighed the several schemes of our projectors, I have always found them grossly mistaken in their computation. It is true, a child just dropped from its dam may be supported by her milk for a solar year, with little other nourishment; at most not above the value of 2s.,* which the mother may certainly get, or the value in scraps, by her lawful occupation of begging; and it is exactly at one year old that I propose to provide for them in such a manner as instead of being a charge upon their parents or the parish, or wanting food and raiment for the rest of their lives, they shall on the contrary contribute to the feeding, and partly to the clothing, of many thousands.

There is likewise another great advantage in my scheme, that it will prevent those voluntary abortions, and that horrid practice of women murdering their bastard children, alas! too frequent among us! sacrificing the poor innocent babes I doubt more to avoid the expense than the shame, which would move tears and pity in the most savage and inhuman breast.

The number of souls in this kingdom being usually reckoned one million and a half, of these I calculate there may be about 200,000 couple whose wives are breeders; from which number I subtract 30,000 couple who are able to maintain their own children (although I apprehend there cannot be so many, under the present distress of the kingdom); but this being granted, there will remain 170,000 breeders. I again subtract 50,000 for those women who miscarry, or whose children die by accident or disease within the year. There only remain 120,000 children of poor parents annually born. The question therefore is, how this number shall be reared and provided for? which, as I have already said, under the present situation of affairs, is utterly impossible by all the methods hitherto proposed. For we can neither employ them in handicraft or agriculture; we neither build houses (I mean in the country) nor cultivate land; they can very seldom pick up a livelihood by stealing, till they arrive at six years old, except where they are of

*2s. = two shillings. Later in the essay, Swift speaks of "l" and "d," that is, of pounds and pence.

towardly parts; although I confess they learn the rudiments much earlier; during which time they can, however, be properly looked upon
only as probationers; as I have been informed by a principal gentleman
in the county of Cavan, who protested to me that he never knew above
one or two instances under the age of six, even in a part of the kingdom
so renowned for the quickest proficiency in that art.

I am assured by our merchants, that a boy or a girl before twelve   7
years old is no saleable commodity; and even when they come to this
age they will not yield above 3l. or 3l. 2s. 6d. at most on the exchange;
which cannot turn to account either to the parents or kingdom, the
charge of nutriment and rags having been at least four times that value.

I shall now therefore humbly propose my own thoughts, which I   8
hope will not be liable to the least objection.

I have been assured by a very knowing American of my acquaintance   9
in London, that a young healthy child well nursed is at a year old a most
delicious, nourishing, and wholesome food, whether stewed, roasted,
baked, or broiled; and I make no doubt that it will equally serve in a
fricassee or a ragout.

I do therefore humbly offer it to public consideration that of the   10
120,000 children already computed, 20,000 may be reserved for breed,
whereof only one-fourth part to be males; which is more than we allow
to sheep, black cattle, or swine; and my reason is, that these children
are seldom the fruits of marriage, a circumstance not much regarded
by our savages; therefore one male will be sufficient to serve four
females. That the remaining 100,000 may, at a year old, be offered in
sale to the persons of quality and fortune through the kingdom; always
advising the mother to let them suck plentifully in the last month, so as
to render them plump and fat for a good table. A child will make two
dishes at an entertainment for friends; and when the family dines alone,
the fore or hind quarter will make a reasonable dish, and seasoned
with a little pepper or salt will be very good boiled on the fourth day,
especially in winter.

I have reckoned upon a medium that a child just born will weigh   11
twelve pounds, and in a solar year, if tolerably nursed, will increase to
twenty-eight pounds.

I grant this food will be somewhat dear, and therefore very proper   12
for landlords, who, as they have already devoured most of the parents,
seem to have the best title to the children.

Infant's flesh will be in season throughout the year, but more plen-   13
tiful in March, and a little before and after: for we are told by a grave
author, an eminent French physician, that fish being a prolific diet, there
are more children born in Roman Catholic countries about nine
months after Lent than at any other season; therefore, reckoning a year

after Lent, the markets will be more glutted than usual, because the number of popish infants is at least three to one in this kingdom: and therefore it will have one other collateral advantage, by lessening the number of papists among us.

I have already computed the charge of nursing a beggar's child (in which list I reckon all cottagers, laborers, and four-fifths of the farmers) to be about 2s. per annum, rags included; and I believe no gentleman would repine to give 10s. for the carcass of a good fat child, which, as I have said, will make four dishes of excellent nutritive meat, when he has only some particular friend or his own family to dine with him. Thus the squire will learn to be a good landlord, and grow popular among the tenants; the mother will have 8s. net profit, and be fit for work till she produces another child. [14]

Those who are more thrifty (as I must confess the times require) may flay the carcass; the skin of which artificially dressed will make admirable gloves for ladies, and summer boots for fine gentlemen. [15]

As to our city of Dublin, shambles may be appointed for this purpose in the most convenient parts of it, and butchers we may be assured will not be wanting: although I rather recommend buying the children alive, and dressing them hot from the knife as we do roasting pigs. [16]

A very worthy person, a true lover of his country, and whose virtues I highly esteem, was lately pleased in discoursing on this matter to offer a refinement upon my scheme. He said that many gentlemen of this kingdom, having of late destroyed their deer, he conceived that the want of venison might be well supplied by the bodies of young lads and maidens, not exceeding fourteen years of age nor under twelve; so great a number of both sexes in every country being now ready to starve for want of work and service; and these to be disposed of by their parents, if alive, or otherwise by their nearest relations. But with due deference to so excellent a friend and so deserving a patriot, I cannot be altogether in his sentiments; for as to the males, my American acquaintance assured me from frequent experience that their flesh was generally tough and lean, like that of our schoolboys by continual exercise, and their taste disagreeable; and to fatten them would not answer the charge. Then as to the females, it would, I think, with humble submission be a loss to the public, because they soon would become breeders themselves: and besides, it is not improbable that some scrupulous people might be apt to censure such a practice (although indeed very unjustly), as a little bordering upon cruelty; which, I confess, has always been with me the strongest objection against any project, how well soever intended. [17]

But in order to justify my friend, he confessed that this expedient was put into his head by the famous Psalmanazar, a native of the island [18]

Formosa, who came from thence to London about twenty years ago: and in conversation told my friend, that in his country when any young person happened to be put to death, the executioner sold the carcass to persons of quality as a prime dainty; and that in his time the body of a plump girl of fifteen, who was crucified for an attempt to poison the emperor, was sold to his imperial majesty's prime minister of state, and other great mandarins of the court, in joints from the gibbet, at 400 crowns. Neither indeed can I deny, that if the same use were made of several plump young girls in this town, who without one single groat to their fortunes cannot stir abroad without a chair, and appear at the playhouse and assemblies in foreign fineries which they never will pay for, the kingdom would not be the worse.

Some persons of a desponding spirit are in great concern about that   19 vast number of poor people, who are aged, diseased, or maimed, and I have been desired to employ my thoughts what course may be taken to ease the nation of so grievous an encumbrance. But I am not in the least pain upon that matter, because it is very well known that they are every day dying and rotting by cold and famine, and filth and vermin, as fast as can be reasonably expected. And as to the young laborers, they are now in as hopeful a condition: they cannot get work, and consequently pine away for want of nourishment, to a degree that if at any time they are accidentally hired to common labor, they have not strength to perform it; and thus the country and themselves are happily delivered from the evils to come.

I have too long digressed, and therefore shall return to my subject.   20 I think the advantages by the proposal which I have made are obvious and many, as well as of the highest importance.

For first, as I have already observed, it would greatly lessen the   21 number of papists, with whom we are yearly overrun, being the principal breeders of the nation as well as our most dangerous enemies; and who stay at home on purpose to deliver the kingdom to the Pretender, hoping to take their advantage by the absence of so many good Protestants, who have chosen rather to leave their country than stay at home and pay tithes against their conscience to an Episcopal curate.

Secondly, The poor tenants will have something valuable of their   22 own, which by law may be made liable to distress and help to pay their landlord's rent, their corn and cattle being already seized, and money a thing unknown.

Thirdly, Whereas the maintenance of 100,000 children from two   23 years old and upward, cannot be computed at less than 10s. apiece per annum, the nation's stock will be thereby increased £50,000 per annum, beside the profit of a new dish introduced to the tables of all gentlemen of fortune in the kingdom who have any refinement in taste.

And the money will circulate among ourselves, the goods being entirely of our own growth and manufacture.

Fourthly, The constant breeders, beside the gain of 8s. sterling per annum by the sale of their children, will be rid of the charge of maintaining them after the first year. 24

Fifthly, This food would likewise bring great custom to taverns, where the vintners will certainly be so prudent as to procure the best receipts for dressing it to perfection, and consequently have their houses frequented by all the fine gentlemen, who justly value themselves upon their knowledge in good eating; and a skilful cook, who understands how to oblige his guests, will contrive to make it as expensive as they please. 25

Sixthly, This would be a great inducement to marriage, which all wise nations have either encouraged by rewards or enforced by laws and penalties. It would increase the care and tenderness of mothers toward their children, when they were sure of a settlement for life to the poor babes, provided in some sort by the public, to their annual profit instead of expense. We should see an honest emulation among the married women, which of them would bring the fattest child to the market. Men would become as fond of their wives during the time of their pregnancy as they are now of their mares in foal, their cows in calf, their sows when they are ready to farrow; nor offer to beat or kick them (as is too frequent a practice) for fear of a miscarriage. 26

Many other advantages might be enumerated. For instance, the addition of some thousand carcasses in our exportation of barreled beef, the propagation of swine's flesh, and improvement in the art of making good bacon, so much wanted among us by the great destruction of pigs, too frequent at our table; which are no way comparable in taste or magnificence to a well-grown, fat, yearling child, which roasted whole will make a considerable figure at a lord mayor's feast or any other public entertainment. But this and many others I omit, being studious of brevity. 27

Supposing that 1,000 families in this city would be constant customers for infants' flesh, besides others who might have it at merry-meetings, particularly at weddings and christenings, I compute that Dublin would take off annually about 20,000 carcasses; and the rest of the kingdom (where probably they will be sold somewhat cheaper) the remaining 80,000. 28

I can think of no one objection that will possibly be raised against this proposal, unless it should be urged that the number of people will be thereby much lessened in the kingdom. This I freely own, and it was indeed one principal design in offering it to the world. I desire the reader will observe, that I calculate my remedy for this one individual 29 kingdom of Ireland and for no other that ever was, is, or I think ever can be upon earth. Therefore let no man talk to me of other expedients: of taxing our absentees at 5s. a pound: of using neither clothes nor household furniture except what is of our own growth and manufacture: of utterly rejecting the materials and instruments that promote foreign luxury: of curing the expensiveness of pride, vanity, idleness, and gaming in our women: of introducing a vein of parsimony, prudence, and temperance: of learning to love our country, in the want of which we differ even from Laplanders and the inhabitants of Topinamboo: of quitting our animosities and factions, nor acting any longer like the Jews, who were murdering one another at the very moment their city was taken: of being a little cautious not to sell our country and conscience for nothing: of teaching landlords to have at least one degree of mercy toward their tenants: lastly, of putting a spirit of honesty, industry, and skill into our shopkeepers; who, if a resolution could now be taken to buy only our native goods, would immediately unite to cheat and exact upon us in the price, the measure, and the goodness, nor could ever yet be brought to make one fair proposal of just dealing, though often and earnestly invited to it.

Therefore I repeat, let no man talk to me of these and the like 30
expedients, till he has at least some glimpse of hope that there will be ever some hearty and sincere attempt to put them in practice.

But as to myself, having been wearied out for many years with 31
offering vain, idle, visionary thoughts, and at length utterly despairing of success, I fortunately fell upon this proposal; which, as it is wholly new, so it has something solid and real, of no expense and little trouble, full in our own power, and whereby we can incur no danger in disobliging England. For this kind of commodity will not bear exportation, the flesh being of too tender a consistence to admit a long continuance in salt, although perhaps I could name a country which would be glad to eat up our whole nation without it.

After all, I am not so violently bent upon my own opinion as to reject 32
any offer proposed by wise men, which shall be found equally innocent, cheap, easy, and effectual. But before something of that kind shall be advanced in contradiction to my scheme, and offering a better, I desire the author or authors will be pleased maturely to consider two points. First, as things now stand, how they will be able to find food and raiment for 100,000 useless mouths and backs. And secondly, there being a round million of creatures in human figure throughout this kingdom, whose subsistence put into a common stock would leave them in debt 2,000,000l. sterling, adding those who are beggars by profession to the bulk of farmers, cottagers, and laborers, with the wives and children who are beggars in effect; I desire those politicians

who dislike my overture, and may perhaps be so bold as to attempt an answer, that they will first ask the parents of these mortals, whether they would not at this day think it a great happiness to have been sold for food at a year old in the manner I prescribe, and thereby have avoided such a perpetual scene of misfortunes as they have since gone through by the oppression of landlords, the impossibility of paying rent without money or trade, the want of common sustenance, with neither house nor clothes to cover them from the inclemencies of the weather, and the most inevitable prospect of entailing the like or greater miseries upon their breed forever.

I profess, in the sincerity of my heart, that I have not the least 33 personal interest in endeavoring to promote this necessary work, having no other motive than the public good of my country, by advancing our trade, providing for infants, relieving the poor, and giving some pleasure to the rich. I have no children by which I can propose to get a single penny; the youngest being nine years old, and my wife past childbearing.

AIMS AND STRATEGIES OF THE WRITER

Comment. First of all, Swift intends to write *satire,* to ridicule hypocrisy by exaggeration and distortion. He uses as his primary tool the device of *verbal irony* (saying one thing while meaning something else). This technique usually angers readers at first but soon enlightens them if they heed the serious underlying message.

Assignment 1. Plan an essay in the Swift tradition. Select an activity that offends you, such as people who throw trash from their car windows or surly and rude salesclerks. Then offer an exaggerated alternative to improve the situation. For example, suggest that *all* traffic offenders be condemned to one small stretch of an interstate highway. Let the careless drivers try to dodge other reckless drivers. Meanwhile, the normal drivers could drive safely on regular streets and highways.

Comment. One danger of irony (as experienced by Swift himself) is that many will take seriously whatever they read in print. When this happens, of course, they receive the opposite impression from that intended by the writer.

Assignment 2. Use the ironic tone carefully and fine tune it for the audience. You may employ some *verisimilitude* (the appearance of being serious) but then you will need plenty of *hyperbole* (exaggerated statements not meant to be taken seriously). That is, be absurd enough in your piece to strip away your cover so that readers can recognize the humor.

Comment. A satirist like Swift needs to awaken and enlighten his readers, but he cannot afford to offend them to the point that they dismiss his essay as insane ranting. Unfortunately for Swift, his fierce pride and angry disposition often cost him the support and recognition he desperately sought.

Assignment 3. Keep the voice of your essay under control so that your readers will listen and believe your fundamental message and perhaps take appropriate action. Your credibility is on the line in verbose displays in which an impassioned voice might become caustic or grating rather than confident.

THE WRITING PROCESS

Comment. Swift considers the deplorable situation in Ireland and offers a solution. He then presents a well-developed list of six *consequences* of his program (see paragraphs 21 through 27).

Assignment 4. Study Swift's deft handling of his absurd proposal and its consequences. Prepare a block of material for your satiric paper that itemizes the "marvelous" consequences that your proposal will bring to fruition.

Comment. In his perverse way, Swift answers the questions of causal analysis (see pages 331–332). He provides a setting: a country ravaged by poverty and oppression. He notes the principal players: women and their children begging in the streets. He tells what to do: allow women to earn money by breeding children for the wealthy. He explains how: sell and feed the children for a profit. He tells us why and to what purpose: to provide for the children, the mothers, and the general economy of the country.

Assignment 5. Apply these fundamental questions to your subject. Are all pieces of your plan intact and operative? Have you supplied answers to all questions?

Comment. Swift enjoys one advantage over logical writers like Carl Sagan or James Jeans: He need not conform to conventions. Swift ignores logic, dismisses sufficient causes, and embraces post hoc argument.

Assignment 6. Keeping your main cause firmly in mind—that you wish to expose corruption or condemn injustice—you may with some degree of impunity ignore the sufficiency of causal forces and disrupt at will any causal chain that develops. After all, exaggeration in form and style can actually support your development of the ironic situation.

Comment. Swift arranges his essay to develop a situation, offer a solution, and discuss its consequences.

Assignment 7. You may follow the order of Swift's plan, but other options are available. You can trace a series of absurd causes to explain a current condition. You can categorize and discuss a number of absurd scientific theories for the current situation. You can build a set of causes and a matching list of consequences, all of them absurd, of course.

Comment. Note the manner by which Swift blends numerous patterns of development into his essay. He uses description, example, narration, comparison and contrast, definition, classification, and process analysis.

Assignment 8. Make a checklist of patterns that will serve your essay. Make journal notes to *describe* a scene. Develop a few *narrative* episodes and even conversations between imaginary persons. Show the *causal process* unraveling. *Classify* the consequences that will flow from your plan. Express or imply a *contrast* between your plan (an exaggerated one of course) and a reasonable plan (which you dismiss as nonsense). (On this latter note see especially Swift's handling in paragraph 29.)

*A*sked *to write a persuasive paper on a topic of her choice, Susan Noland chose a topic used in many college essays: the death penalty.*

In this case she blends persuasive discourse with expressive writing of a position paper to explain her sentiments on the subject. She is more interested in discovering her own ideas and less concerned with the audience. Therefore, the essay is not a speech, not a call to action but a private reflection that she shares with readers.

She uses a past-to-present pattern to launch the paper, listing several ancient customs to introduce her position that the death penalty should be abolished. She uses the pattern of cause and effect to build the body of the paper, saying that imposing a death penalty produces three erroneous effects.

Although weak in its logic at times and somewhat deficient in its use of evidence and proof, the essay demonstrates the fundamental role of essay writing: to explore problems and face issues. Noland presents her position for inspection, takes the risks of persuasive expression, and invites criticism.

As you read, make marginal notes to record Noland's conscientious attention to the essay's structure, as established by her final sentence of paragraph 1. Write marginal notes that summarize the content of each of her paragraphs.

SUSAN NOLAND, STUDENT

 Legalized Murder

The ancient law and custom of "an eye for an eye, a tooth for a tooth," which demanded that slanderers have their tongues torn out and thieves have their hands amputated, is now considered harsh and uncivilized. Today in many American states, however, a similar form of criminal punishment, known as the death penalty, legally exists. Ineffective as a crime deterrent, unequally applied, and irreversible in the event of an error of justice, the death penalty, in my opinion, should be abolished.   1

The causal relationships of crime and punishment get very cloudy in murder cases. Even with its threatening severity, the death penalty is no more effective than imprisonment as a deterrent for major crimes. For a deterrent to work, a person must logically consider the consequences of his actions. If a potential criminal is drunk, high on drugs, or mentally ill, however, such rational thinking might be impossible.   2

Also, many capital crimes are impulsively committed in a moment of passion, without thought to the possible results.

Supposedly an act of justice, the death penalty is often applied to court cases unequally. Only a small selection of convicted offenders are sentenced to death, while more persons guilty of the same or even more atrocious crimes are simply imprisoned. Those criminals who do receive capital punishment are usually the poor members of society who are at a disadvantage since they cannot afford to hire expert lawyers or to appeal their convictions. 3

Because human judgment is not infallible, the death penalty poses the terrifying possibility of executing an innocent person. Even if the person is not innocent, an error, due to such circumstances as framed evidence or perjury, may result in the application of capital punishment rather than an appropriate lesser sentence. Yet whether it's right or wrong, after the execution is performed, the court decision becomes final and irreversible. 4

Thus, I condemn the use of the death penalty since it has no meaningful purpose and since it may be unjustly and mistakenly administered. Violent and inhumane, capital punishment is a primitive practice that should be banished from our modern society. 5

SUSAN NOLAND TALKS ABOUT HER AIMS AND STRATEGIES

I chose this topic after reading an article in the local newspaper. Because of its controversial nature, the death penalty seemed to be a subject well suited for a persuasive essay.

I did not begin writing my paper immediately, however. Instead, I made two lists, one containing arguments for the death penalty and one, arguments against it. Up to this point, I had been relatively sure about which position I would take, but, by considering both sides, I was able to make a definite decision.

Having already developed an outline of arguments in support of my position, I simply used this outline as the basis for my essay. In separate paragraphs, I examined each argument. Then, for the conclusion, I restated my position in a concise and direct manner.

If given the chance to rewrite this paper, I would include reference material from outside sources. I feel that such material would be of great benefit since it would lend authoritative strength and validity to my personal opinions.

Thus, I chose a controversial issue, examined both sides, and took a stand. Then, I wrote an essay presenting support for my position.

366   *Cause and Effect*

Comment. Noland's aim is exploratory discourse that will advance a persuasive proposition. In effect, she blends two aims in search of a proposition.

Assignment 1. List topics or freewrite on a few issues to discover a topic. Consider one of these: abortion, genetic engineering, gun control laws, seat belt laws, speed limit laws, pressure to get good grades, or college expenses.

Comment. Noland chooses one side of a controversy and defends her position by attacking the consequences of the law, which she finds ineffective, irreversible, and unequally applied.

Assignment 2. After selecting your subject for a paper, list the causal forces at work. For example, list reasons for genetic engineering, both pro and con, and also list positive and negative consequences. Your list may help you decide your position.

Comment. Noland's essay is shaped by her list of consequences: ineffectiveness (paragraph 2), unequal application (paragraph 3), and irreversibility (paragraph 4). These paragraphs are sandwiched between her opening and closing.

Assignment 3. Use your lists (see assignment 2) to set the pattern of your writing. Select key reasons and/or fundamental effects and then devote a full paragraph of development to each one.

Comment. Noland makes her position clear in the closing, calling the death penalty a "primitive practice that should be banished from our modern society."

Assignment 4. Write a closing for your essay that, like Noland's, announces clearly your position on a controversial subject. Then, with your opening and the paragraphs developed for assignment 3, write a preliminary draft.

CHAPTER TEN

Induction and Deduction

Inductive reasoning requires that you work from evidence in order to examine a problem and reach a general conclusion. For example, you might conduct a poll prior to an election and thereby discover that candidate B is favored over candidate A by 65 percent of those interviewed. You could then make your inductive leap to a conclusion: Candidate B will win the election. If your samples represent a good cross section of the eligible voters, your prediction will probably become fact.

Deductive reasoning requires that you reach your conclusions by applying known laws to a particular case. Deductive reasoning uses generalizations. For example, without conducting a poll, you might announce: "Democratic candidates have always won in this county; candidate B is the Democratic candidate; therefore candidate B will win the election with 60 to 70 percent of the votes."

In neither case does inductive or deductive reasoning *prove* anything; the election will do that, and it might even surprise the prognosticators. Yet we depend daily on both inductive and deductive reasoning. Your doctor might give you a flu shot and you would probably receive it willingly because your deductive reasoning suggests to you that "Flu shots have been used successfully by my friends to avoid serious illness; I want to avoid influenza; therefore, I too will get a flu shot." You have based your deductive thinking on valid relationships of the statements. In contrast, the physician's confidence in the immunization program depends on inductive evidence, which consists of thousands of tests on laboratory animals and humans.

Robert Pirsig offers this comparison and contrast of inductive and deductive thinking.

> This morning I talked about hierarchies of thought—the system. Now I want to talk about methods of finding one's way through these hierarchies—logic.

367

Two kinds of logic are used, inductive and deductive. Inductive inferences start with observations of the machine and arrive at general conclusions. For example, if the cycle goes over a bump and the engine misfires, and then goes over another bump and the engine misfires, and then goes over another bump and the engine misfires, and then goes over a long smooth stretch of road and there is no misfiring, and then goes over a fourth bump and the engine misfires again, one can logically conclude that the misfiring is caused by the bumps. That is induction: reasoning from particular experiences to general truths.

Deductive inferences do the reverse. They start with general knowledge and predict a specific observation. For example, if, from reading the hierarchy of facts about the machine, the mechanic knows the horn of the cycle is powered exclusively by electricity from the battery, then he can logically infer that if the battery is dead the horn will not work. That is deduction.

Solution of problems too complicated for common sense to solve is achieved by long strings of mixed inductive and deductive inferences that weave back and forth between the observed machine and the mental hierarchy of the machine found in the manuals. The correct program for this interweaving is formalized as scientific method.*

As Pirsig points out, use your common sense to solve most problems. Depend on the scientific method for complex issues.

PREPLAN YOUR ESSAY USING DEDUCTIVE REASONING

A thesis paper usually grows from deductive thinking. You must select a subject and begin prewriting your essay with commonsense ideas. For example, one student began by asserting, "Children watch television excessively." Using that idea as a basis, she worked her way logically to this thought: "Excessive television watching detracts from a child's reading and studying." She then searched for a conclusion. Does it follow that watching television is detrimental to a child's education? "No," she decided, "television is not at fault, nor is the programming." Cautiously, she looked for an assertion she could defend, namely: "Unlimited and unsupervised television watching by children may be detrimental to their education." She then had a reasonable thesis that would not offend those who use television effectively for educational purposes.

She had, in effect, worked deductively to reach a conclusion through her two premises. These stages of logic represent a process called *syllogism*, which has three parts.

*Robert M. Pirsig, *Zen and the Art of Motorcycle Maintenance* (New York: Morrow, 1974), 107.

Major premise:	Some children watch television excessively.
Minor premise:	Television watching detracts from reading and studying.
Conclusion:	Unlimited and unsupervised television watching by children may be detrimental to their general education.

This deductive reasoning asks readers to accept the premises. If they do so, then readers must also accept the validity of the conclusion. Deductive conclusions are *valid* because they follow logically from the premises. Of course, if the premises are faulty (some common fallacies are discussed later), then the building blocks of logic begin to tumble.

In preparing a paper, you may or may not respond to all links in the chain of deductive logic. After all, persuasive discourse differs from argument in that persuasion attempts to win the audience with ethical and emotional appeals while argument must *prove* the claims with logical appeals. For example, you might argue that use of animals in research experiments is wrong by basing your decision on the rights of animals to a full and productive life. You could probably develop a reasonable paper without confronting other factors (such as that medical benefits to humans derive from drug testing on animals, suggesting that human welfare takes precedence over animal rights). It is enough that you defend your basic position in a short essay. However, in a formal argument you would need in-depth examination of a host of issues and closely related premises.

PREPLAN YOUR ESSAY USING INDUCTIVE REASONING

You will use inductive reasoning whenever you study the available evidence and reach conclusions. In one case, a student took a poll to predict the outcome of an impending election. In another case, a doctor administered a flu shot on the basis of scientific evidence and extensive testing. The conclusions, drawn only after examination of the evidence, are probabilities.

While the validity of deductive reasoning rests on the accuracy of the thesis or the basic premises, the validity of inductive reasoning rests on the accumulated evidence. For example, insurance companies charge high rates for teenage male drivers based on inductive evidence. If you apply for insurance and you are a nineteen-year-old male, the insurance company inductively concludes that you are a high risk. In effect, your reputation as a good driver has been tarnished by other teenage drivers before you even get behind the steering wheel.

The *inductive leap* becomes necessary at some point during your investigation. This means that you must at some point stop gathering evidence and reach a conclusion. For example, if enough automobiles crash at an intersection, city officials will post warning signs or lights. Traffic authorities will have used evidence to reach a conclusion: The intersection is dangerous and needs warning signals for all drivers.

APPEAL TO REASON AND EMOTION

A blend of logical thought and emotional feelings will give substance to your essay. If you feel strongly about the topic, you can appeal to reason with force and conviction. At the same time, if your reasoning and evidence are adequate, your appeal to emotion will move the audience toward accepting the ideas.

For example, John Holt in one of the essays that follows later in this chapter explains how he forced his student Nell to copy her work again and again only to see more and more errors creep into the writing. He then offers this comment, which mixes logical reasoning with emotional responses.

> We must beware of making a virtue of necessity, and cooking up high-sounding educational reasons for doing what is done really for reasons of administrative economy or convenience. The still greater danger is that, having started to do something for good enough reasons, we may go on doing it stubbornly and blindly, as I did that day, unable or unwilling to see that we are doing more harm than good.

As shown by the paragraph above, Holt adds an emotional element with the phrase "we may go on doing it stubbornly and blindly." He appeals to reason by the logic of his argument: "We must beware of making a virtue of necessity."

Finally, keep in mind the needs of your audience. Raw emotion cannot win the day against opponents who demand factual evidence, yet a dull recitation of statistical facts may be meaningless unless you motivate readers and get them involved.

FEATURE CONCLUSIONS EITHER EARLY OR LATE

One model plan for an essay of this type features a general opening, then the evidence, and finally a conclusion. With this plan you start the essay with an introductory thesis: "History textbooks may have inaccuracies that distort our sense of the past." You are giving the readers, in effect, your original starting point that began the project. The body of the paper then sets forth the evidence, citing passages of history texts as necessary. You would present your final conclusion only after all facts are before the readers. This model plan follows the order of inductive reasoning: from subject, to evidence, to conclusions.

A second model plan begins with presenting your conclusion in the opening and using the remainder of the essay to defend the conclusion with evidence and findings. The closing generally offers suggestions and recommendations. With this arrangement, for example, your fundamental position, one reached after careful research, will open the essay: "Ethnic bias distorts some history textbooks." In another example, one student opened with this statement: "Animal rights are violated daily in our campus laboratories." In both cases the writers open with final judgments. They must then defend them and offer recommendations.

USE OTHER PATTERNS OF DEVELOPMENT

You will need *examples* to defend your thesis in most instances. For example, proving textbook bias requires that you reproduce several examples. Also, you might *classify* your reasons or divide your evidence into segments. You might need *comparison* and *contrast* to show treatment of history by different writers. A segment of *historical narration* might reveal inaccuracies in the reporting of facts. You could discuss the *effects* of textbook bias as one section of your essay. Use the patterns of development for writing blocks of material that will fit the scheme of your essay.

AVOID LOGICAL FALLACIES

In general, inductive fallacies result from an improper use of evidence. Deductive fallacies result from a breakdown in the logic of the premises.

Hasty generalization happens when you draw conclusions from insufficient evidence. Libel suits in the courts, for example, attest to the haste of some journalists in pursuit of a story.

Improper use of authority occurs when a writer fails to check carefully the credentials of a person. Political, religious, and social status may prejudice the opinion of even some apparent authorities who have written articles or books on the subject. Check the writer's credentials, which are usually provided as a note to a published essay. If experts disagree, find a source that presents sufficient and appropriate evidence.

The *post hoc* fallacy is one of doubtful cause. *Post hoc, ergo propter hoc* means "after this, therefore because of this." Just because one event follows another does not mean that the first caused the second. (See also page 331 for additional discussion.)

False analogy means that the writer uses a comparison that, while descriptive, offers no proof of a serious connection. For example, if an animal rights paper exclaims that "the soul of a rat fetus will be destroyed by scientific experiments," the writer makes an assumption that rats, like humans, have souls.

Ad hominem means "against the person" and refers to those instances when writers attack another person, not the person's position, responsibilities, and the issues involved. For example, holding the football coach accountable for drug abuse among players would be reasonable only if you had proof that he knowingly ignored the problem or, worse, supplied the drugs. In truth, the coach may have vehemently argued against drug use.

False dilemma is the fallacy of arguing an either/or situation when, in truth, several options are available. Sometimes referred to as the white-black fallacy, it reflects oversimplification of the issue under discussion. For example, one writer said, "At this university you either join a sorority or fraternity to enter the mainstream of social activity or you remain an outsider, isolated and lonely." Such simplification ignores other possible elements.

Begging the question means that you assume the issue at hand has already been proved, as when a writer says, "Higher salaries for teachers will improve the education of my two children." (But the issue is just that—will better pay make better teachers?)

Two wrongs make a right diverts attention from one side, as with an athlete who responded to mandatory drug testing of scholarship athletes by stating, "This proposal discriminates against athletes because I know several nonathletes of this student body who use drugs."

Non sequitur, which means "it does not follow," is a fallacy of irrelevance because it draws a conclusion that does not follow from the premises, as with one writer's assertion: "Many students don't need a liberal arts core curriculum. After all, I'm going to be a businessman, not an artist."

Appeals to the basic values and emotions of your audience are appropriate and necessary, but *faulty emotional appeals* are fallacious because they confuse the issues. One writer appealed for volunteers to help with the Special Olympics on the grounds that volunteers would learn lessons in courage, dedication, and willpower from the children, rather than on the fallacious grounds that poor little handicapped children are owed support.

To review: Conform to these guidelines when writing with an inductive or deductive pattern.

1. Use inductive reasoning for investigative papers that work from evidence to conclusions.

2. Use deductive reasoning for thesis papers that apply general, well-known laws to predict an outcome. If possible, write out your complete syllogism to test the premises and conclusion.

3. Cautiously make inductive leaps after examination of all readily available evidence.

4. Balance your appeals to reason with appeals to emotion.

5. Feature your conclusion last if you want the readers to work through progressively important evidence in a cumulative fashion.

6. Feature your conclusion first if you wish to confront the readers and challenge them to examine the facts.

7. Blend into your essay all necessary patterns of development, especially example, definition, and cause and effect.

8. Avoid hasty generalization and other logical fallacies.

John Holt writes on educational theory and practice. He draws on his breadth of experience in teaching, from the elementary levels through graduate programs. He reaches his generalizations about teaching by inductive reasoning. That is, he listens to his students, observes them, and learns from them.

His expressive writing on personal experiences builds a foundation for his conclusions on how children learn and how instructors teach. He makes discoveries by observation: Penmanship did not serve Nell's writing; Jane displayed good character, not just good behavior; and terms of endearment usually irritate children.

Holt represents the teacher-scientist. He takes samples, observes, interviews, and then makes his generalizations. His book How Children Fail *(1964), from which this segment is excerpted, began as a journal in which he recorded his observations and conclusions when teaching a fifth-grade class.*

In general, Holt blends several patterns to build his inductive arguments about teachers and the education of fifth graders, offering examples of his experiences with the children, narrating various happenings, and conducting causal analysis.

As you read, make marginal notes to Holt's evidence. Determine its sufficiency. Where does he appeal to reason? To emotion?

JOHN HOLT

 How Children Fail

Nell, February 27, 1958

A few days ago Nell came up to the desk, and looking at me steadily and   1
without speaking, as usual, put on the desk her ink copy of the latest composition. Our rule is that on the ink copy there must be no more than three mistakes per page, or the page must be copied again. I checked her paper, and on the first page found five mistakes. I showed them to her, and told her, as gently as I could, that she had to copy it again, and urged her to be more careful—typical teacher's advice. She looked at me, heaved a sigh, and went back to her desk. She is left-handed, and doesn't manage a pen very well. I could see her frowning with concentration as she worked and struggled. Back she came after a while with the second copy. This time the first page had seven mistakes, and the handwriting was noticeably worse. I told her to copy it again. Another bigger sigh, and she went back to her desk. In time the third

374

copy arrived, looking much worse than the second, and with even more mistakes.

At that point Bill Hull asked me a question, one I should have asked myself, one we ought all to keep asking ourselves: "Where are you trying to get, and are you getting there?" 2

The question sticks like a burr. In schools—but where isn't it so?— we so easily fall into the same trap: the means to an end becomes an end in itself. I had on my hands this three-mistake rule meant to serve the ends of careful work and neat compositions. By applying it rigidly was I getting more careful work and neater compositions? No; I was getting a child who was so worried about having to recopy her paper that she could not concentrate on doing it, and hence did it worse and worse, and would probably do the next papers badly as well. 3

We need to ask more often of everything we do in school, "Where are we trying to get, and is this thing we are doing helping us to get there?" Do we do something because we want to help the children and can see that what we are doing is helping them? Or do we do it because it is inexpensive or convenient for school, teachers, administrators? Or because everyone else does it? We must beware of making a virtue of necessity, and cooking up high-sounding educational reasons for doing what is done really for reasons of administrative economy or convenience. The still greater danger is that, having started to do something for good enough reasons, we may go on doing it stubbornly and blindly, as I did that day, unable or unwilling to see that we are doing more harm than good. 4

Jane, March 20, 1959

Today Jane did one of those things that, for all her rebellious and annoying behavior in class, make her one of the best and most appealing people, young or old, that I have ever known. I was at the board, trying to explain to her a point on long division, when she said, in self-defense, "But Miss W. (her fourth-grade teacher) told us that we should take the first number . . ." Here she saw the smallest shadow of doubt on my face. She knew instantly that I did not approve of this rule, and without so much as a pause she continued, ". . . it wasn't Miss W., it was someone else . . ." and then went on talking about long division. 5

I was touched and very moved. How many adults would have seen what she saw, that what she was saying about Miss W.'s teaching was, in some slight degree, lowering my estimate of Miss W.? Even more to the point, how many adults, given this opportunity to shift the blame for their difficulties onto the absent Miss W., would instead have instantly changed their story to protect her from blame? For all our yammering 6 about loyalty, not one adult in a thousand would have shown the loyalty that this little girl gave to her friend and former teacher. And she scarcely had to think to do it; for her, to defend one's friends from harm, blame, or even criticism was an instinct as natural as breathing.

Teachers and schools tend to mistake good behavior for good char- 7 acter. What they prize above all else is docility, suggestibility; the child who will do what he is told; or even better, the child who will do what is wanted without even having to be told. They value most in children what children least value in themselves. Small wonder that their effort to build character is such a failure; they don't know it when they see it. Jane is a good example. She has been a trial to everyone who has taught her. Even this fairly lenient school finds her barely tolerable; most schools long since would have kicked her out in disgrace. Of the many adults who have known her, probably very few have recognized her extraordinary qualities or appreciated their worth. Asked for an estimate of her character, most of them would probably say that it was bad. Yet, troublesome as she is, I wish that there were more children like her.

Terms of Endearment, April 11, 1959

The things children talk about in class, when they are allowed to talk at 8 all, are seldom close to their hearts. Only once in a great while do I feel, at the end of a class discussion, that I have come close to the real life of these children. One such discussion was about hiding places; another, just a few days ago, was about names.

This latter came up in Roman history. The time arrived in Rome 9 when the mob gained political power, so that the ability to arouse and inflame the mob was a sure key to high office. The kids wanted to know how this was done. I said it was done mostly with names. The way to arouse a mob against your political opponent was to call him names, the kind of names the mob hates most, or can be talked into hating. The mob spirit is weaker in these children than it will be in a few years, and they were skeptical; they wanted to know what kind of names would arouse a mob.

For answer, I asked them, "Well, what kind of names do you hate to 1 be called?" We were off. Before the end of the period the board was covered with names. About half were what I expected, the usual ten-year-old insults—idiot, stupid, nuthead, fat slob, chicken, dope, scaredy-cat, etc. The rest surprised me. They were all terms of endearment.

It was quite a scene. There were all these bright-faced, lively chil- 1 dren, eyes dancing with excitement and enthusiasm, seeing who could most strongly express their collective contempt and disgust for all the names that adults might suppose they like most. Someone would say, "Dearie—ug-g-g-g-gh!" Chorus of agreement. Someone else would say, "Honey—ic-c-c-c-ch!" More agreement. Every imaginable term of affection and endearment came in for its share. Not one was legitimate, not one was accepted. Nobody said of any term, "Well, that's not too bad." To some extent the children may have been carried away by the excitement of the game, but from the way they looked and sounded I felt sure, and do now, that they really meant what they were saying, that their dislike of these terms of endearment was genuine and deeply felt.

Why should this be? Of course, ten is a heroic age for most kids.   12
They remind me in many ways of the Homeric Greeks. They are quarrelsome and combative; they have a strong and touchy sense of honor; they believe that every affront must be repaid, and with interest; they are fiercely loyal to their friends, even though they may change friends often; they have little sense of fair play, and greatly admire cunning and trickery; they are both highly possessive and very generous—no smallest trifle may be taken from them, but they are likely to give anything away, if they feel so disposed. Most of the time, they don't feel like little children, and they don't like being talked to as if they were little children.

But there is more to it than this. They suspect and resent these terms   13
of endearment because they have too often heard them used by people who did not mean them. Everyone who deals with children these days has heard the dictum that children need to be loved, must be loved. But even to those who like them most, children are not always a joy and delight to be with. Often they are much like older people, and often they are exasperating and irritating. It is not surprising that there are many adults who do not like children much, if at all. But they feel that they ought to like them, have a duty to like them, and they try to discharge this duty by acting, particularly by talking, as if they liked them. Hence the continual and meaningless use of words like *honey, dearie,* etc. Hence, the dreadful, syrupy voice that so many adults use when they speak to children. By the time they are ten, children are fed up with this fake affection, and ready to believe that, most of the time, adults believe and mean very little of what they say.

AIMS AND STRATEGIES OF THE WRITER

Comment. Holt observes the children in his classroom and then reaches certain conclusions. He has an open mind, he is willing to listen, and he can adjust his thinking accordingly. That talent is necessary for inductive discoveries; a closed mind dismisses the evidence before it.

Assignment 1. Begin a regimen of personal observation and record keeping in a notebook or writing journal. Your aim will be honesty in your objective responses. For example, you might study the social mannerisms of others. What do people do with their hands when conversing with you? You will need to watch closely, objectively, and keep a written record of your observations. One student, for example, touched an arm of everybody (male and female) he talked with for a period of two days, and he kept notes on the reactions of each person.

Comment. Expressive writing, when based on inductive reasoning, differs from formal scientific reporting. Holt, for example, is directly involved in the investigation. These are his personal findings, not the results of objective, nonbiased experiments. Consequently, the results have limited authority. Holt's experiments cannot be replicated; someone else cannot duplicate exactly the same tests.

Assignment 2. Keep in mind the personal nature of your own investigations. Your pronouncements will probably interest others but will not represent the final word. Your purpose will be accurate reporting of your personal observations. For example, your comparison of students who sit in the front row of classrooms with those who sit in the back row might offer interesting insights, but it represents only your personal reactions to limited situations.

Comment. One purpose of inductive reasoning is to arrive at conclusions based on interviews and discussions with others. Holt demonstrates this technique in "Terms of Endearment," which describes a classroom session that taught him that children react negatively to "the dreadful, syrupy voice" of some adults.

Assignment 3. In your search for a topic, consider interviews or questionnaires as special methods for reaching inductive discoveries. Ask several people to respond to your questions (fifteen people or more will form a representative sample). Then tabulate and analyze the results.

THE WRITING PROCESS

Comment. Holt reports his findings in journal form, listing the date and then describing his discoveries of that day.

Assignment 4. Consider the advantages of note-taking during your investigations. Keep a log for as many days or for as many people interviewed as possible. The accumulation of data is crucial. For example, if you ask people to describe their first automobile accident, you need enough samples to make some reasonable conclusions.

Comment. Holt arranges the format of his presentation as a series of independent observations, combining these into a book on why children fail.

Assignment 5. Carefully format your inductive investigation in one of several ways: (1) State your findings early and then provide the evidence; (2) present all the evidence and reach one major conclusion; or (3) like Holt, present each observation as a separate finding and an independent conclusion but with all items tied to a general theme.

Comment. Holt appeals to reason and emotion. Of course, in a discourse on children, he could not escape some emotional issues, but he maintains a rational, balanced attitude to make serious statements about these children.

Assignment 6. Consider carefully your own appeals to reason and emotion. Will your study say, "The lazy and shiftless students usually occupy the back row of classrooms"? Or will it say, "Those students without any apparent motivation usually sit in the back row of classrooms"? The latter is more objective, less emotional, and probably less offensive to readers. In either case, you will need evidence to defend your statement.

Comment. Holt uses his evidence to make inductive leaps that explain adult relationships to the children. His message addresses the needs of his audience—teachers and school administrators.

Assignment 7. Consider the needs of your audience. Are you writing for your fellow students, your associates in the research project, your supervisors, or the public in general? Formulate your conclusions for that audience.

Comment. Holt blends several patterns of development into his discussions. He provides three *narrative* episodes with the children. Jane and Nell serve as specific *examples*. *Causal analysis* leads Holt to some conclusions about the children. He *describes* the three scenes with specific imagery. He *classifies* three episodes that demonstrate his overall point. He *compares* the children; he examines the *process* of teaching techniques; he *defines* "terms of endearment" in a new light. He blends all patterns effectively.

Assignment 8. Consider the patterns of development that are most essential for your presentation. Define your terms, give examples, compare and contrast the different results, analyze causal elements and discuss consequences, narrate a few of the more interesting episodes of your investigation, explain your methods and process for conducting the study, and, if necessary, classify the materials into appropriate divisions.

The following three essays represent the efforts of three different writers to present logical, coherent reasons for their positions on affirmative action and the use of quotas for hiring members of minority groups. Some proponents of affirmative action argue that enforcement of quotas to hire a specific number of blacks, Hispanics, native Americans, and women can guarantee fairness. Opponents, however, disagree with the quota system because undue favoritism to the group violates the rights of other individuals.

Jesse Jackson uses argument by analogy, saying that slavery and past discrimination are like weights on the ankles of a runner; even after the weights are removed, the runner cannot catch up with others. Wilcomb Washburn challenges the definition of "minority group" and is concerned about the logical necessity but moral absurdity of "reducing the numbers of high-achieving minorities in order to bring up those of the lower-achieving minorities." Sidney Hook wishes to avoid emotion and to look rationally at the consequences of "imposing any criterion other than that of qualified talent" so that emphasis in hiring is placed on qualifications and not on quotas.

"Why Blacks Need Affirmative Action" by Jesse Jackson appeared in the September/October 1978 issue of Regulation; *"Quotas Are Tough If All Are Minorities" by Wilcomb E. Washburn appeared in* The Wall Street Journal *(1984); "Discrimination, Color Blindness, and the Quota System" by Sidney Hook is from* Reverse Discrimination *(1977), Barry R. Gross, editor.*

JESSE JACKSON

 Why Blacks Need Affirmative Action

Let me illustrate the point [this] way, using the familiar athletic example. 1
"Runners to your mark, get set, go!" Two world-class distance runners begin the grueling human test of trying to run a sub-four-minute mile. Two minutes into the race, officials observe that one runner, falling far behind, still has running weights on his ankles. They stop the race, and hold both runners in their tracks. The weights are removed from the runner far behind, the officials re-fire the starting gun, and both runners continue from the points where they were when the race was stopped. Not surprisingly, the runner who ran the entire race without the ankle weights comes in with a sizable lead.

The fundamental moral question one could ask about that theoreti- 2
cal race must be, Would anyone call it fair? Again, not surprisingly, the

answer would certainly be a simple and resounding no. If one could devise some means of compensating the second runner (for example, comparing the runners' times for the last two laps and projecting them over the entire race), a more accurate appraisal of each runner's ability and performance could be made. And if a reasonable means of compensation could be devised, no one would say that such compensation constituted "reverse discrimination" against the first runner or "preferential treatment" for the second. All would agree that compensation was fair and just.

Everyone can follow this example and see the "reasonableness" and   3 morality of the solution because racial attitudes are not involved. Yet this is similar to the position in which blacks find themselves in the United States. We have been running the race with weights on our ankles—weights not of our own choosing. Weights of "no rights that a white must respect," weights of slavery, of past and present discrimination in jobs, in education, housing, and health care, and more.

Some argue that there now are laws forbidding discrimination in   4 education, in public accommodations and employment, in politics, and in housing. But these laws only amount to removing the weights after years of disadvantage. Too often, when analyzing the race question, the analysts start at the end rather than at the beginning. To return to the track meet example, if one saw only the last part of the race (without knowing about the first part), the compensation might seem unreasonable, immoral, discriminatory, or a form of preferential treatment. Affirmative action programs (in light of the history and experience of black people in the United States) are an extremely reasonable, even conservative, way of compensating us for past and present discrimination. According to a recent publication of the Equal Employment Opportunity Commission (*Black Experience and Black Expectations*, Melvin Humphrey), at the present rate of "progress" it will take forty-three years to end job discrimination—hardly a reasonable timetable.

If our goal is educational and economic equity and parity—and it   5 is—then we need affirmative action to catch up. We are behind as a result of discrimination and denial of opportunity. There is one white attorney for every 680 whites, but only one black attorney for every 4,000 blacks; one white physician for every 649 whites, but only one black physician for every 5,000 blacks; and one white dentist for every 1,900 whites, but only one black dentist for every 8,400 blacks. Less than 1 percent of all engineers—or of all practicing chemists—is black. Cruel and uncompassionate injustice created gaps like these. We need creative justice and compassion to help us close them.

Actually, in the U.S. context, "reverse discrimination" is illogical and   6 a contradiction in terms. Never in the history of mankind has a majority, with power, engaged in programs and written laws that discriminate against itself. The only thing whites are giving up because of affirmative action is unfair advantage—something that was unnecessary in the first place.

Blacks are not making progress at the expense of whites, as news 7 accounts make it seem. There are 49 percent more whites in medical school today and 64 percent more whites in law school than there were when affirmative action programs began some eight years ago.

In a recent column, William Raspberry raised an interesting question. Commentating on the *Bakke* case, he asked, "What if, instead of setting aside 16 of 100 slots, we added 16 slots to the 100?" That, he suggested, would allow blacks to make progress and would not interfere with what whites already have. He then went on to point out that this, in fact, is exactly what has happened in law and medical schools. In 1968, the year before affirmative action programs began to get under way, 9,571 whites and 282 members of minority groups entered U.S. medical schools. In 1976, the figures were 14,213 and 1,400 respectively. Thus, under affirmative action, the number of "white places" actually rose by 49 percent: white access to medical training was not diminished, but substantially increased. The trend was even more marked in law schools. In 1969, the first year for which reliable figures are available, 2,933 minority group members were enrolled; in 1976, the number was up to 8,484. But during the same period, law school enrollment for whites rose from 65,453 to 107,064—an increase of 64 percent. In short, it is a myth that blacks are making progress at white expense.

WILCOMB E. WASHBURN

 ## Quotas Are Tough If All Are Minorities

Minority preferences/quotas/affirmative action are emerging as critical 1 issues dividing Republicans and Democrats in this presidential election year. While the ambiguity surrounding such concepts allows for vague and evasive responses to questions concerning candidate commitment to "minority rights," there seems to be a clear division on the issue.

In the fight over minority rights, whether in the form of rigid quotas 2 or more flexible affirmative-action measures to enlarge the opportunities for minorities, one of the strongest arguments against minority preferences has been overlooked: There is no "majority" in the U.S. against which "minority" rights can be measured. All elements of the

American population constitute minorities, the largest being the English at 14 percent, followed by the German at 13 percent, the black at 12 percent, the Irish at 8 percent and the Hispanic at 7 percent. Only the term "white" keeps the concept of a majority alive. By combining the wide variety of groups traditionally designated white, one masks the enormous inequalities among such minorities in the proportions represented in the professions, school admissions and the like.

By breaking down the stereotypical opposition of minority/majority, 3
opponents of quotas could more easily note the logical necessity—but moral absurdity—of reducing the numbers of higher-achieving minorities in order to bring up those of the lower-achieving minorities. If Jews, who are usually lumped into the category of whites, have a disproportionate achievement in many areas (which they do) not only against blacks, but against all other whites, then the implications of such inequality of results should be argued either in terms of its essential justice in a society in which all have equal opportunity but no guarantee of equal results, or in terms of the need to bring Jews (and Orientals) down so that more Poles and Italians, as well as blacks and Hispanics, can achieve equivalent rates of success.

It is now time for the candidates, as well as for those who question 4
them, to confront the basic definitional as well as philosophical implications of minority preferences.

SIDNEY HOOK

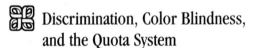 Discrimination, Color Blindness, and the Quota System

It is not hard to demonstrate the utter absurdity of the directives issued 1
by the Office of Civil Rights of the Department of Health, Education, and Welfare. I shall use two simple instances. A few years ago, it was established that more than 80 percent of the captains of tugboats in the New York Harbor were Swedish. None were black. None were Jewish. And this in a community in which blacks and Jews outnumbered Swedes by more than a hundred to one. If one were to construe these figures along the lines laid down by the Office of Civil Rights of HEW, this would be presumptive proof of crass discrimination against Negroes and Jews. But it is nothing of the sort. Negroes and Jews, for complex reasons we need not here explore, have never been interested

in navigating tugboats. They have not applied for the positions. They have therefore never been rejected.

The faculties of many Negro colleges are overwhelmingly black out   2
of all proportion to their numbers in the country, state, or even local community. It would be a grim jest therefore to tax them with discriminatory practices. Until recently, they have been pathetically eager to employ qualified white teachers, but they have been unable to attract them.

The fact that HEW makes a distinction between women and minor-   3
ities, judging sexual discrimination not by simple proportion of women teachers and researchers in universities to their proportion in the general population, but only to their proportion among *applicants*, shows that it has a dim understanding of the relevant issue. There are obviously various occupational fields—military, mining, aeronautical, and so forth, for which women have, until now, shown little inclination. Neither the school nor the department can be faulted by the scarcity of female applications. But the main point is this: no matter how many applicants there are for a post, whether they are male or female, the only relevant criterion is whether or not they are qualified. Only when there is antecedent determination that the applicants, with respect to the job or post specifications are equally or even roughly equally qualified, and there is a marked and continued disparity in the relative numbers employed, is there legitimate ground for suspicion and inquiry.

The effect of the ultimata to universities to hire blacks and women   4
under threat of losing crucial financial support is to compel them to hire *unqualified* Negroes and women, and to discriminate *against* qualified nonblacks and men. This is just as much a manifestation of racism, even if originally unintended, as the racism the original presidential directive was designed to correct. Intelligent, self-respecting Negroes and women would scorn such preferential treatment. The consequences of imposing any criterion other than that of qualified talent on our educational establishments are sure to be disastrous on the quest for new knowledge and truth as well as subversive of the democratic ethos. Its logic points to the introduction of a quota system, of the notorious *numerus clausus* of repressive regimes of the past. If blacks are to be hired merely on the basis of their color and women merely on the basis of their sex, because they are *under*represented in the faculties of our universities, before long the demand will be made that Jews or men should be fired or dismissed or not hired as Jews or men, no matter how well qualified, because they are *over*represented in our faculties.

After Jackie Robinson broke the color bar, the vicious and immoral   5
system of racial discrimination in professional sports was abandoned.
Today, the best players, regardless of race, are chosen without quotas
or affirmative action, numerical goals, and timetables. Why not univer-
salize the practice?

AIMS AND STRATEGIES OF THE WRITERS

Comment. The controversy over issues of affirmative action have focused recently on the quota system, which requires that employers hire
(or at least show a good faith effort to hire) a percentage of blacks,
women, and other members of a racial minority. The three essays by
Jackson, Washburn, and Hood address this issue.

Assignment 1. Begin work on your own essay to address this issue.
After all, women are angry, blacks are enraged, whites scream of reverse
discrimination, and nobody appears very happy. How you approach
the problem is your choice. You might use personal experience, interview several people, read additional essays on the topic, study the
reasoning of the courts in their opinions, or do all of the above.

Comment. The aim of most writers on this issue focuses on methods
of achieving affirmative action and equality for all races. Most agree
with measures that prohibit discrimination by employers, but they disagree with methods for carrying out the Civil Rights Act of 1964.

Assignment 2. Clarify in your own mind the issue that you wish to
address by developing a writing situation. If possible, tie your thesis to
a local issue, perhaps the fact that your college's faculty of three
hundred has only three black faculty members and only eight women.
Or you may wish to defend the black identity of traditional black institutions, such as Howard University, Tennessee State University,
Grambling, and others.

THE WRITING PROCESS

Comment. Jackson uses analogy and statistics to support his defense
of quotas in achieving affirmative action. Washburn approaches the
problem as one of definition that would explain the nature of a minority
in comparison with a majority. Hook approaches the issue deductively,
saying that quotas will function well for the balanced hiring of qualified
applicants but will fail if employers are forced to hire unqualified
blacks and women.

Assignment 3. Find an effective way to develop your essay on affirmative action. You might explore the process, discuss the effects, define the terms, compare this decade with the last, classify types of quotas or types of discrimination. You will also need plenty of examples and perhaps some historical narration. A blend of rhetorical patterns can greatly enhance your general thesis.

Comment. Jackson, Washburn, and Hook are all authorities on this subject. Jackson is founder of Operation PUSH and in 1984 was a candidate for president of the United States. Washburn is a noted historian and sociologist who serves as director of the Office of American Studies of the Smithsonian Institution. Hook is a senior research fellow at the Hoover Institution and a former president of NAACP.

Assignment 4. You cannot speak from experience like these three men, but you can speak with expertise that you gain by research. Therefore, consider writing this essay as a process of scholarly research and draft a persuasive essay based on ethical appeals. To this end, examine source materials on the topic. Consult *Social Sciences Index* for articles under such headings as "discrimination in employment," "sex roles," "sexism," "women's rights," "race," and so on.

Comment. These three writers work from a deductive assumption, which features, in general, this syllogism: Every person should have an equal opportunity; blacks and other minority members have been denied equality; therefore, members of a minority should receive preferential treatment in their search for jobs.

Assignment 5. Determine in advance how you will approach the problem. You might start with a fundamental syllogism, such as this: Humans are not created equal; some blacks may have exceptional athletic abilities; therefore, an intercollegiate team composed entirely of blacks may represent good recruiting by the coach, not racial prejudice. In another case, you might start by gathering inductive evidence, such as: statistics on black-white ratios in, for instance, the Big 10 conference; quotations from players, fans, and coaches; and evidence from journal articles on the subject. After that, make the inductive leap to a conclusion.

Inductive reasoning need not always be serious. Writers of humor often look with a questioning eye at the absurd world around them. They accumulate a bit of evidence, reach inductively for ironic conclusions, and write their findings. Russell Baker, a newspaper columnist, has long been noted for his witty observations of the American scene and for his satiric thrusts at pretense, ostentatiousness, and bigotry.

"Fedgush" represents his term for the pretentious language of some government bureaucrats: "Speech became a dangerous tool down there, because it made it too easy for people to understand what Government people were talking about. So they moved up to gush, and now they can't even tell what they're talking about themselves."

In effect, Baker takes the evidence before him—the unusual, unorthodox language of the bureaucrat—and reaches his conclusion that many persons use language to confuse, not to enlighten, issues. (You might also consult William Zinsser's essay "Clutter," on pages 282–283, which defines wording that confuses and obscures meaning rather than clarifying.)

As you read, note Baker's use of characterization and dialogue. He creates a fictional person, Cummings, who motivates the discourse on language. Mark sections that represent Baker's position.

Baker writes for The New York Times *and has published several books, including* All Things Considered *(1965) and* Poor Russell's Almanac *(1972). "Fedgush" is reprinted from* The New York Times *(1 June 1975).*

RUSSELL BAKER

 Fedgush

Cummings, who is finicky about the language, burst into the office and stood aghast. I sat aglectricked, for I sensed that he had just watched a Congressman strangling the English language with his bare tongue, and was outraged. 1

"Define 'energy crunch,'" Cummings said. 2

"A breakfast cereal. Tasty, invigorating, packed full of wholesome goodness. Keeps you going hours after higher-priced antiperspirants have quit keeping you safe twice as long." 3

"Then how can an 'energy crunch' be 'down the road,'" he demanded. 4

"It can't. It can only be at your grocer's (2 cents off), on the table, or down your gullet." 5

"Exactly," said Cummings, turning red with rage, white with anger, 6
purple with fury, and slipping into a blue funk. I wanted to turn green
with envy at his ability to run the spectrum, but couldn't, so stayed puce
with indifference.

I told him to quit mincing words, get to the point, and give me the 7
thrust of his argument. He said he couldn't possibly mince words because he had lost his mincer, and had sent his saber and foil to the
cleaner, which left him without a point or a thrusting device to bear his
argument.

"Quit trying to speak sensibly and talk like everybody else," I 8
screamed. "Tell me about the breakfast cereal down the road."

"It is going to hit us right between the eyes," Cummings said. 9

"Get out of here, Cummings." 10

"It is not only going to hit us right between the eyes, but it is also 11
going to shake us to the roots."

I expressed incredulity, which inflamed Cummings because he be- 12
lieves incredulity travels faster if air-freighted. After smothering the
flames, I pushed him toward the door. He was a fire hazard and an
alarmist.

I told him there was no breakfast cereal down the road, and even 13
if there were it couldn't possibly hit me right between the eyes,
much less shake me to the roots, since I had just had my annual root
checkup and been assured that they were as sound as a two-month-old
dandelion's.

"Congressman Al Ullman says differently," Cummings replied. 14

Suddenly, the scales fell from my eyes. Cummings pounced on them 15
and weighed himself. "You need new scales," he said. "These things are
eight pounds off."

I was not going to be sidetracked to the hardware store that easily, 16
for everything had become clear. "Congressman Ullman," I explained
to Cummings, "is the powerful chairman of the powerful House Ways
and Means Committee, which handles oil law. As a Congressman, he
does not speak English. He speaks munchy, crunchy, down-the-road,
right-between-the-eyes, root-shaking Fedgush."

Cummings cringed and whined when the word "Fedgush" rasped 17
across his word ends, but I showed him no mercy. "In the Federal
center of civilization, Cummings, speech has been superseded by gush.
Speech became a dangerous tool down there, because it made it too
easy for people to understand what Government people were talking
about. So they moved up to gush, and now they can't even tell what
they're talking about themselves."

"Ghastly," Cummings ghasted. 18

"Not necessarily. As long as no two of them understand each other, 19
it's harder for them to gang up against us."

"Energy crunch isn't a breakfast cereal?" Cummings asked. 20

"Probably not. In Fedgush 'energy' usually means 'oil.' 'Crunch' can 21
mean almost anything except 'crunch,' and 'down the road' can mean
'next week' or 'next century.' When Ullman says there is an 'energy
crunch down the road,' he probably means the oil problem is going
to get worse next week or twenty-five years from now. All the rest
about being hit right between the eyes and shaking us to the roots is
added only to make the sentence more musical with ridiculous metaphor. Fedgush relies heavily on ridiculous metaphor to heighten the
confusion."

Cummings wept. "Energy crunch," he sobbed. "Down the road. Hit 22
us right between the eyes. Shake us to the roots."

"Don't take on so, Cummings. All it means is what it always means 23
in Washington. Things are going to get worse."

Cummings's spirit was broken, so I put the pieces in a plastic bag 24
for him, told him he was going through a spirit crunch and asked him
to come see me down the road if it didn't hit him right between the
eyes with root-shaking consequences.

He tried to hit me right between the eyes, but there wasn't enough 25
space left, what with all the other crunches already lodged there.

AIMS AND STRATEGIES OF THE WRITER

Comment. As a humorist, Baker must meet the expectations of his
readers, who expect a light, ironic touch on serious issues. Thus Baker
often treats subjects that are deadly serious and even depressing with
deft strokes, thereby elevating them to comedy. By laughing at pretense
and bigotry, he accomplishes as much, or more, than a writer who
condemns in stern, unrelenting language.

Assignment 1. Begin preliminary plans for an essay in the style of
Baker's. Consider excesses in social behavior as your target: rough-and-
tough football players who pat each other on their rumps, the unisex
look, body shapes and sizes, or any other subject that lends itself to the
accumulation of inductive data.

Comment. Underlying any piece of satire there exists a serious purpose. The aim of Baker's essay is to protest the distortions of the English
language by federal bureaucrats.

Assignment 2. Write a note that explains the serious nature of your essay in the satiric mode. Rather than merely condemn, poke fun at, or ridicule a class of people, make clear your appeal to universal values that have an effect on all readers. For example, Baker may ridicule the Washington establishment, but his message reaches all who clutter their speech with obtuse, distorted language. Your focus should be on the *excess* in human activities, not on specific persons.

Comment. The aim of many humorous writers is to reveal something incongruous, humorous, or foolish about themselves as well as others. This self-deprecating attitude softens the satire because it shows the writer as one who is also fallible. Baker does this by playing word games, as with his "color" words in paragraph 6.

Assignment 3. You might consider a satiric topic that involves you and your life-style. You could involve yourself as a target and thereby mute the ridicule. If you poke fun at yourself as well as others, you avoid offending your audience, who can laugh with you as well as at themselves. For example, you might admit, first, that you sometimes get stuck with blind dates and then, second, reach satiric conclusions about blind dates by using your personal experiences as well as evidence drawn from interviews with others.

THE WRITING PROCESS

Comment. Baker's style in this essay features a fictional person named Cummings, who serves as a sounding board for Baker's observations. Cummings is the foil. The technique is used regularly in the columns of another humorous writer, Art Buchwald.

Assignment 4. Consider using in your essay a fictional character. Imagine interviewing a football player or have a conversation with a spaced-out dope addict.

Comment. Baker's use of an imaginary character requires dialogue. The technique works as a type of comparison and contrast. Cummings expresses his outrage to Baker, and then Baker, the moderate voice, explains how, why, and where the language became distorted.

Assignment 5. Develop your satiric essay with a short section of such dialogue. For example, have an imaginary student approach you in a state of distress over, for instance, a set of chemistry assignments and then moderate the conversation in the manner of Baker.

Comment. Baker uses one phrase as his inductive evidence of "fed-gush": the statement by a congressman that "an energy crunch down the road is going to hit us right between the eyes and shake us to the roots." That one example is sufficient for Baker's purposes.

Assignment 6. Consider carefully the needs of your audience and use the amount of evidence that can justify your ironic attack on pretense, racism, bigotry, or any other excess of social behavior that you decide to examine. One instance might serve your purposes, as with Baker, or you may need many examples.

Comment. Humor and satire are difficult to write. Finding the right touch, in the manner of Baker, can be difficult. Too much bitterness about social conditions will ruin a lighthearted, ironic tone. Yet if your tone gets too fluffy, silly, and lighthearted, you lose the serious point of the essay.

Assignment 7. As you develop your essay in the style of Baker, permit a few of your peers to read the draft. Let them tell you if it makes a good point while being light and humorous. It should do both.

*Kaye Crouch writes a persuasive essay on the feminist movement. She
advances a positive thesis that equality should be a responsible state of
mind, something earned by hard work. Her inductive reasoning tells
her that equality does not come easily. It also tells her that mouthing
platitudes will not bring it about. She asks women to live their equality.*

*Although inductive reasoning serves as her primary pattern of de-
velopment, Crouch's persuasive aim of discourse requires a blending
of several other patterns. She uses cause and effect, example, comparison and contrast (especially for the section about black freedom
marchers), and indirectly defines the entire feminist movement.*

*As a good essayist, she presents controversial ideas for her readers,
knowing they will agree on a few points but disagree, perhaps even
strongly, about some others.*

*As you read this essay, write marginal notes to record her major
points and her methods for defending them. Also note her persistent
use of the first-person voice, which you should avoid in explanatory
discourse but can use regularly in expressive writing and on occasion
in persuasive writing.*

KAYE CROUCH, STUDENT

▣▣ Equality Is a State of Mind

If I hear one more word about the liberated American woman, I think   1
I will scream. There, I said it. Lightning bolts didn't fall from the sky;
Gloria Steinem did not appear in a ghost-like apparition to doom me
to eternal total-womanhood, and no whimpy, liberated man tried to be
supportive of my wishes. The women's movement has reached a point
when it no longer stirs fires in the souls of women—heartburn maybe,
but not fire. Why are so many women ignoring the fearless leaders and
so many men cringing at the very mention of the name Gloria Steinem?
Probably for the same reason Jesse Jackson is no longer viewed as the
new leader in the civil rights movement, for there comes a point when
a person or group goes too far. The feminists of the 70s reached and
passed that point. Now in the 80s we need balance.

The women's movement has run aground because it lost sight of its   2
goals. Yes, feminists want full equality among the sexes, but how can
we achieve that when the blacks have been working for equality for
over one hundred years and *still* face discrimination? The key word
here is "work." Equality must be earned. It also must be a state of mind.

Channel 4 news last night reported on the lunch counter sit-ins of   3
the 1960s in Nashville. What impressed me the most was how prepared
and organized these black students were. They had read Thoreau and
Gandhi and held meetings to plan their actions, and they even went so
far as to rehearse their actions and reactions to white extremists. Also
impressive were the expressions on the faces of these students as they
sat at the white lunch counter. They knew they were equal to any person
in the room, and they seemed to have ten times the character of the
good-old-boys who pulled them off the stools and beat them. It's a sure
bet that none of those roughnecks had studied Gandhi.

The leaders of the women's movement have failed to prepare and   4
plan. The suffragettes of the turn of the century, like the blacks of the
60s, knew that equality would not come in one bold stroke but in many
small steps. We live in the real world, not the best of all possible worlds
of Voltaire's imagination. Women need to organize and decide what
they want. They need to define particular steps rather than merely cry,
"We want total equality."

Florence King wrote in one of her essays that the only goal she could   5
determine the feminists had was "an abortion performed by a gay black
doctor under an endangered tree on an Indian reservation." The minorities should stick together and work together for the common cause,
but again, this is not the best of all possible worlds we live in; it's
America where the establishment is the White-Anglo-Saxon-Protestant
male. The more he gets forced, the more prejudiced he becomes. Some
men do support the feminists, but these are not establishment men (for
instance, Phil Donahue is almost as offensive as the bra-burners).

The feminists have also instilled the idea, albeit subconsciously,   6
that women are not equal and that some miracle, namely the passing of
the ERA, will make all women brilliant, successful, and fulfilled. This
attitude cannot bring social revolution. We are only as repressed as we
let others make us feel. The founding fathers did not contend that it
would take a revolt toward England to make the colonists equal to the
British. They operated on the theory that all men are created equal and
that shopkeepers in Boston had just as many rights as the dukes and
earls in England. Instead of telling women that they are not equal
and should demand equality, the feminists should spend more time
living equally instead of shouting for it from the rooftops.

If women don't know what women want, it's no wonder men are so   7
confused by the changing roles. Feminists wish to claim the popular
role of conquering hero. They fail to realize that men have no more
desire to be conquered than women. Radical feminists try to castrate
men until they become submissive eunuchs. They forget that the submissive role is not fun. They fail to recognize the fact that they have

adopted the very role of oppressor that they so fervently denounced in men.

I am not against equal rights for women. We have to realize, though,   8 that with rights come responsibilities—to respect the beliefs of others, to avoid tyranny, to accept the responsibilities of equality. It means that when we get all the good stuff, we take the bad, too. It means accepting the draft, paying alimony and child support when we are the family's main support, and making decisions from state capitals and, one day, the White House. We must live our sermon, not just preach it.

KAYE CROUCH TALKS ABOUT HER AIMS AND STRATEGIES

My instructor asked me to make a critical response to an issue that I felt strongly about. So I did, not holding back ideas or trying to please anybody. In fact, after I got started, I rather enjoyed the tendency to provoke my readers, make them take notice, and perhaps rile them just a bit.

Others can judge the validity of my position, but the point I wanted to make is a positive one, not a negative harping against extremists. If we women lead our lives in a state of mind that reflects our confidence, we will send out powerful signals without needing to preach, teach, burn bras, or create meek house-husbands.

Writing stuff like this can be fun. I read one version of this paper to my speech class, and the students, even the guys, applauded. I may try another version of it in logic class, but that professor may clobber me because I scatter my thoughts around without maintaining "logical discipline," as he loves to say. One thing about it, if you get a good paper going, you can spread it around for different assignments.

Comment. Crouch looks at the evidence around her and makes an inductive leap to her conclusion that, loosely translated, suggests that women must stop screaming hysterically for equal rights and live life fully and equally.

Assignment 1. In your notes or writing journal begin formulating ideas and pieces of freewriting that might open up your topic, one that duplicates the Crouch model. Search out a group of complainers and examine their behavior in order to justify it or, like Crouch, condemn it. At issue is a negative view of life or a positive one.

Comment. Crouch makes reference to Thoreau, Gandhi, and the black movement of the 1960s in comparison with the modern feminist movement. Underlying that comparison rests her deductive thinking.

Major premise:	A nonviolent social revolt requires careful planning and many years to accomplish.
Minor premise:	The contemporary women's movement is poorly planned and too impatient.
Conclusion:	It therefore appears hysterical and short-sighted.

Readers will accept her conclusion if they accept her premises. Crouch probably expected some readers to agree and others to disagree, for her minor premise is vulnerable and subject to attack.

Assignment 2. You should consider developing a deductive scheme for your essay. Jot down the premises on which you will base your major idea or thesis. Are they valid? Will readers accept them?

Comment. Crouch makes her appeal to emotion as well as reason. She feels strongly about the issues, and her personal vitality adds force and conviction to the writing.

Assignment 3. Get involved in your subject, release your feelings in a first draft, and show your emotional commitment. Crouch doesn't back away from offending readers, nor should you.

Comment. In her comments after the essay, Crouch admits that she fails to exercise "logical discipline," by which she recognizes her hasty generalizations, *ad hominems*, and *non sequiturs*. Yet she gains respect of readers because she expresses honest emotional appeals, not faulty ones.

Assignment 4. As you develop a rough draft, examine again the list of logical fallacies on pages 371–373. Your best interests are served by avoiding all of these errors in reasoning, but like Crouch, you may wish to dive headfirst into the fray and throw caution to the wind. If so, be ready for rebuttal by peer reviewers and your instructor.

Acknowledgments

Muhammad Ali, "Why Ali Whipped Patterson," is from Muhammad Ali with Richard Durham, *The Greatest—My Own Story*. Copyright © 1975 by Muhammad Ali, Herbert Muhammad, Richard Durham. Reprinted with permission of Random House, Inc.

Isaac Asimov, "The Difference between a Brain and a Computer" is from Isaac Asimov, *Please Explain*. Copyright © 1973 by Isaac Asimov. Reprinted with permission of Houghton Mifflin Company.

Isaac Asimov, "'Universe' and 'University'," is from Isaac Asimov, *Words of Science*. Copyright © 1959 by Isaac Asimov. Reprinted with permission of Houghton Mifflin Company.

Russell Baker, "Fedgush," is from *The New York Times*, June 1, 1975. Copyright © 1975 by The New York Times Company. Reprinted with permission of The New York Times Company.

Robert Bly, "The Hockey Poem," is from *The Morning Glory* (New York: Harper & Row, 1975). Reprinted with permission of Robert Bly.

Thomas Boswell, "The View from the Dugout," is from Thomas Boswell, *Why Time Begins on Opening Day*. Copyright © 1982 by Washington Post Writer's Group. Reprinted with permission of Doubleday & Company.

Suzanne Britt, "That Lean and Hungry Look," is from *Newsweek*, October 9, 1978. Reprinted with permission of Suzanne Britt.

Bruce Catton, "Grant and Lee: A Study in Contrasts," is from Earl Schenck Miers, editor, *The American Story: The Age of Exploration to the Age of the Atom* (Great Neck, N.Y.: Channel Press, 1956). Copyright © 1956 by Broadcast Music, Inc.

Alan Devoe, "Snapping Turtle," is from Alan Devoe, *Speaking of Animals*. Copyright 1947 by Alan Devoe. Copyright renewed © 1974 by Mary Devoe Guinn. Reprinted with permission of Farrar, Straus & Giroux, Inc.

Joan Didion, "Marrying Absurd," is from Joan Didion, *Slouching towards Bethlehem*. Copyright © 1967, 1968 by Joan Didion. Reprinted with permission of Farrar, Straus & Giroux, Inc.

Annie Dillard, "Untying the Knot," is from Annie Dillard, *Pilgrim at Tinker Creek*. Copyright © 1974 by Annie Dillard. Reprinted by permission of Harper & Row, Publishers, Inc.

397

Peter Farb, "Linguistic Chauvinism," is from Peter Farb, *Word Play: What Happens When People Talk*. Copyright © 1973 by Peter Farb. Reprinted with permission of Alfred A. Knopf, Inc.

Julius Fast, "Winking, Blinking and Nods," is from Julius Fast, *Body Language*. Copyright © 1970 by Julius Fast. Reprinted with permission of the publishers, M. Evans and Company, Inc., 216 East 49 Street, New York, N.Y. 10017.

Robert Frost, "Fire and Ice," is from Edward Connery Lathem, editor, *The Poetry of Robert Frost*. Copyright 1922, © 1969 by Holt, Rinehart and Winston. Copyright 1951 by Robert Frost. Reprinted with permission of Henry Holt and Company, Inc.

Ellen Goodman, "The Long Transition to Adulthood," is from Ellen Goodman, *At Large*. Copyright © 1981 by The Washington Post Company. Reprinted with permission of Summit Books, a division of Simon & Schuster, Inc.

Dick Gregory, "If You Had to Kill Your Own Hog," is from Dick Gregory, *The Shadow That Scares Me*. Copyright © 1968 by Dick Gregory. Reprinted with permission of Doubleday & Company.

Lorraine Hansberry, "To Be Young, Gifted, and Black," is from *To Be Young, Gifted, and Black: Lorraine Hansberry in Her Own Words*, adapted by Robert Nemiroff. © 1969. Reprinted with permission of the publisher, Prentice-Hall, Inc., Englewood Cliffs, N.J.

Ernest Hemingway, "Christmas in Paris," is from "Christmas on the Roof of the World," in William White, editor, *By-Line: Ernest Hemingway*. Copyright © 1967 Mary Hemingway. Reprinted with permission of Charles Scribner's Sons.

John Holt, "How Children Fail," is from John Holt, *How Children Fail*, Revised Edition. Copyright © 1964, 1982 by John Holt. Reprinted with permission of Delacorte Press/Seymour Lawrence.

Sidney Hook, "Discrimination, Color Blindness, and the Quota System," is from Barry R. Gross, editor, *Reverse Discrimination* (Buffalo, N.Y.: Prometheus Books, 1977). Reprinted with permission of Sidney Hook.

Langston Hughes, "Salvation," is from Langston Hughes, *The Big Sea*. Copyright 1940 by Langston Hughes. Copyright renewed © 1968 by Arna Bontemps and George Houston Bass. Reprinted with permission of Farrar, Straus & Giroux, Inc.

Jesse Jackson, "Why Blacks Need Affirmative Action," is from Jesse Jackson, "Reparations Are Justified for Blacks," *Regulation*, September/October 1978. Copyright 1978 The American Enterprise Institute. Reprinted with permission of *Regulation*.

James Jeans, "Why the Sky Is Blue," is from James Jeans, *The Stars in Their Courses* (Norwood, P.A.: Telegraph Books, 1982). A reprint of the 1931 edition, copyrighted by Cambridge University Press. Reprinted with permission of Cambridge University Press.

Thomas Jefferson, "Declaration of Independence," July 4, 1776.

Rachel L. Jones, "What's Wrong with Black English," *Newsweek*, December 27, 1982. Reprinted with permission of Rachel L. Jones.

Helen Keller, "Three Days to See." Reprinted with permission of the American Foundation for the Blind, Inc., 15 West 16 Street, New York, N.Y. 10011.

John F. Kennedy, "Inaugural Address," January 20, 1961.

Thomas Kinsella, "First Light," is from Thomas Kinsella, *Nightwalker and Other Poems* (New York: Alfred A. Knopf, 1968). Reprinted with permission of Thomas Kinsella.

Harold Krents, "Darkness at Noon," is from *The New York Times*, May 26, 1976. Reprinted with permission of James D. Fornari of Jarblum, Solomon & Fornari, Attorneys at Law, as agent for Harold Krents.

John McPhee, "Grizzly," is from John McPhee, *Coming into the Country*. Copyright © 1976, 1977 by John McPhee. Originally appeared in *The New Yorker*. Reprinted with permission of Farrar, Straus & Giroux, Inc.

N. Scott Momaday, "My Kiowa Grandmother," is from N. Scott Momaday, *The Way to Rainy Mountain*. © 1969 The University of New Mexico Press. Reprinted with permission of The University of New Mexico Press.

Carin Quinn, "The Jeaning of America—and the World," is from *American Heritage*, April/May 1978. © *American Heritage*, a division of Forbes, Inc. Reprinted with permission of *American Heritage*.

Richard Rodriguez, "Aria: A Memoir of a Bilingual Childhood," is from Richard Rodriguez, *Hunger of Memory*. Copyright © 1983 by Richard Rodriguez. Reprinted with permission of David R. Godine, Publisher.

Bertrand Russell, *The Autobiography of Bertrand Russell* (London: Unwin Hyman Ltd., 1968), pp. 3–4. Reprinted with permission of Unwin Hyman Ltd.

Carl Sagan, "The Nuclear Winter," is from *Parade*, October 30, 1983. Copyright © 1983 by Dr. Carl Sagan. Reprinted with permission of the Scott Meredith Literary Agency, as agent for Carl Sagan.

Jonathan Schell, "A Description of the Effects of a One-Megaton Bomb," is from Jonathan Schell, *The Fate of the Earth*. Copyright © 1982 by Jonathan Schell. Originally appeared in *The New Yorker*. Reprinted with permission of Alfred A. Knopf, Inc.

L.S. Stavrianos, "Myths of Our Time," is from *The New York Times*, May 8, 1976. Copyright © 1976 by The New York Times Company. Reprinted with permission of The New York Times Company.

Jonathan Swift, "A Modest Proposal," 1729.

Judy Syfers, "I Want a Wife," is from Judy Syfers, "Why I Want a Wife," *Ms* Magazine, December 1971. Copyright 1971 by Judy Syfers. Reprinted with permission of Judy Syfers.

Index